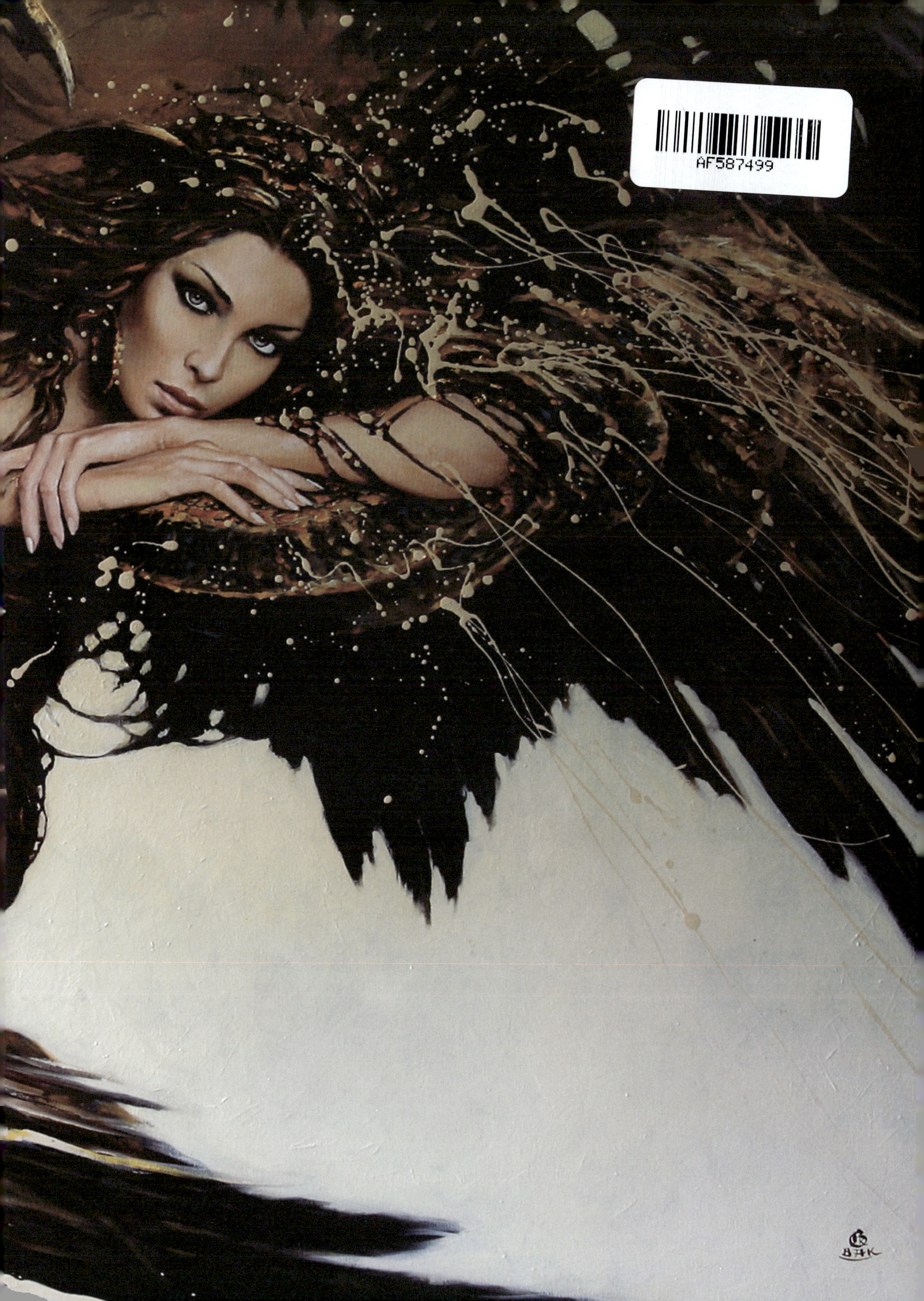

IMAGINAIRE IV

Contemporary Magic Realism

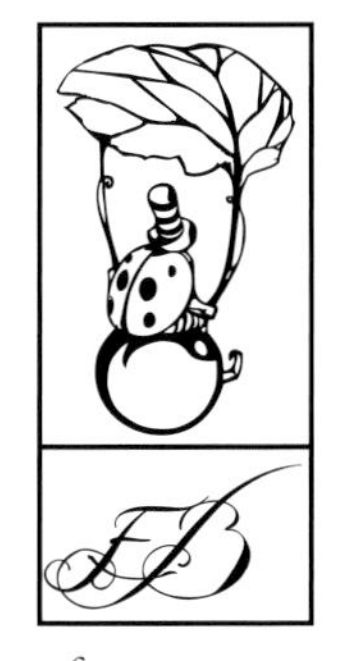

www.fantasmus-art.com

INTRODUCTION

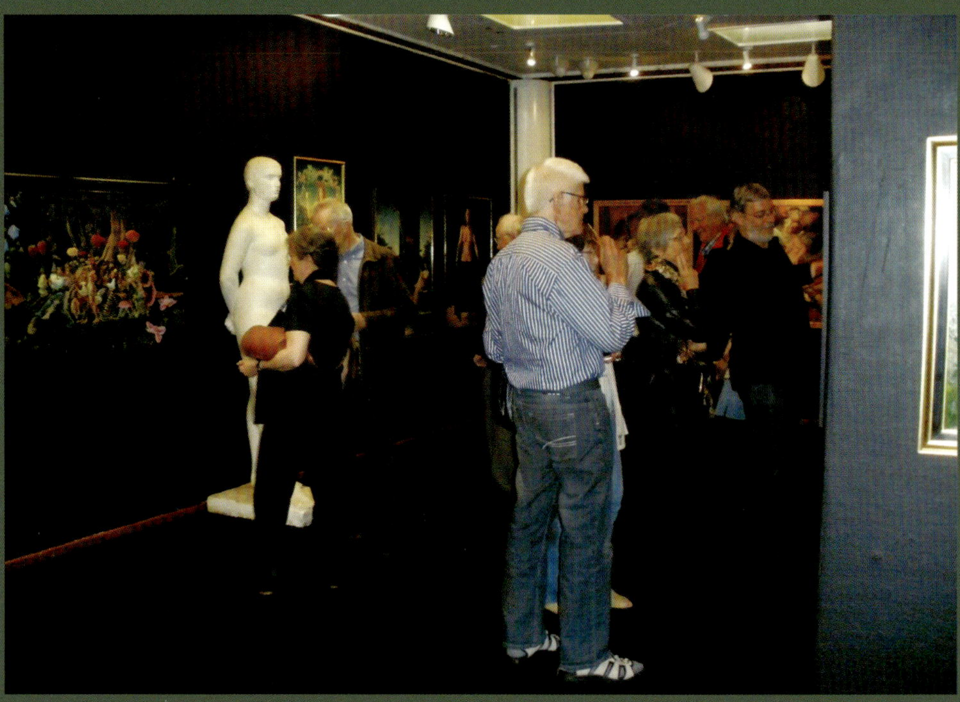

From opening reception June 23rd. 2011. Memorial exhibition for Carsten Svennson at Skive Art-museum, Denmark

This issue features German artist Wolfgang Harms. He is a master in not just paintings, but also mureals & trompe l'oeil. He is creating beautiful landscapes, strange birds and flowers coming to life, in short a true creator of dreamscapes, a good word for this artists work. I have had the pleasure of showing Harms work several times here in Denmark and people are blown away by his skill and he ability to create hundreds of items appearing in his images, often people playing instruments, like you can almost hear the music when watching his work, in my ears it is always classical music that starts when getting the flow of his brushstrokes. Everything in his paintings appears to excist like he just took a photo from a beautiful landscape, but nothing has ever been seen before and therefore it is fabulous and breathtaking.

We have a feature on Lukas Kandl and his Libelulle group, some 32 artists from around the globe, always doing an image in a special size on a special theme, this make these exhibitions very powerful and give a certain strenght to the entire exhibition. despite the theme and size are fixed, it still gives a huge variaty for the spectator, the overall is fenomenal. Some artists have made several on each theme and others have made just one, especially for the Angel show, all 32 have contributed.

I am also pleased in this book to show so many new artists, never seen before in this or other books like these, I am specially pleased to find that here in Denmark the younger female artists have taken on this kind of art and wish to join in for the fight for recognition of our genre, I would like here to mention Anja Altenburg, Coco Electra and Billie Bailey. Bailey is Australia, but lives and have her family in Denmark. It is as if we here in Denmark finally are getting somwhere as this summer I was asked to curate an exhibition for Skive Art-museum. This was to be in memory of Carsten Svennson with those artists he admired the most and this became a beautiful exhibition with artists: Michael Hiep, Patrick Woodroffe, Steven Kenny, Lamy, José Roosevelt, Eli Tiunine, Rigge Gorm Holten,

Gerard Willemenot, Daron Mouradian and Claus Brusen. Most of the works presented was from the **Fantasmus** collection and Skive Art-museum's collection. The exhibition went on for a period of 5 months and was well visited and very commented by visitors.

2 artists I have been knowing and working with have died since last **Imaginaire**, January 31st, 2011 Voytek Nowakowski past away. March 16th, 2011 Carsten Svennson died. Both artists I have known through a number of years, so it is with sadness I announce this here, but both artists will be remembered forever through their art. Last finished painting by Carsten Svennson, *next pages*, this vere done for next biennale I am to curate **Freakshow**, which will take place i Hilleroed near Copenhagen, March 2012, Carsten worked very hard to finish this piece because he knew about his passing long before the rest of us realized this.

It seems that the financially crises will not stop, at least what art is concerned, it is holding on with a strong grib and depriving artists a stabil income, it seems very few countries maintain a good selling of art, or at least our art, art of the imaginary, fantastic art.

I need to make an excuse to Dutch artist Peter van Oostzanen, as last edition I mentioned all great Dutch artists by name, but forgot Peter. Peter I am sorry for this, you should have had your name on here with the rest of the great Dutch artists, my mistake!!

The first museum for Fantastic art has finally opened, January 15th 2011. PhantastenMuseum Wien. It is placed in Vienna at the beautiful Palais Palffy. A beautiful catalogue is published showing a varaity of artists represented there, with names as Ernst Fuchs, Rudolph Hausner just to mention a few, and of course with a great number of younger living artists from around the world, it is definately worth visiting for anyone travelling around Europe.

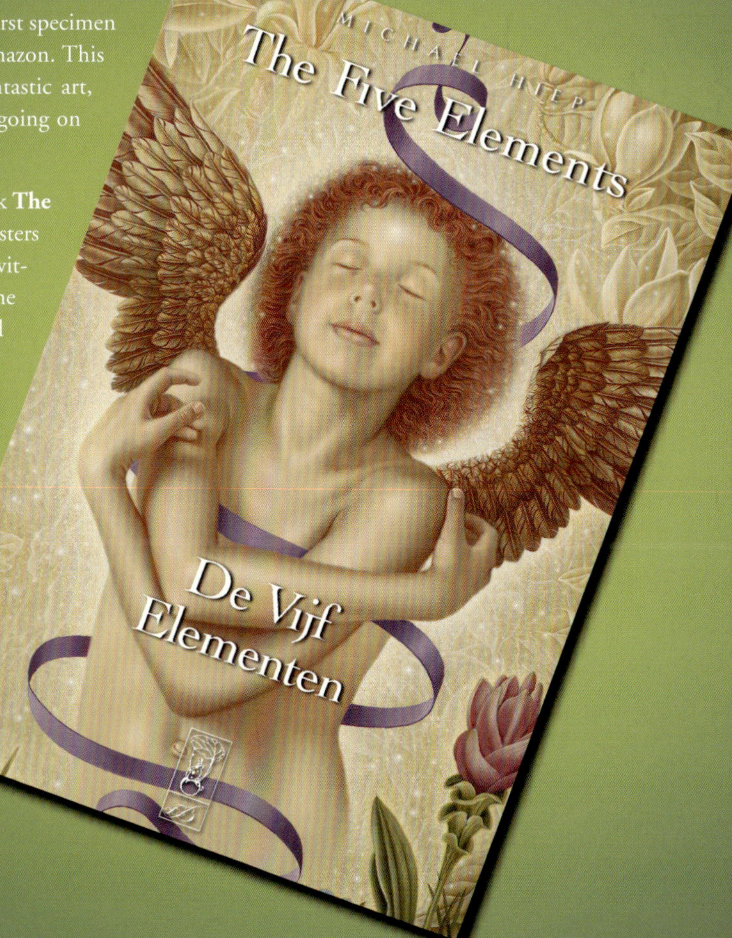

New Books since last, Spectrum 17. has to be mentioned on op of all, every year since I got my first specimen back in 2003, back then first try, buying through amazon. This is still a great showcase of what goes on in the Fantastic art, especially in the Illustration world they show whats going on present.

Michael Hiep, Dutch master has made a beautiful book **The 5 Elements** an oversized format book with 5 mini posters inside to frame and decorate your wall with, this even without destroying the book as they are loose inside. The book is a beautiful celebration of the five elements and a tribute to his Muse, his daughter Eva. The book is published by FANTASMUS-ART Books.

December 2010 we were proud to be able to have the presentation of **Imaginaire III**. Almost all participants were presented at this huge exhibition, this exhibiton was done with the help of Artist Gert Brasque and Hilleroed Library, this library is one of the bigger, some 1.000 people visit this place each day seven days a week and once again this was an exhibition the audience liked very much and commented on frequently

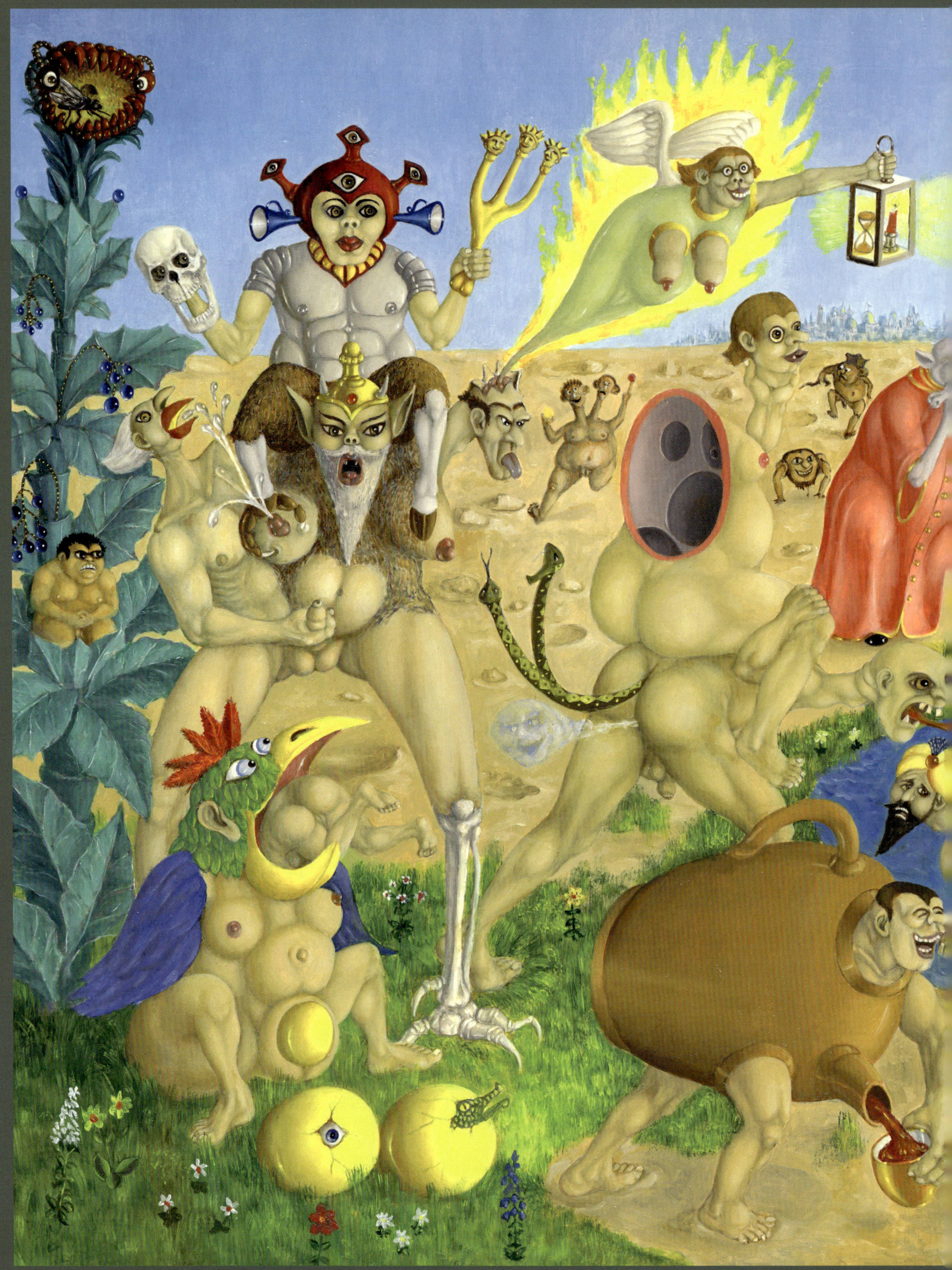

Carsten Svenssons last work made for the Freakshow exhibition · Temptation of St. Anthony · 55 x 85 cm · Tempera/oil on panel · 2010

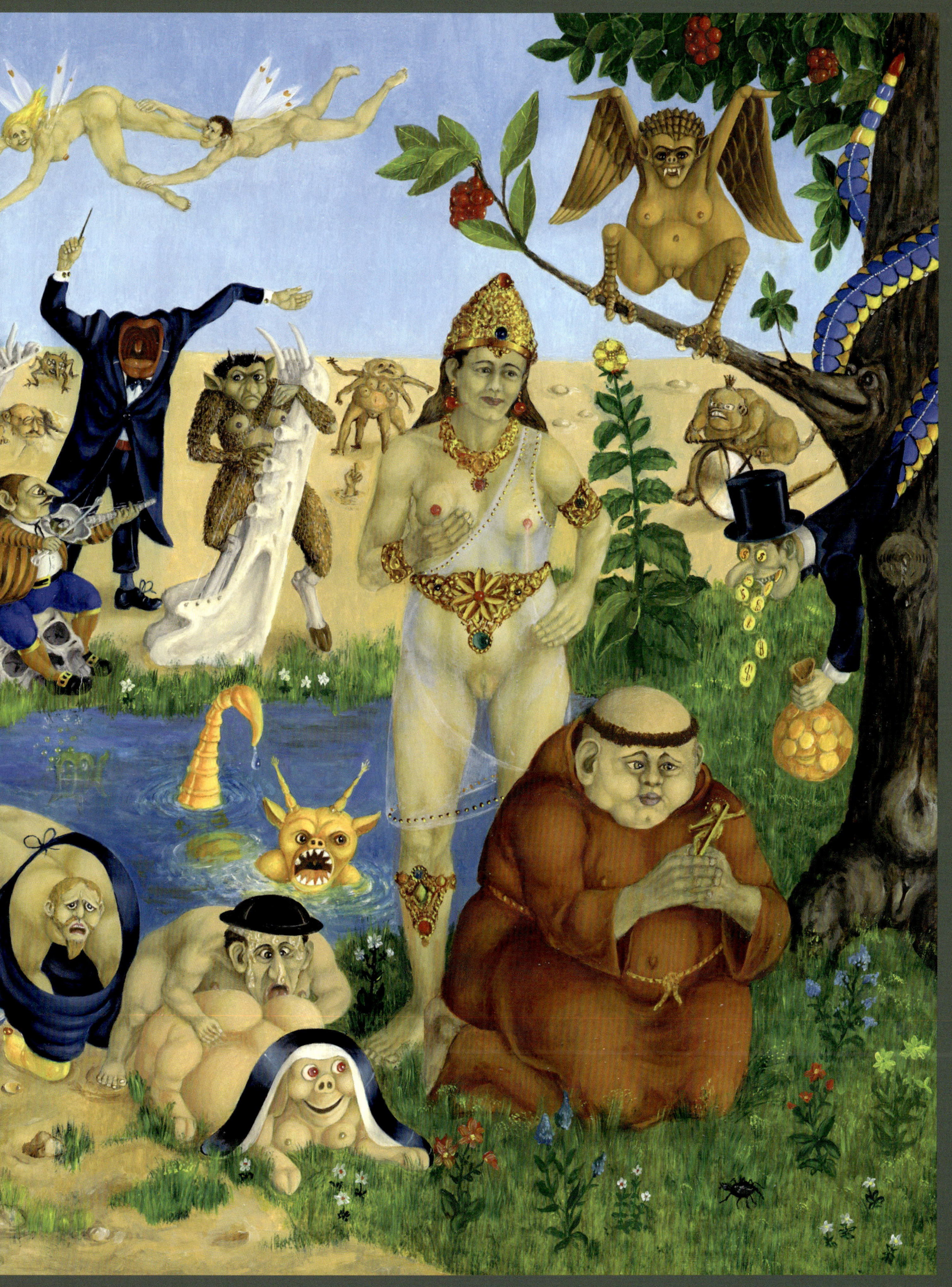

LIBELLULE

www.libellulart.com

In 2004, Lukáš Kándl, internationally renowned French Magic Realist painter, brings together a group of the best contemporary international artists to present a fantastic, surreal, imaginary and visionary world, around a set of fundamental values based on openness, sharing, group spirit, superb technical quality and master of the craft.
In a twinkling to the game "Cadavre Exquis" ("Exquisite Corpse") played by the Surrealists, the artists rally to realize a monumental work made of same format, same theme « être ange, étrange » paintings and so realize a huge « Ange exquis » slowly spreading his wings on the 21st century.

Libellule group was born!

String in artists' enthusiasm, Kándl, head of the group "Visioniric Strange" in Comparaisons salon, which takes place yearly in the Grand Palais in Paris, decides to give a specific theme and format every year to his group, in order to create, every time, a new event.
2006 shows the start of the Ange exquis, 2007 Exclamations !, 2008 Divine Comedy, 2009 Black and White, 2010 One million dollars banknotes, 2011 Phoenix and Dragons.

Don't think that this choice is only due to chance. There is a real link between the labyrinth of our group's themes.

The Angels link us to the spiritual world. They are the go-between the divine and the profane world. With them, we go into an ascending path which goes up to the light while respecting the complexity and the diversity of the individuals.
The guardian Angels protect us, the **Anges Exquis** guide us, the fallen Angels show us how we must be vigilant, while their gender concerns us for thousands of years. (2006)

In order to express vehemently, the artists have to put their feet down, to spell out and speak loudly, in order their voices get through the darkness and reach the ears, too often blocked with pieces of pink cotton, saturated by an ordinary and trivial perfume.
Our **Exclamation**! are there to blow off these tampons. (2007)

Then under our eyes various worlds take place: the hell or ordinary world, wherein we are stuck, the purgatory or intermediate world which opens our mind even if often we make a faux pas, and finally the paradise or divine world, where we walk, when we reach it (sometimes by chance), on tiptoe, walking backwards and looking behind. **The Divine Comedy**.
We get perfectly used to the first step, at ease in our hell, where we can cuss, piss through the windows or even knock out our alcoholic sleeping neighbour. On the contrary, paradise suggests us to take a walk, nude, inhaling the perfume of unknown flowers which encourages our souls to rise up towards the light of an eternal life. (2008)

Later, things become bipolar, defined, **Black and White**, black or white, forming this chessboard of the life where chance pushes the pieces of a subtle game which escapes us, and where the creator is not there, or, rather is invisible for us. Often we blame him for being bad, unpleasant or unfair, when we cannot understand his reasons.
But, is it really chance which manages all of this? Would it be possible that everything was premeditated, in order to make us grab the mirror in which our face is reflected? And after the first reaction to throw away our narcissistic images, we realize that we may be could be responsible of our future, and that could gradually (and definitively?) modify the sentence "checkmate", "the king is dead, long live to the queen" into "the king is still alive, long live to the queen". (2009)

Alchemy is also one of our concerns. All the ancient, esoteric texts describe the transmutation, which, when successful, will transform the dark metals into shining gold, thus fulfilling all our desires, allo-

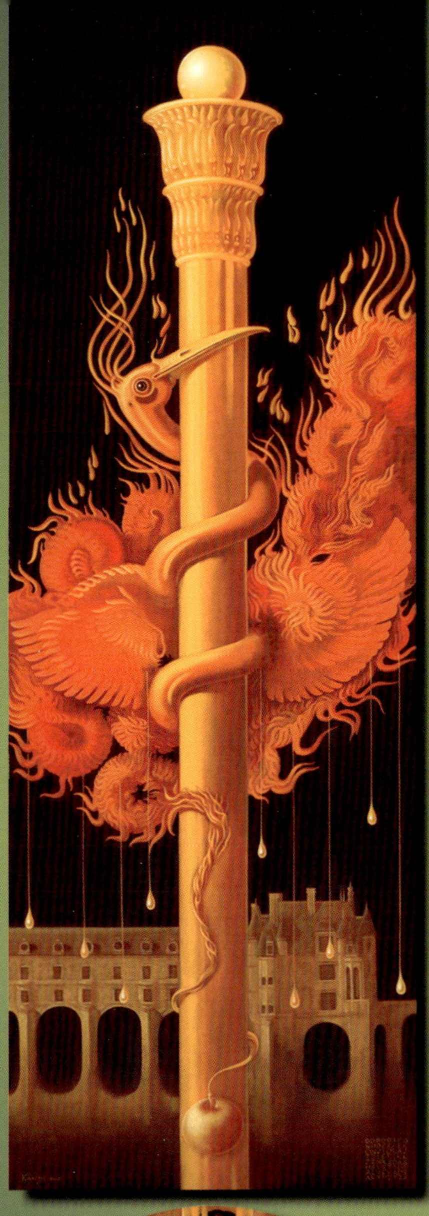

Lukáš Kándl
Calques
180 x 60 cm + 60 cm dia.
Oil on canvas

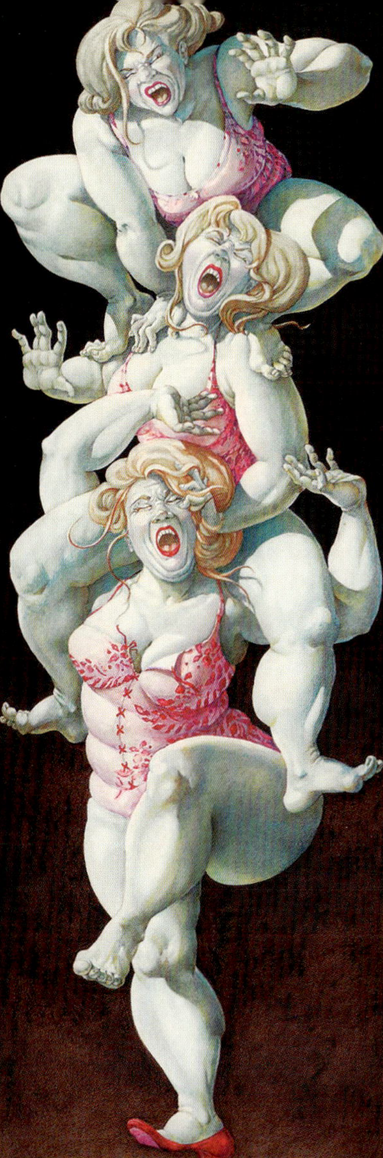

Patrizia Comand
Aiuto!!
180 x 60 cm + 60 cm dia.
Acrylic on canvas

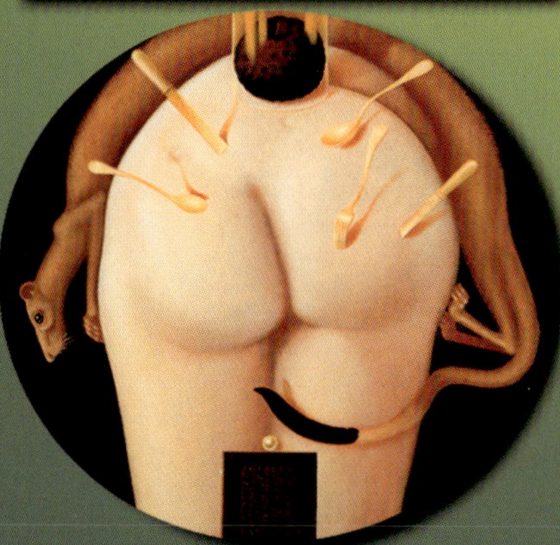

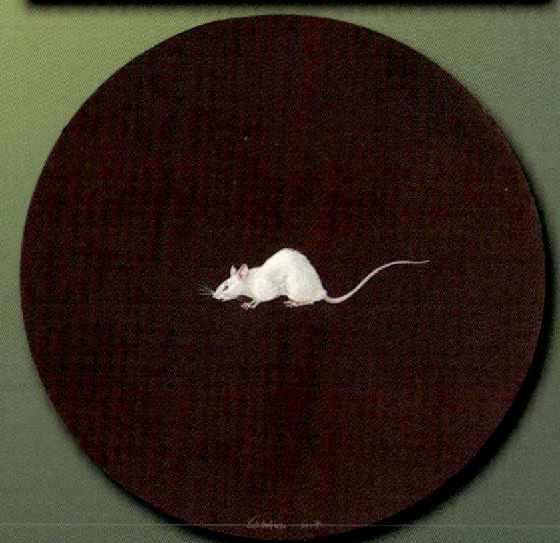

wing us to satisfy all our dreams.
But, paradoxically, we don't realize that the transmutation is real since a long time, that we widely exceeded the dose, and that everything, even the human soul, is now made of solid gold.
Blue birds are becoming very rare and coming backward will be even more complex than succeeding the transmutation.
In French we often say "for one buck you get nothing", but what can we get for **One Million Dollars Banknote?** (2010)

Phoenix and Dragons (2011) The Phoenix, bird of fire, has shined for centuries from its inner light and, when we are fortunate, we can access it. In the alchemical process, there is a time when everyt-hing must be purified by fire. It is then that the dragon breathes and we encounter the risk that the

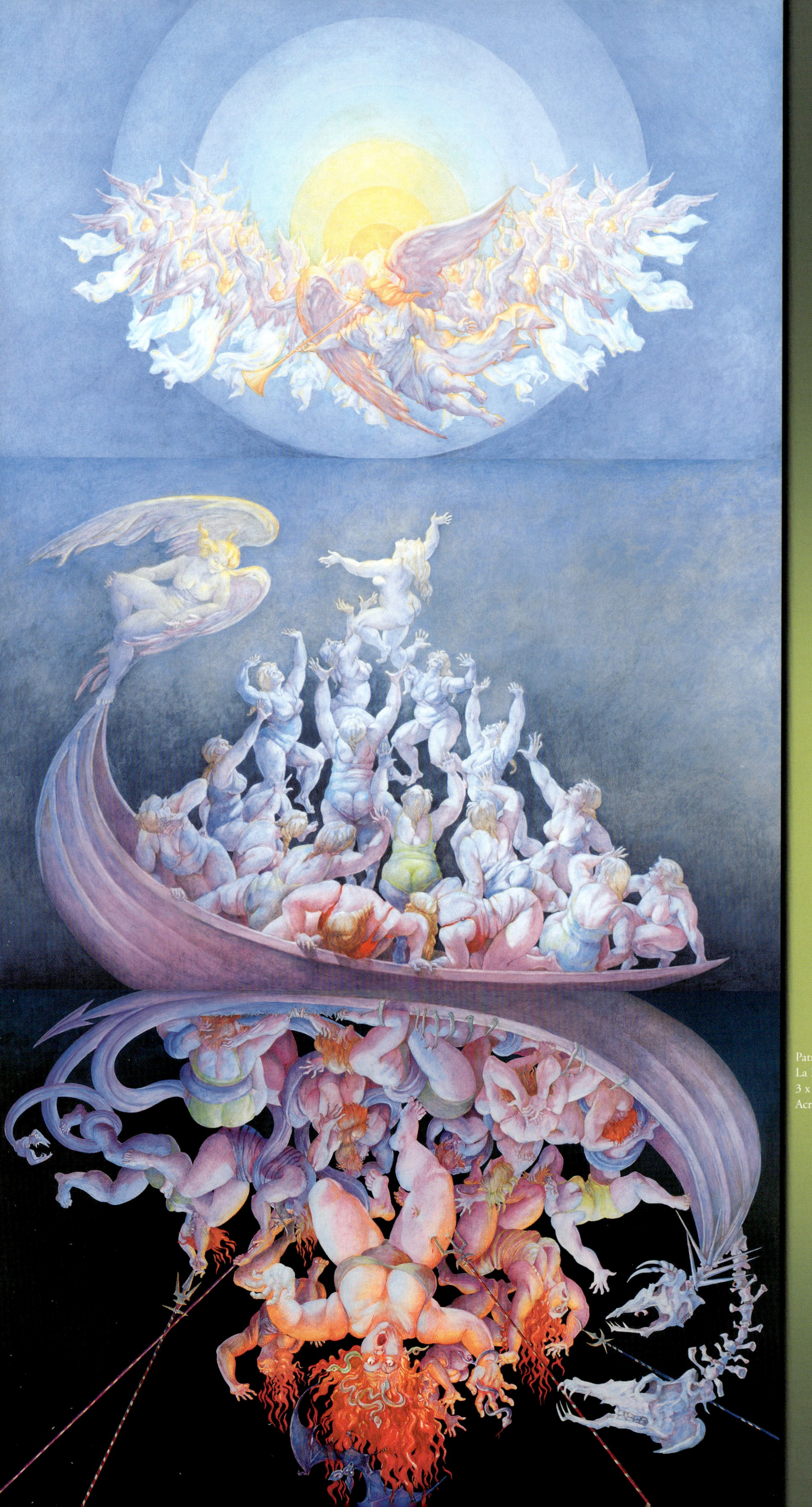

Patrizia Comand
La Divina Comedia
3 x 85 x 130 cm (Triptych)
Acrylic on tablet

dragon's breath will scorch us, as we have only one face against a danger with multiple faces. Only a sharp and pure consciousness has the power to lead us through this ordeal. After, when all matter has been consumed and only a small pile of burning ash is left, comes the rebirth and its accompanying new, more elevated visions. The cycle of the Phoenix starts again for life anew and, as acknowledged by ancient writings, the bird of fire declares, "I am the God of fire, the one who lives from truth."

Libellule group representatives are in charge to find locations for these shows in France and abroad, sometimes adding a few invitees, while staying very elitist about the artists' choice.

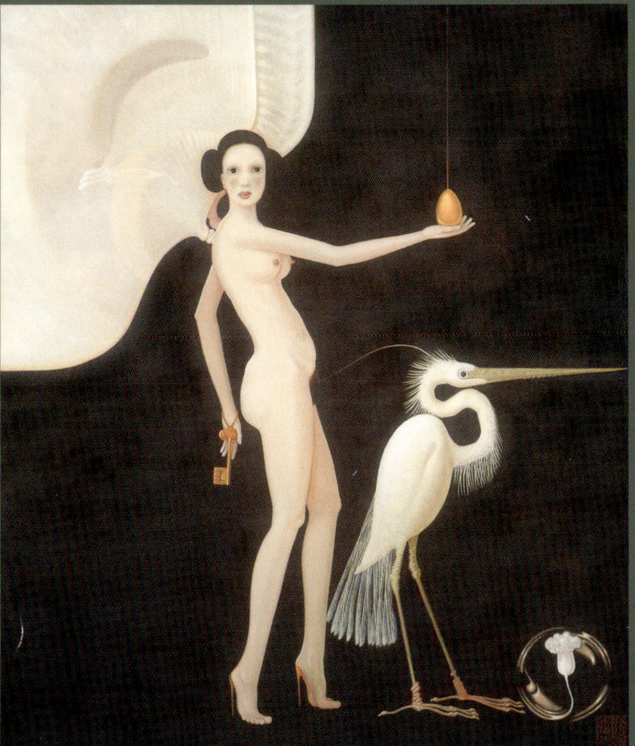

Lukáš Kándl
Ange Annonciation
195 x 162 cm
Oil on canvas

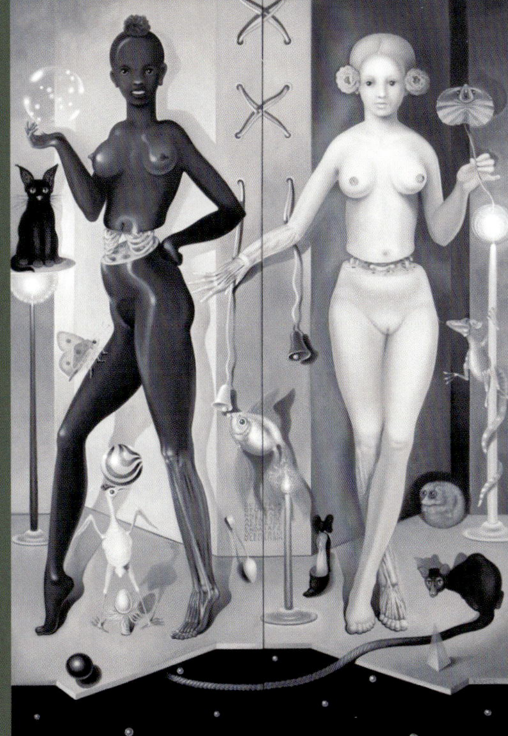

Lukáš Kándl
Black and White Metamorphosis
195 x 2 x 65 cm
Oil on canvas

In 5 years we organized a lot of shows:

Ange exquis: Paris – Grand Palais (F), Saint-Germain-des-Angles (F), Sedan (F), Rosny-sur-Seine (F), Chaumont (F), Viechtach (D), Viroflay (F), Firenze (I), Piombino (I), Vascoeuil (F), Riegersburg (A)

Exclamations!: Paris – Grand Palais (F), Rosny-sur-Seine (F), Vascoeuil (F), Chaumont (F), Viechtach (D), Wien (A), ...

Divine Comedy: Paris – Grand Palais (F), Sedan (F)

Black and White: Paris – Grand Palais (F), Orleans (F)

One Million dollars Banknote: Paris – Grand Palais (F), Chamalières (F)

With our Libellule group of artists we succeeded to bring together the highest level of technique and craft, while bringing an extended portfolio of diversity of interpretations and visions in the contents of the artworks.

LIBELLULE Artists: *Alaux (F), Aparin (Ru/Serbia), Arnas (SP), Bachelier (F), Baddeley (UK/NL), Bailly (F), Bassot (F), Cacace (I), Comand (I), Coquelin (F), De Rosa (I), Djurovic (Montenegro/Serbia), Ivanovic (Serbia), Janda (Czech Rep.), Jontschewa (Bulgaria/D), Kopera (PL/UK), Kortan (Czech Rep./D), Kándl (Czech Rep./F), Krejča (Czech Rep.), Kuksi (USA), Levita (I), Müller (D), Oscity (SK/D), Ravski (Belarus), Schmid (D), Shapiro (Ukraine/Israël), Sugawara (Japan), Tiunine (PL/F), Velicu (Romania/F), Žáček (Czech Rep.), Zademack (D), Zappelli (CH).*

Our main aim is to show to the spectators that this type of art is worldwide well alive.

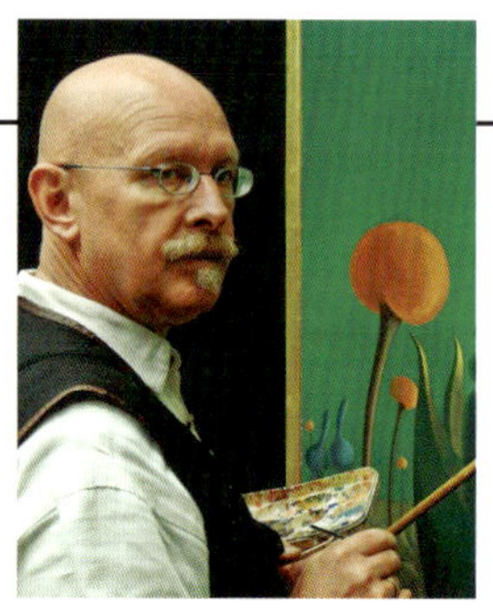

WOLFGANG HARMS

1950 Germany

www.harms-malereien.de

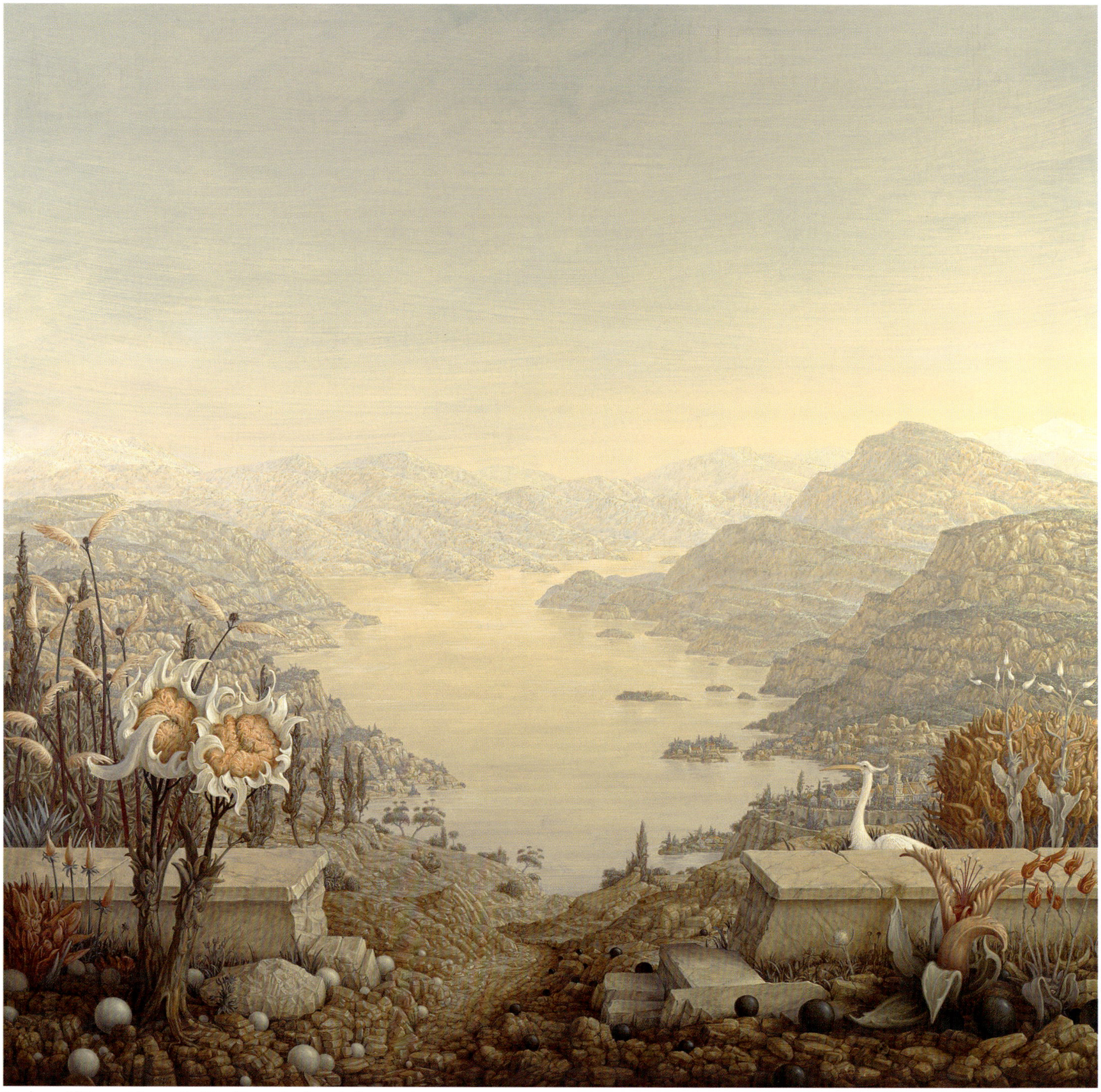

Landscape Without a Motorcycle · 76 x 82 cm · Acrylic and oil on panel

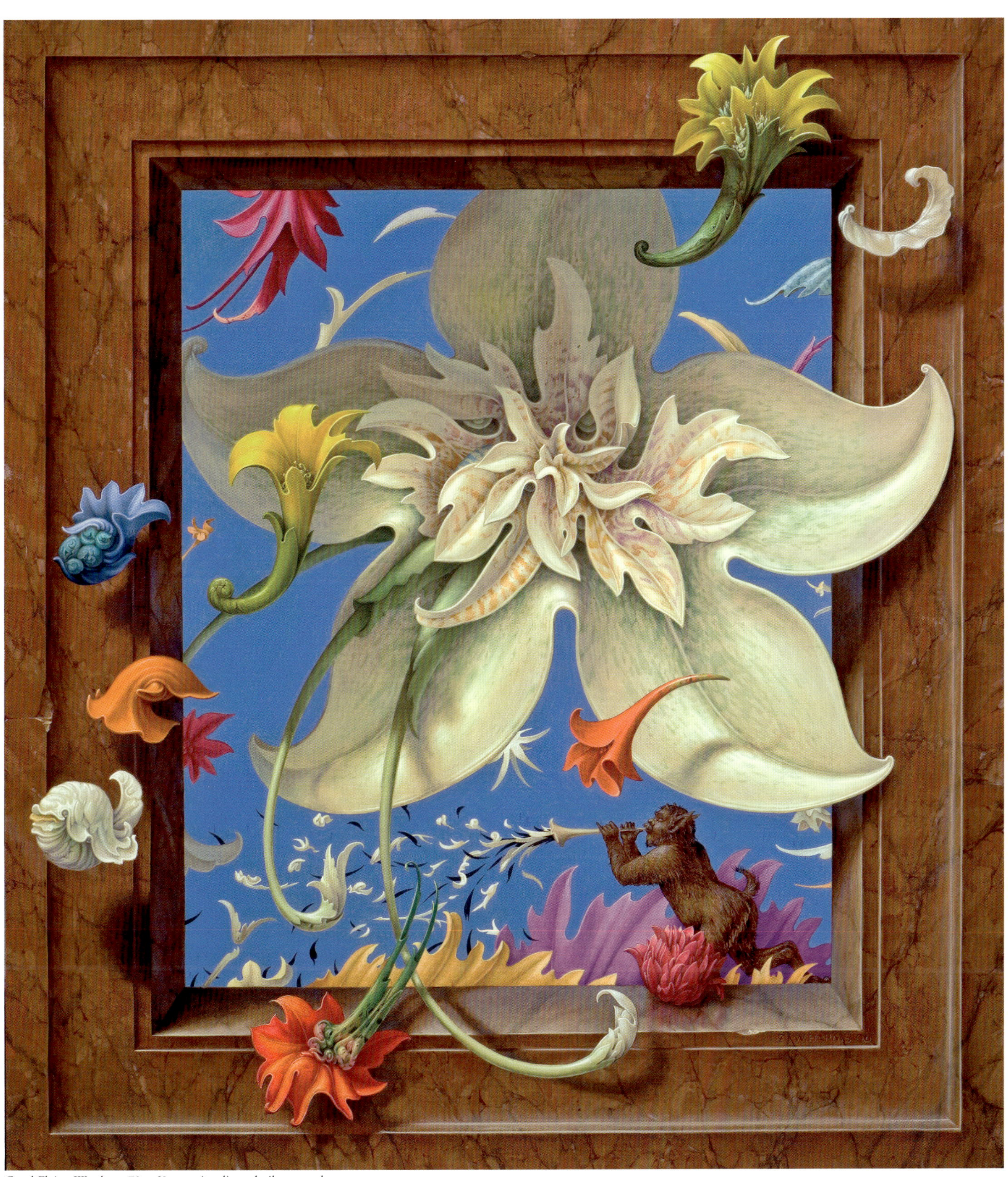

Good Flying Weather · 70 x 60 cm · Acrylic and oil on panel

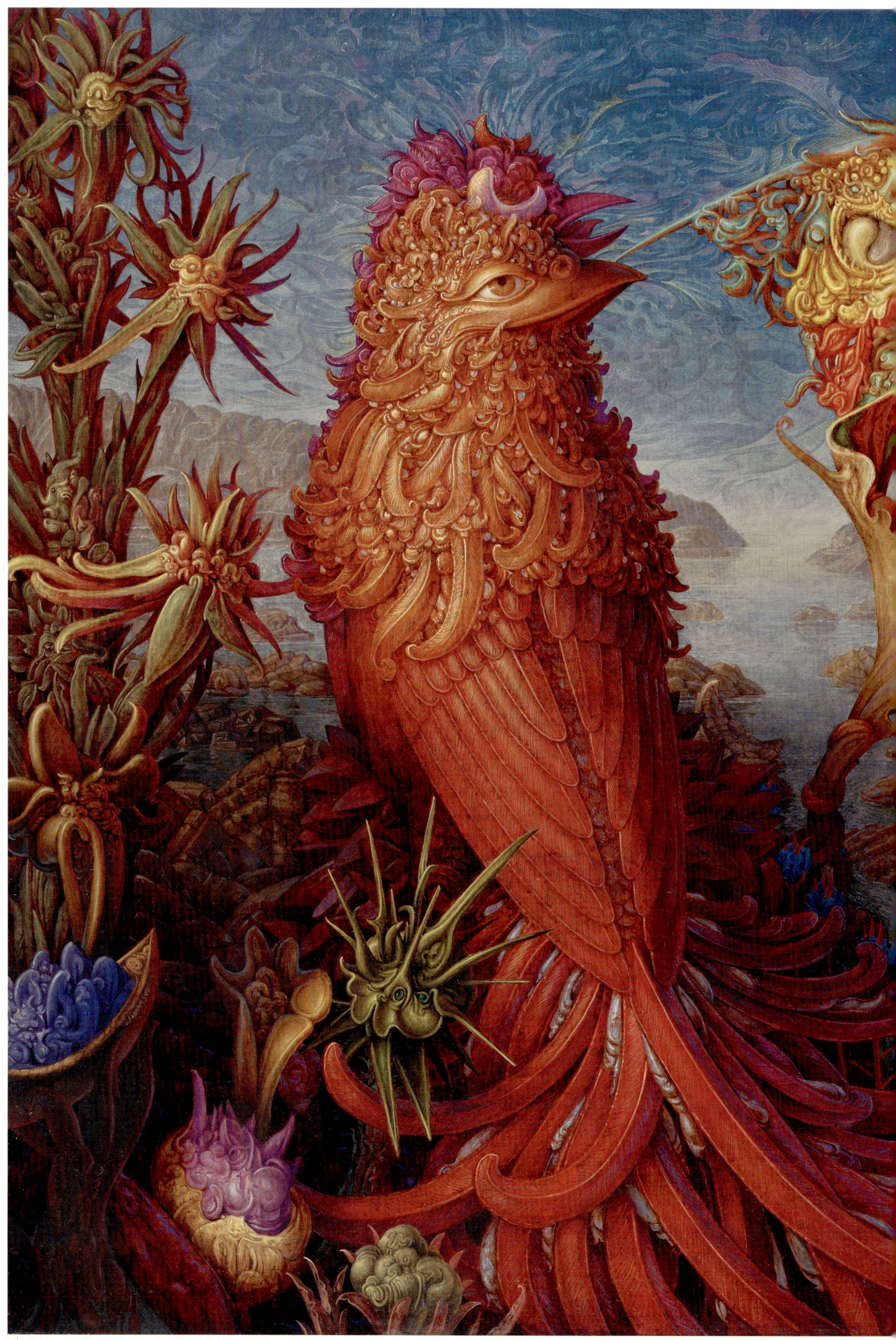

The Massage · 62 x 85,5 cm · Acrylic and oil on panel

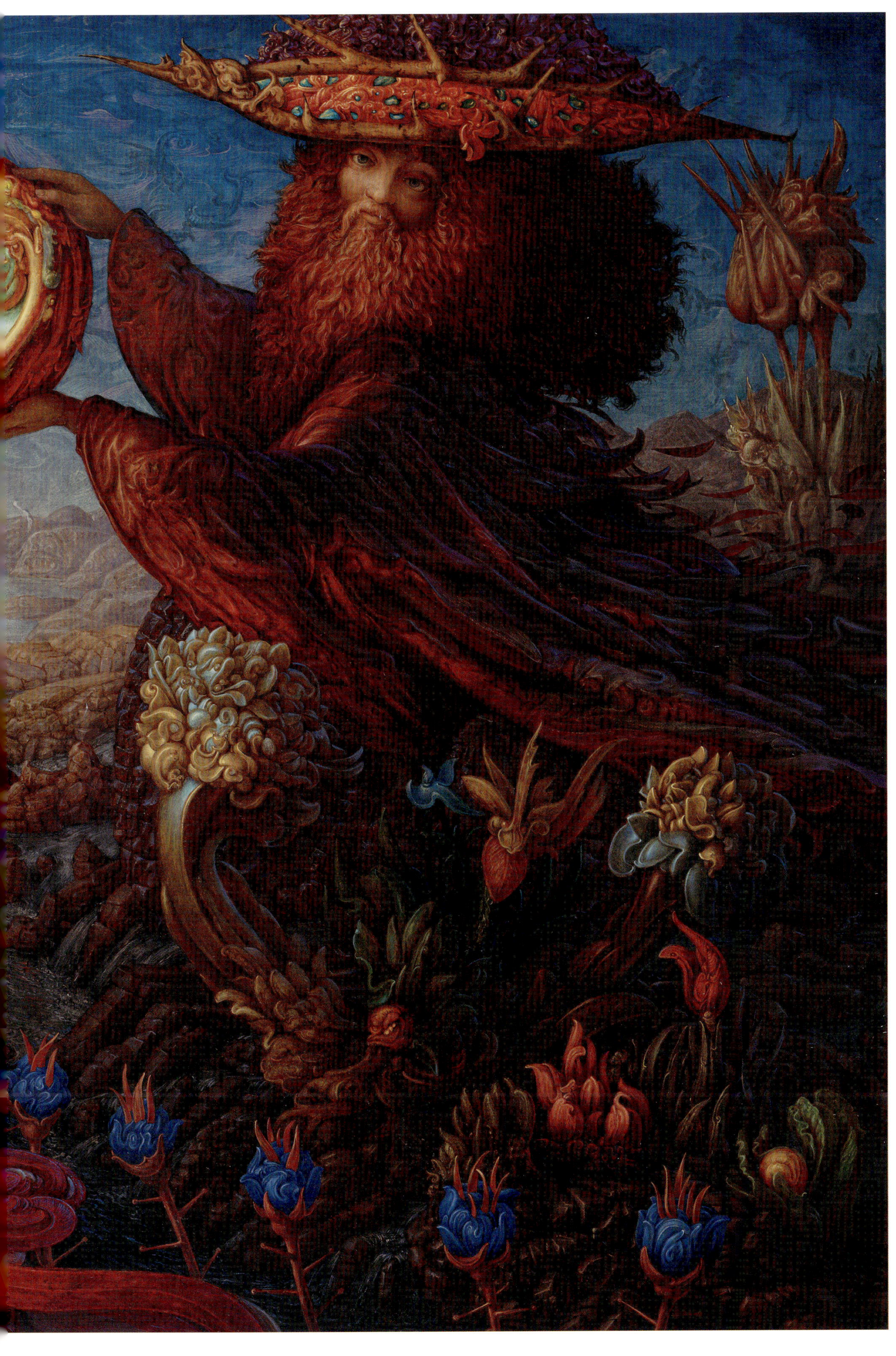

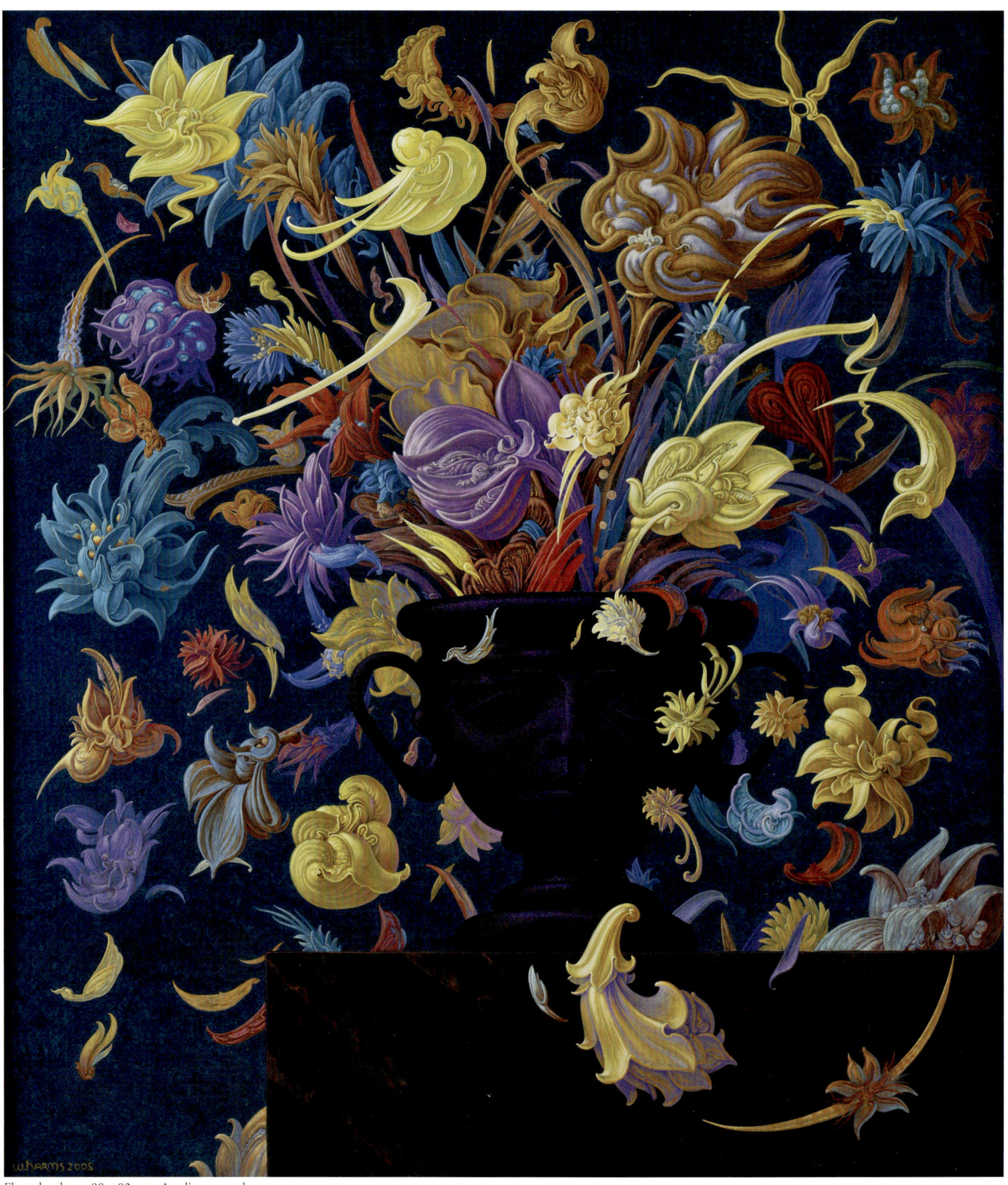

Flowerheadpot · 98 x 82 cm · Acrylic on panel

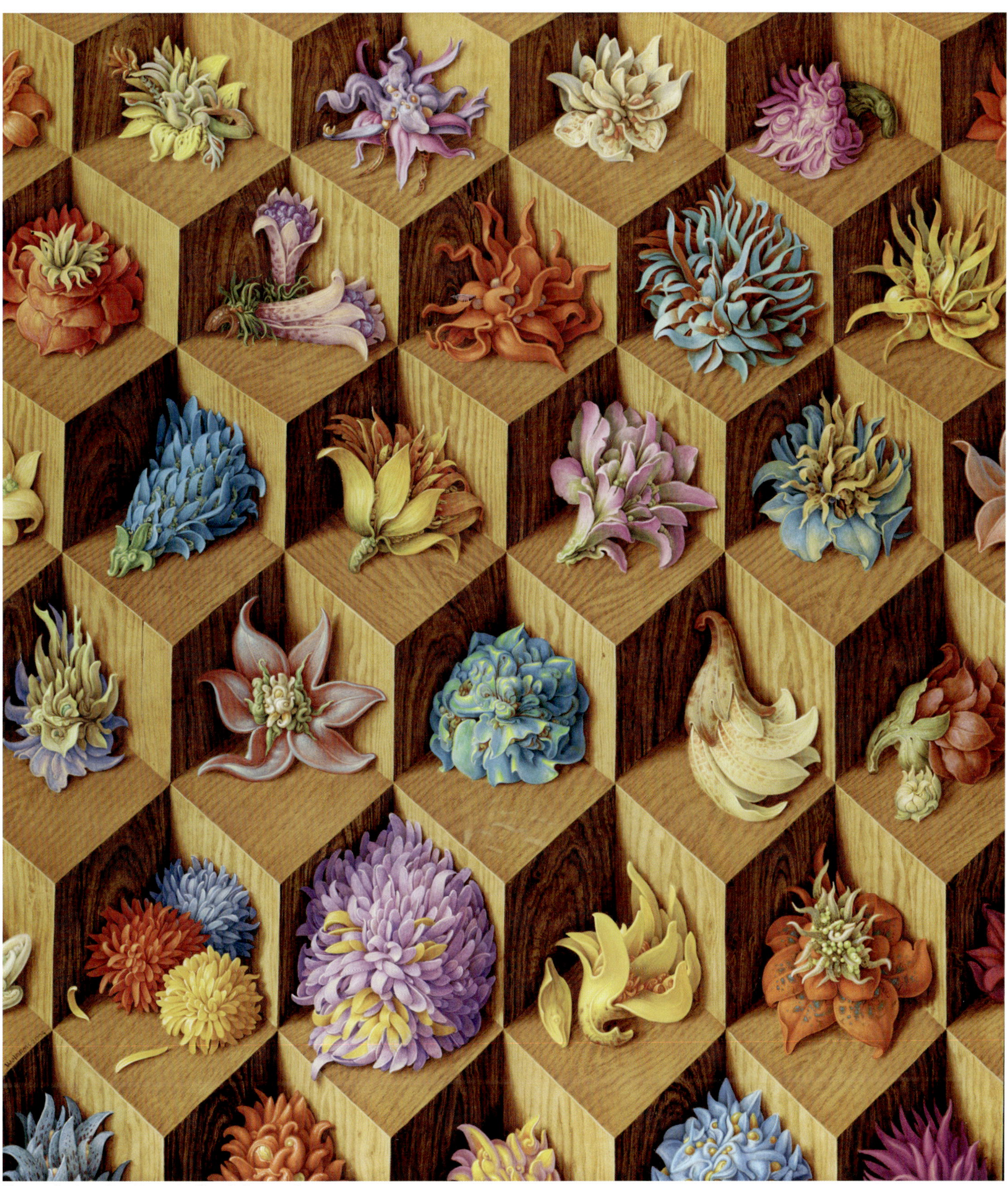

Flower-collection · 65 x 55 cm · Acrylic and oil on panel

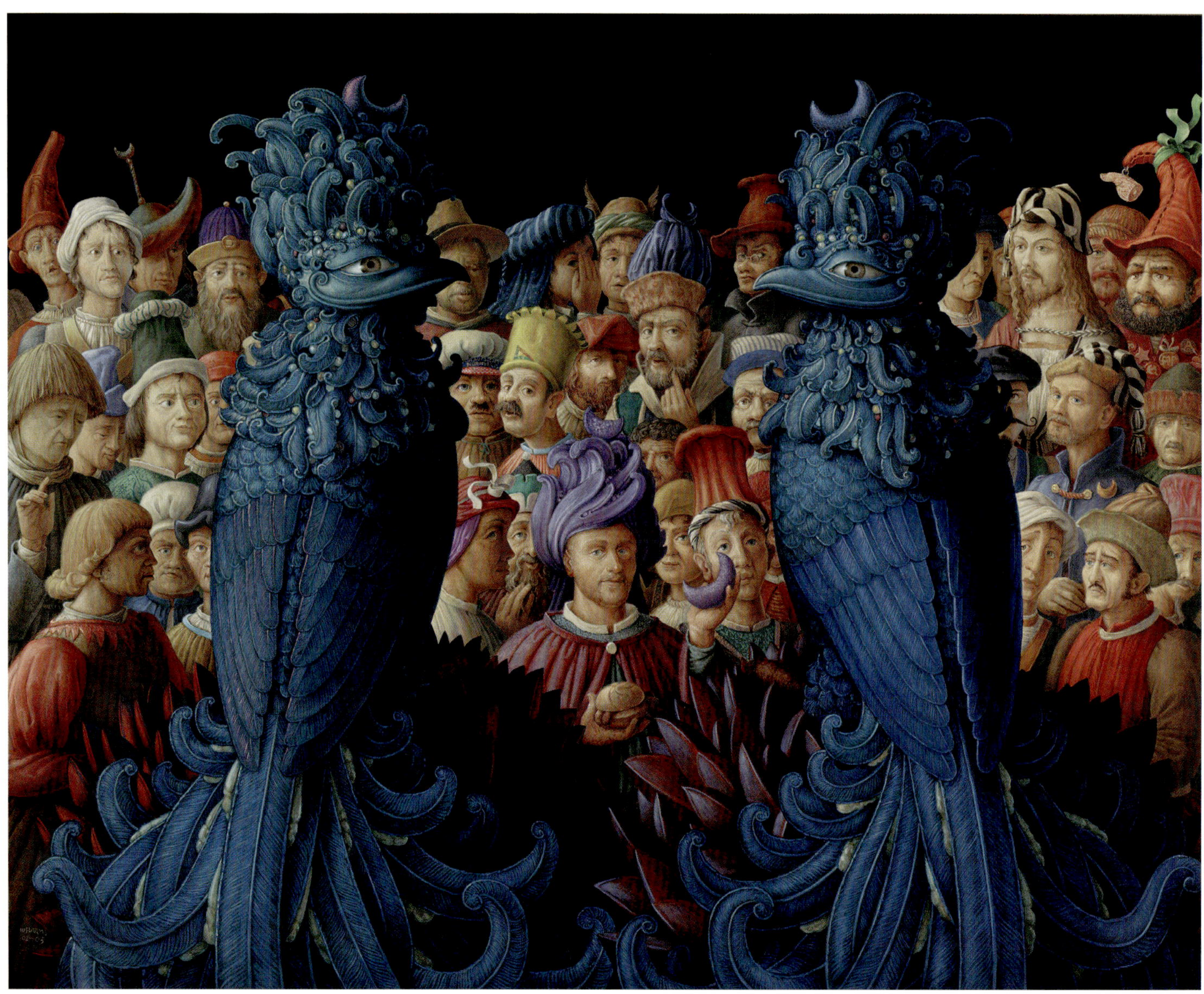

Observed Moonbirds · 45 x 55 cm · Acrylic and oil on panel

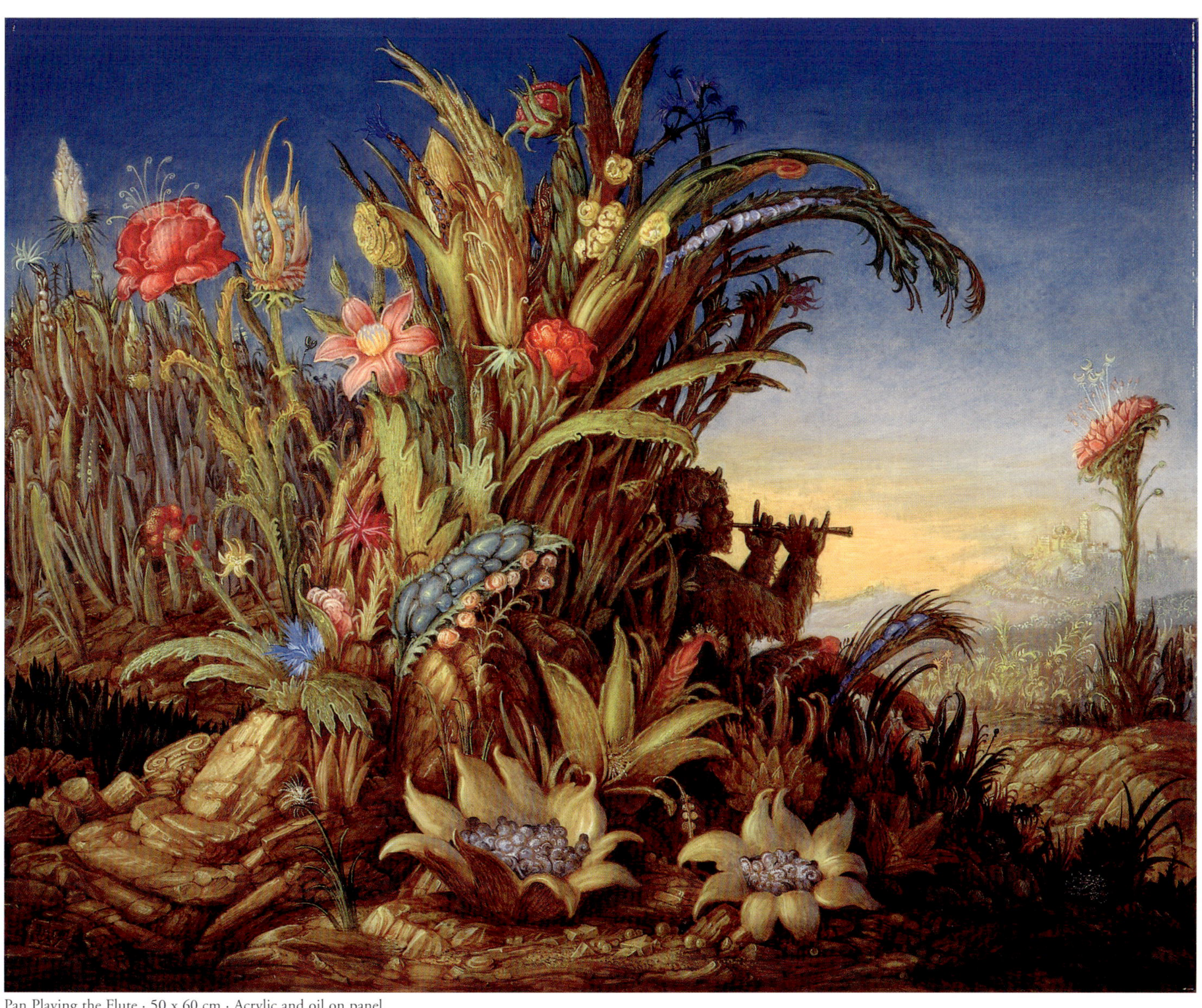
Pan Playing the Flute · 50 x 60 cm · Acrylic and oil on panel

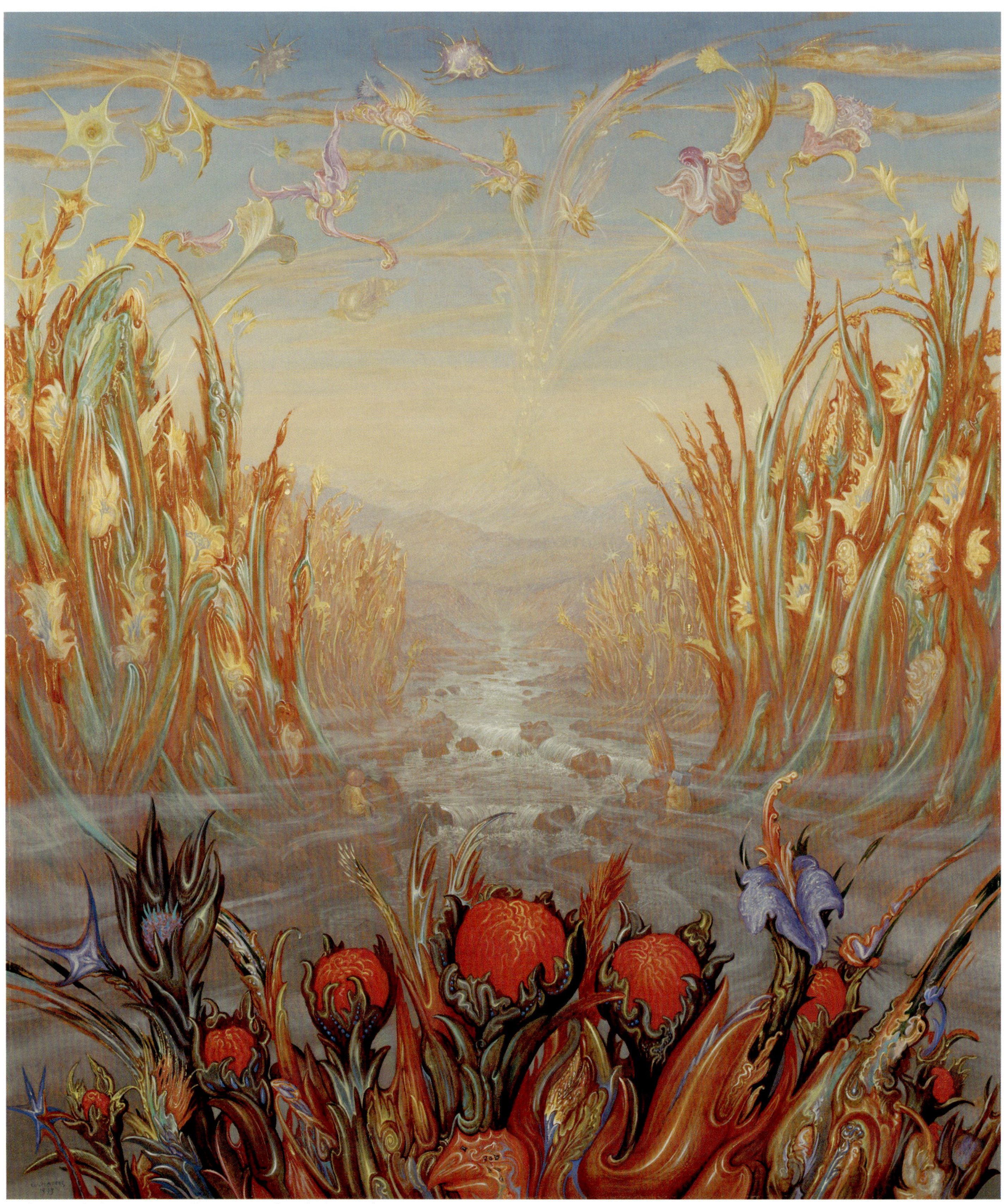

Landscape With Flowereruption · 84 x 70 cm · Acrylic and oil on panel

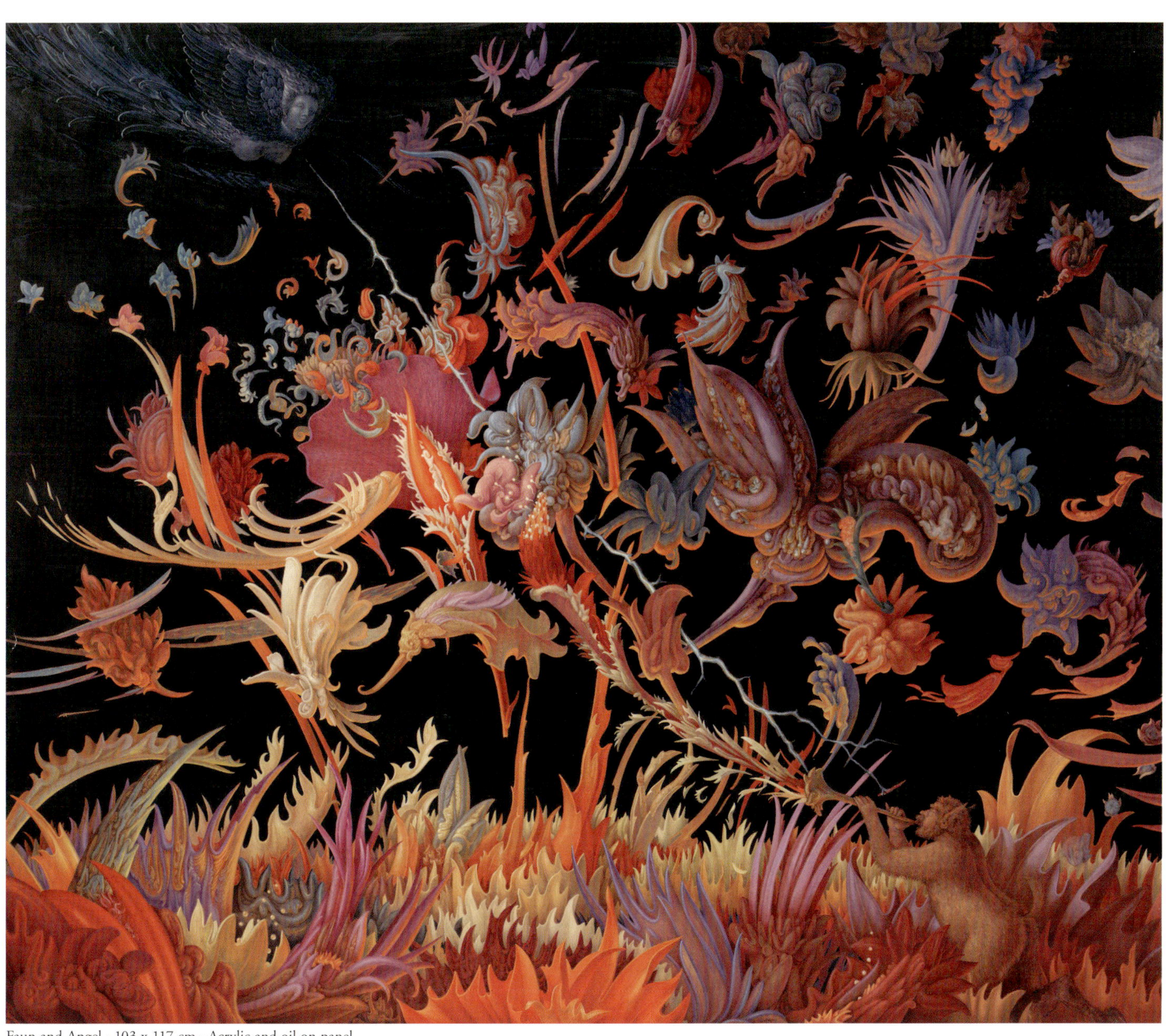
Faun and Angel · 103 x 117 cm · Acrylic and oil on panel

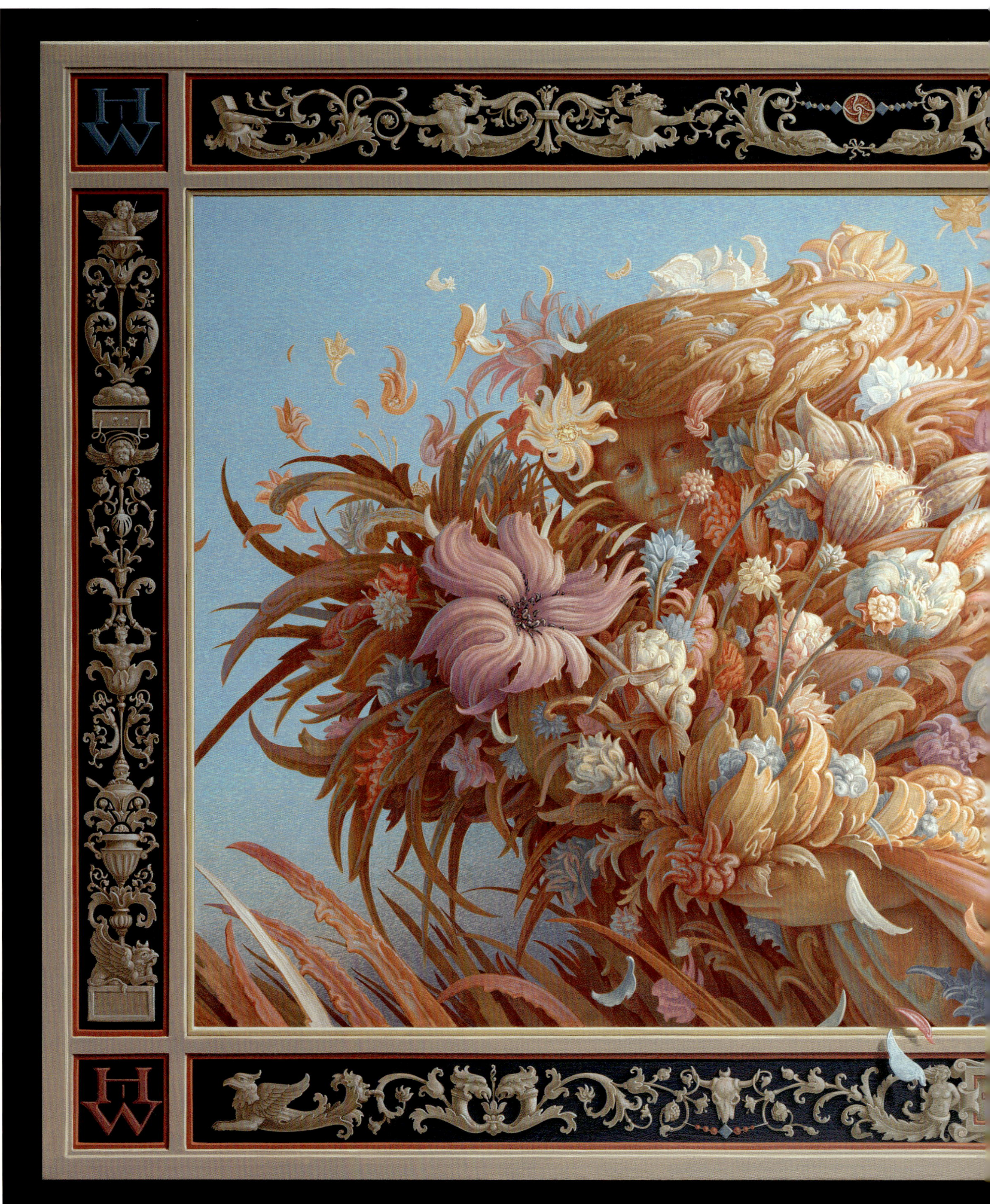
Flowerthief · 99 x 169 cm · Acryli and oil on panel

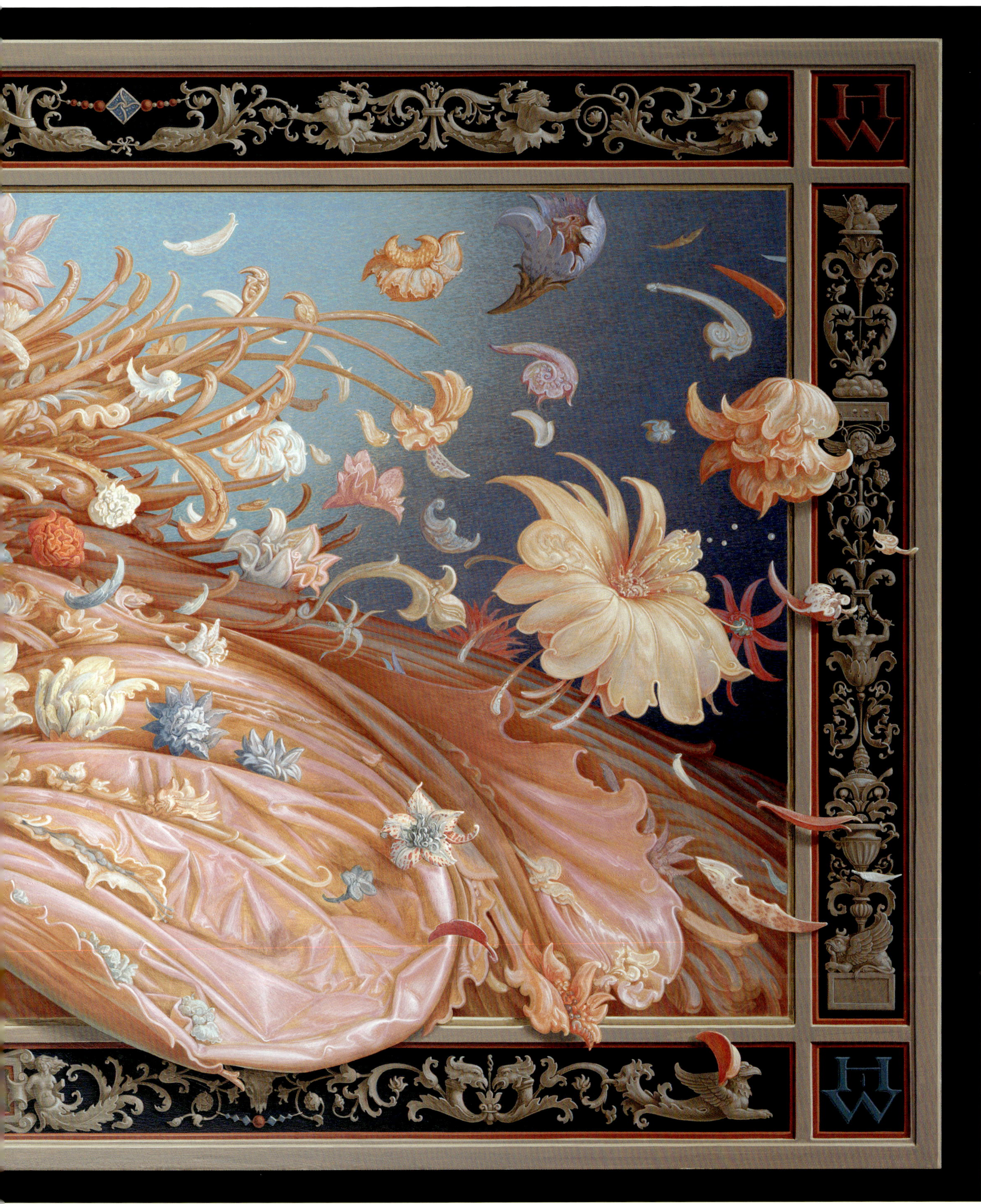

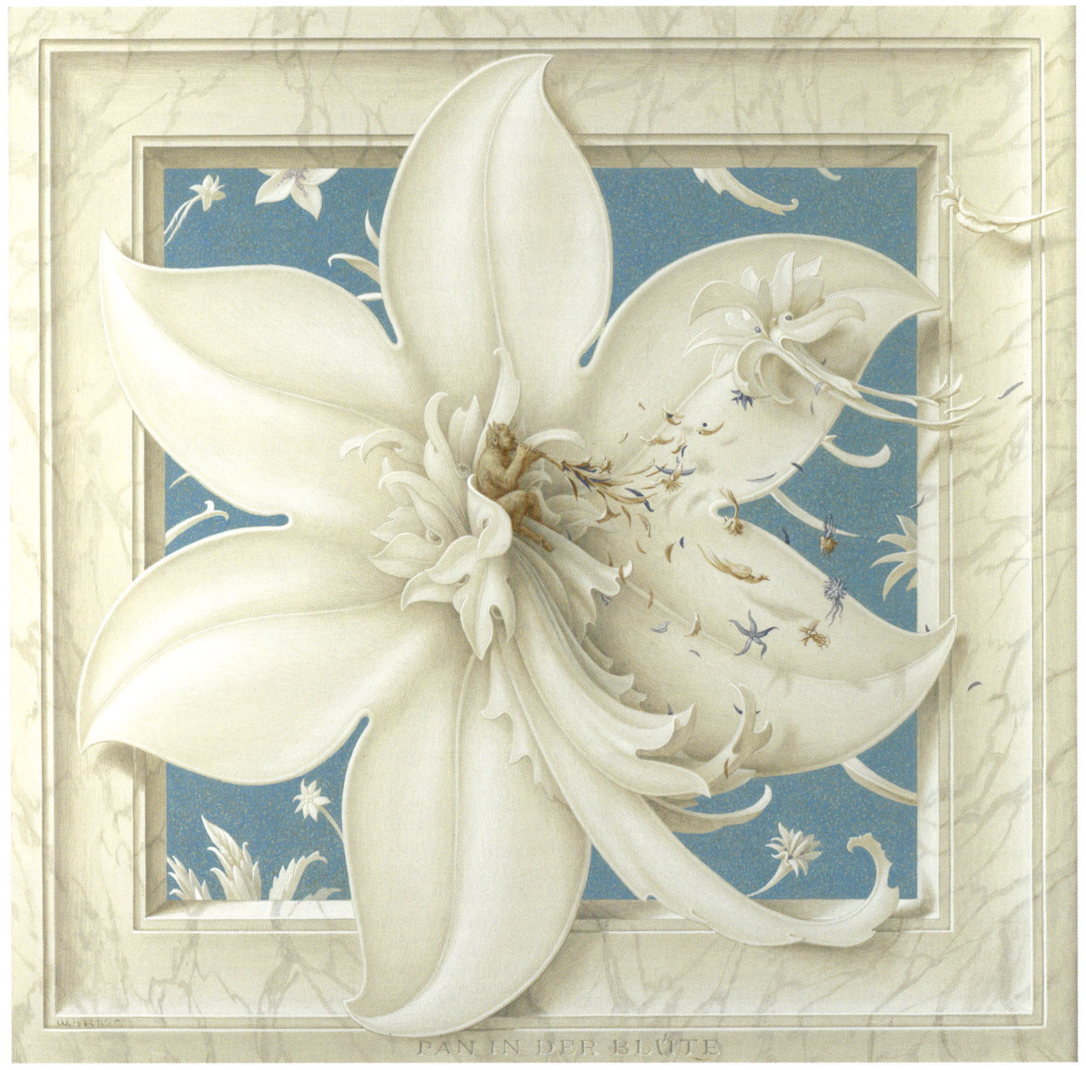

Faun, Sitting in a Flower · 67,5 x 64,5 cm · Acrylic on panel

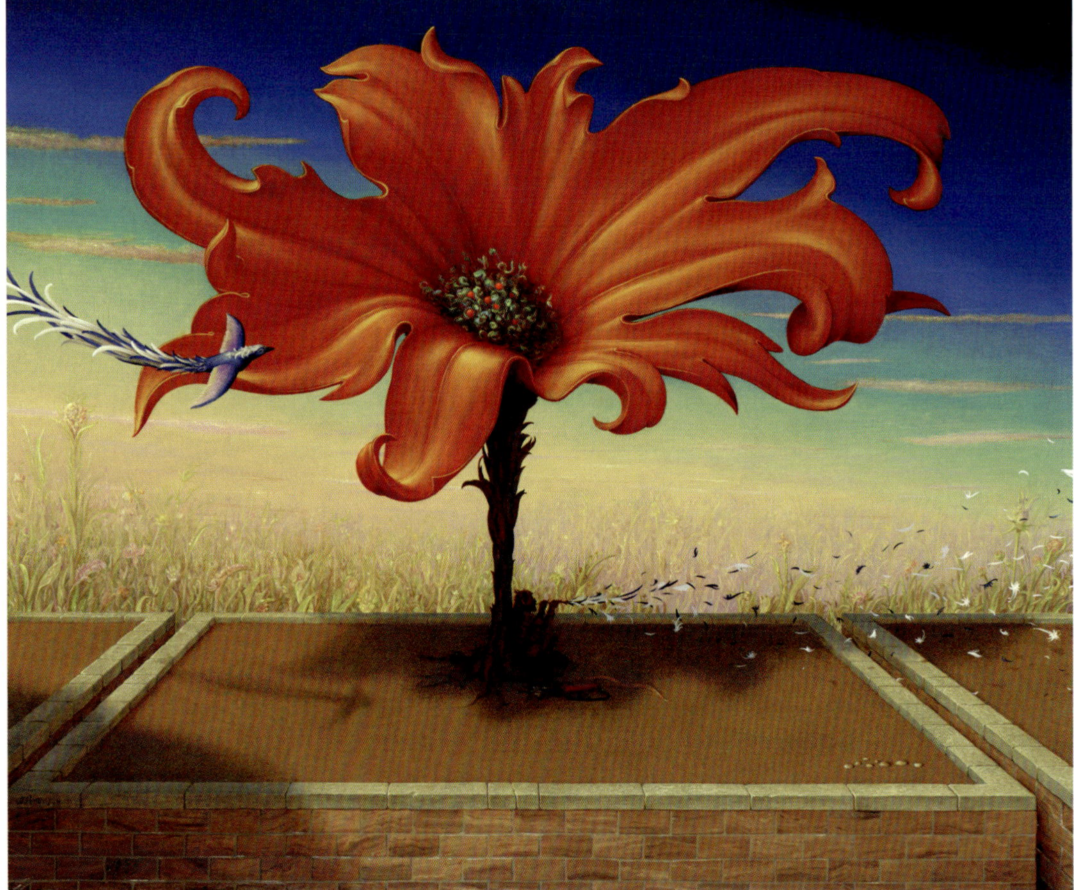

A Nice Place in the Shadow · 60 x 70 cm · Acrylic and oil on panel

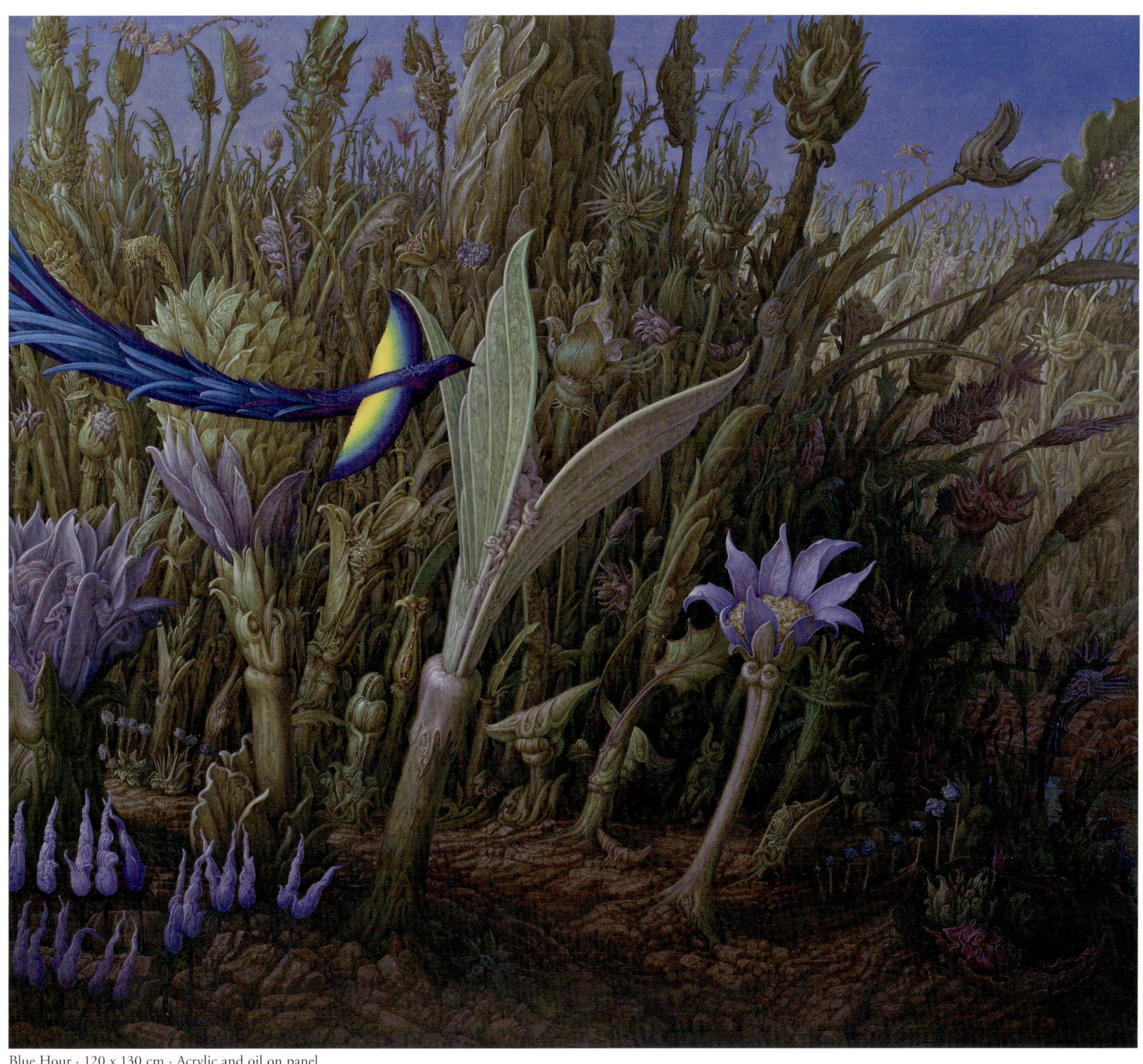

Blue Hour · 120 x 130 cm · Acrylic and oil on panel

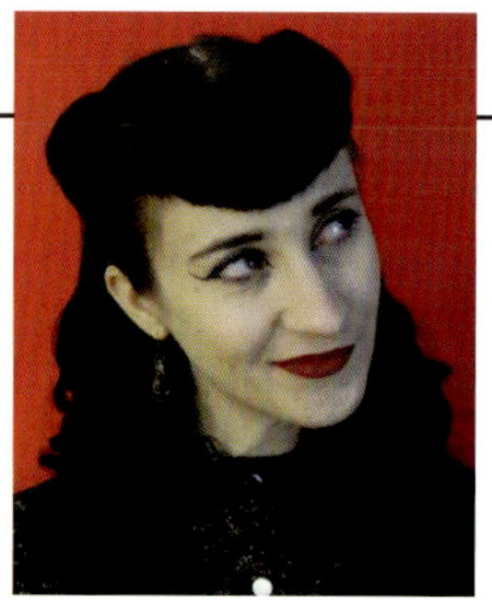

ANJA ALTENBURG

1980 Denmark

www.abenart.dk

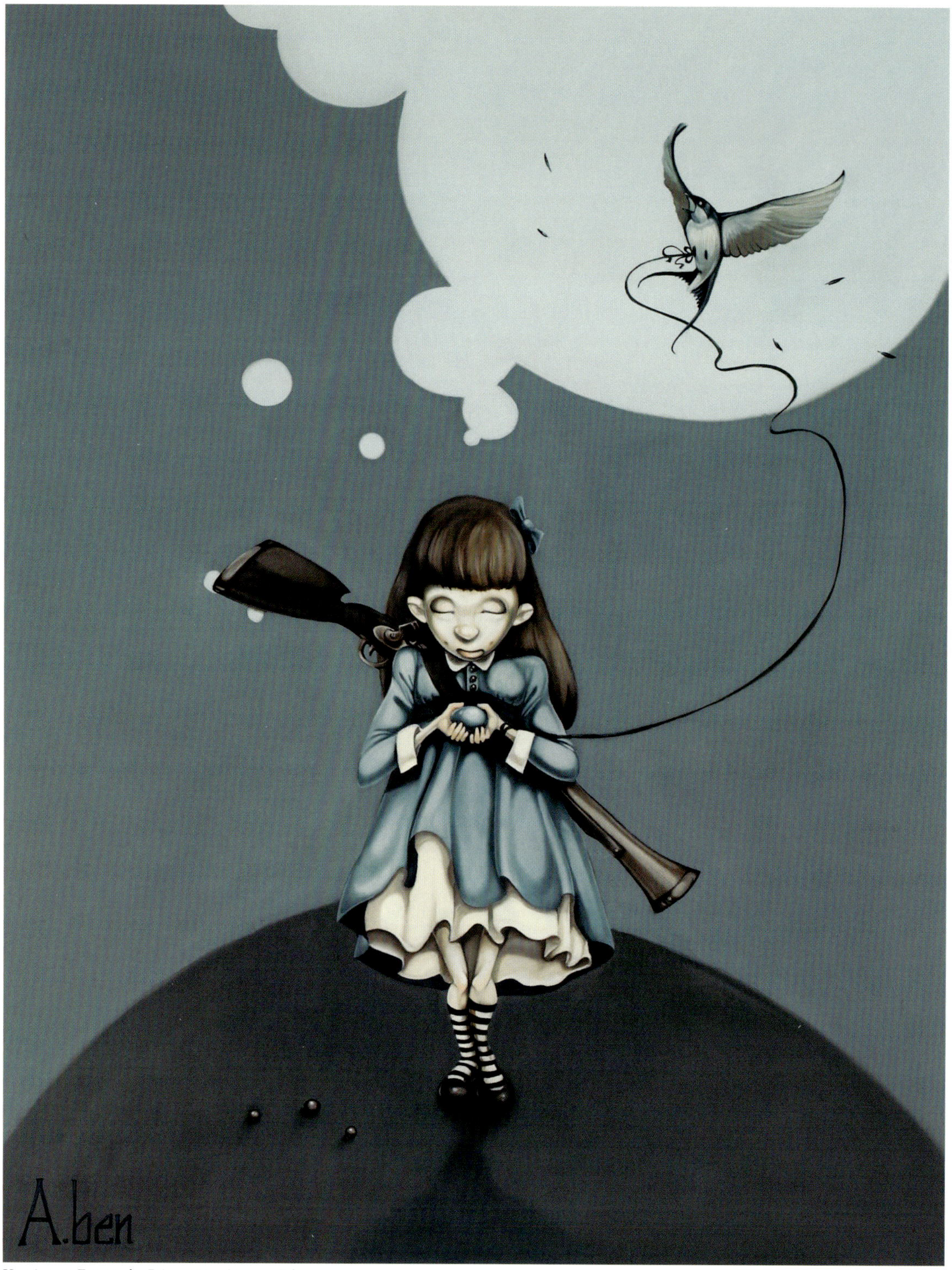

Keeping an Eye on the Prize · 80 x 60 cm · Oil on canvas

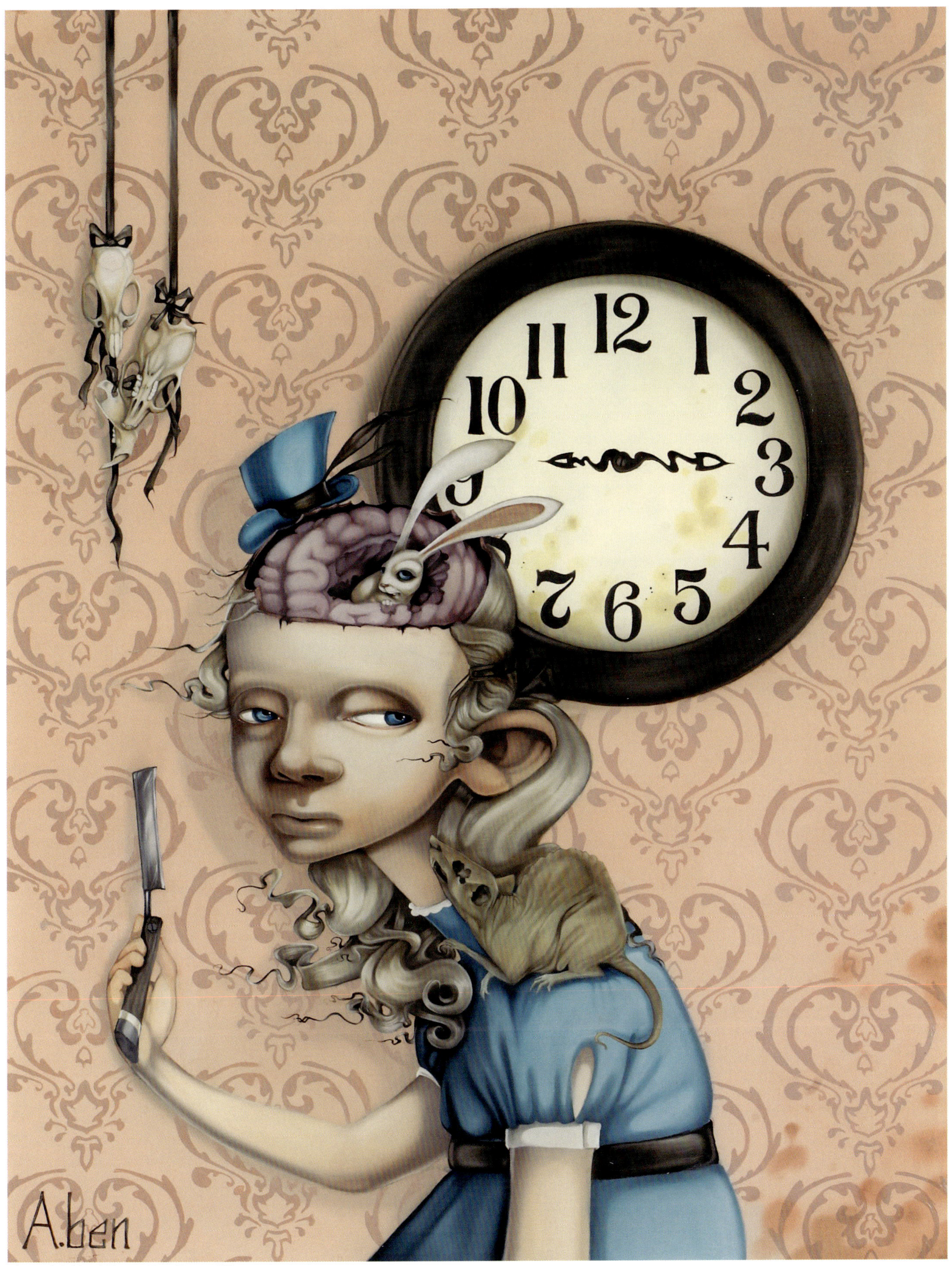

Alice and Ockham's Razor · 80 x 60 cm · Oil on canvas

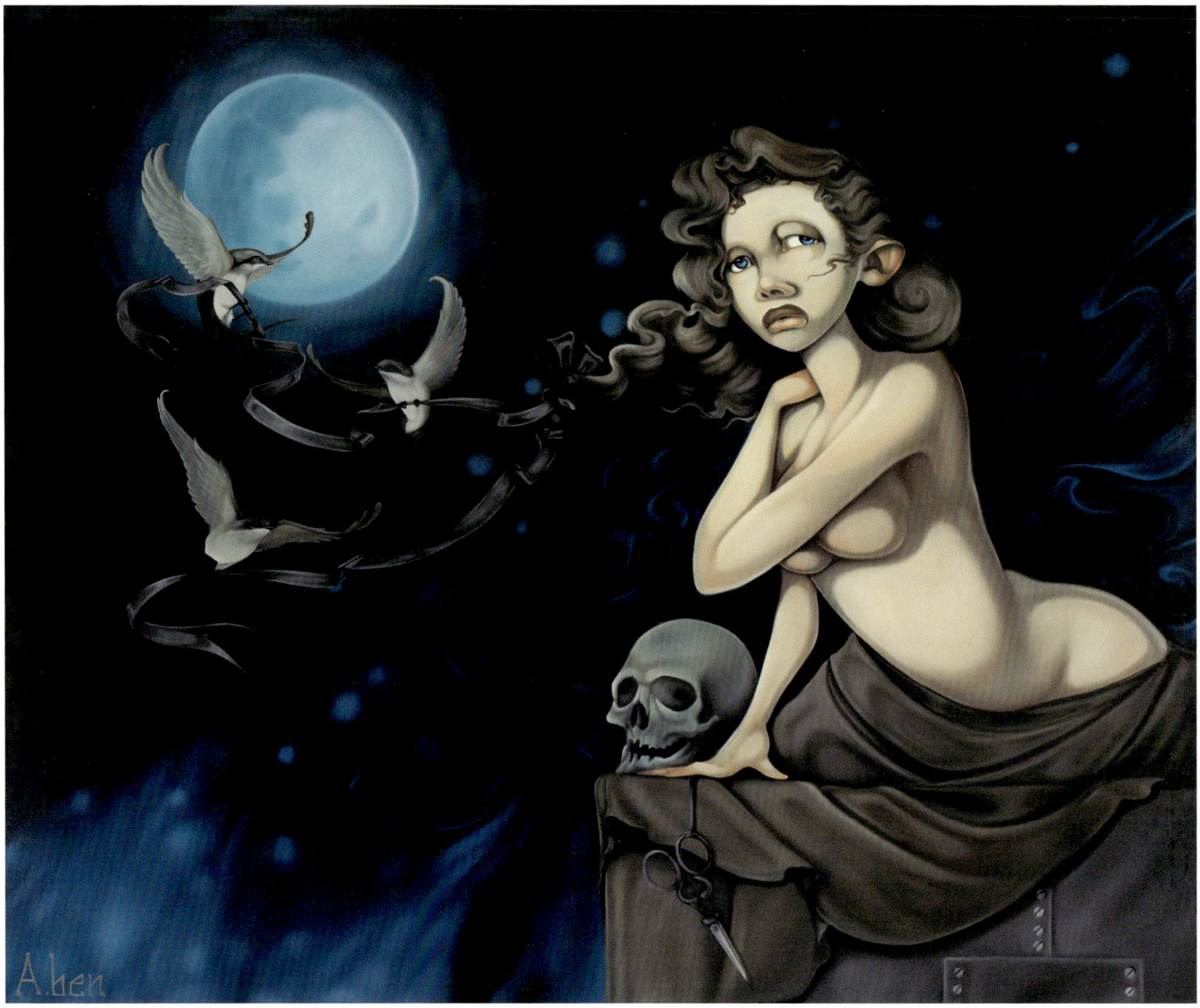

Morphean Dreaming, Like the wind through my Bones · 110 x 130 cm · Oil on canvas

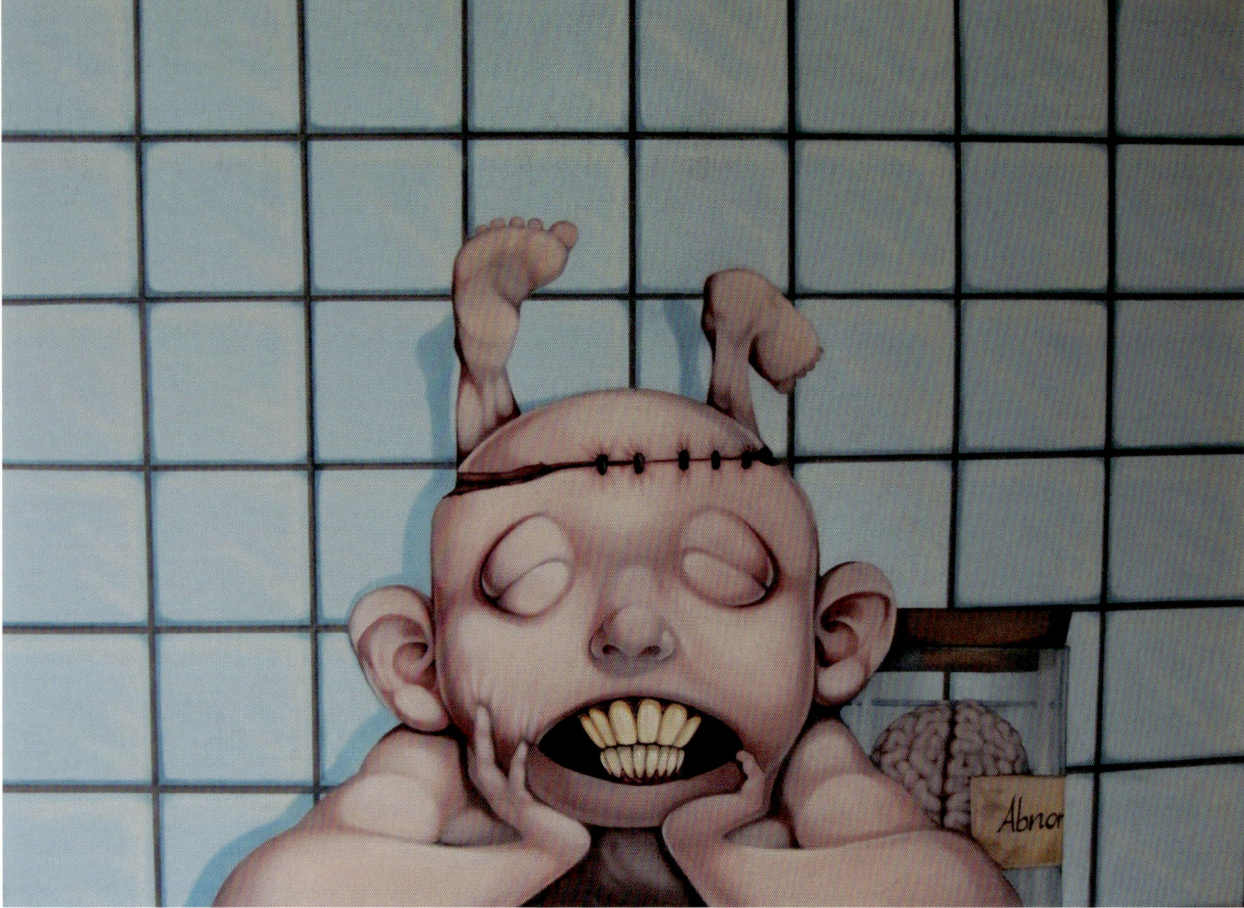

A & E · 60 x 80 cm · Oil on canvas

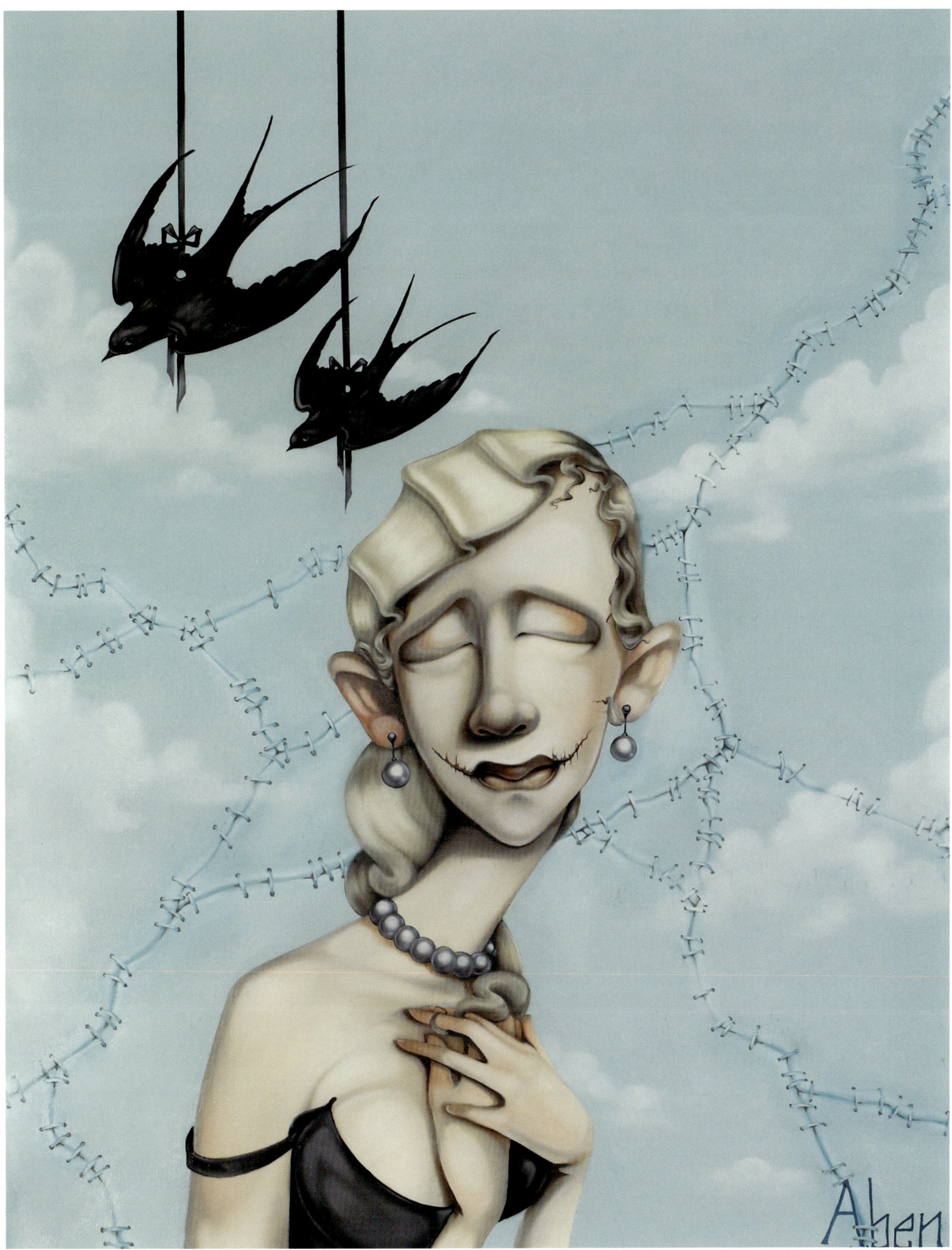

Picure Perfect · 80 x 60 cm · Oil on canvas

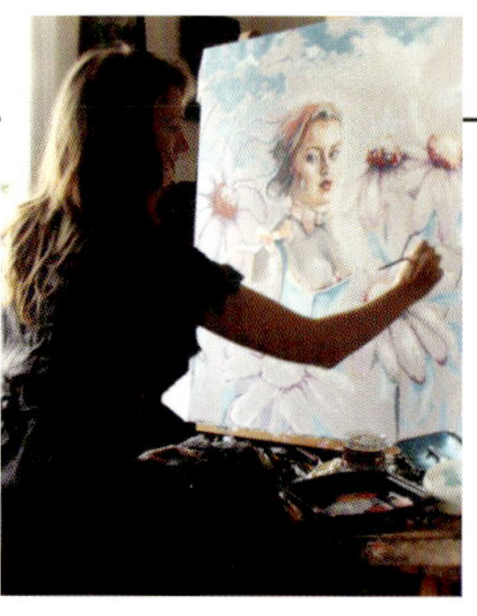

BILLIE BAILEY

1974 Australia/Denmark

www.billiebailey.com

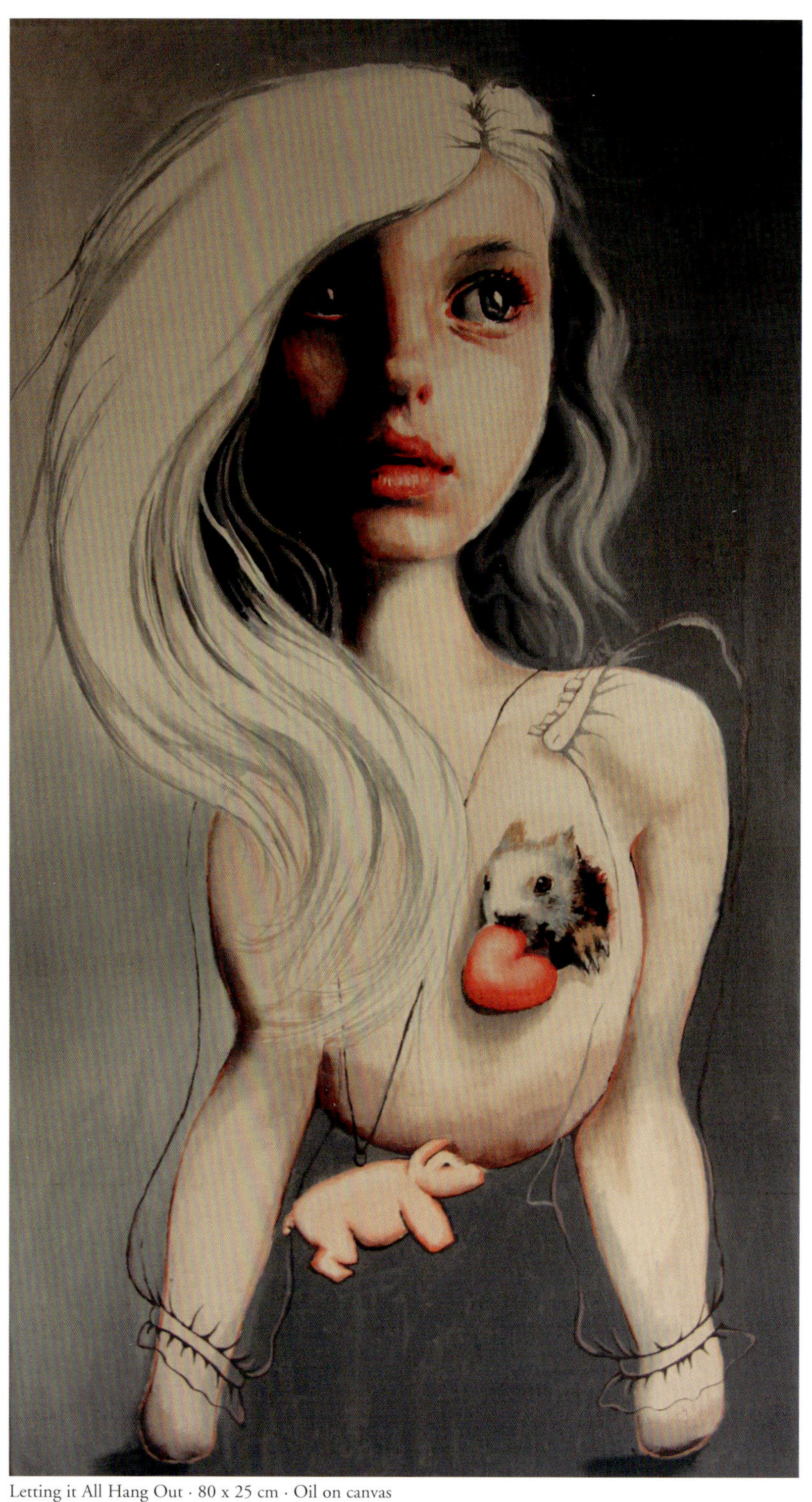

Letting it All Hang Out · 80 x 25 cm · Oil on canvas

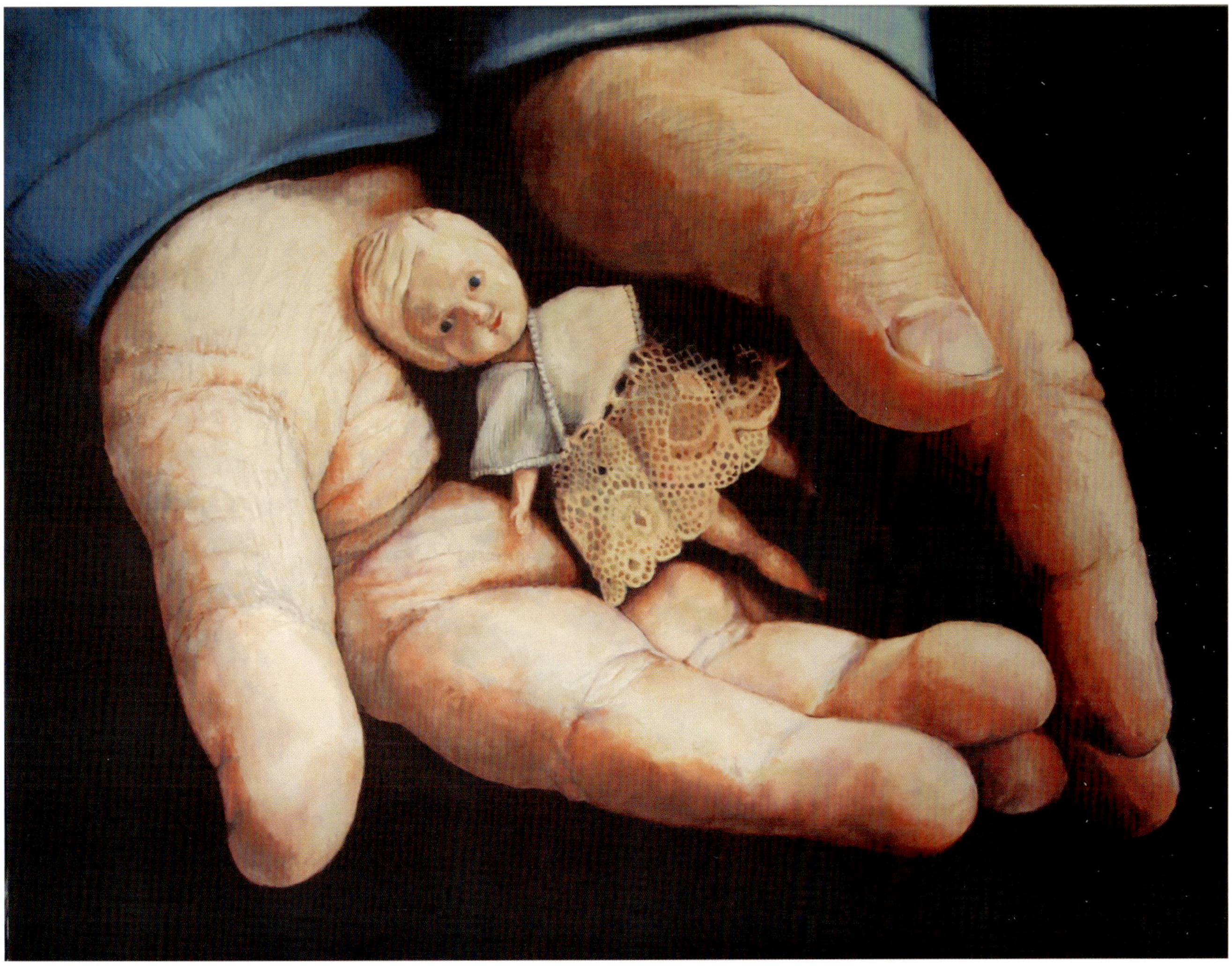

In Your Hands · 85 x 115 cm · Oil on canvas

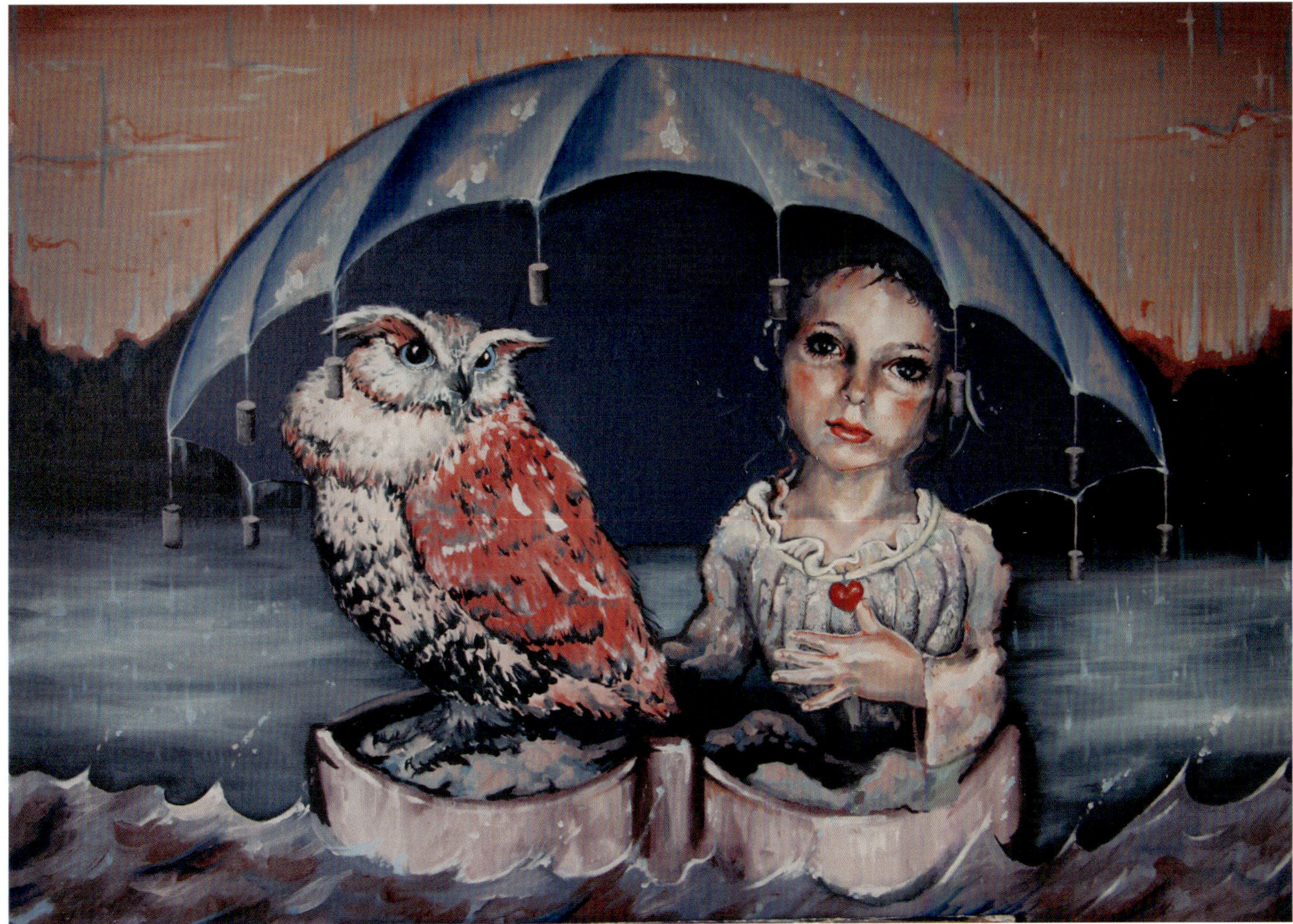

Long Way · 80 x 110 cm · Oil on canvas

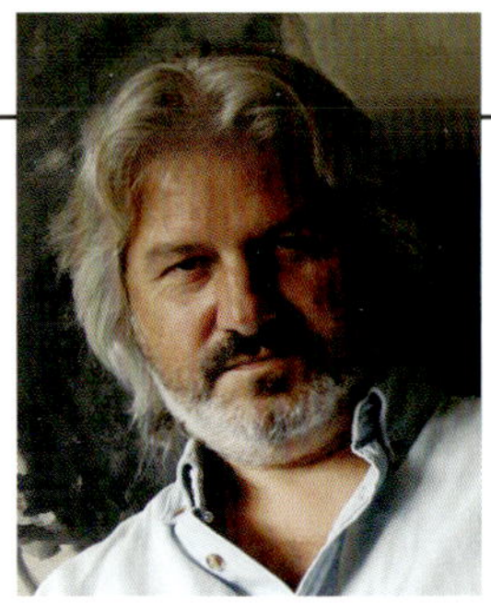

KAROL BĄK

1961 Poland

www.karolbak.com

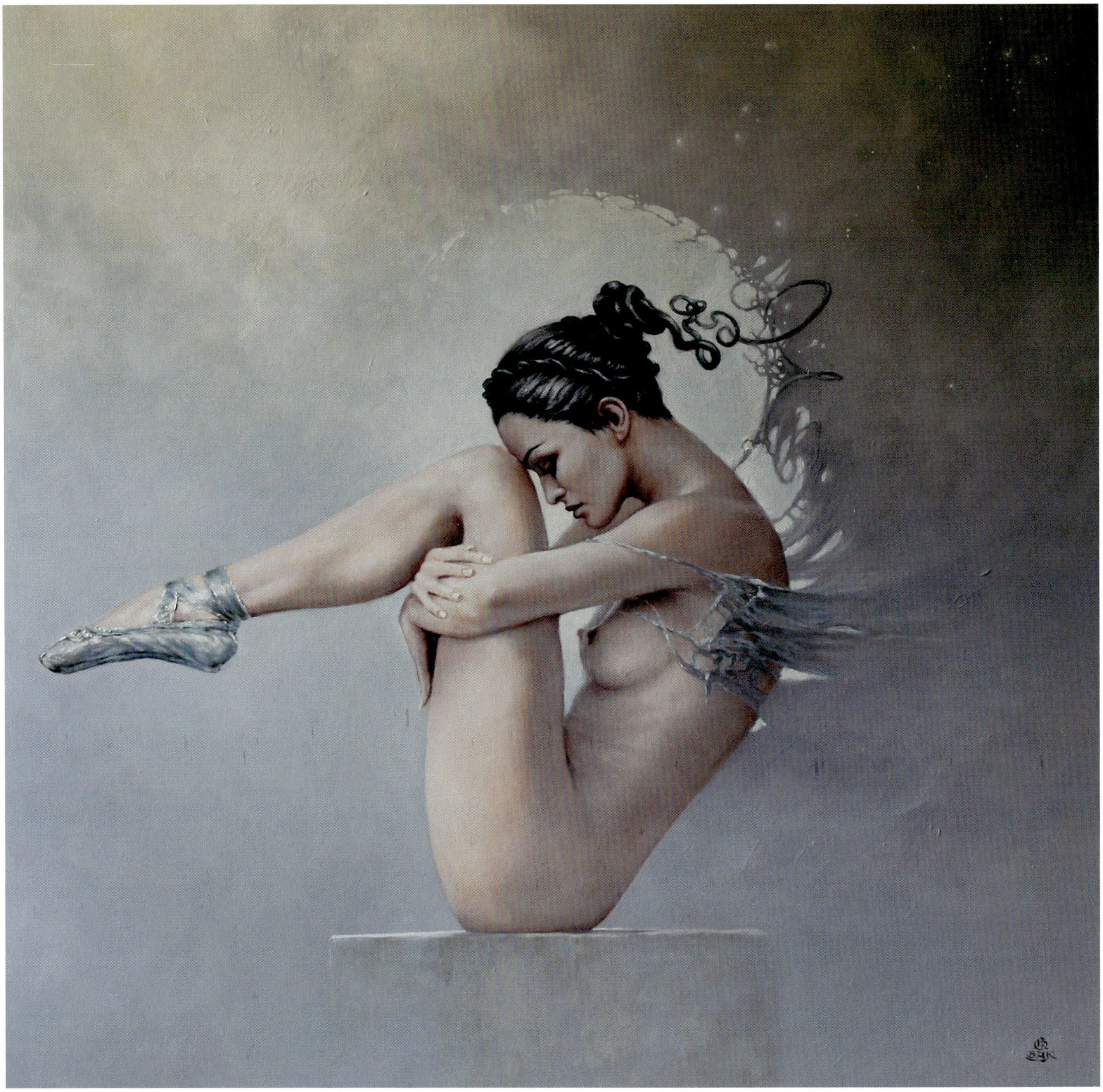

Disappointment · 100 x 100 cm · Oil on canvas

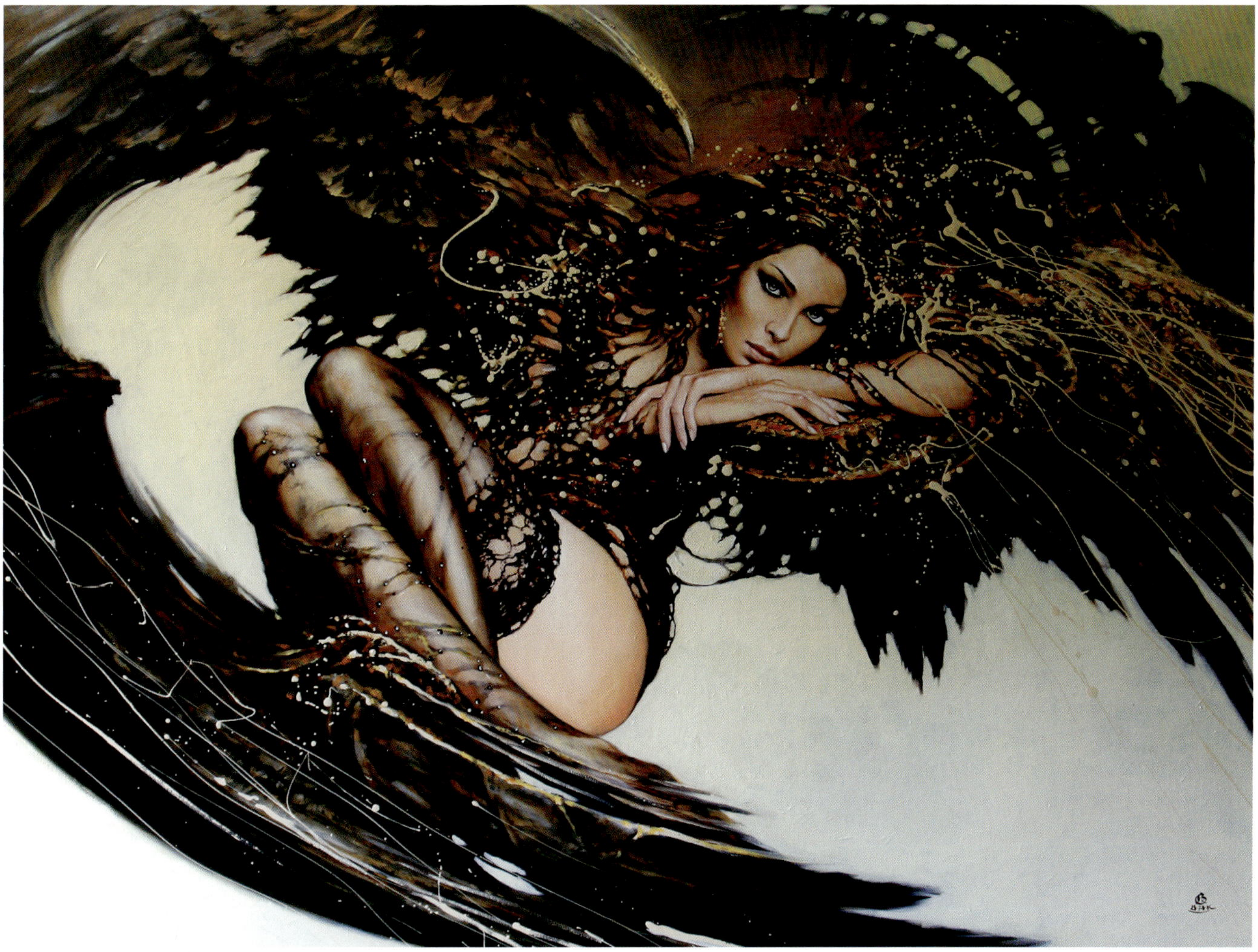

Causa · 100 x 130 cm · Oil on canvas

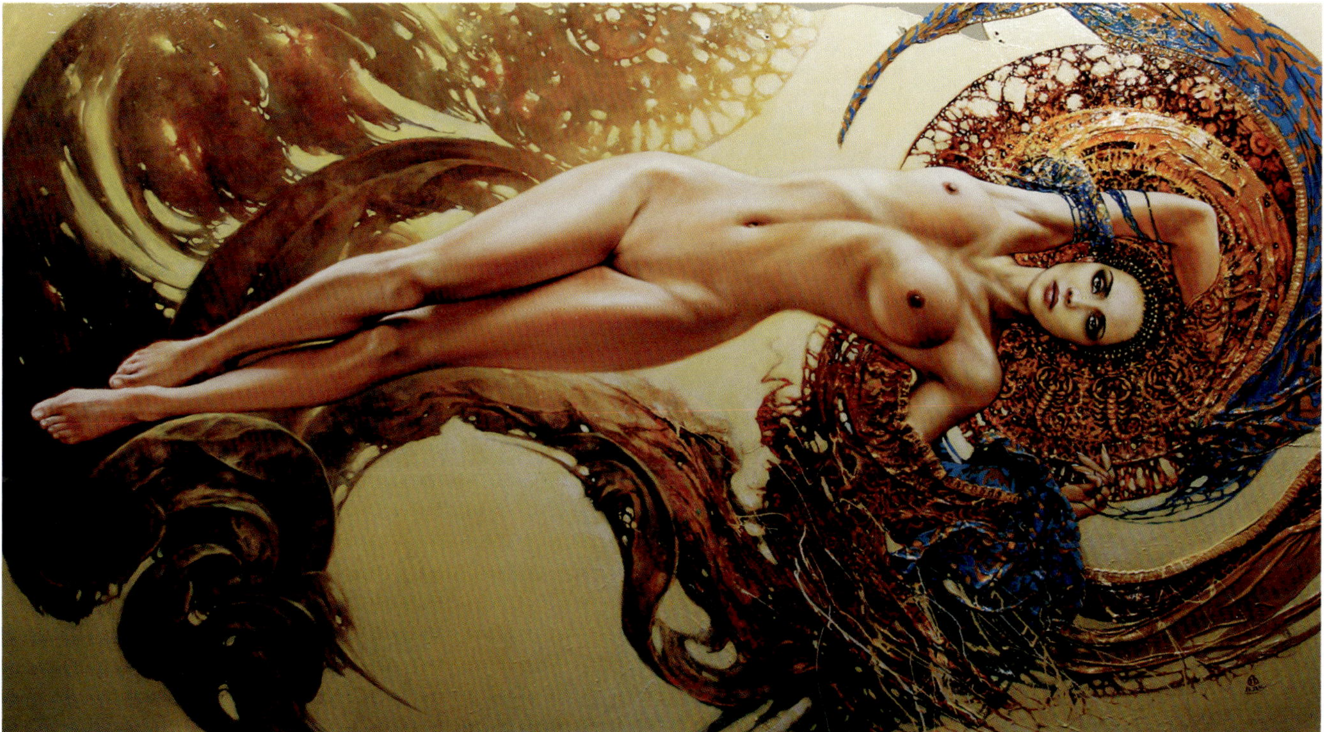

Golden Dawn · 100 x 180 cm · Oil and mixed media on hard board

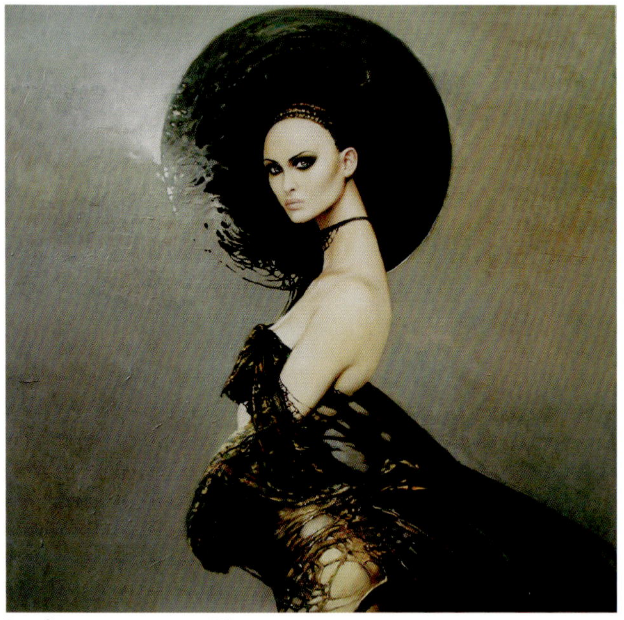

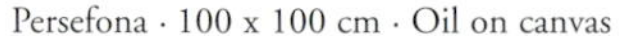

Persefona · 100 x 100 cm · Oil on canvas

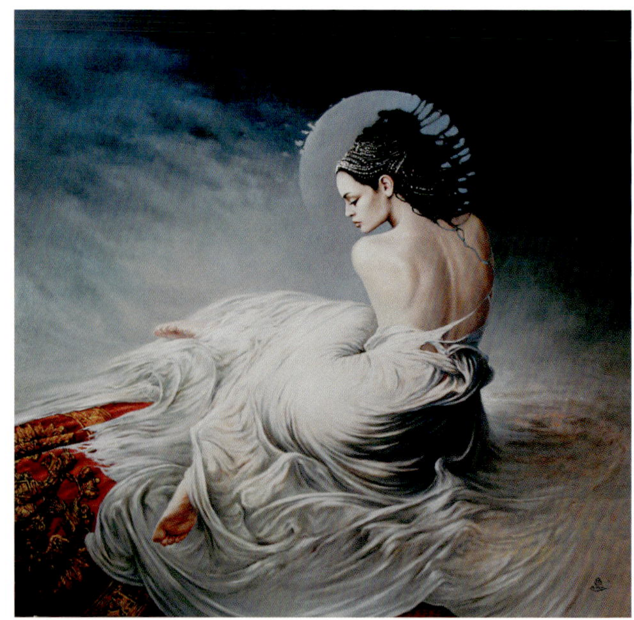

Nocturn No2 · 120 x 120 cm · Oil on canvas

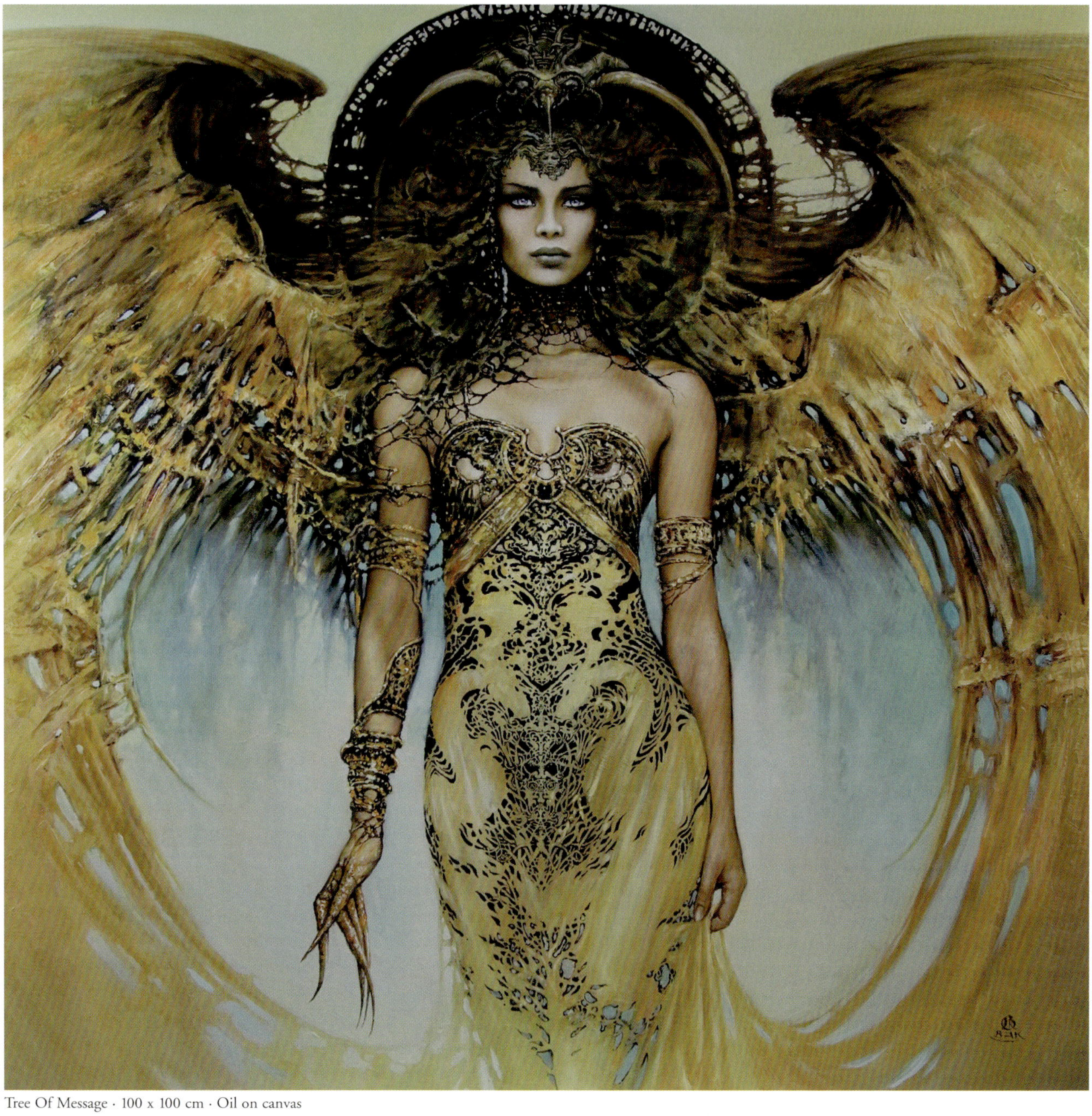

Tree Of Message · 100 x 100 cm · Oil on canvas

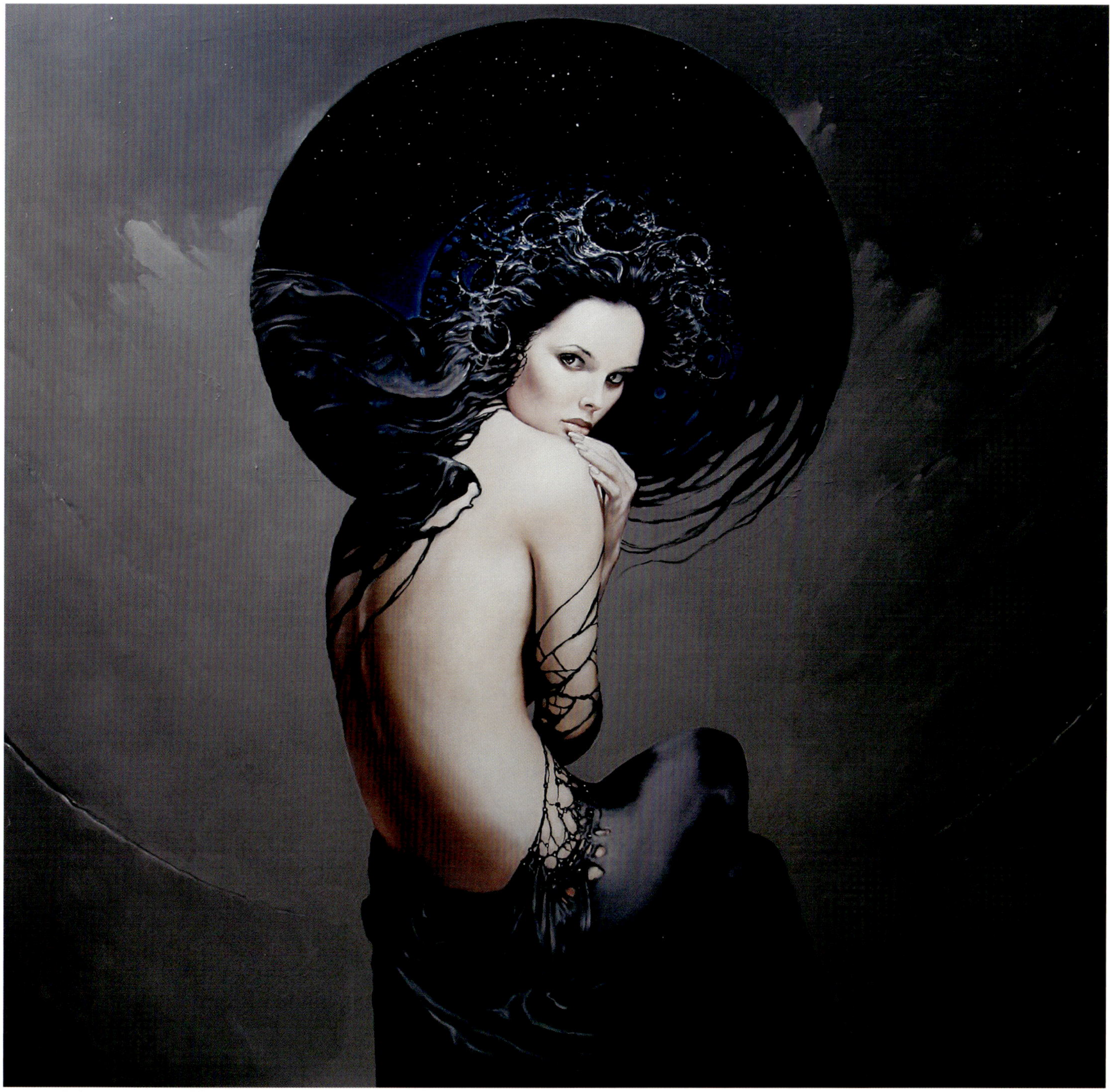

Nocturn No4 · 100 x 100 cm · Oil on canvas

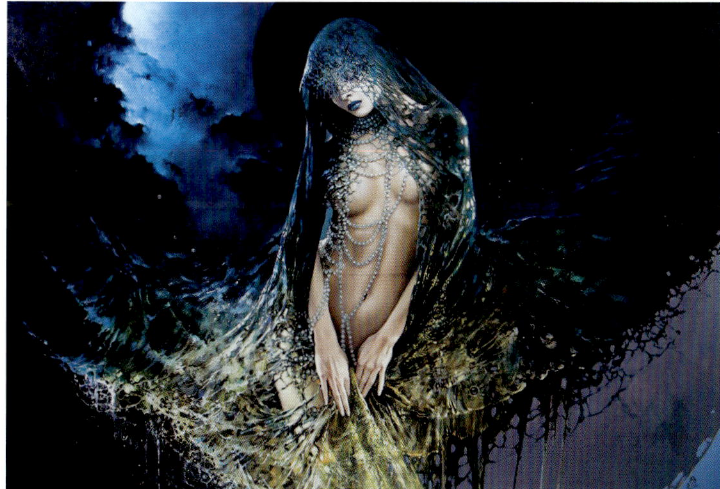

Nocturn No20 · 90 x 130 cm · Oil on canvas

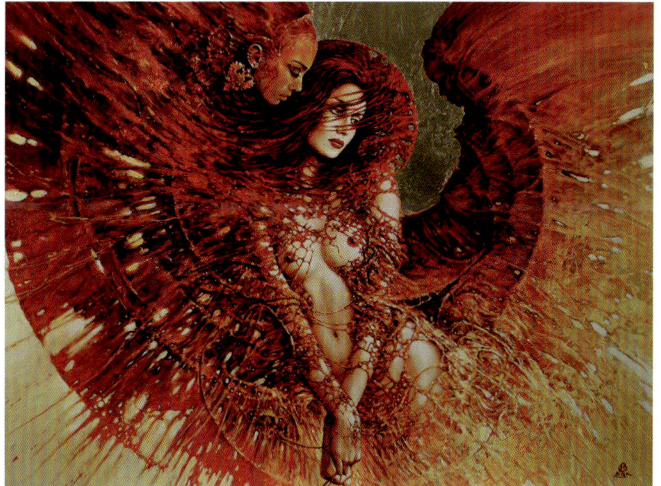

Crimson Etude · 90 x 120 cm · Oil on canvas

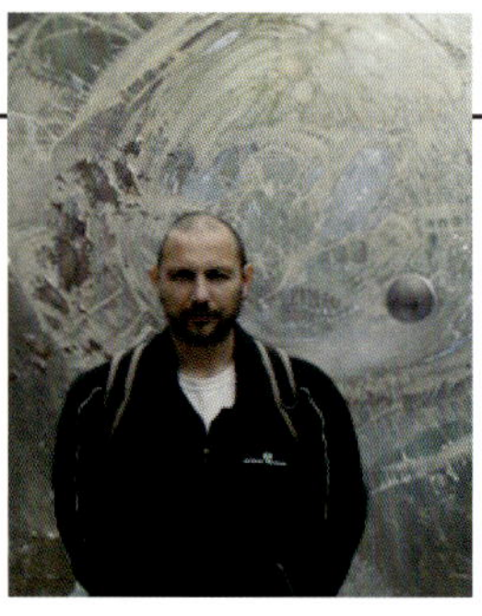

JEF BERTELS

1961 Belgium

www.jefbertels.be

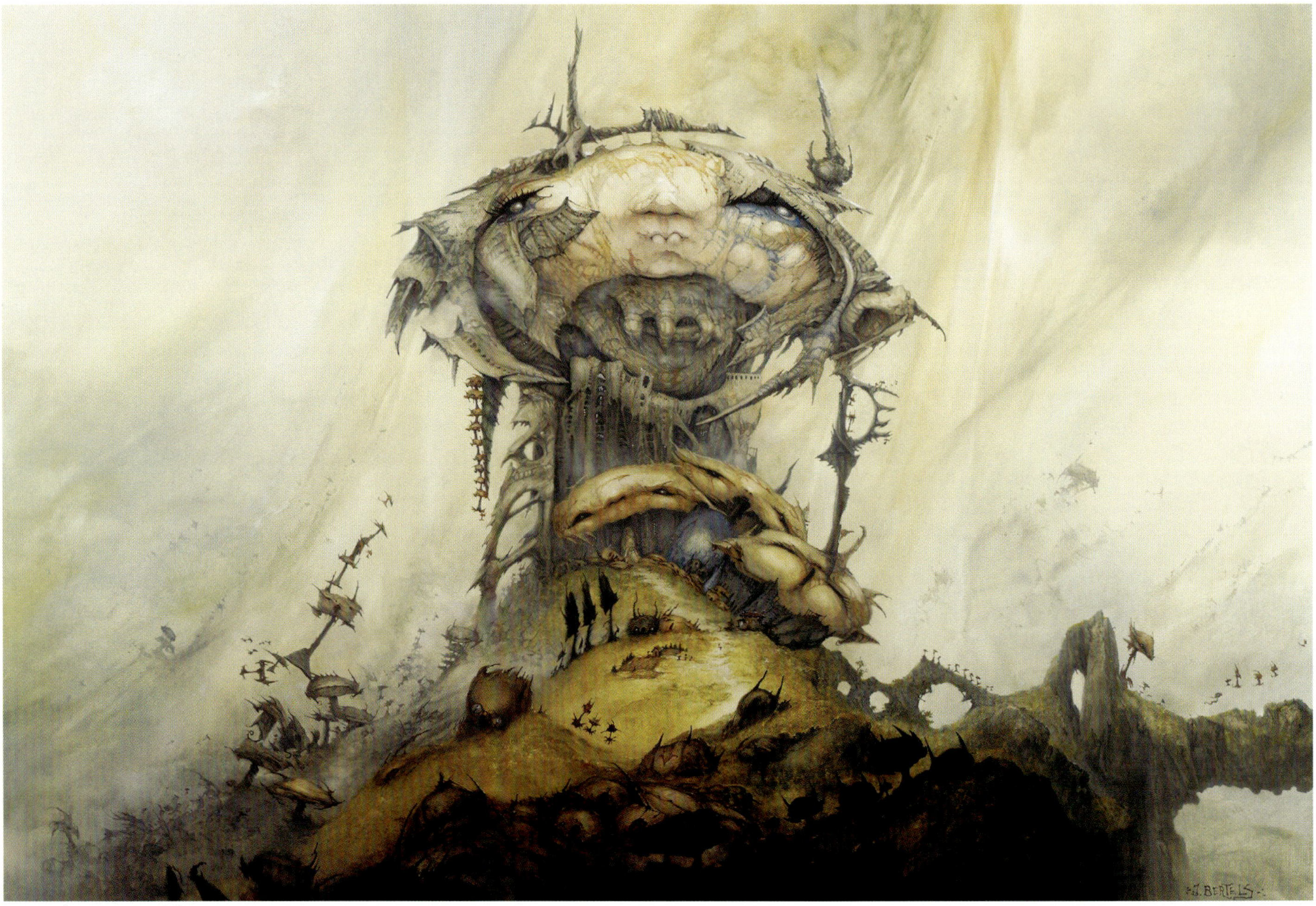

Diva · 140 x 200 cm · Oil on canvas

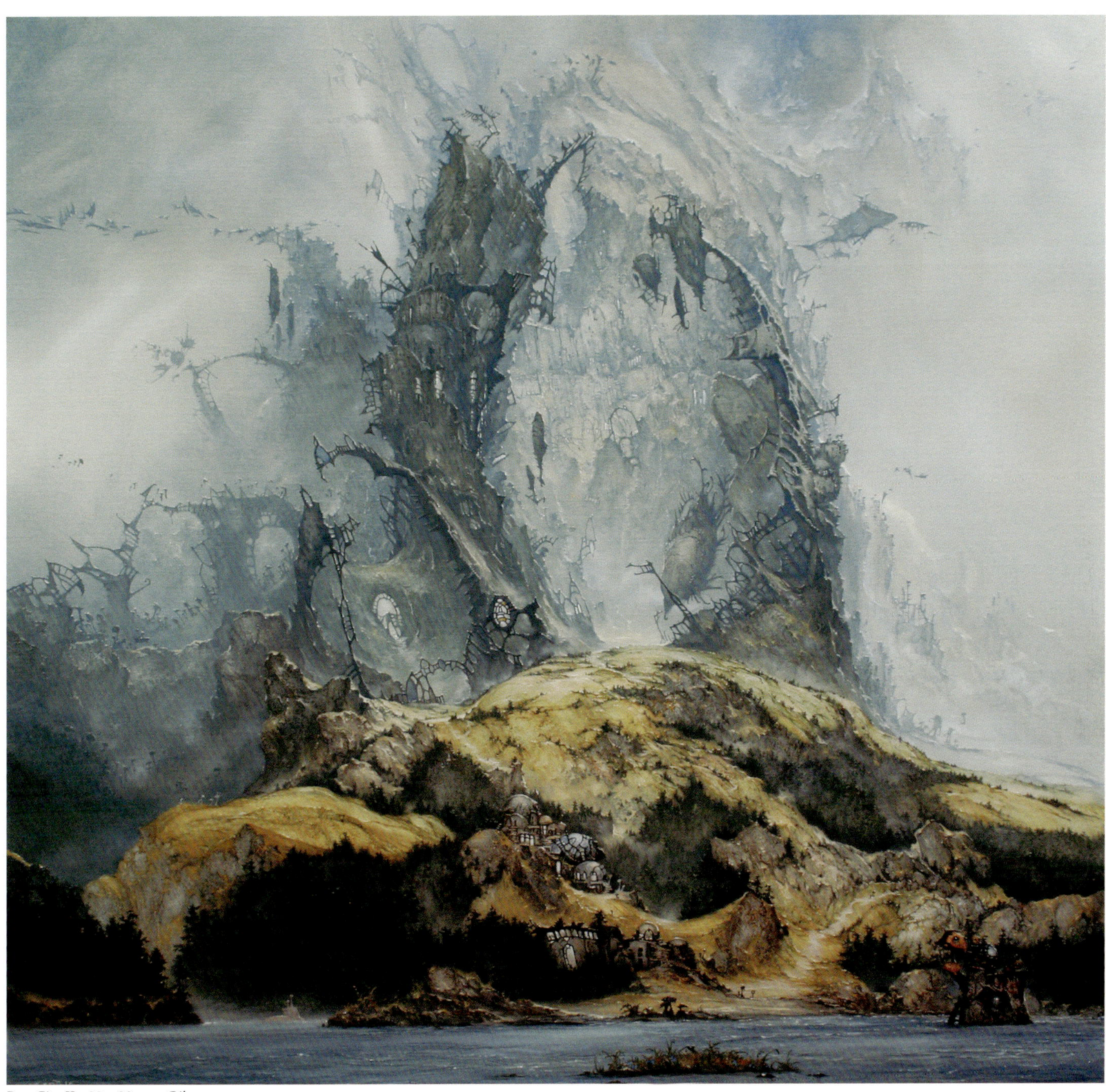

Port City II · 90 x 90 cm · Oil on canvas

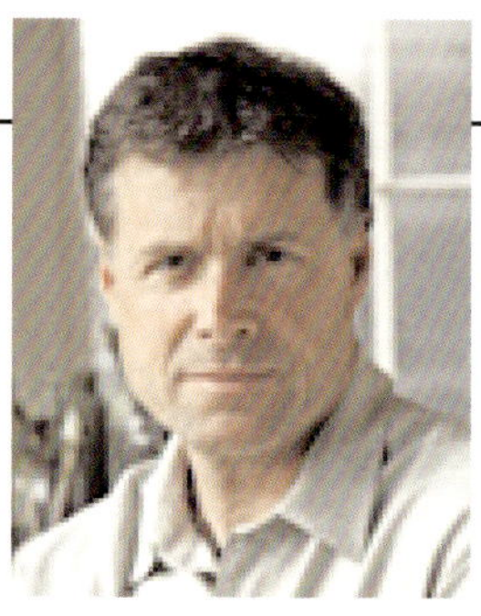

ROBERT BISSELL

1952 USA

www.robertbissell.com

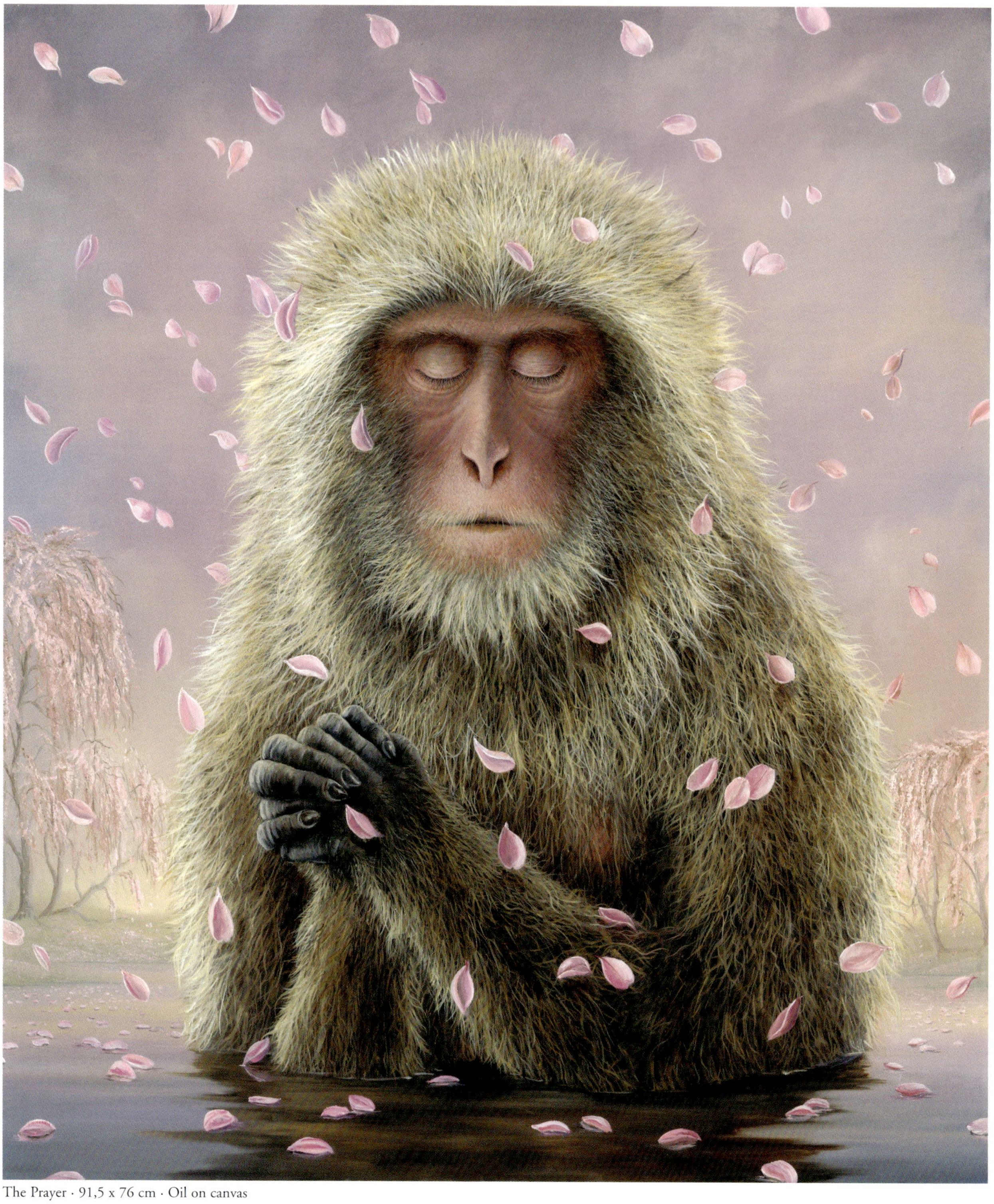

The Prayer · 91,5 x 76 cm · Oil on canvas

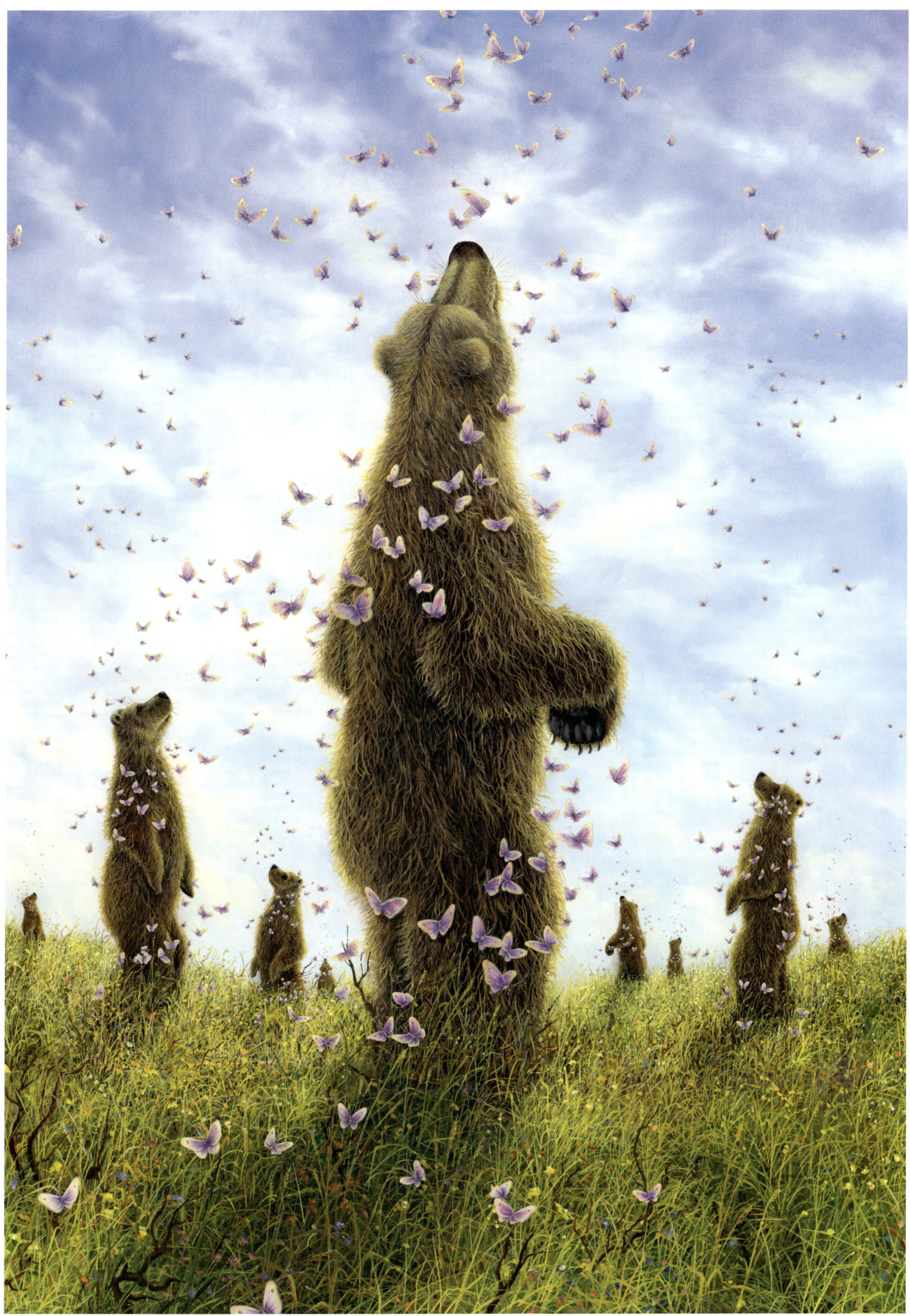

The Enchantment · 147 x 101,5 cm · Oil on canvas

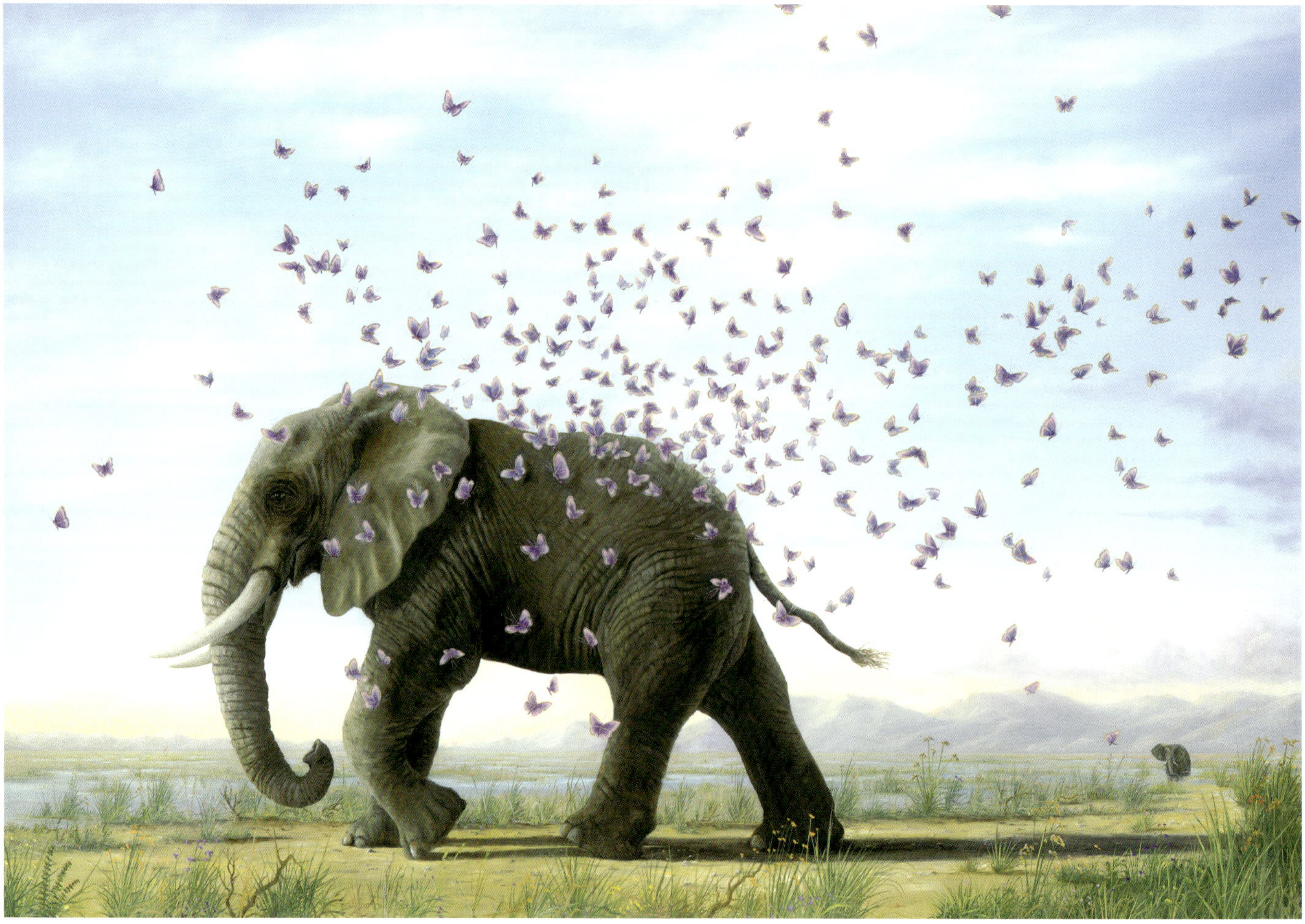

Metamorphosis · 101,5 x 142 cm · Oil on canvas

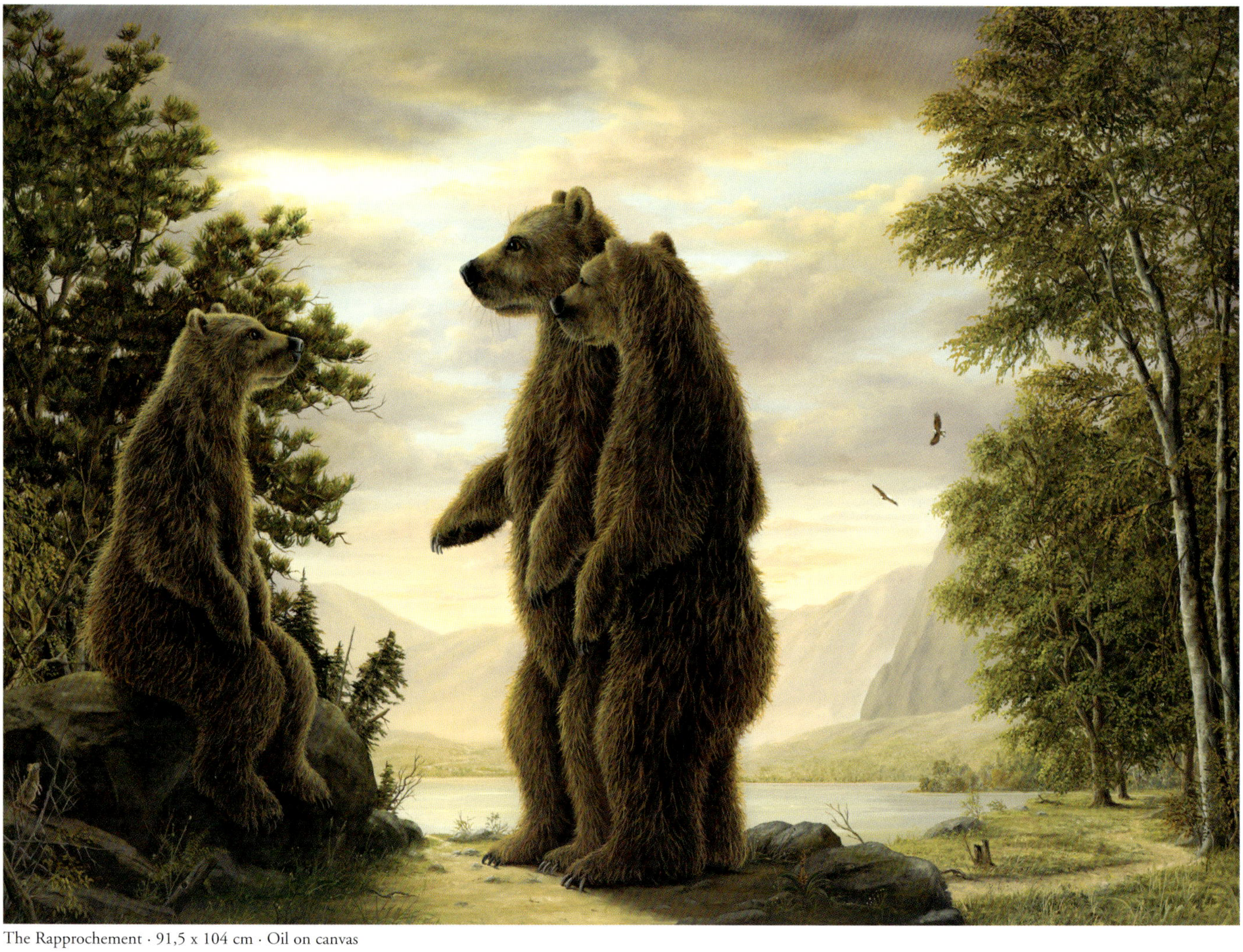

The Rapprochement · 91,5 x 104 cm · Oil on canvas

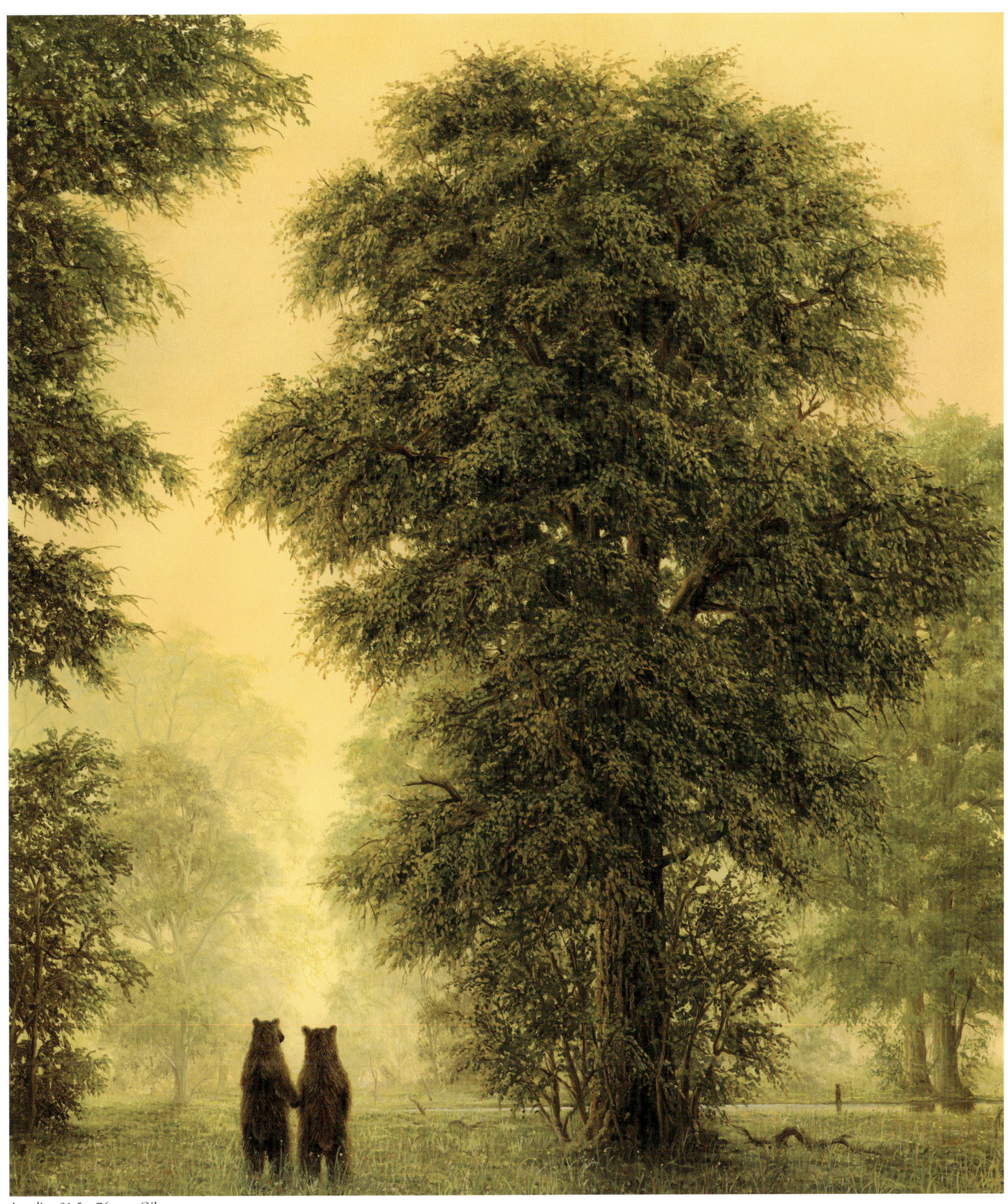

Arcadia · 91,5 x 76 cm · Oil on canvas

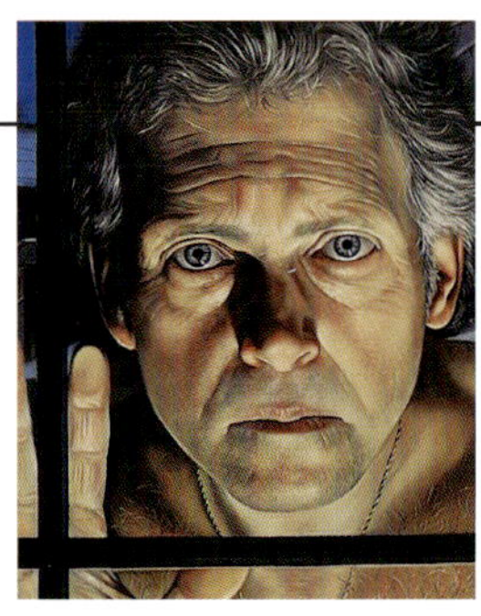

DAVID M. BOWERS

1956 USA

www.dmbowers.com

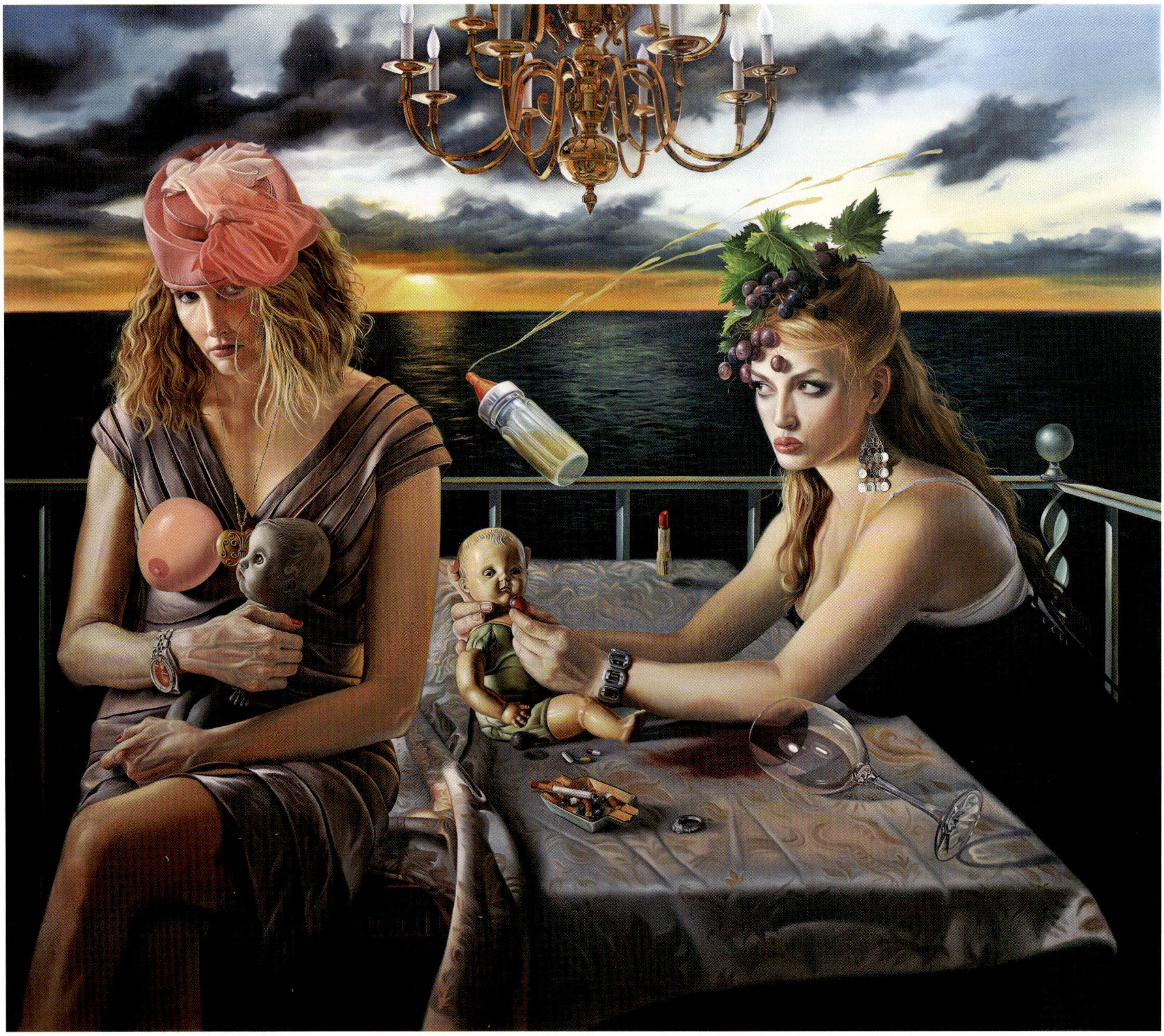

Blonde's Have More Fun · 96,5 x 86 cm · Oil on canvas

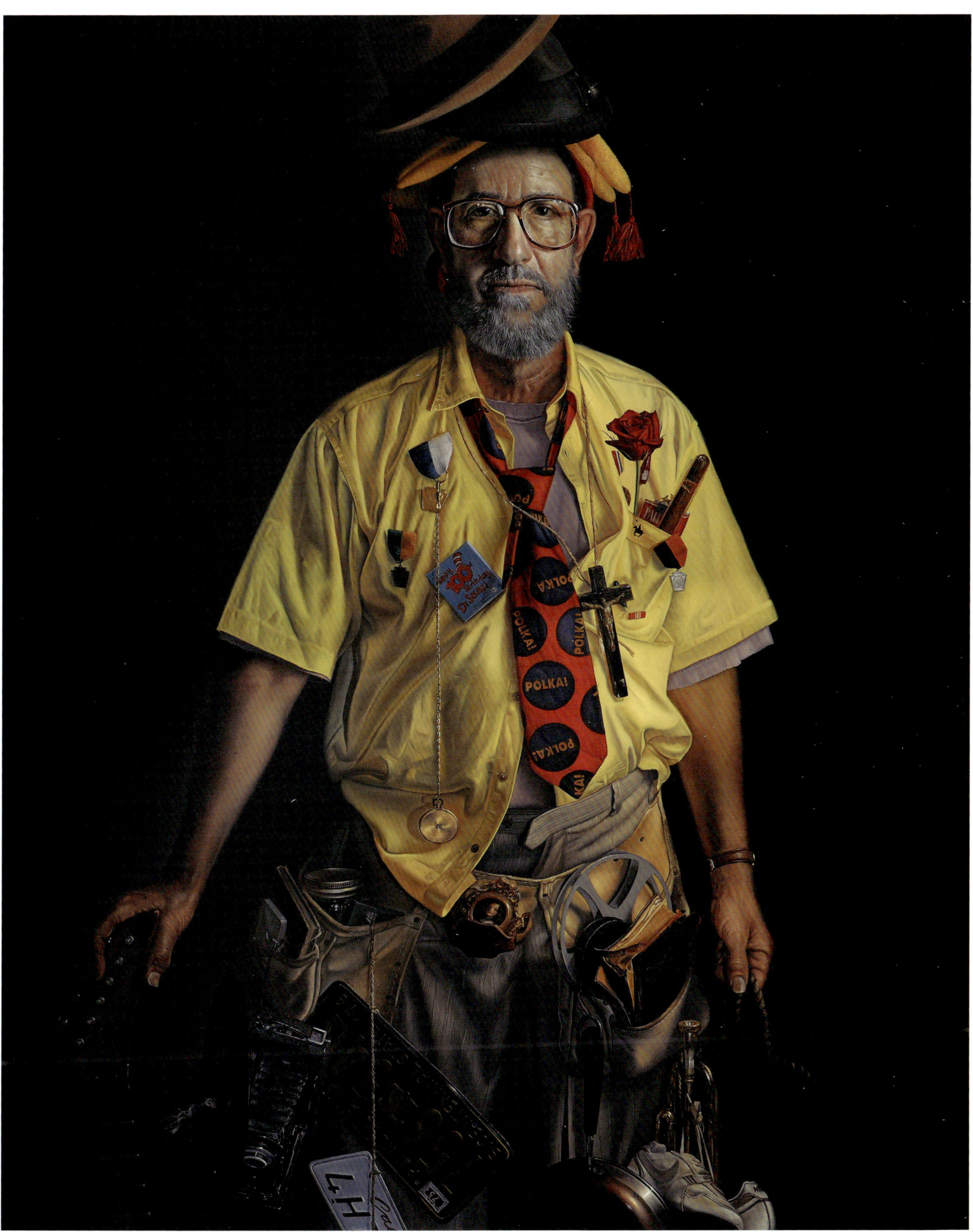

The Collector · 96,5 x 76 cm · Oil on canvas

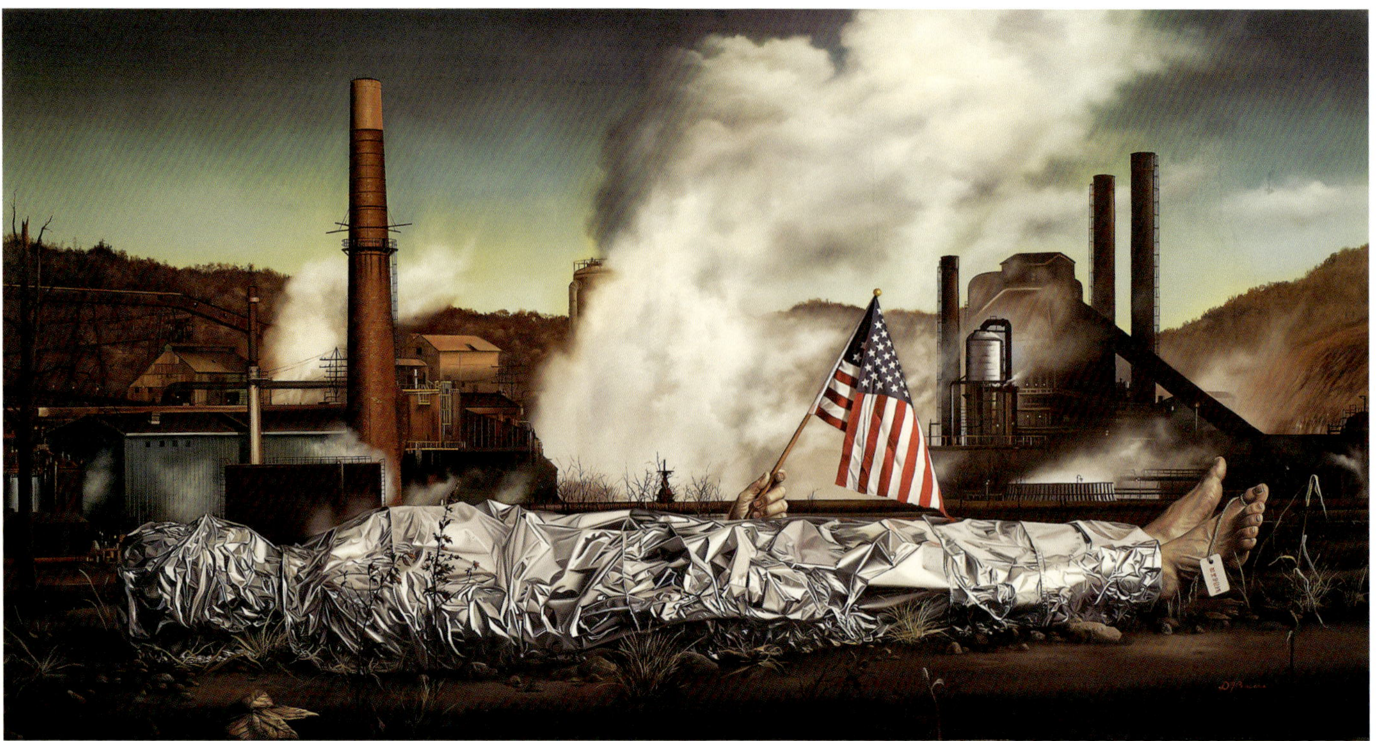

Made in America · 113 x 61 cm · Oil on canvas

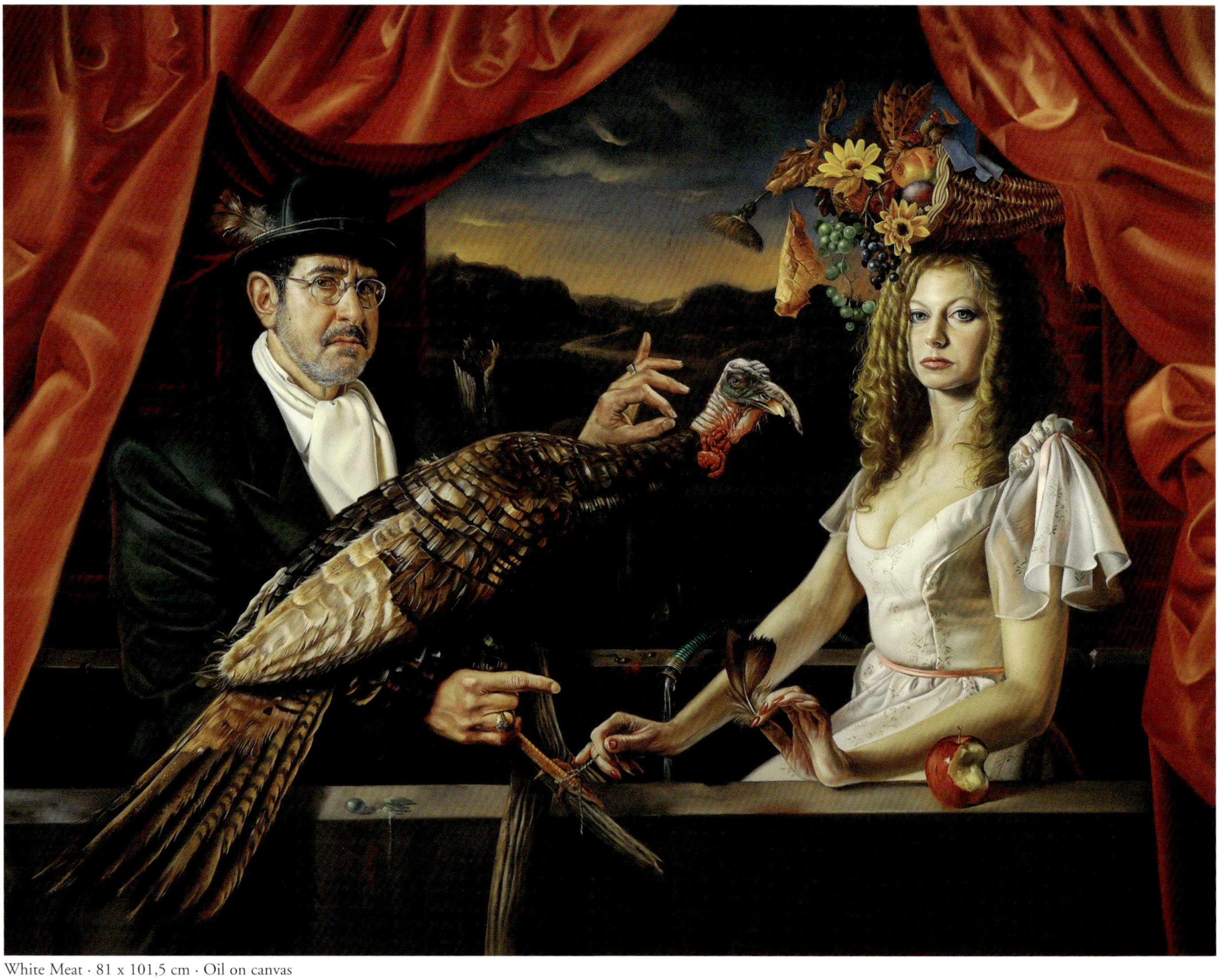

White Meat · 81 x 101,5 cm · Oil on canvas

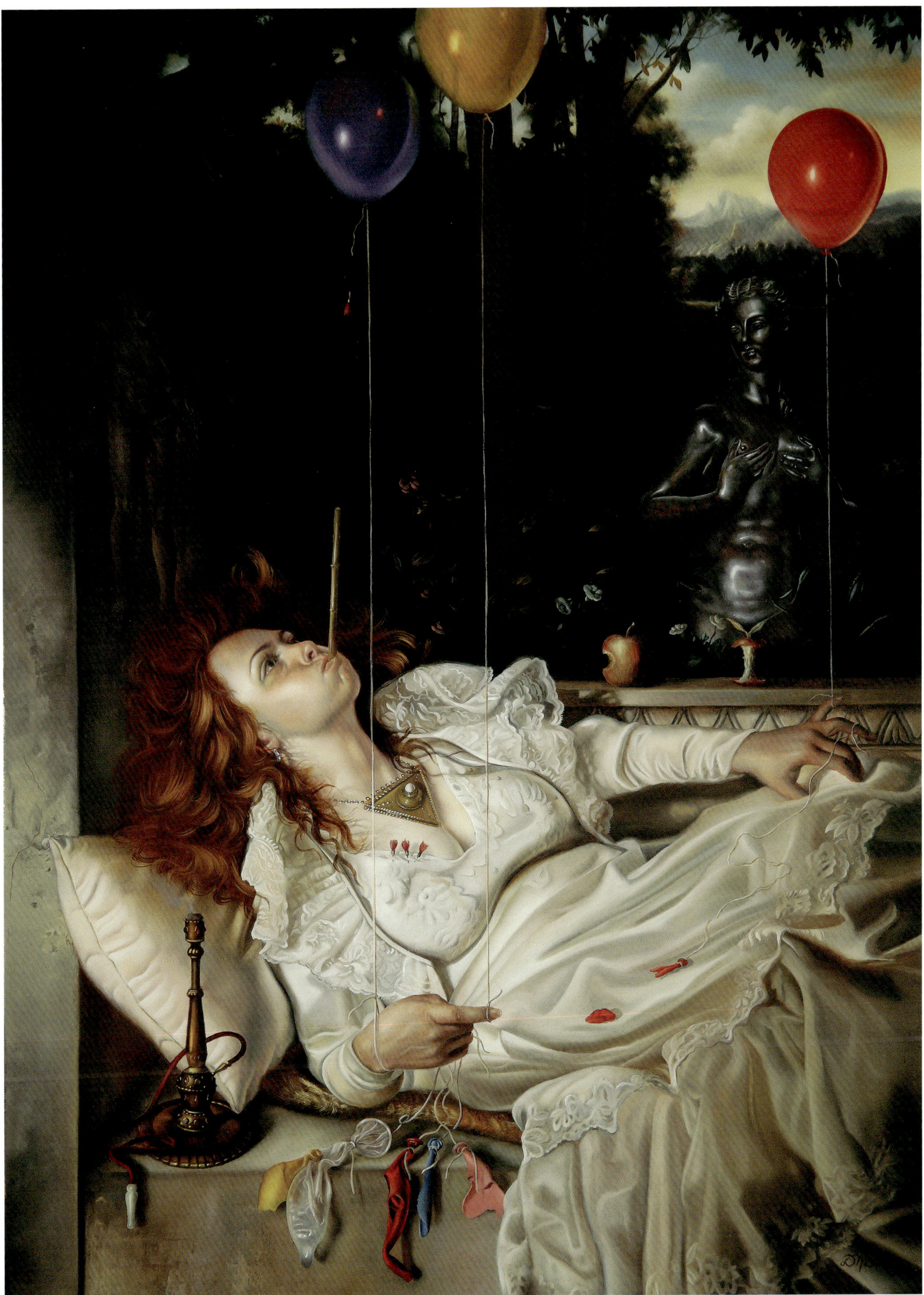

Fragile Ego's · 43 x 30,5 cm · Oil on canvas

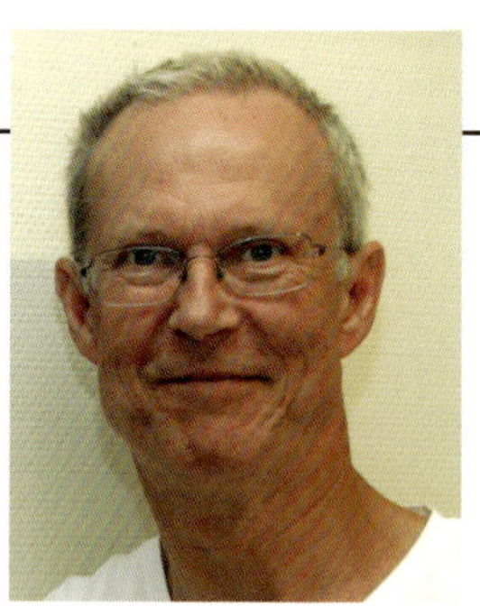

CLAUS BRUSEN

1960 Denmark

www.clausbrusen.com

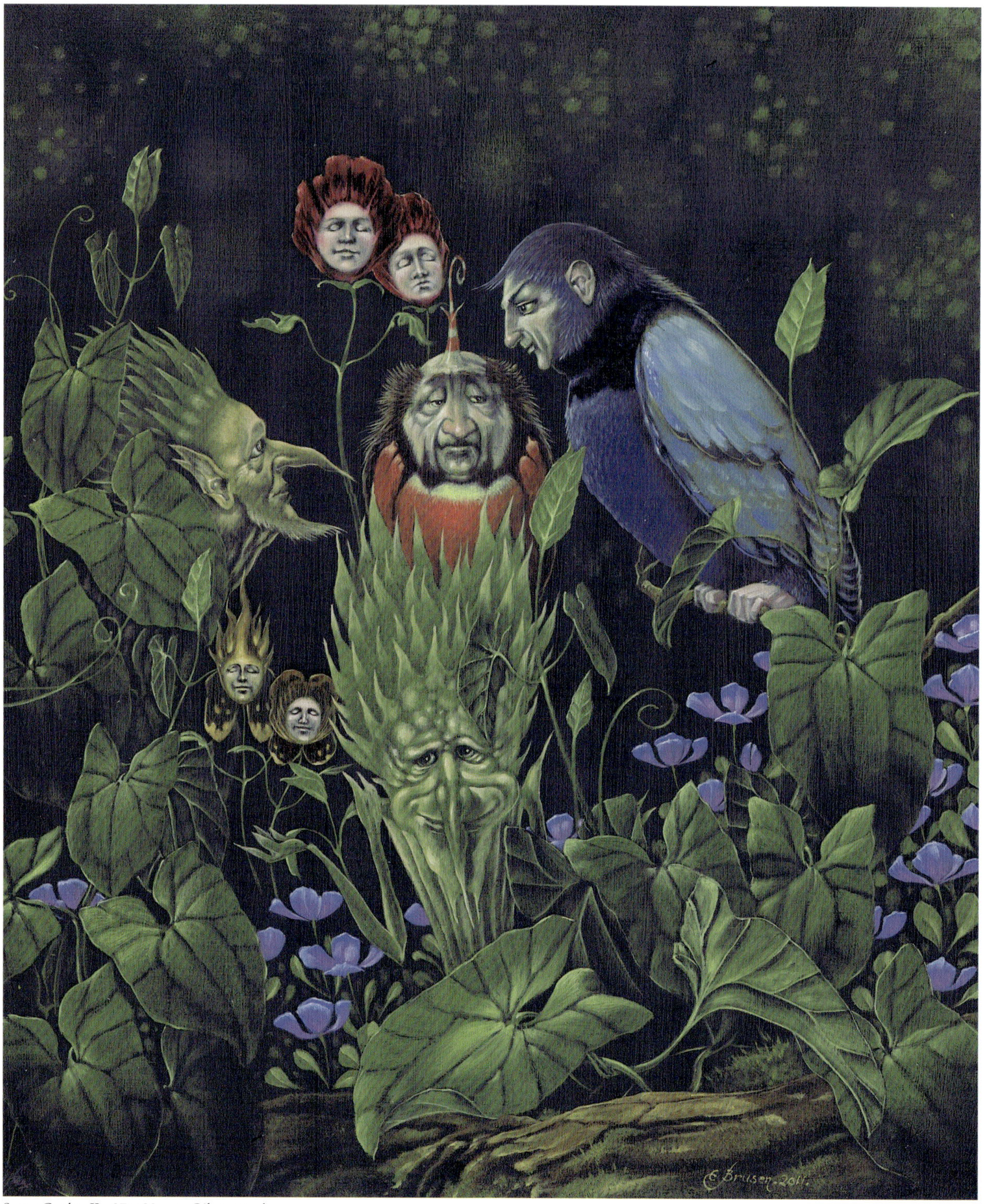

Secret Garden II · 27 x 22 cm · Oil on panel

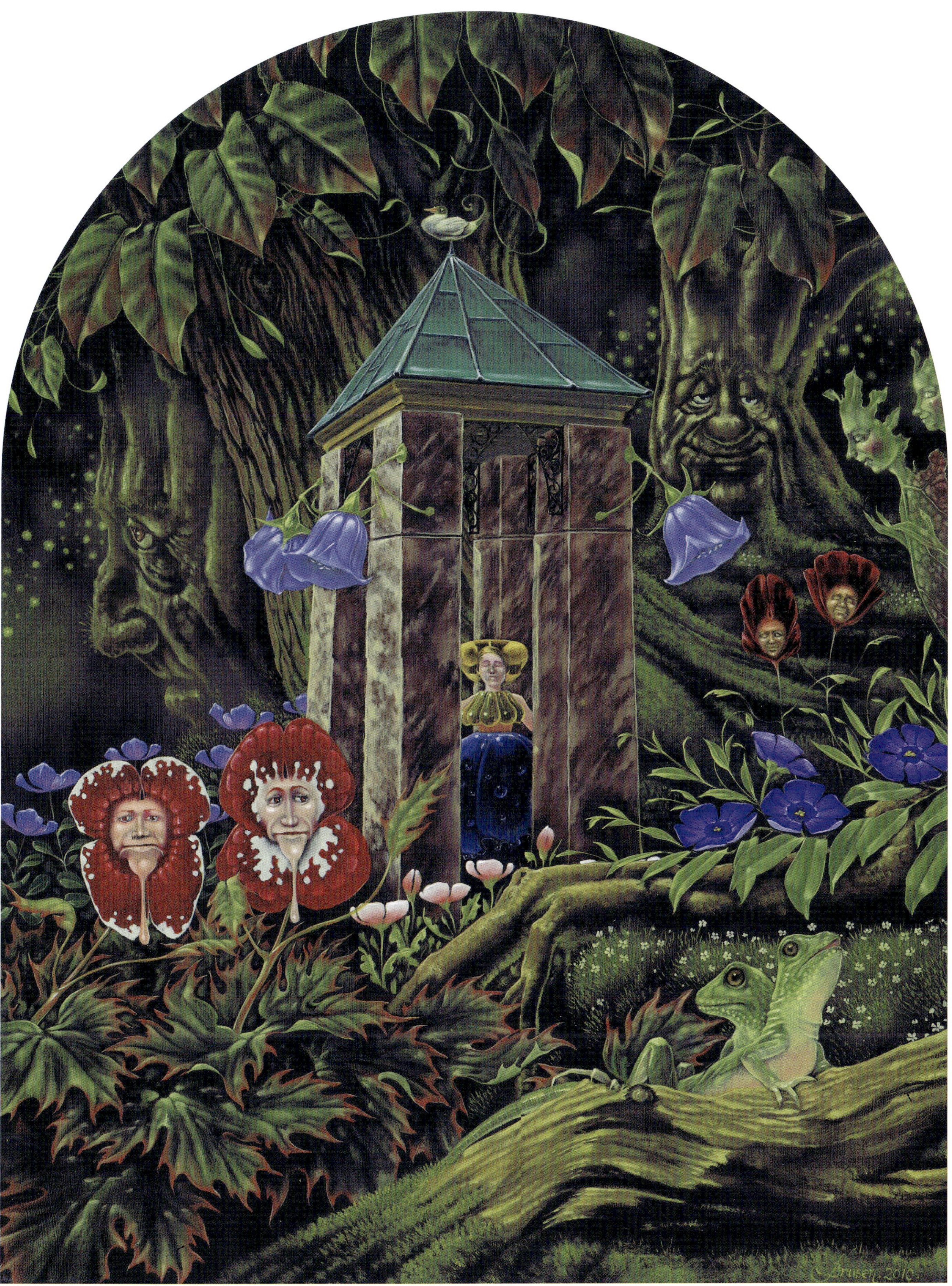

Secret Garden I · 40 x 30 cm · Oil on panel

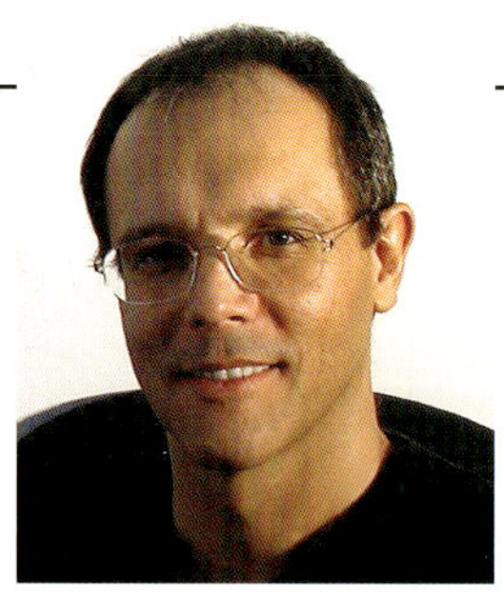

GIL BRUVEL

1959 USA

www.bruvel.com

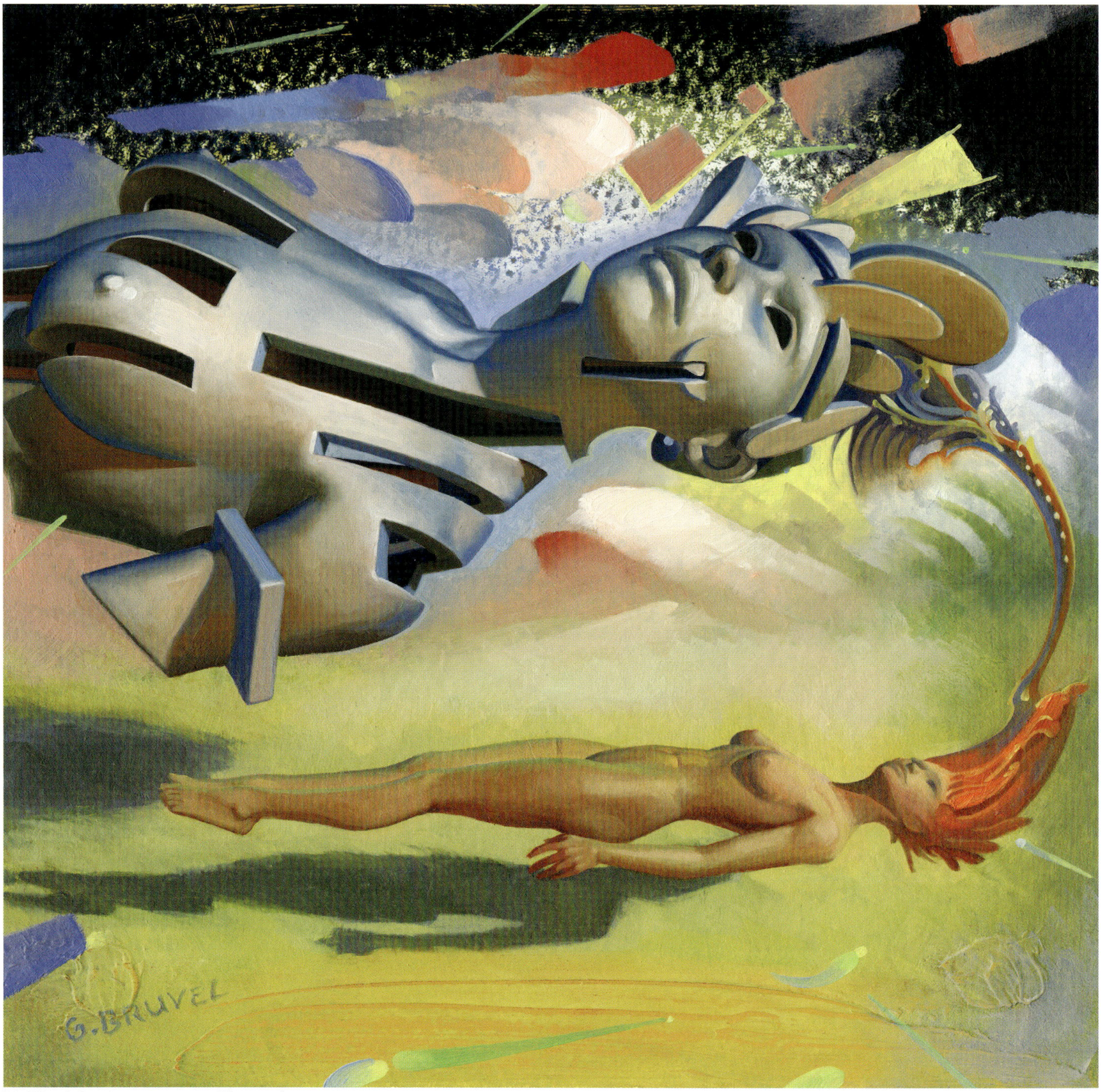

My Mirror's Remains · 20 x 20 cm · Oil on panel

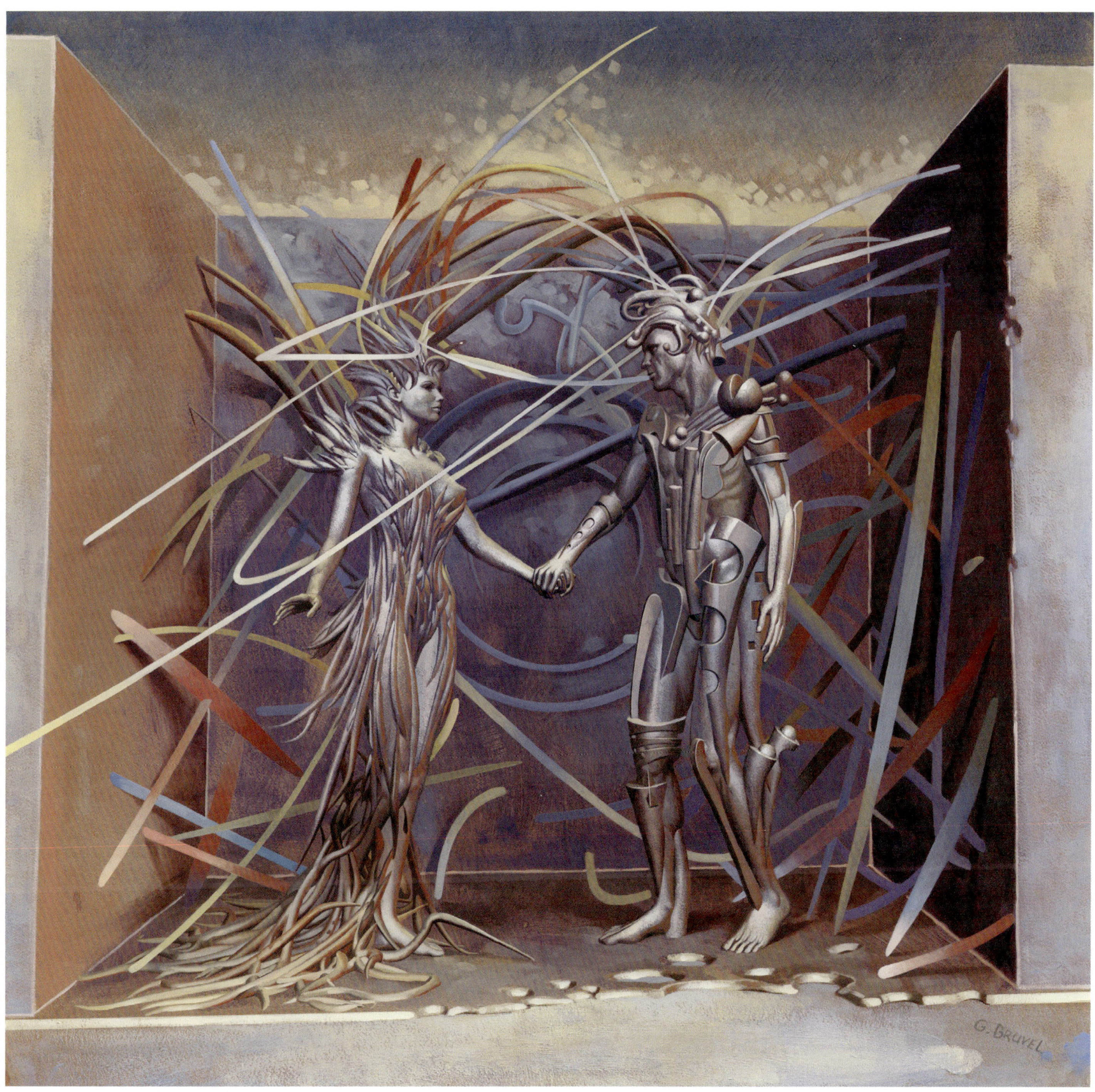

Trajectories · 60 x 60 cm · Oil on panel

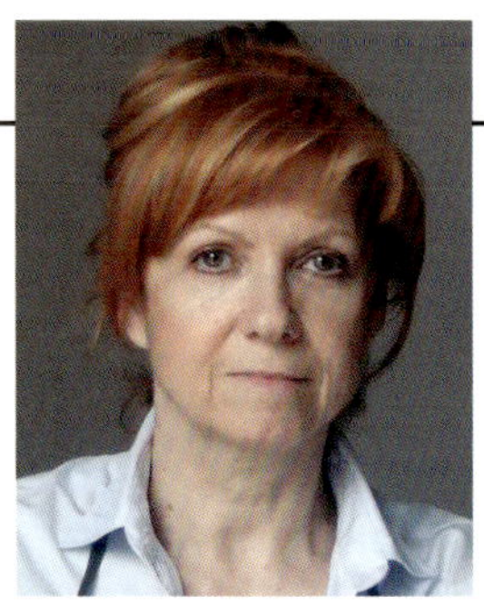

PATRIZIA COMAND

1950 Italy

www.patriziacomand.com

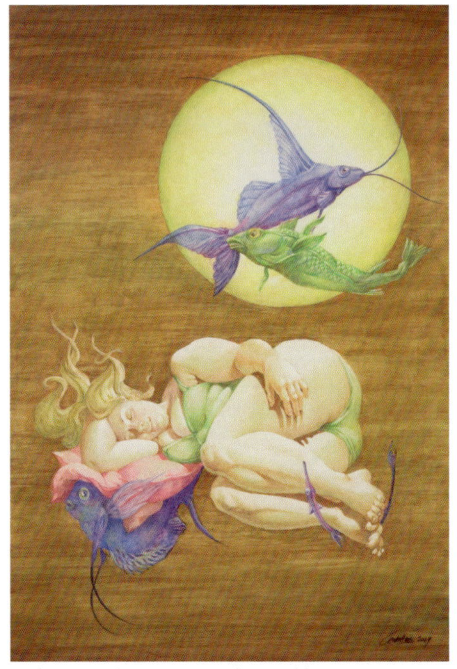

Evolutions · 74 x 50 cm · Acrylic on tablet

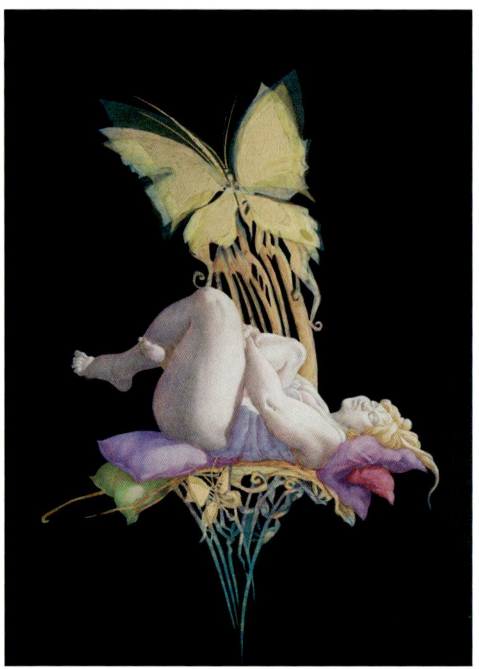

Like a Flore · 70 x 50 cm · Acrylic and gold on tablet

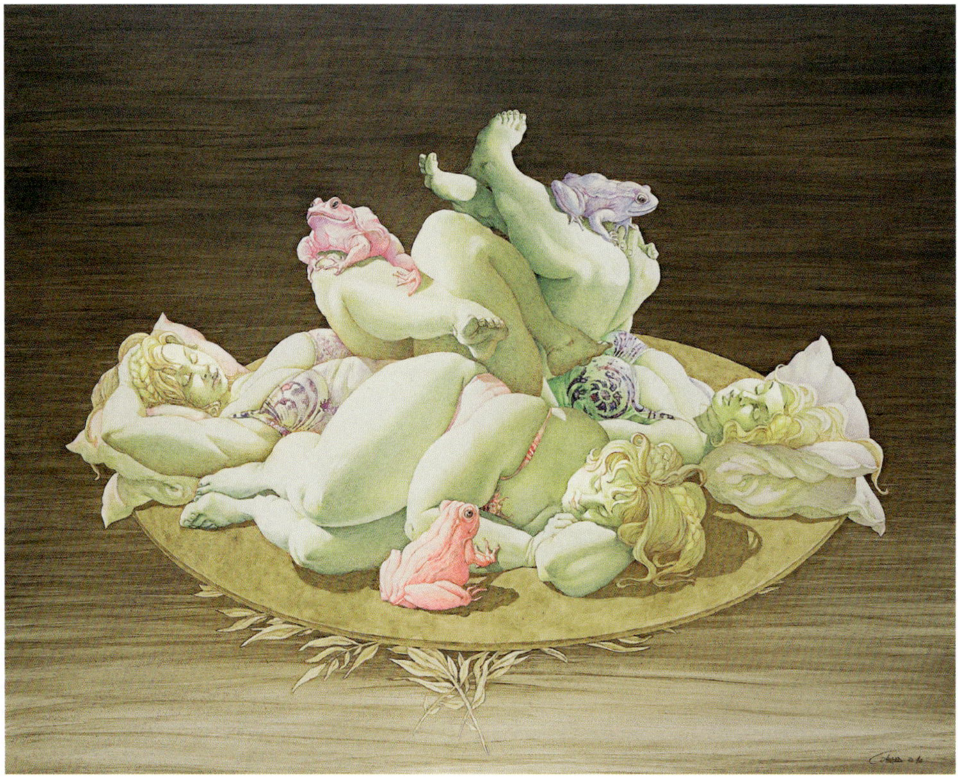

Prince and Princess · 100 x 120 cm · Acrylic on canvas

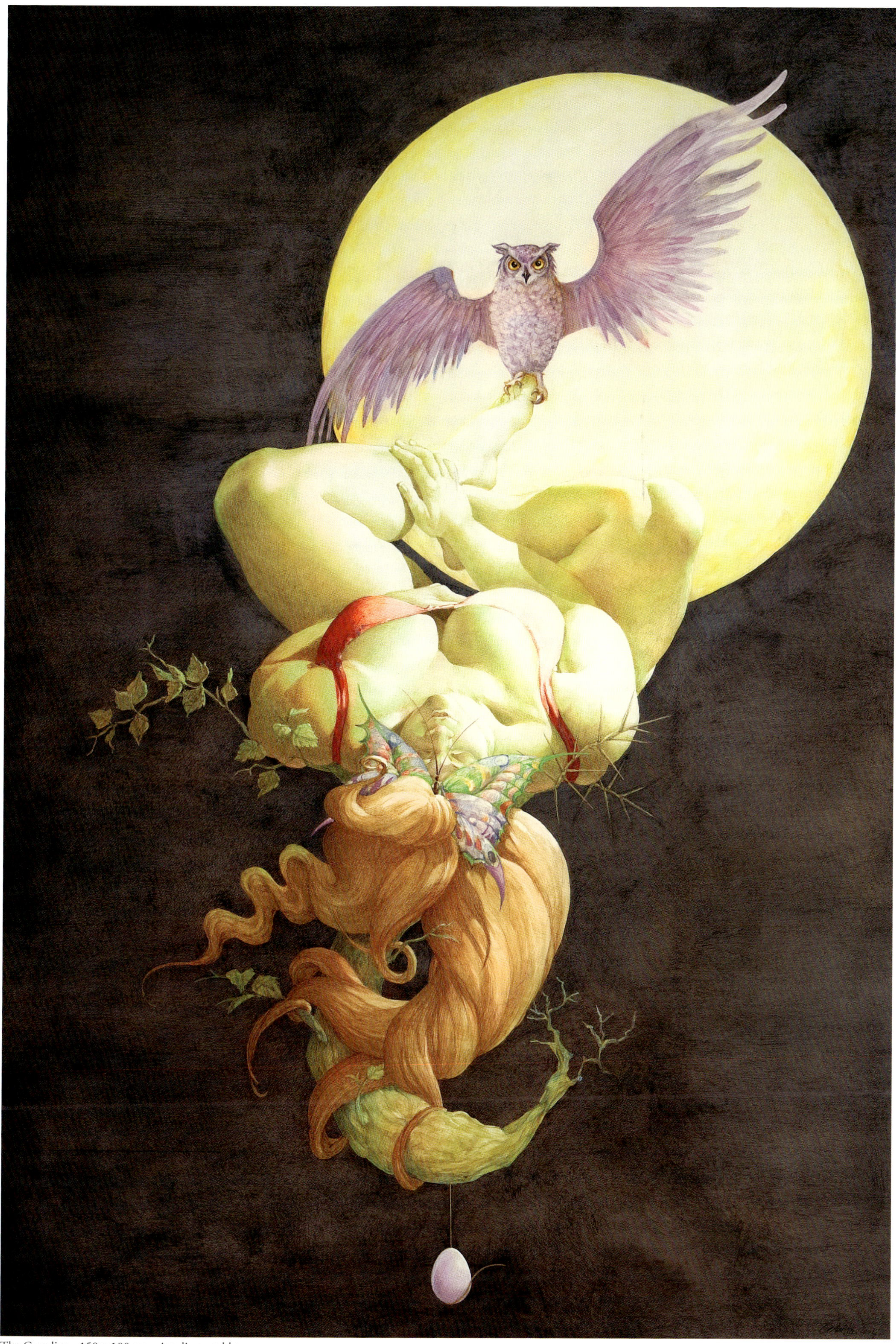

The Guardian · 150 x 100 cm · Acrylic on tablet

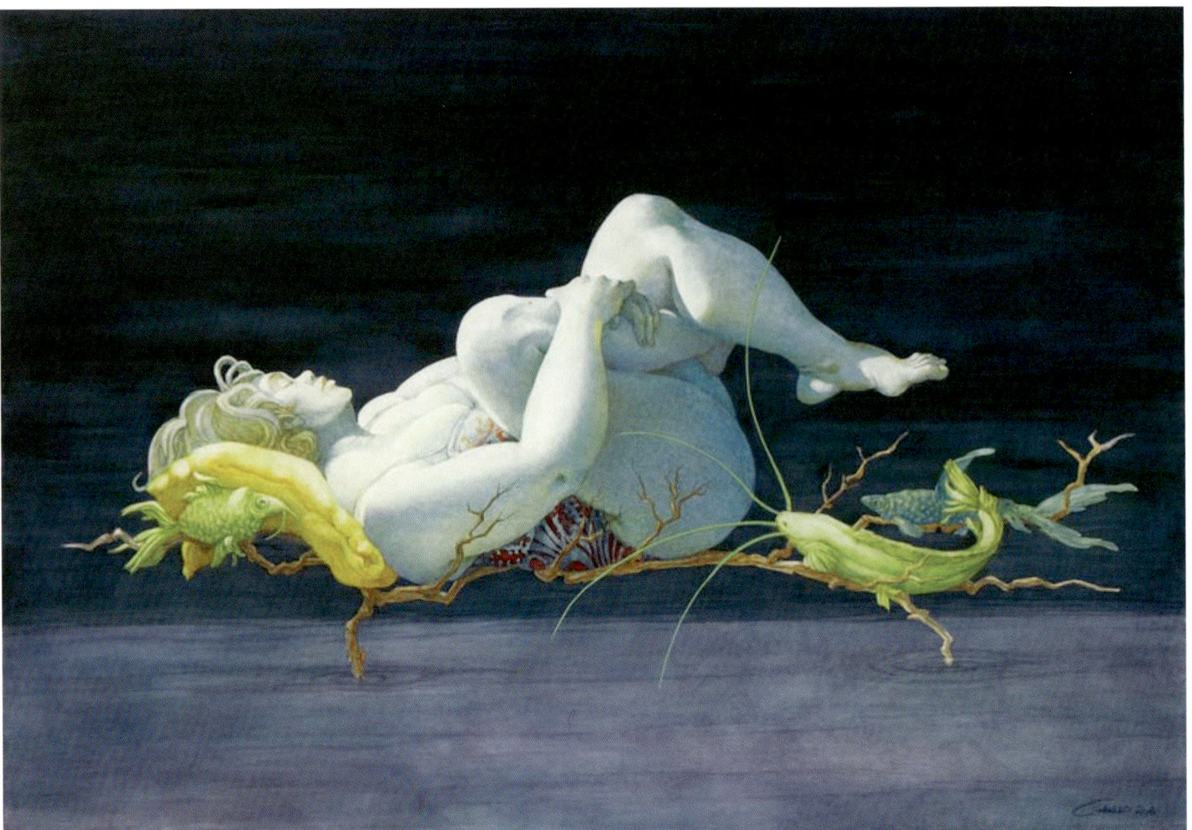
Do not awake her · 70 x 90 cm · Acrylic on tablet

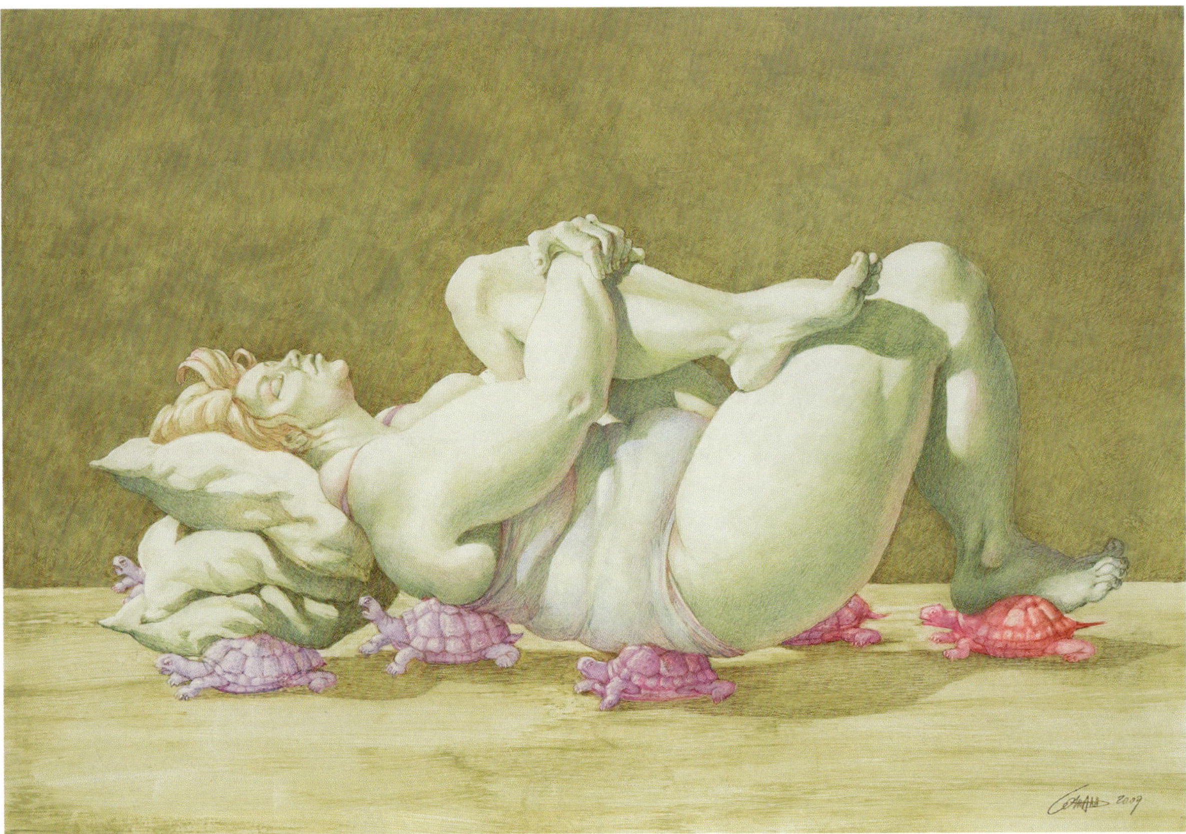
Exceptional Transport · 50 x 70 cm · Acrylic on tablet

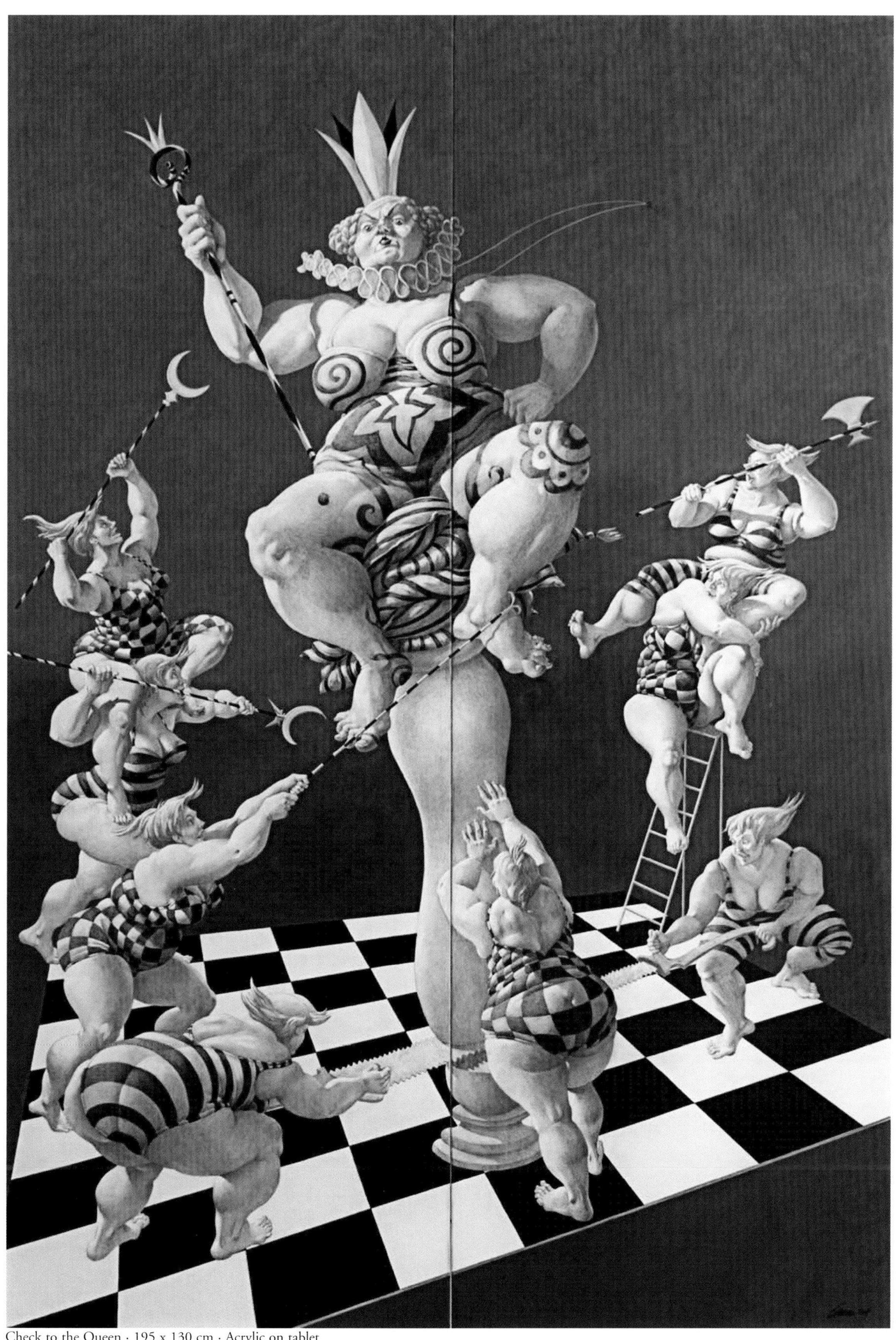

Check to the Queen · 195 x 130 cm · Acrylic on tablet

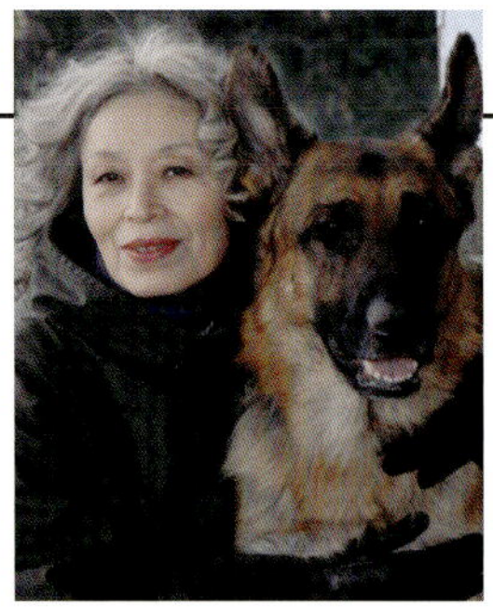

KINUKO Y. CRAFT

USA

www.kycraft.com

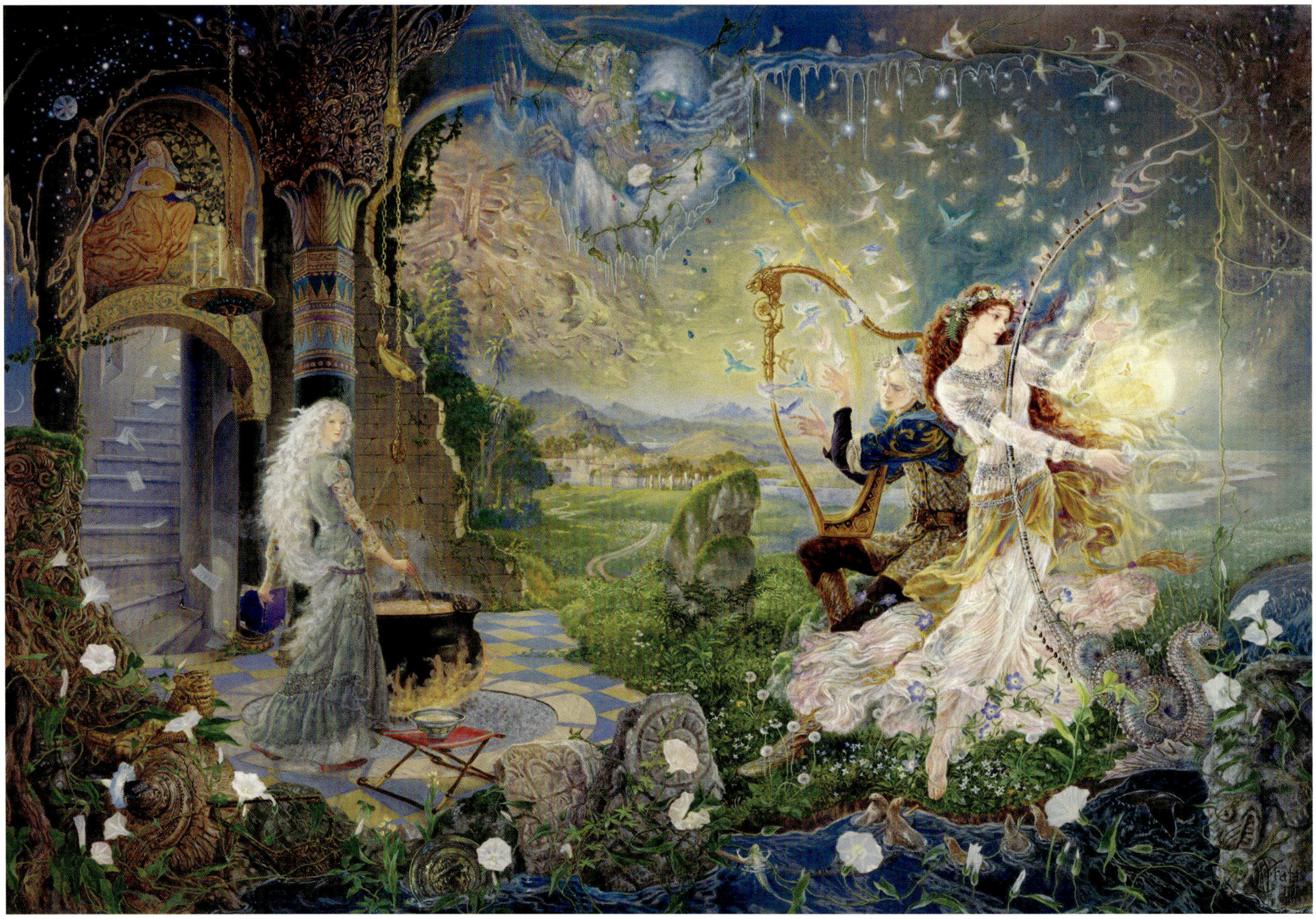

The Bards Of Bone Plain · 53 x 76 cm · Oil on panel

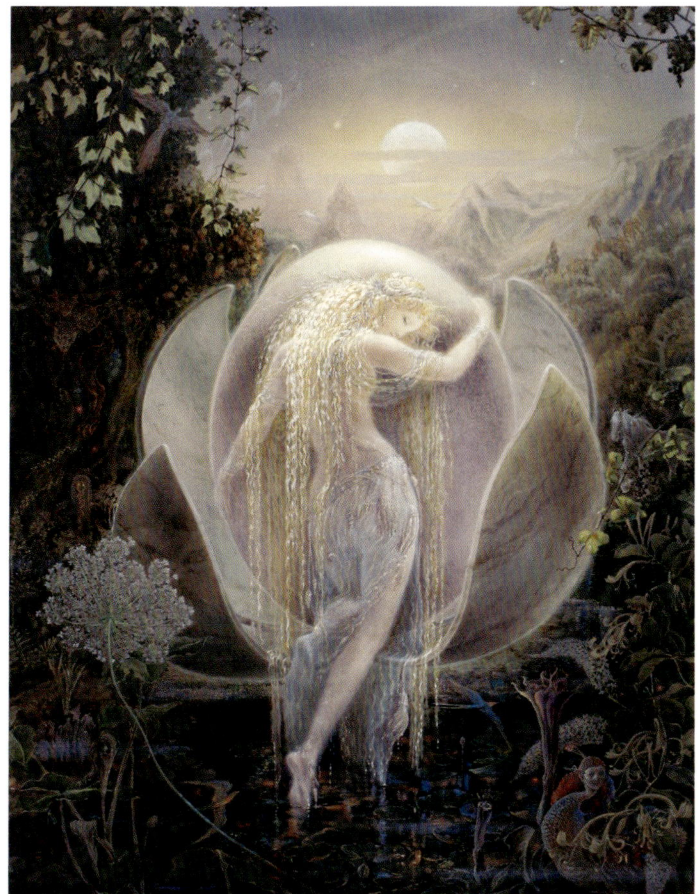
Midsummer Night · 61 x 45,5 cm · Oil on panel

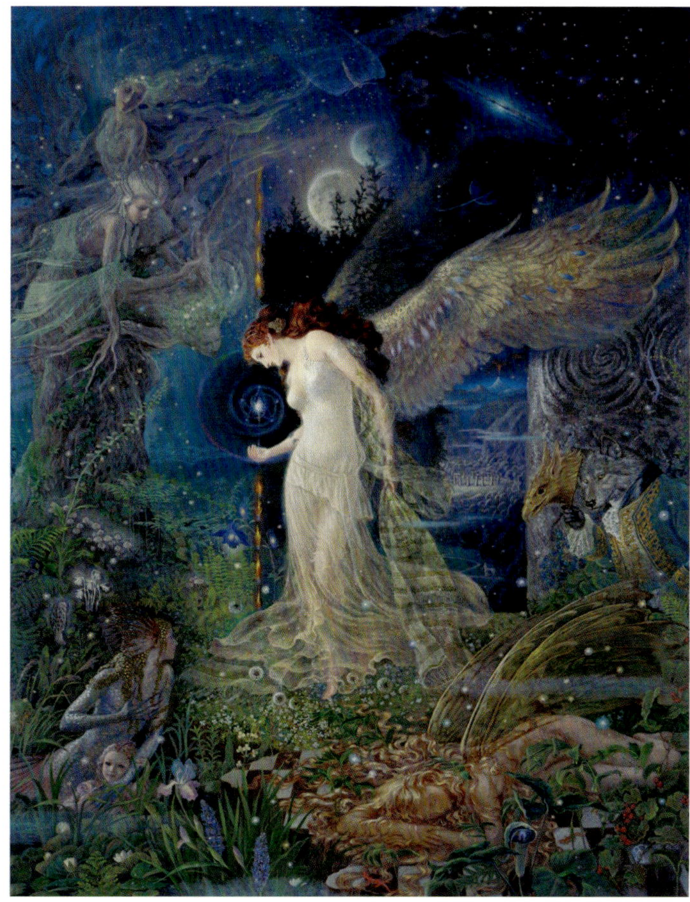
Luna · 59,5 x 44,5 cm · Oil on panel

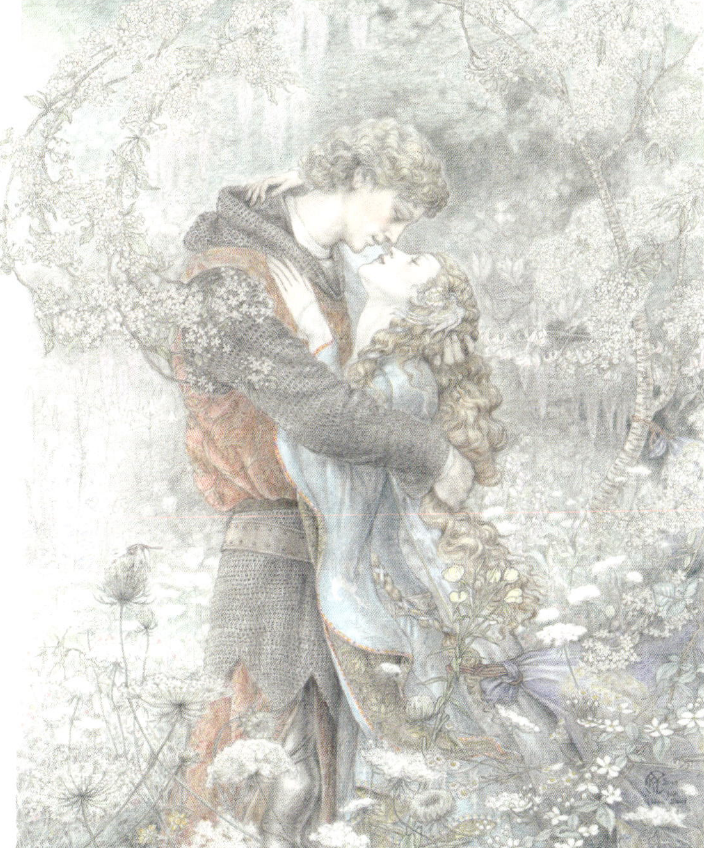
Love Story: Aucassin and Nicolette · 48 x 38 cm
Graphite and color pencil on Arches watercolor paper

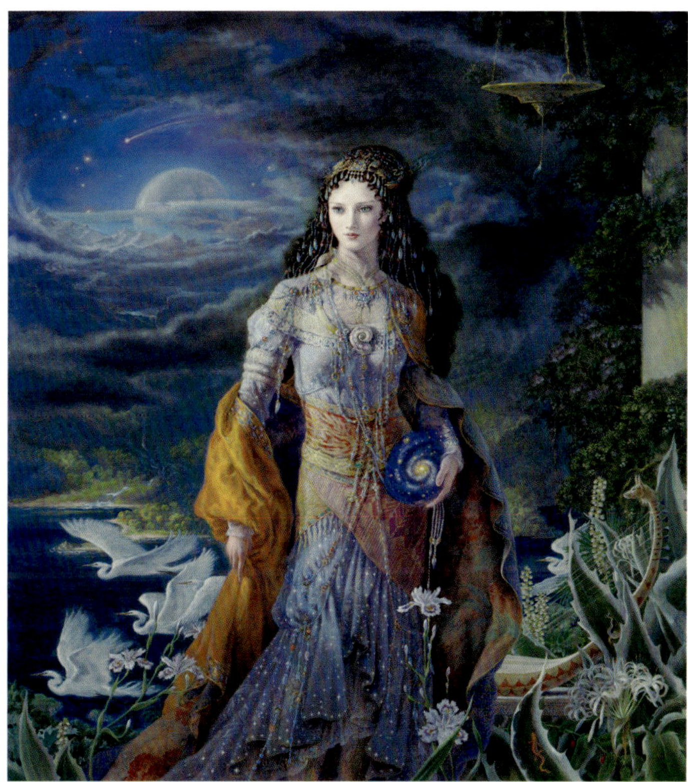
Isis · 60 x 68,5 cm · Oil on panel

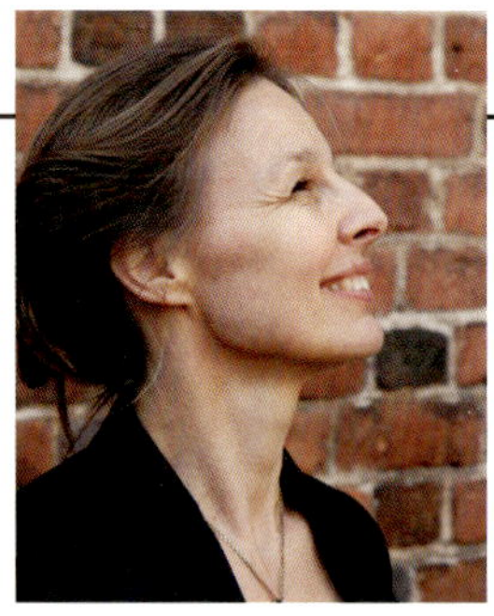

HELLE RASK CRAWFORD

1964 Denmark

www.helleraskcrawford.dk

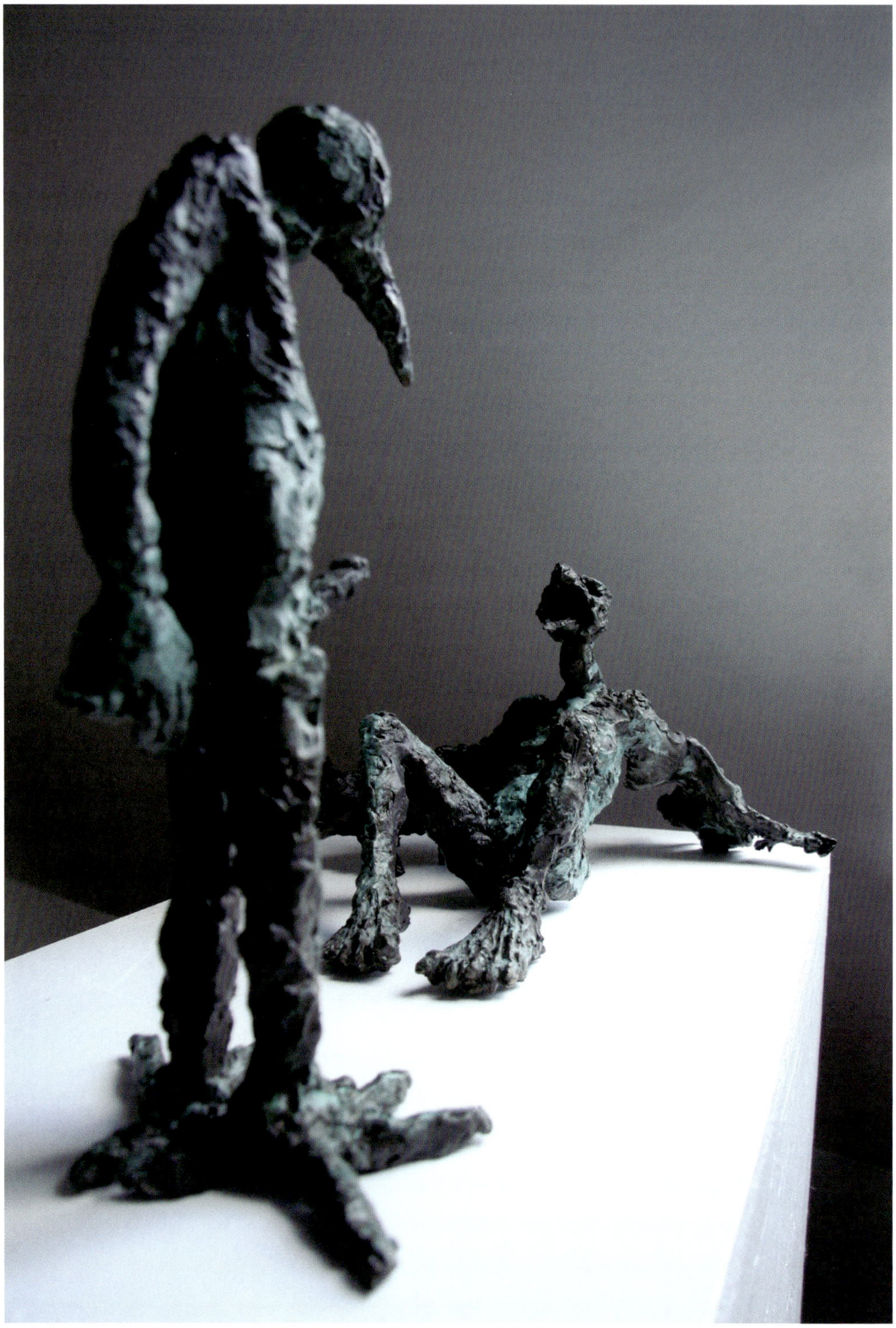

Fowl Play · 35 x 60 x 30 cm · Bronze

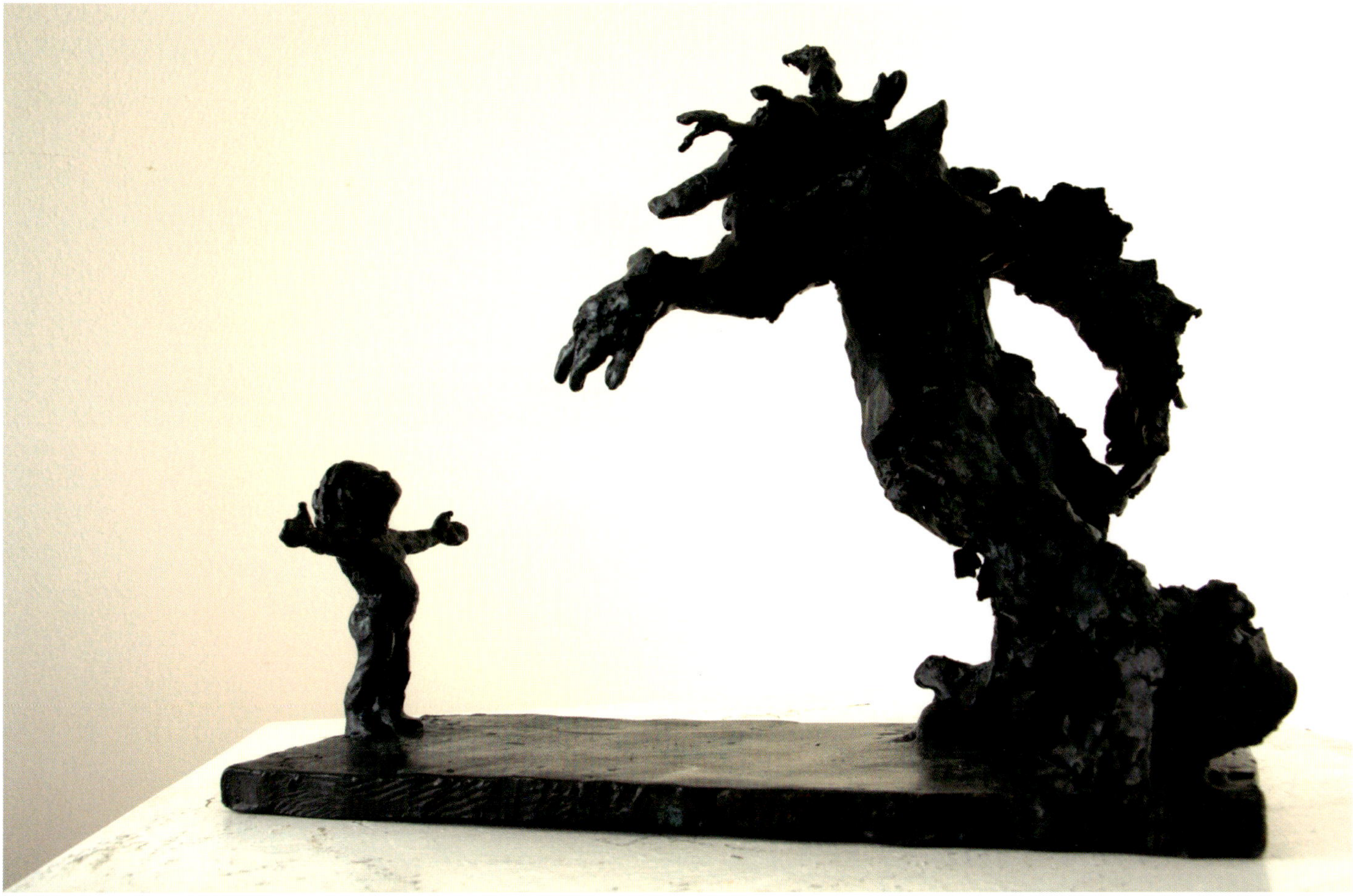

Thou shalt not pass! · 30 x 10 x 30 cm · Bronze

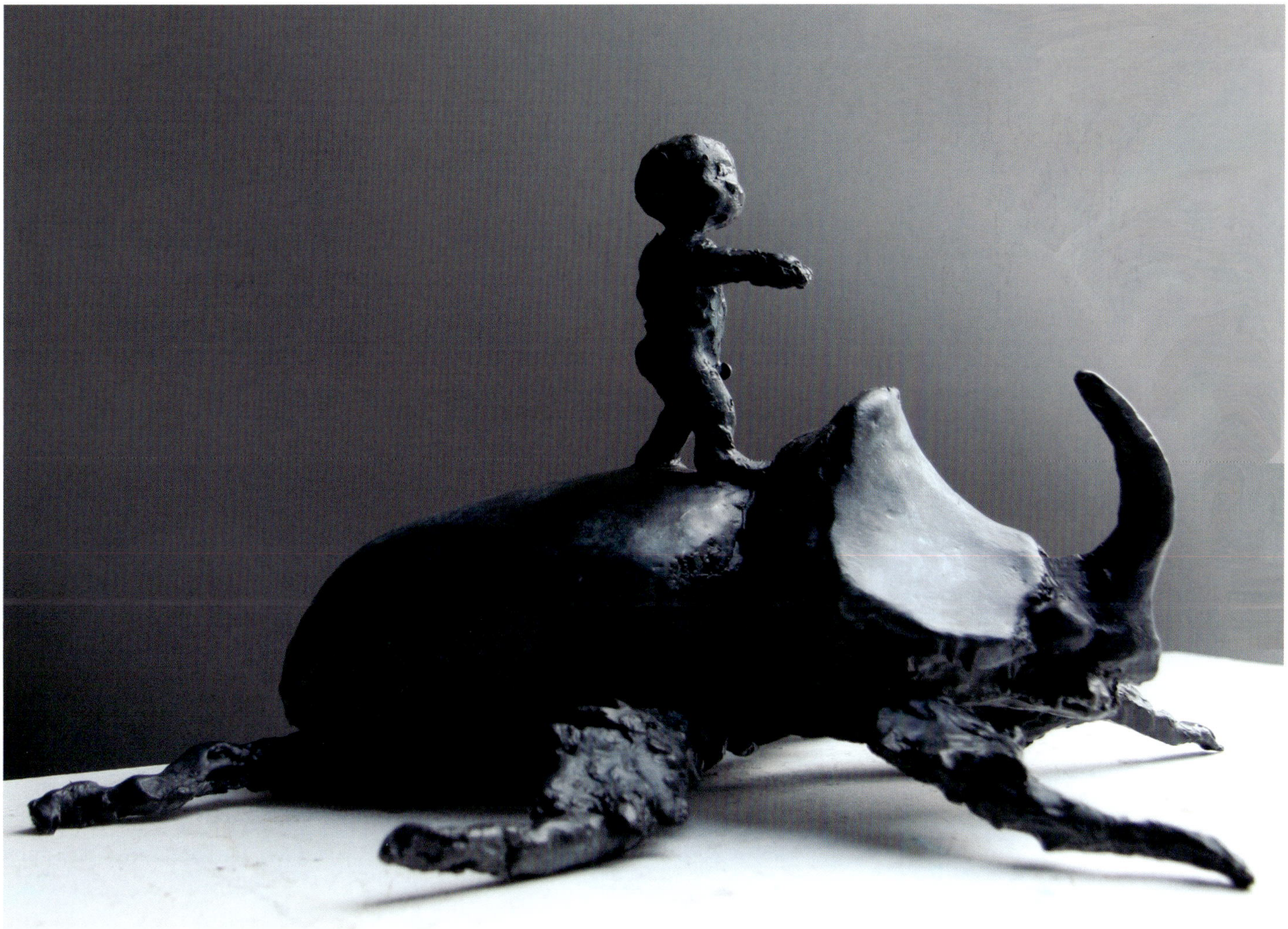

Beetle Surfer · 25 x 30 x 25 cm · Bronze

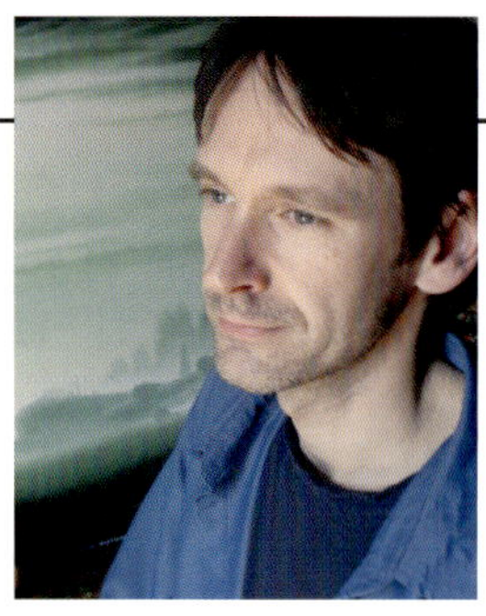

PATRICK VAN DER LINDE

1972 The Netherlands

www.patrickvanderlinde.nl

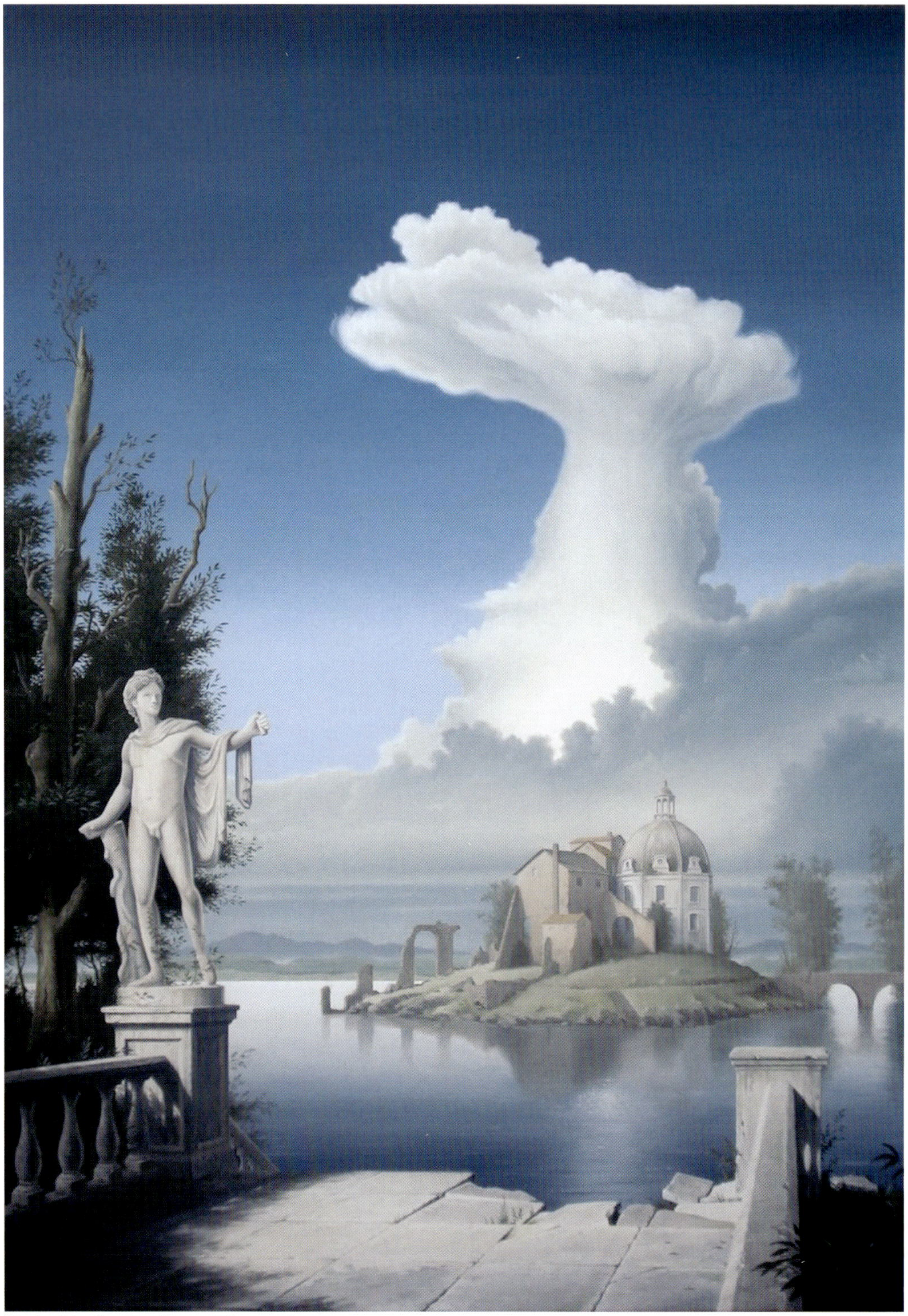

Wrath of Apollo · 65 x 45 cm · Oil on panel

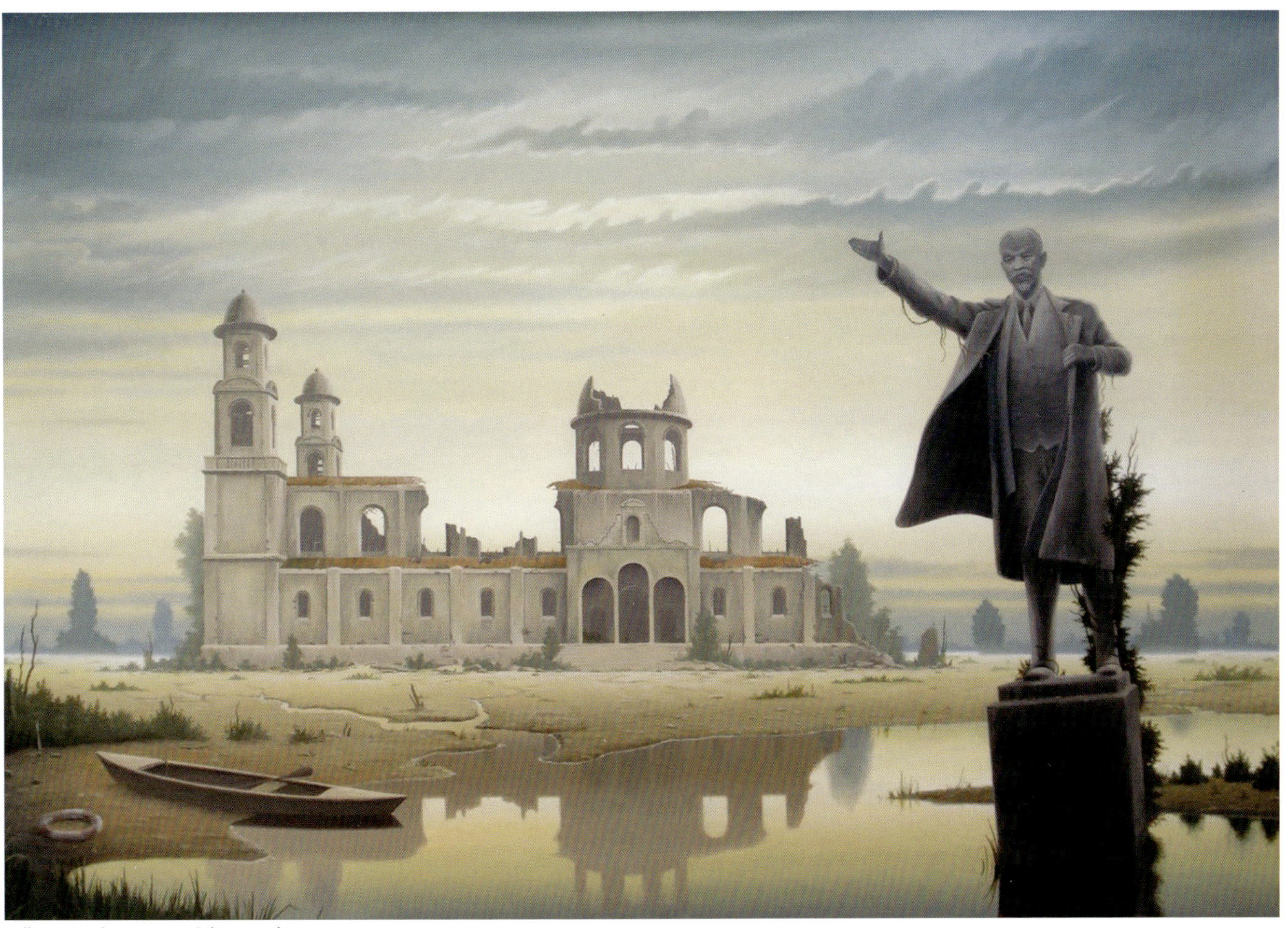

Follow Me · 40 x 55 cm · Oil on panel

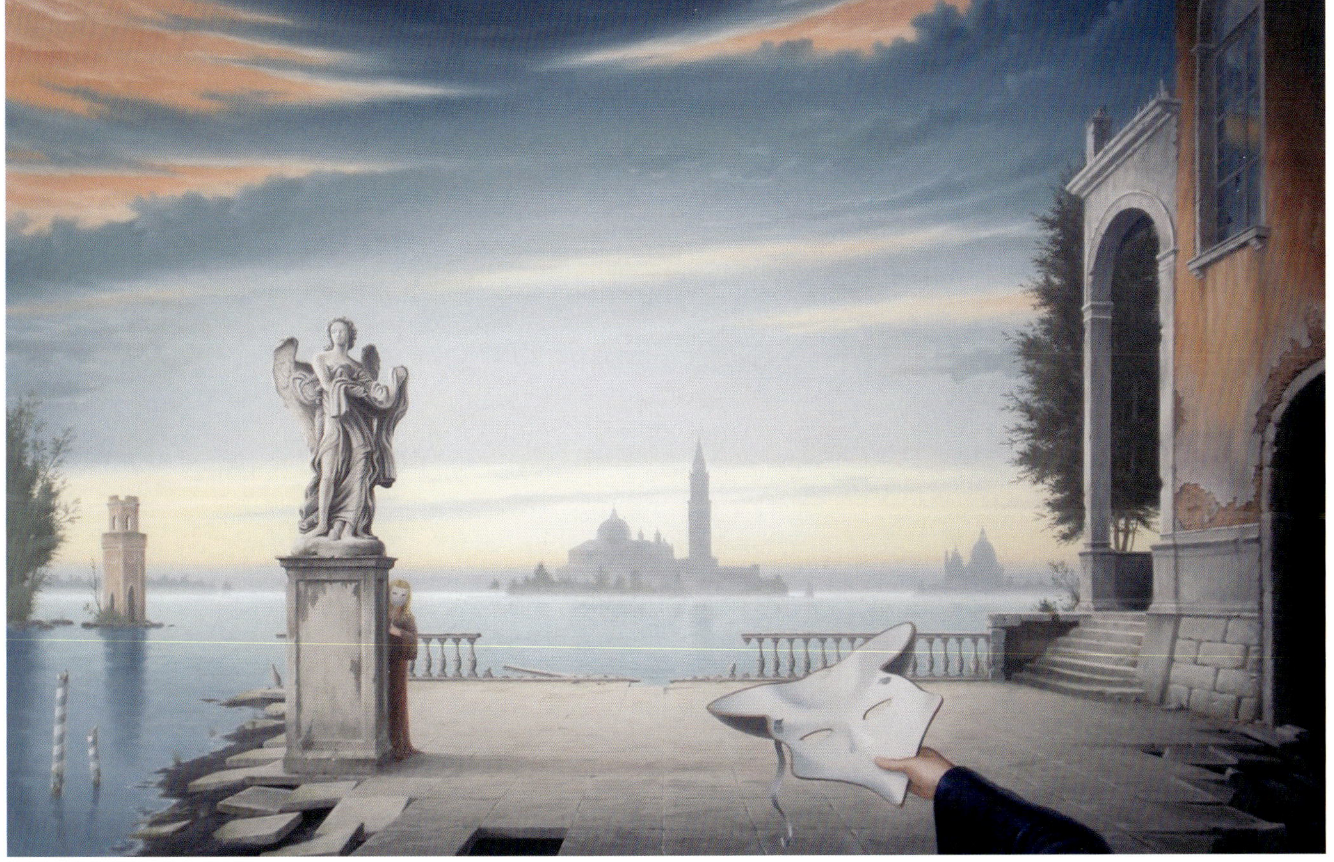

You First · 40 x 60 cm · Oil on panel

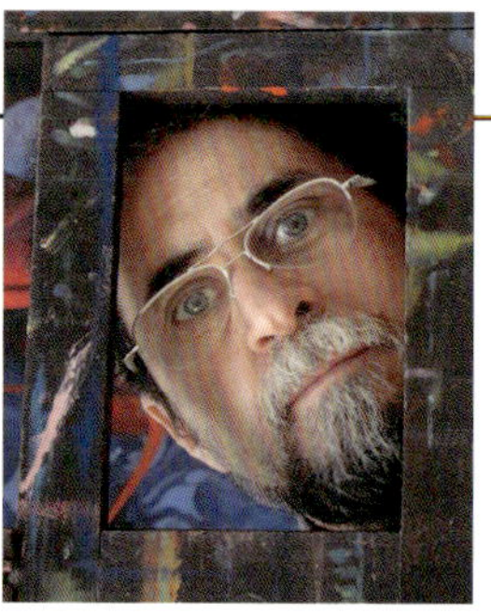

ZELJKO DJUROVIC

1956 Serbia

www.zeljkodjurovic.com

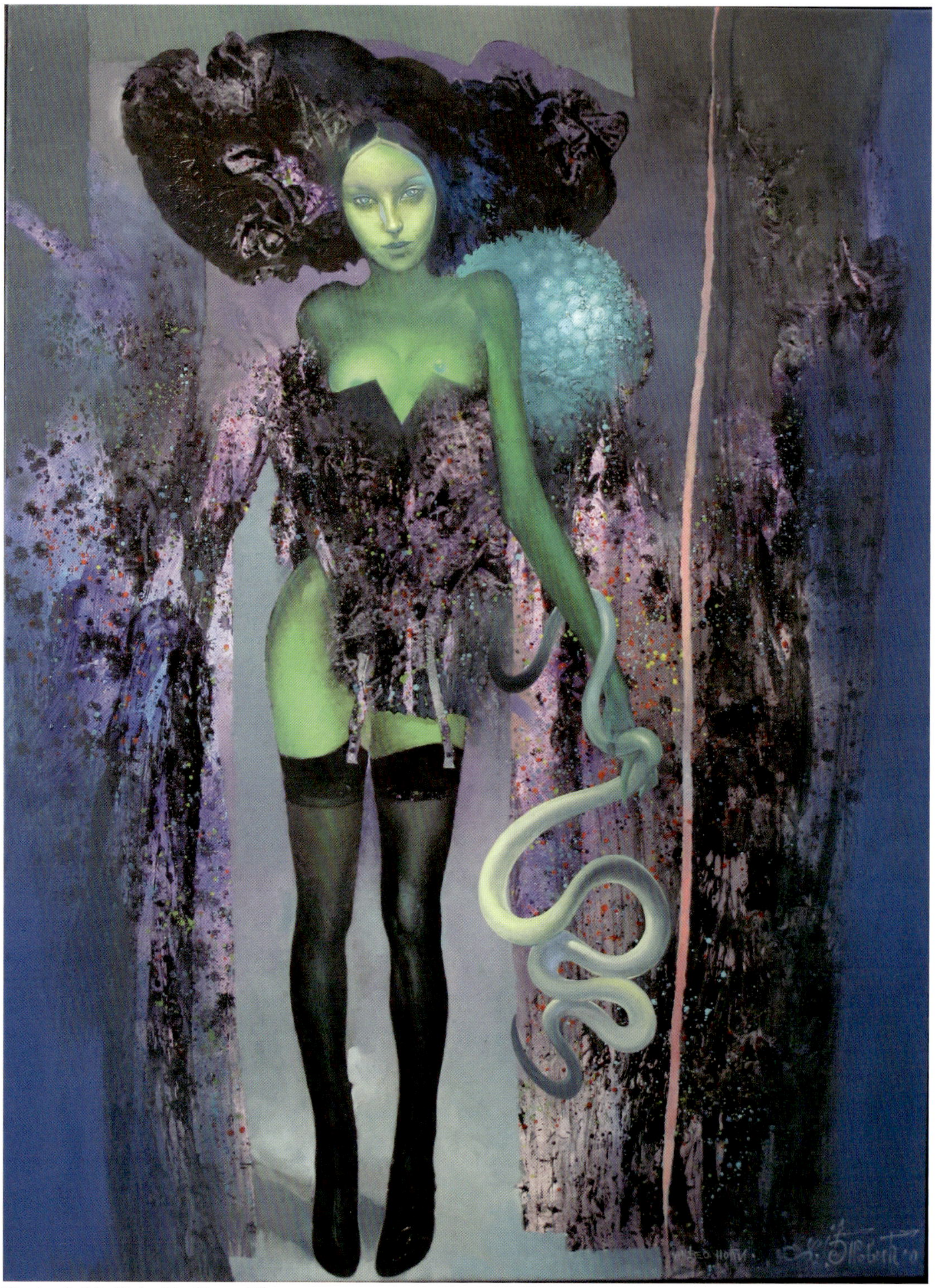

The Angel of the Dark · 90 x 65 cm · Oil on canvas

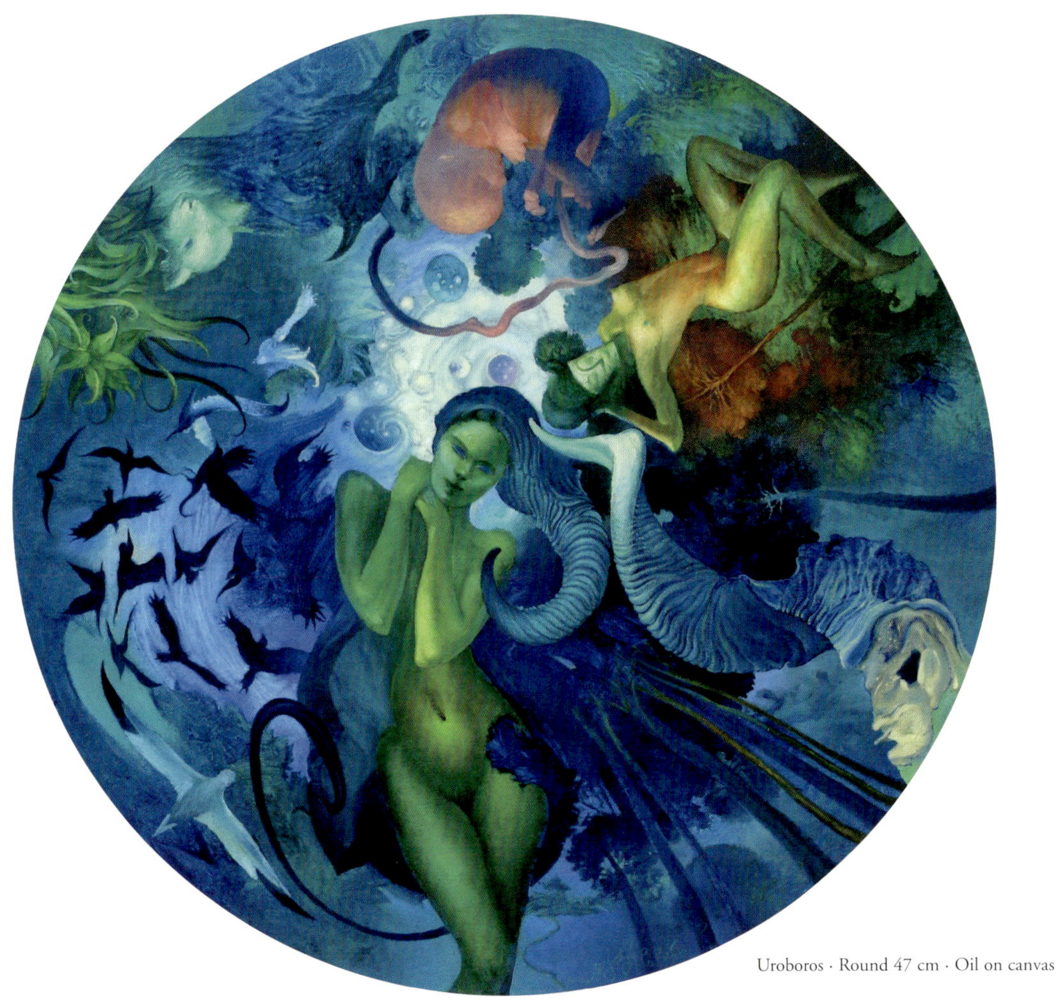

Uroboros · Round 47 cm · Oil on canvas

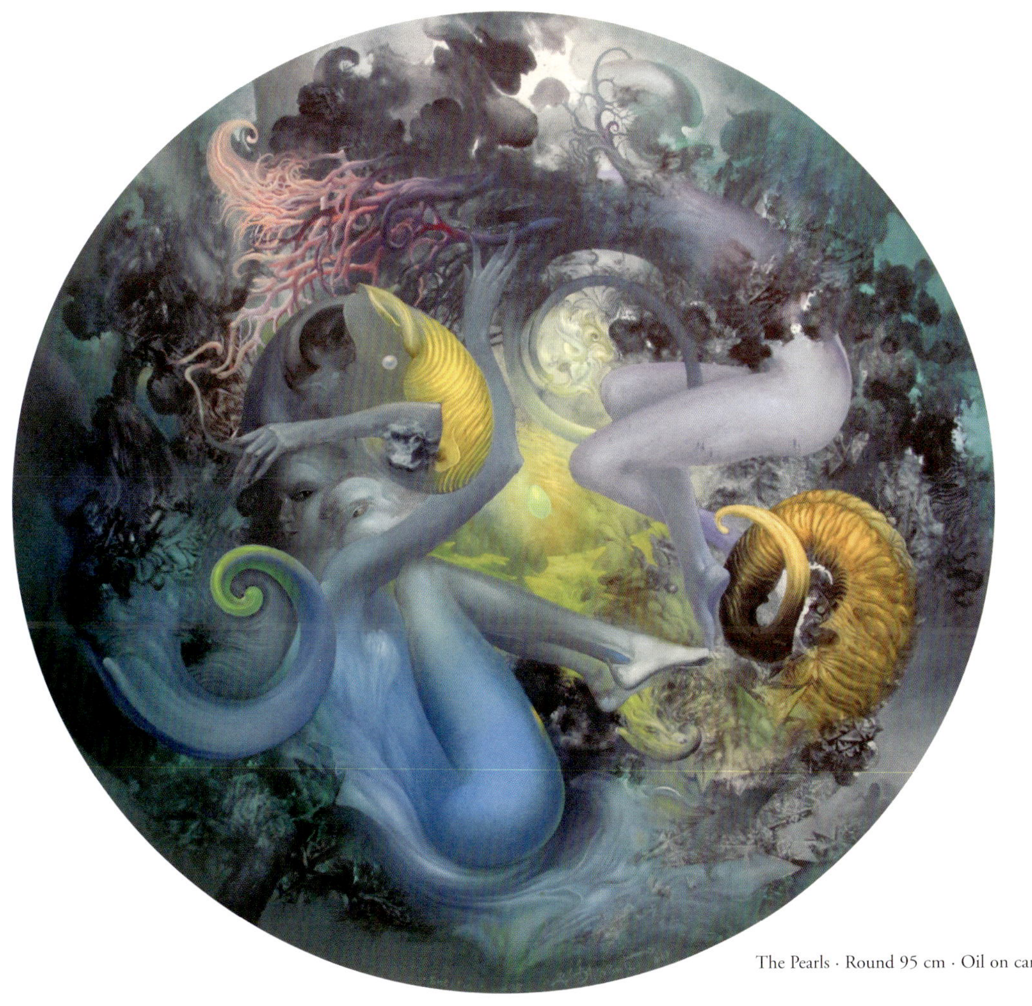

The Pearls · Round 95 cm · Oil on canvas

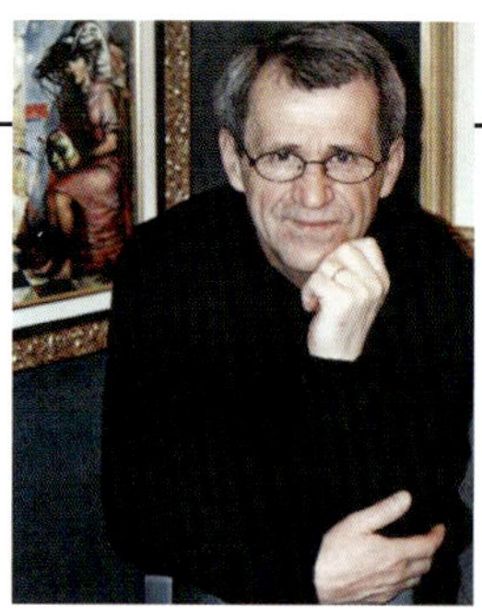

VAL DYSHLOV

1950 USA

www.valdyshlov.com

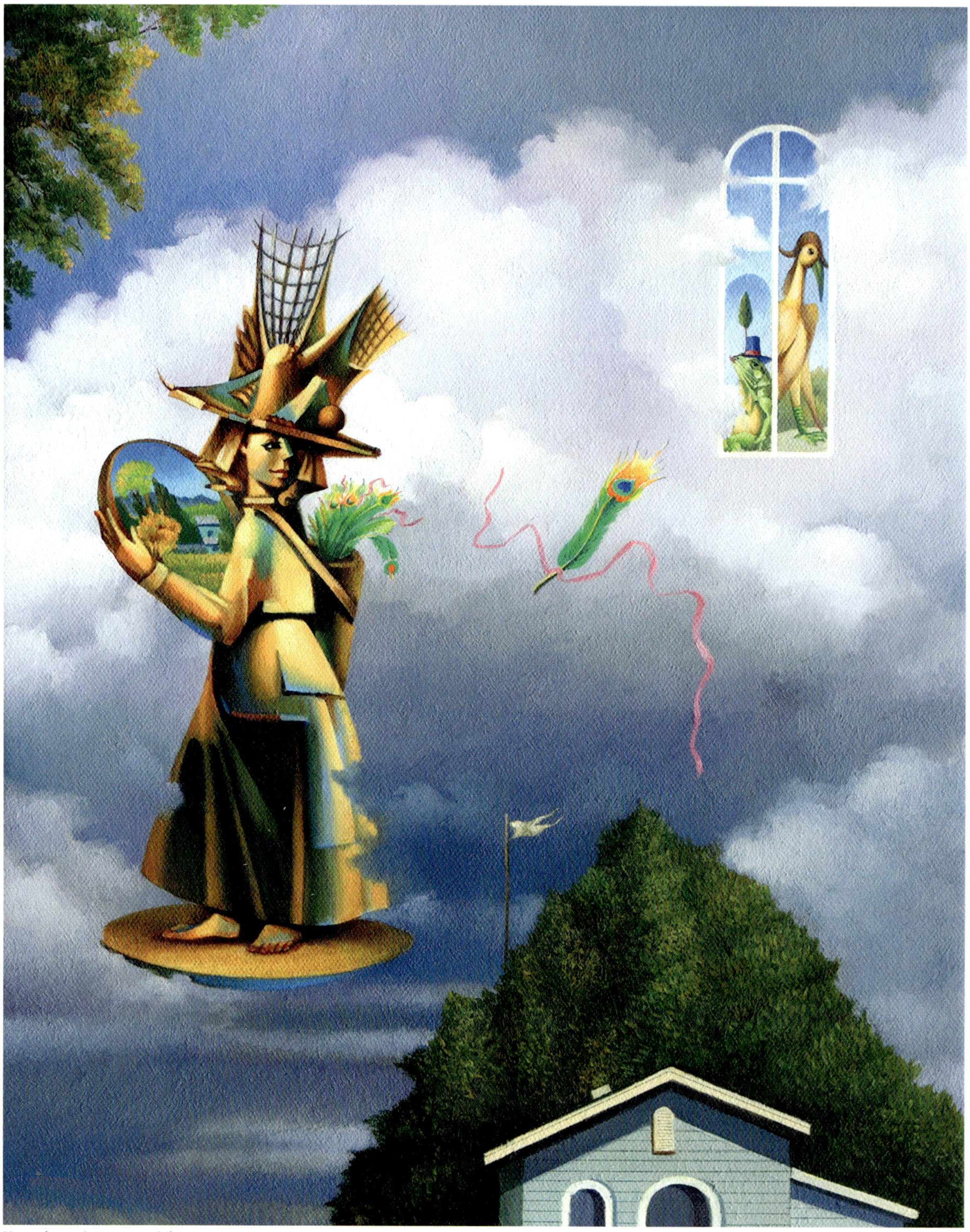

Keepsake · 36 x 28 cm · Oil on canvas

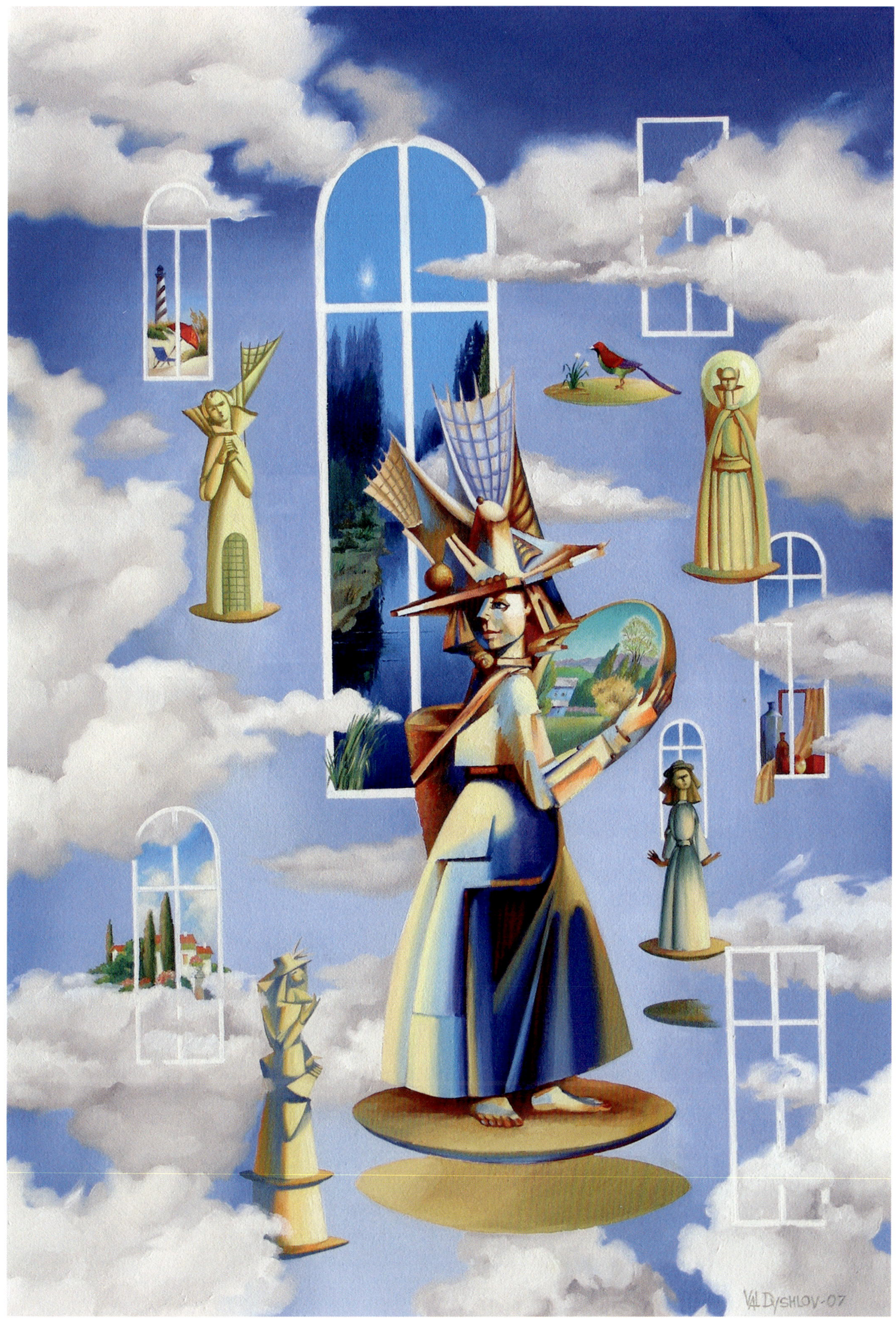

Flying Windows · 90 x 60 cm · Oil on canvas

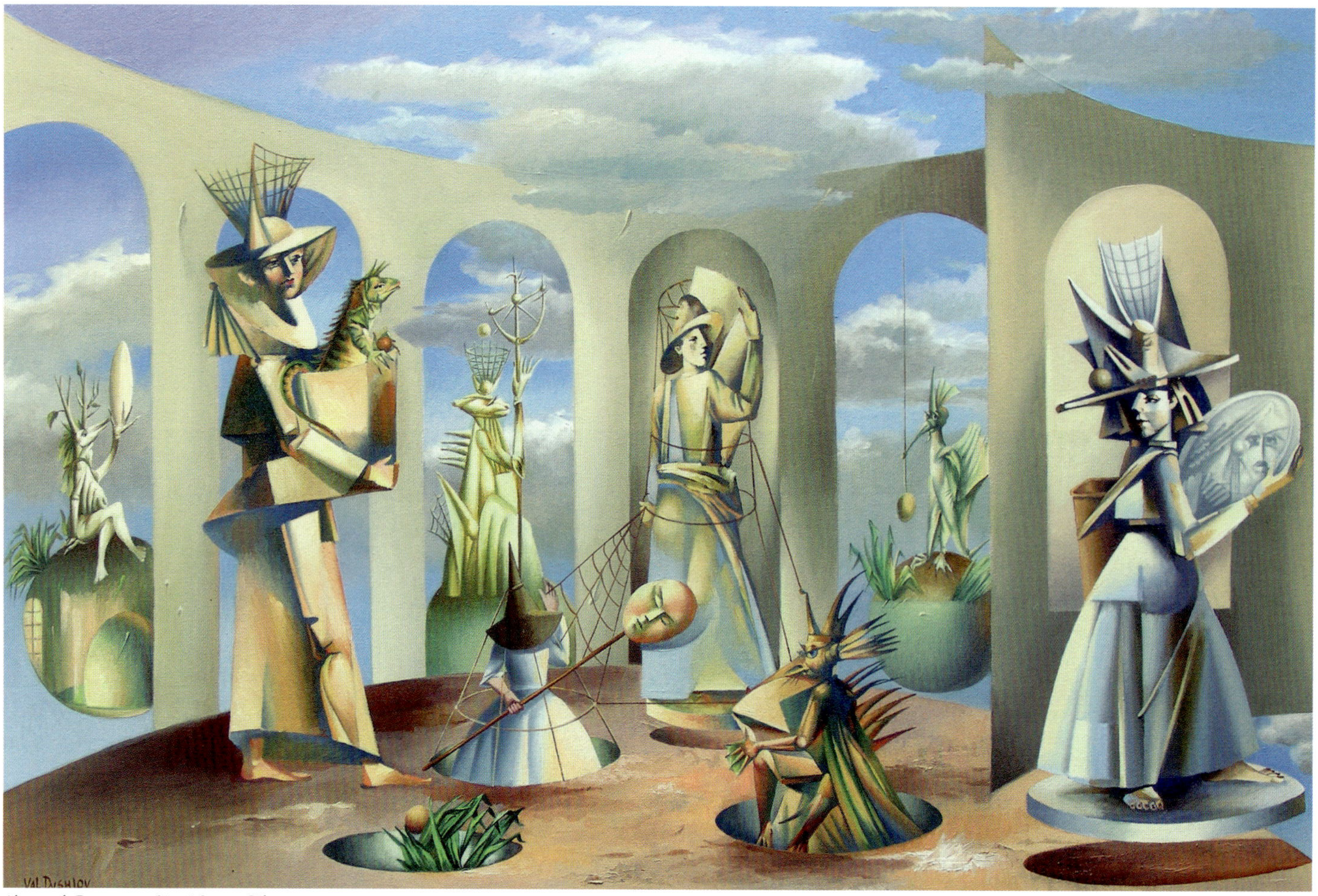

Alon and Gorgeous · 61 x 96 cm · Oil on canvas

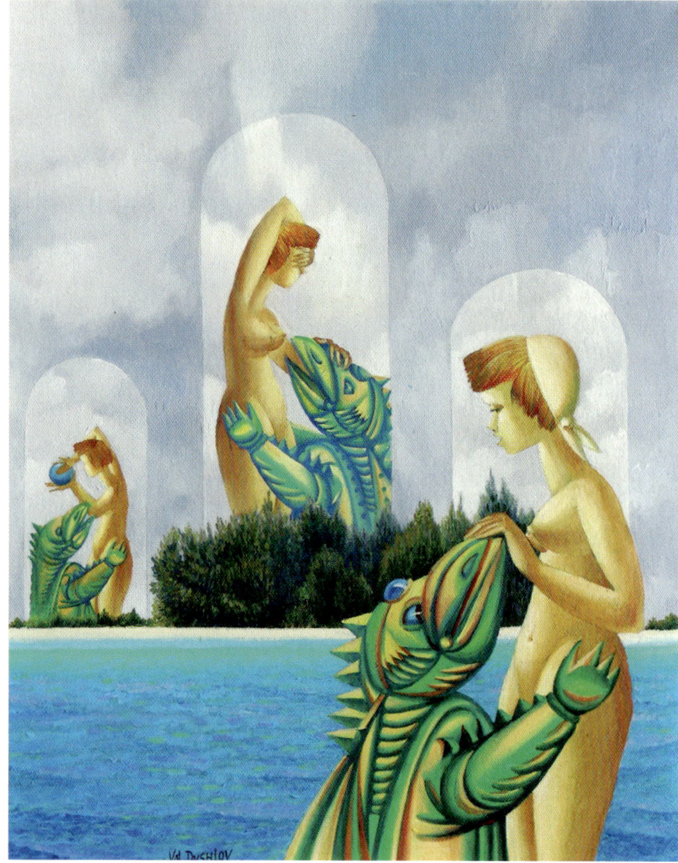

Aruba · 36 x 28 cm · Oil on canvas

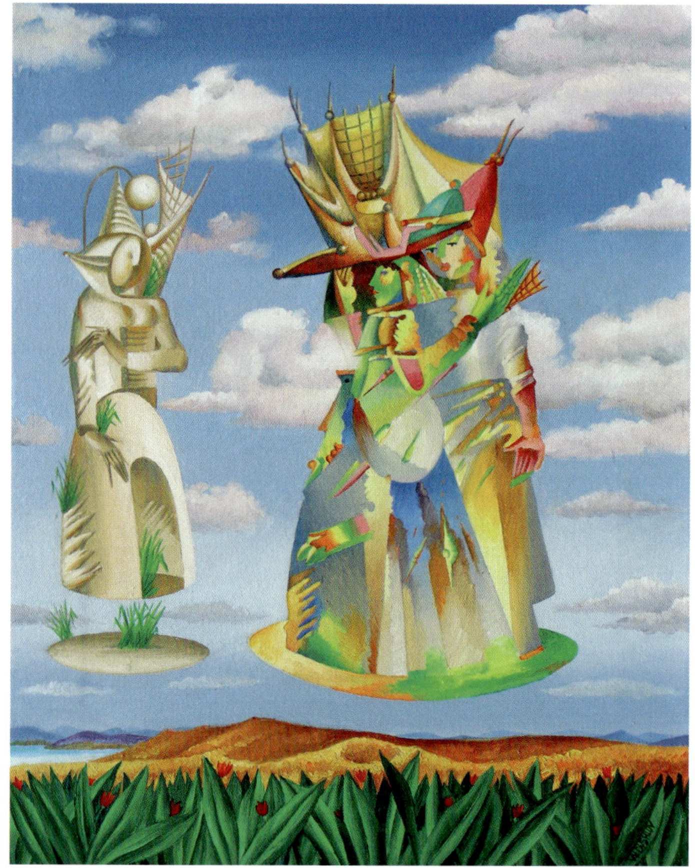

Ethernal · 45 x 35 cm · Oil on canvas

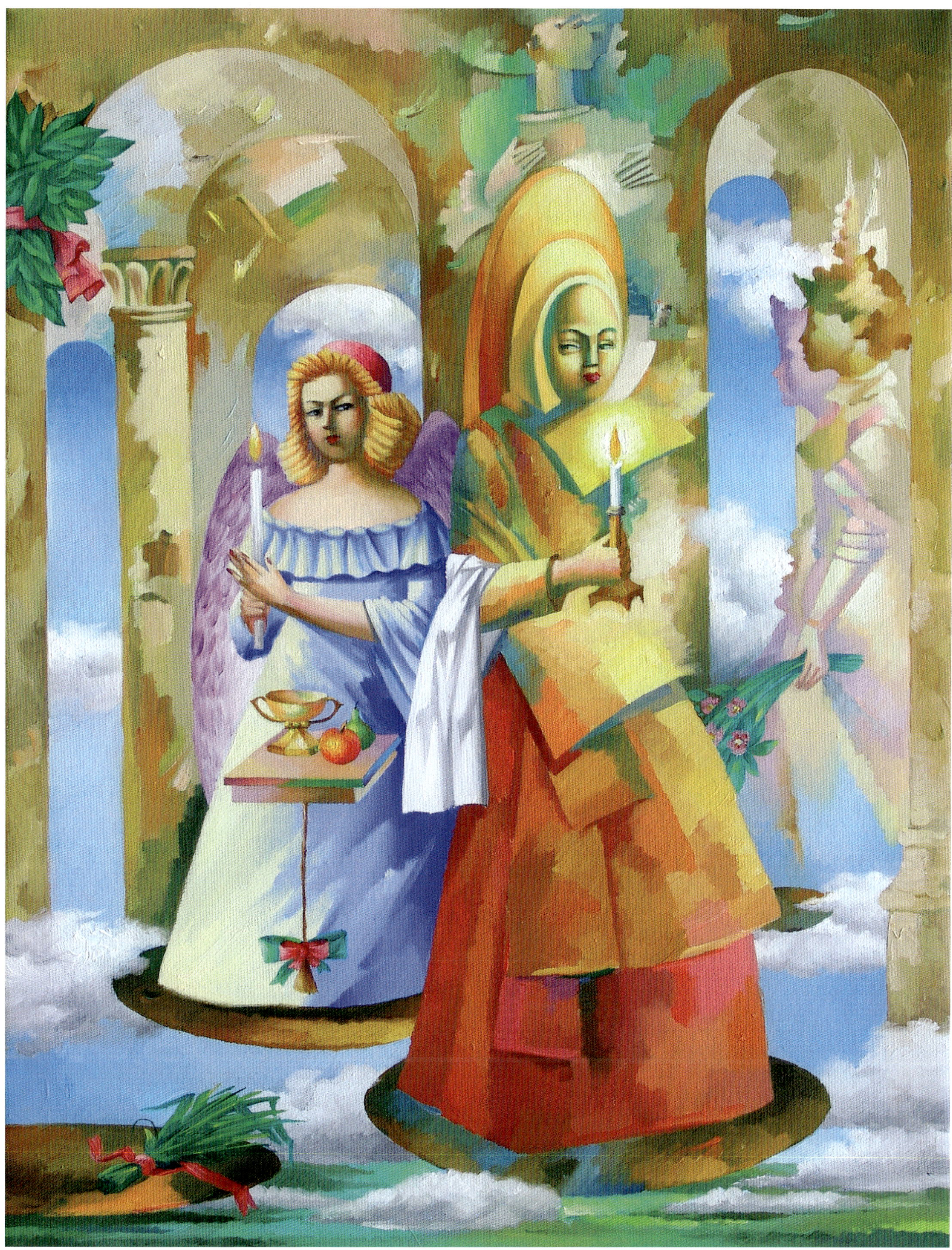

Daydream · 41 x 31 cm · Oil on canvas

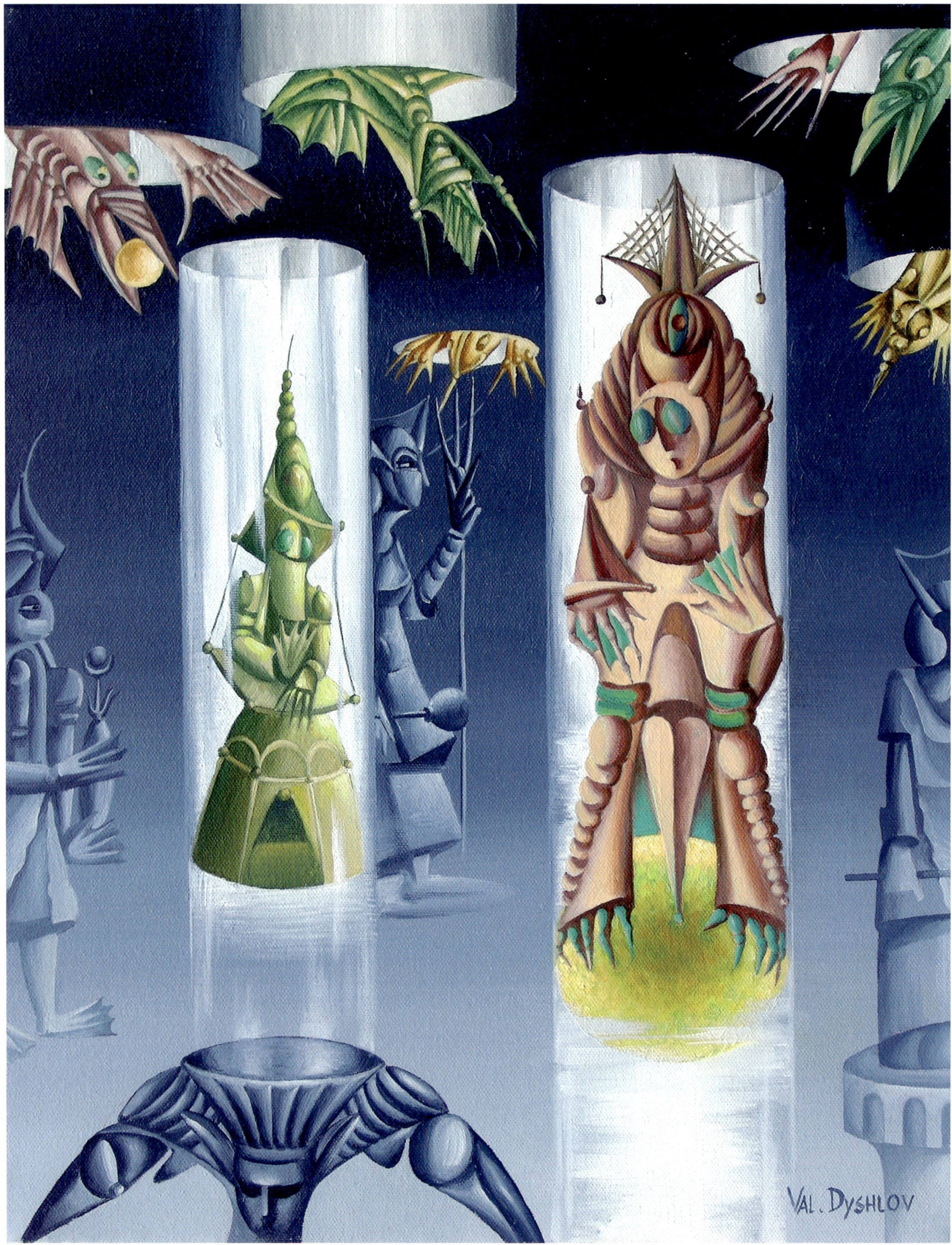

Visitors · 45 x 35 cm · Oil on canvas

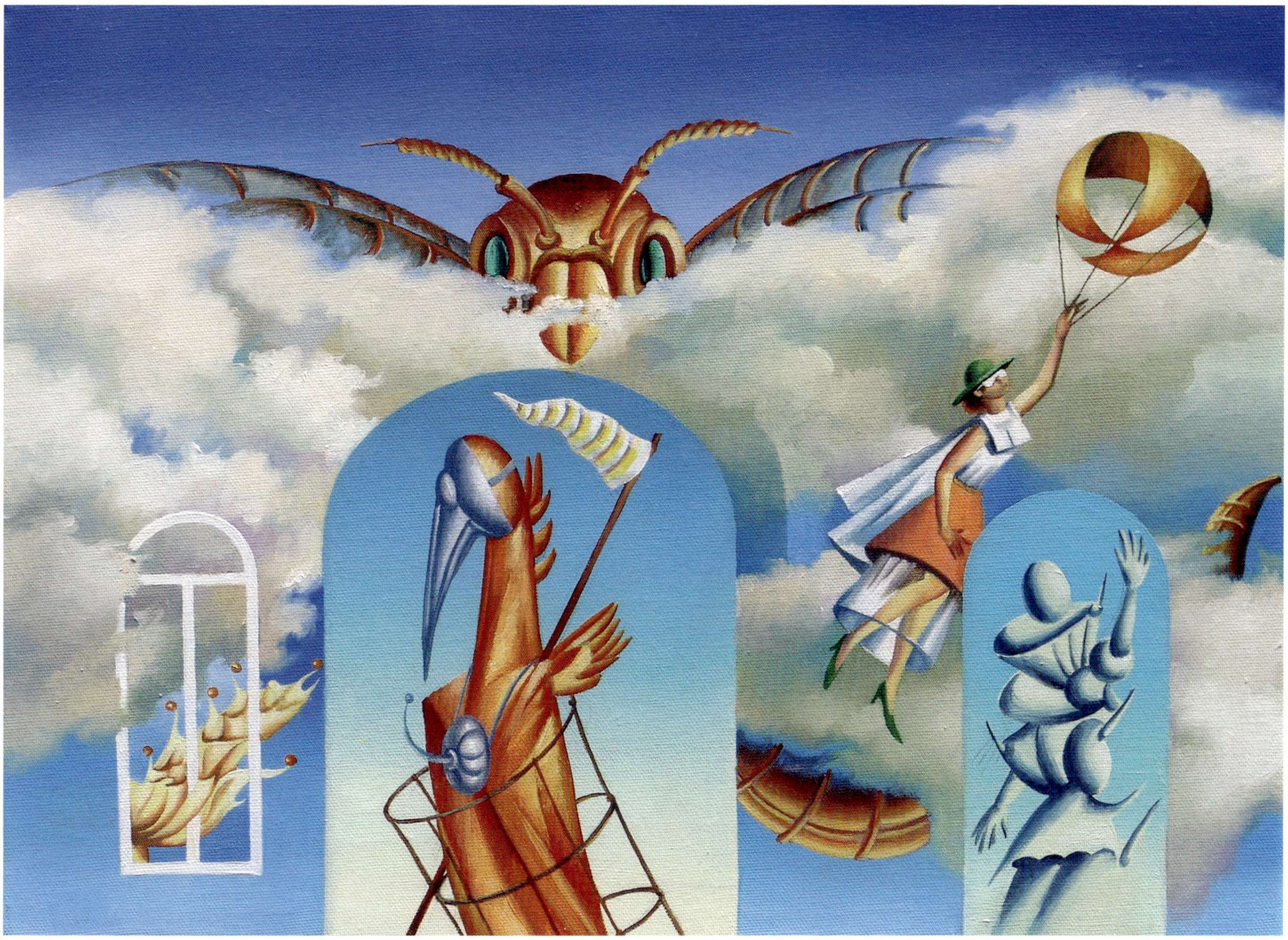

Flight of Fancy · 30 x 40 cm · Oil on canvas

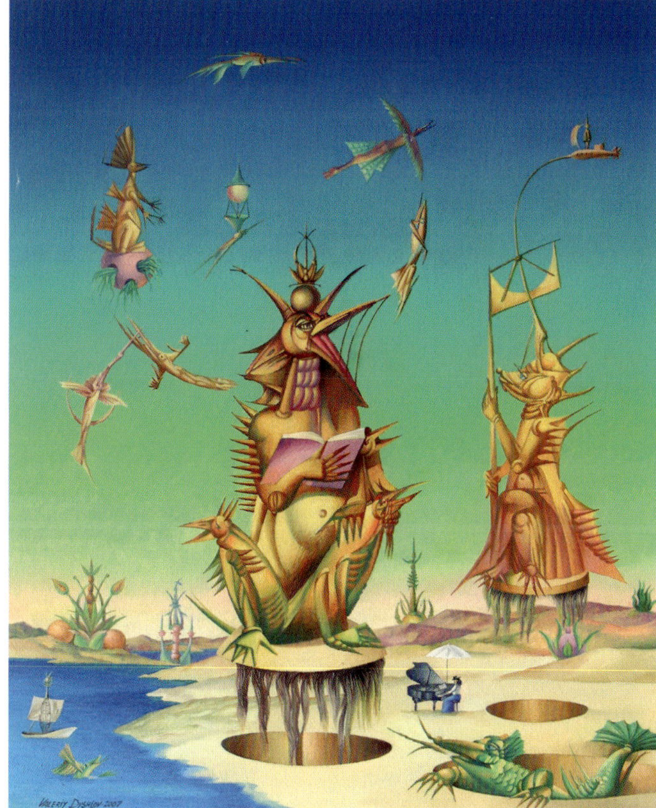

Soaring · 76 x 61 cm · Oil on canvas

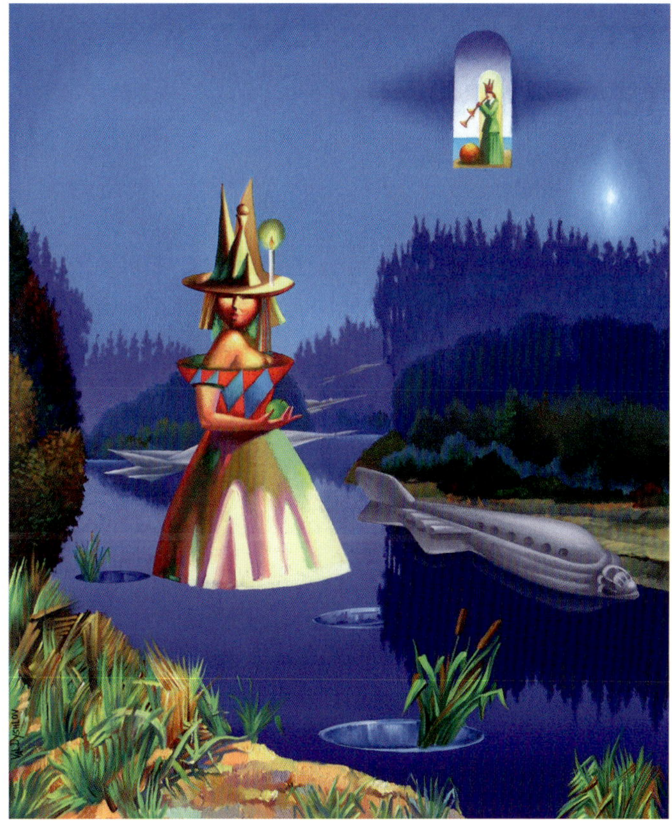

Nightime in May · 50 x 40 cm · Oil on canvas

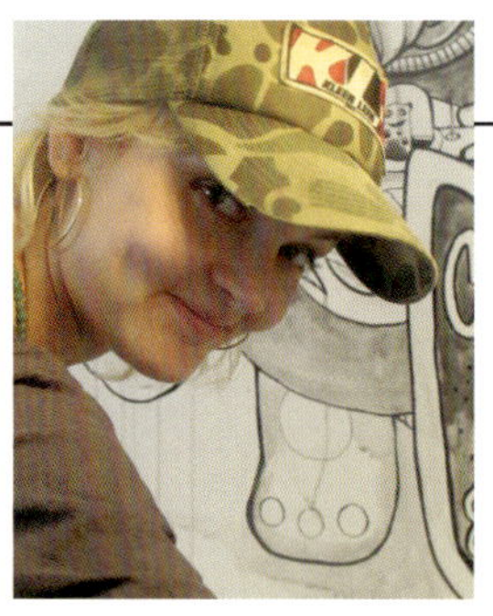

COCO ELECTRA

1977 Denmark

www.electraladyland.com

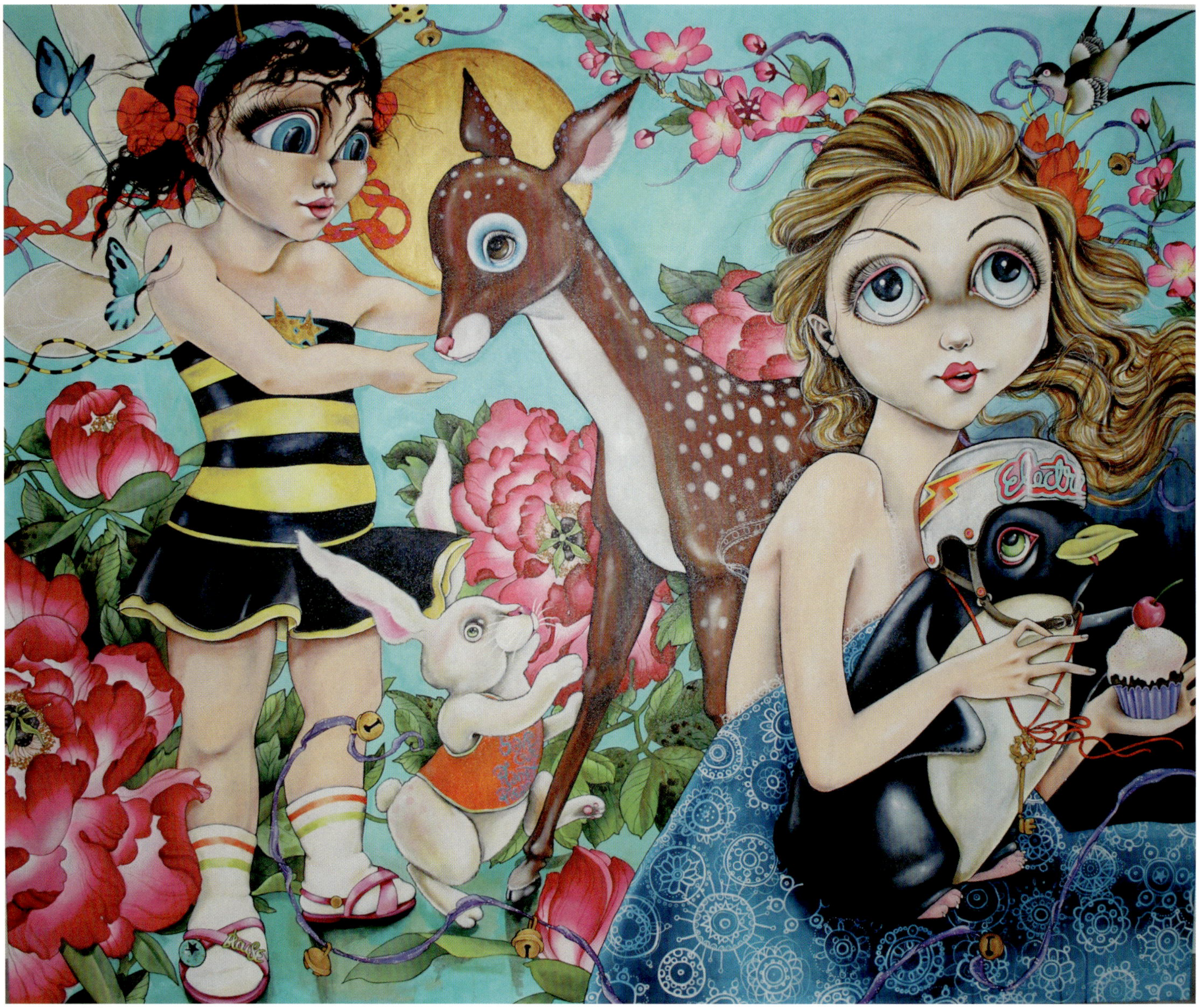

Summer Holliday · 170 x 200 cm · Acrylic on canvas

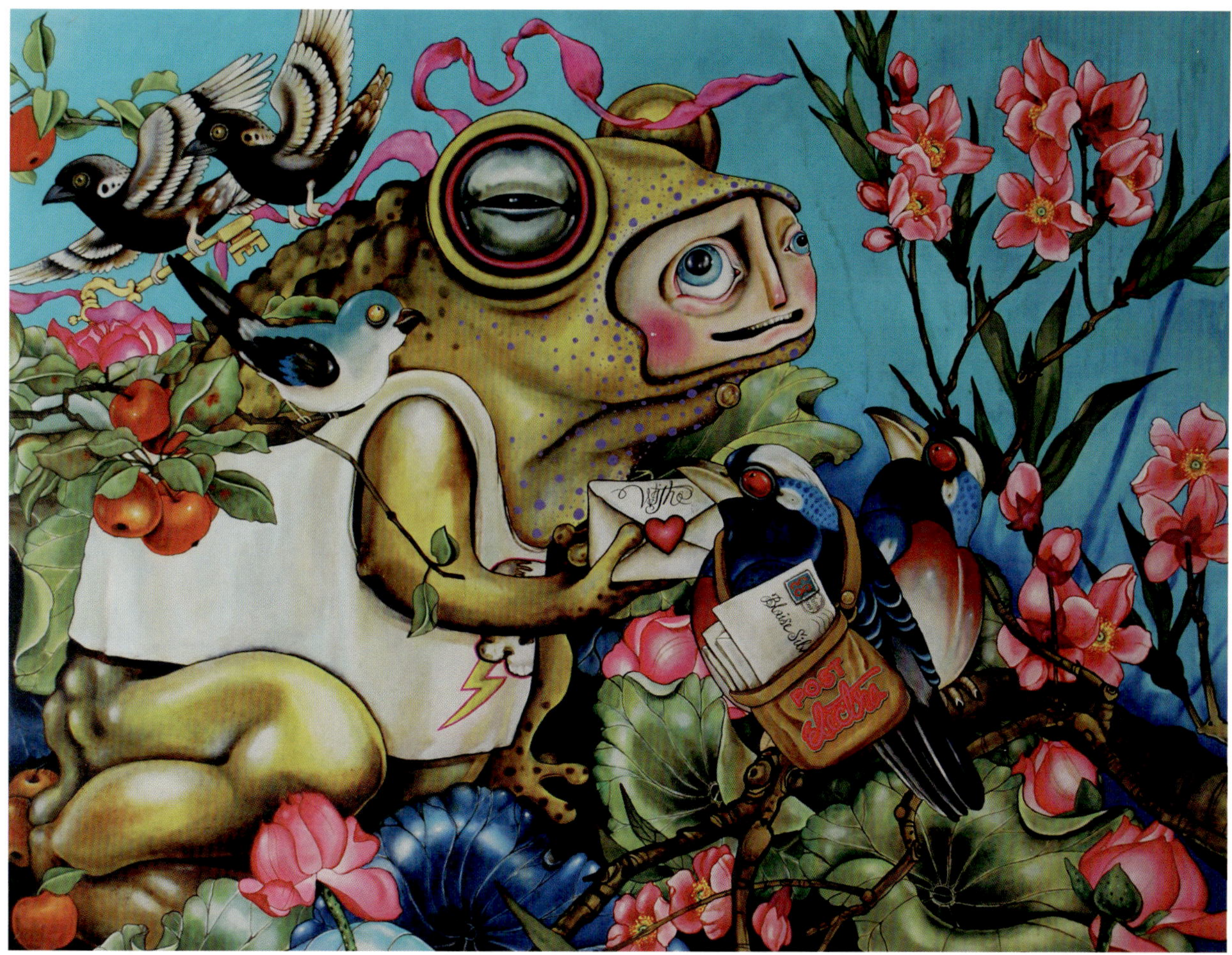

My Cousin the Toad 120 x 150 cm · Acrylic on canvas

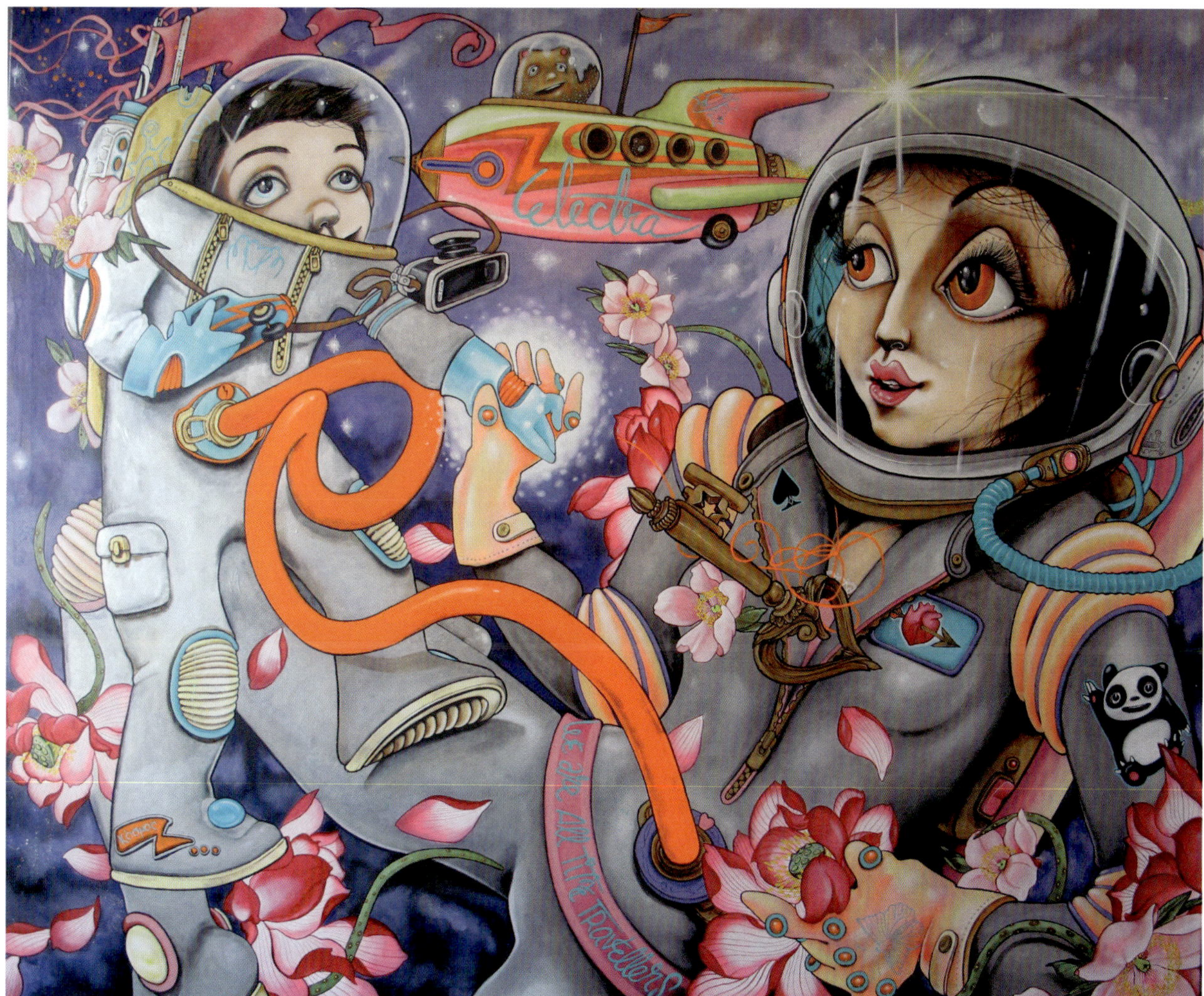

Cosmos · 170 x 200 cm · Acrylic on canvas

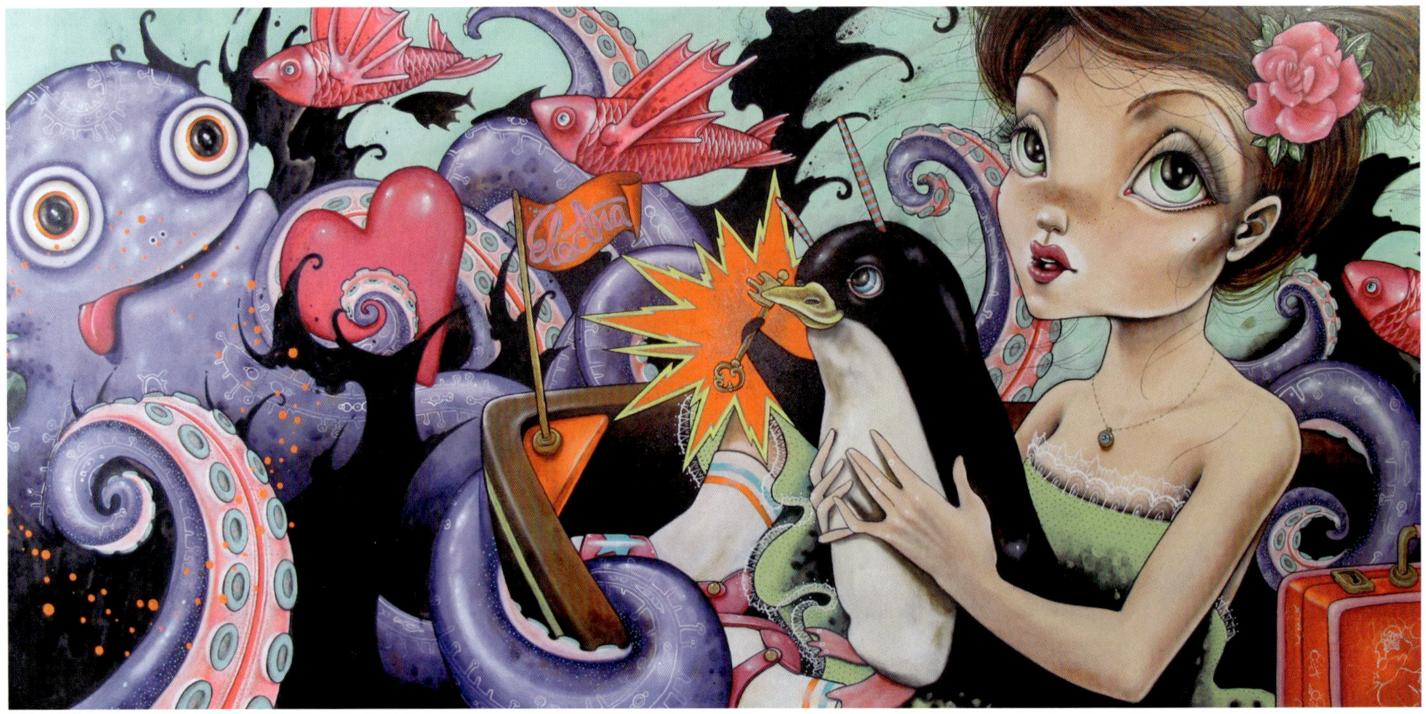

Moonligh Dream · 50 x 100 cm · Oil on canvas

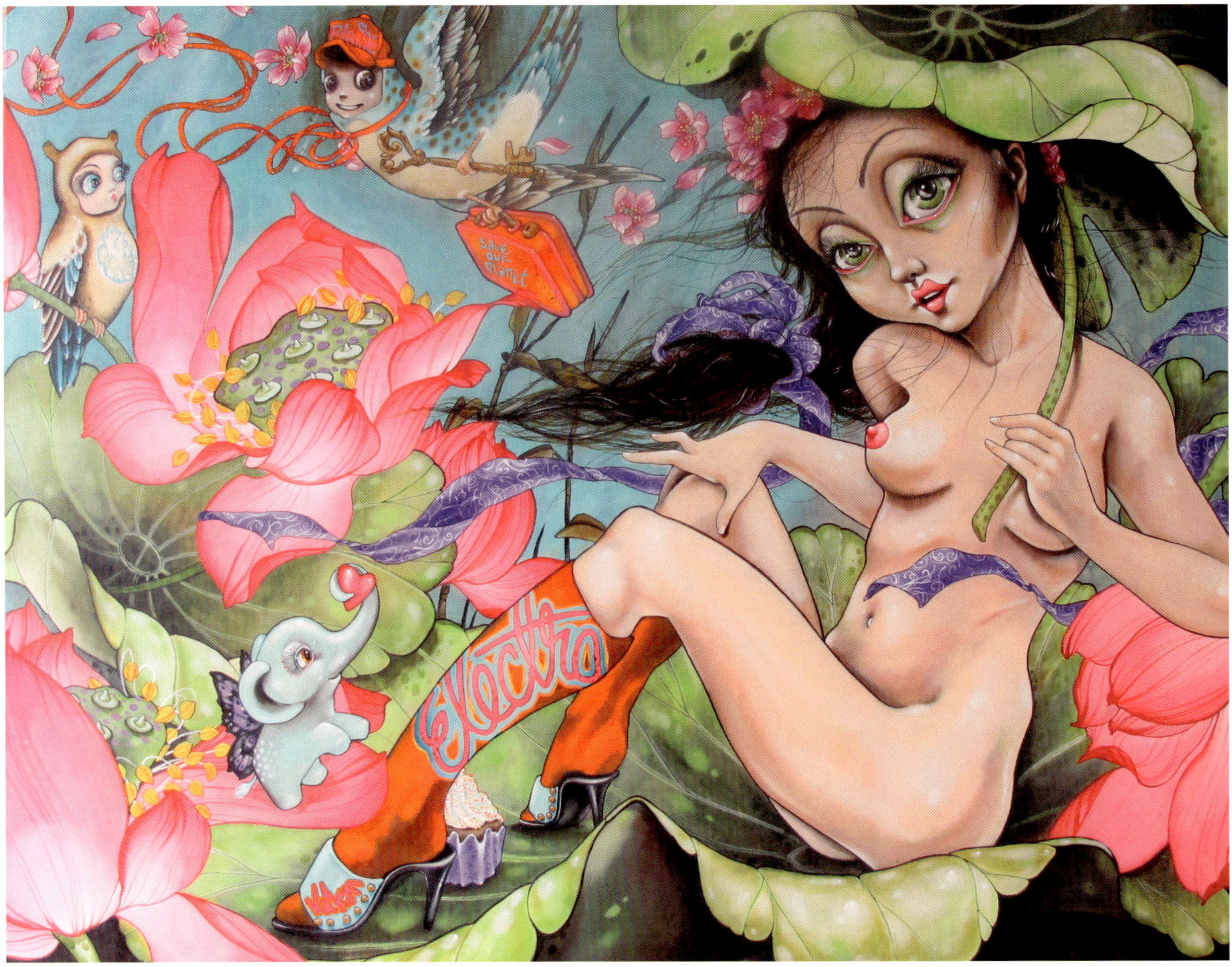

Vera · 120 x 150 cm · Oil on canvas

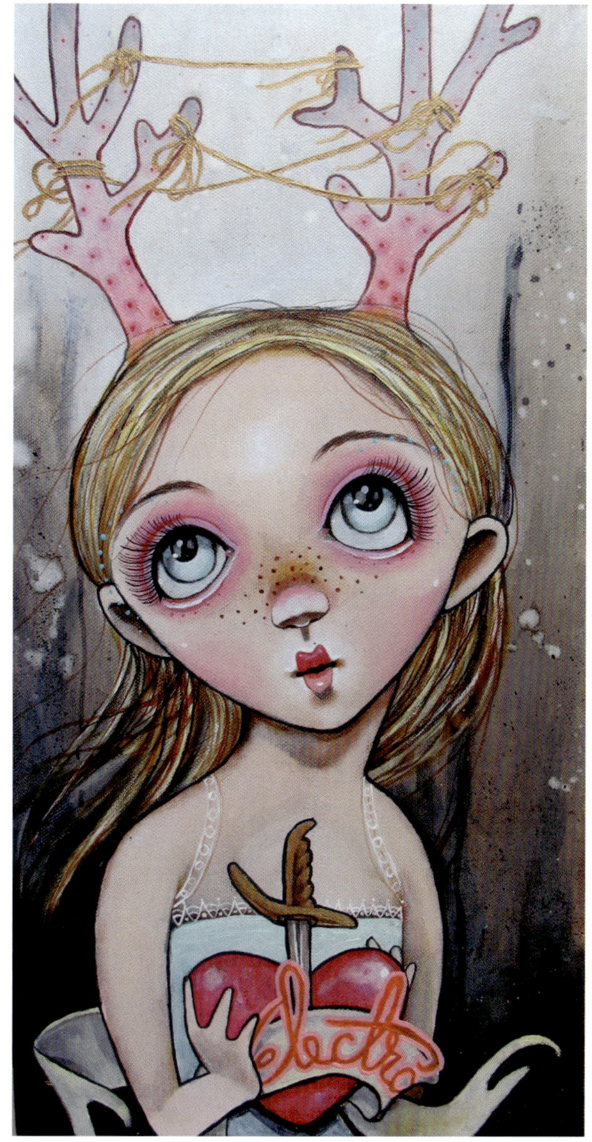

Have my Heart · Acrylic on canvas

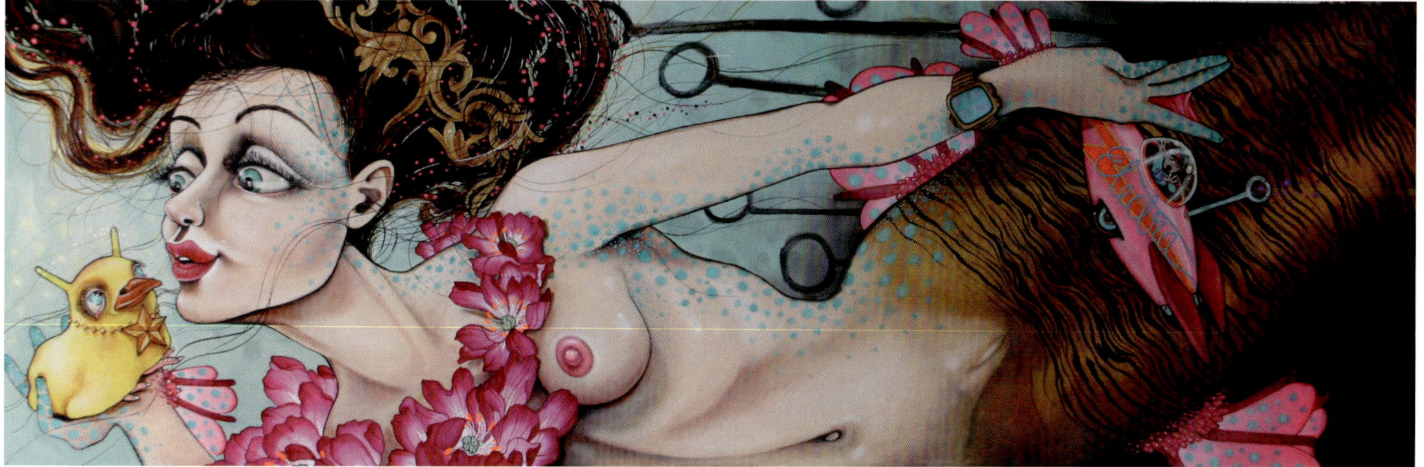

Lillith · 50 x 150 cm · Acrylic on canvas

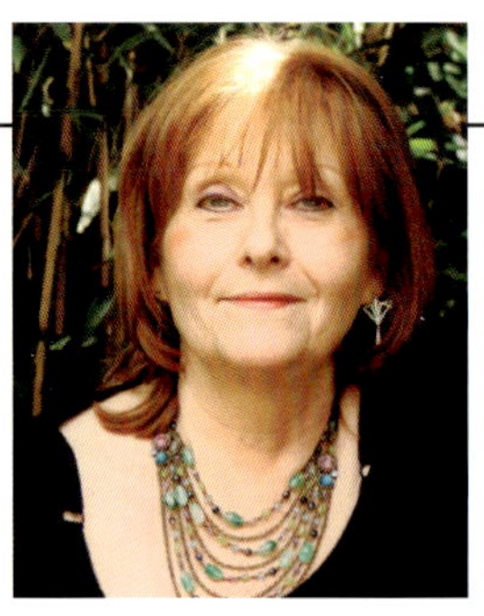

MAGDA FRANCOT

1942 Belgium

www.magda-francot-art.com

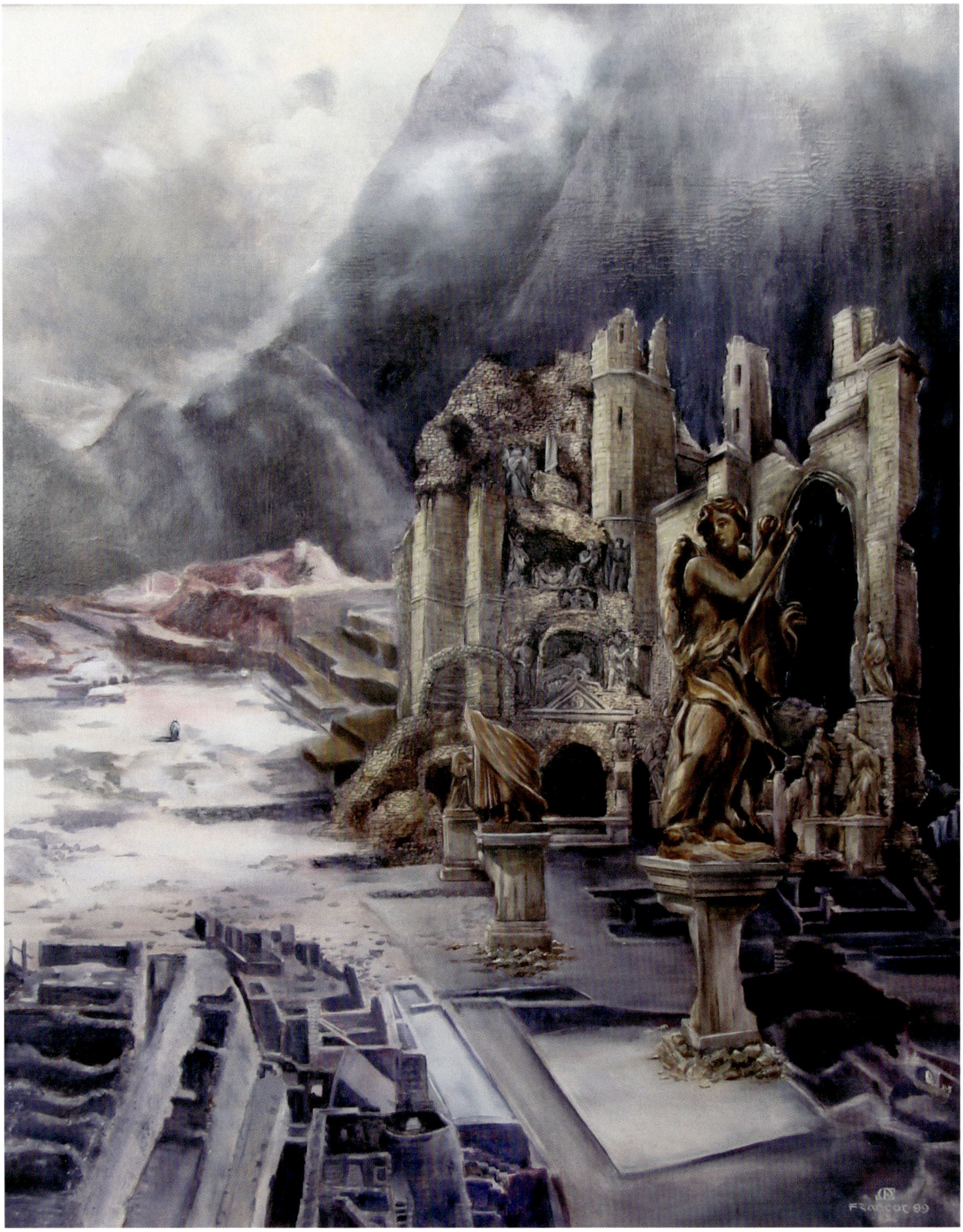

The Spirit of the Ruin · 78 x 63 cm · Oil on panel

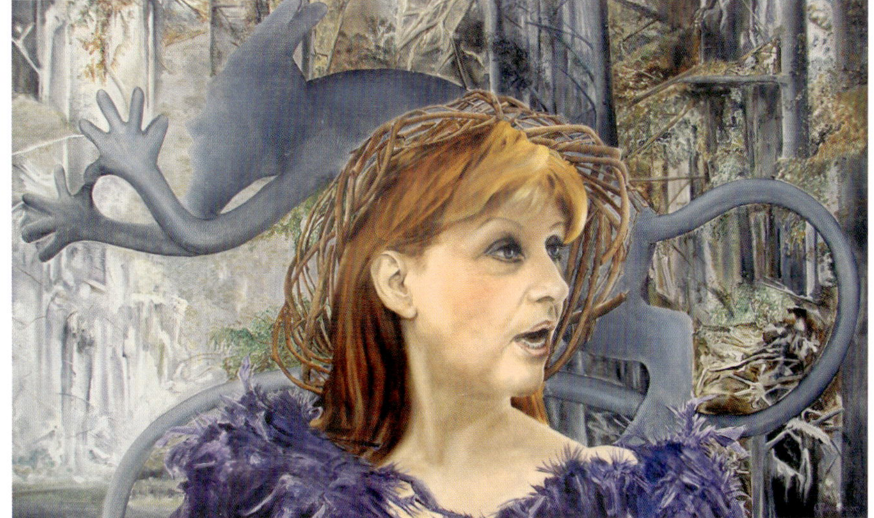

Waiting for he Imagination · 63 x 100 cm · Oil on canvas glued to panel

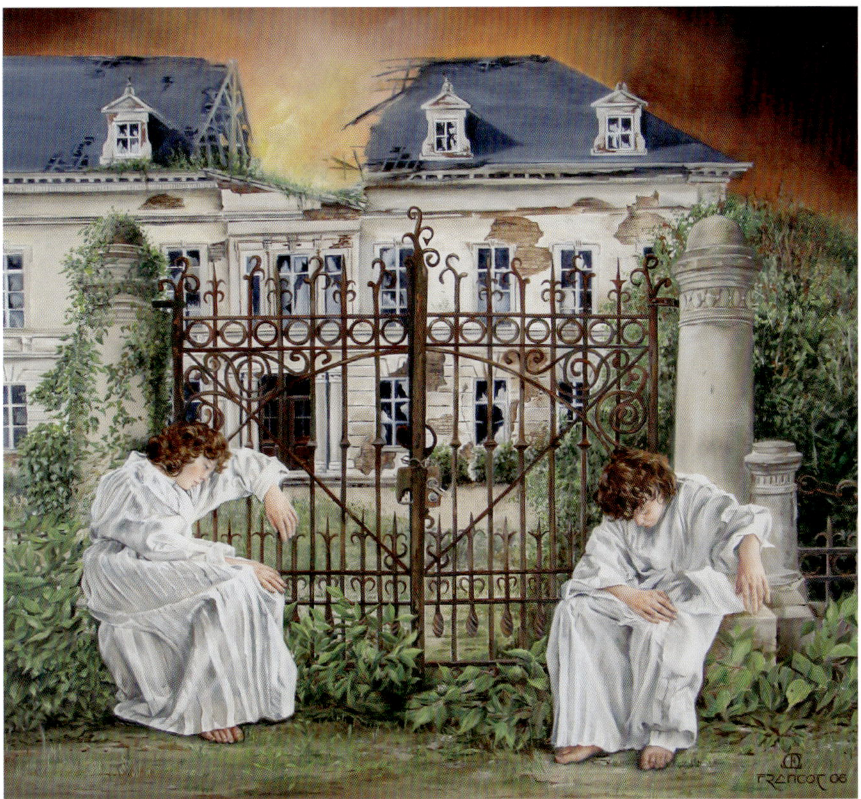

The lost Civilization · 39 x 42 cm · Oil on panel

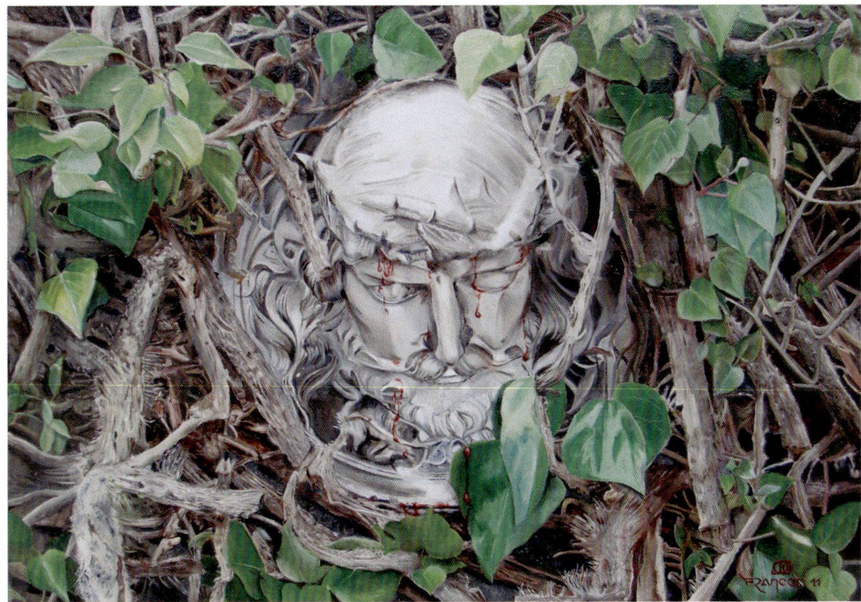

Magician · 30 x 45 cm · Oil on panel

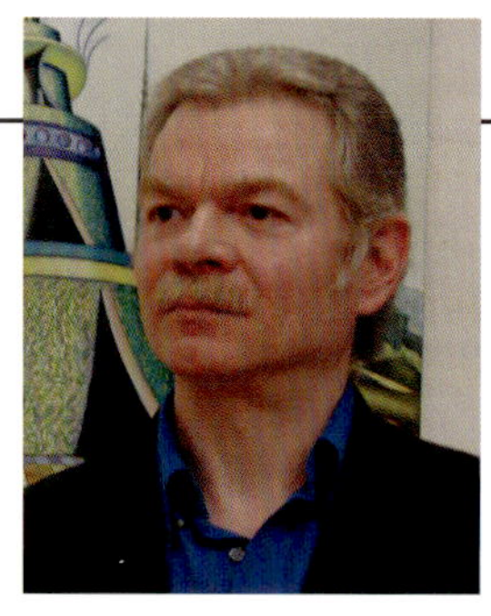

ANDREAS N. FRANZ

1956 Germany

www.andreas-nikolaus-franz.de

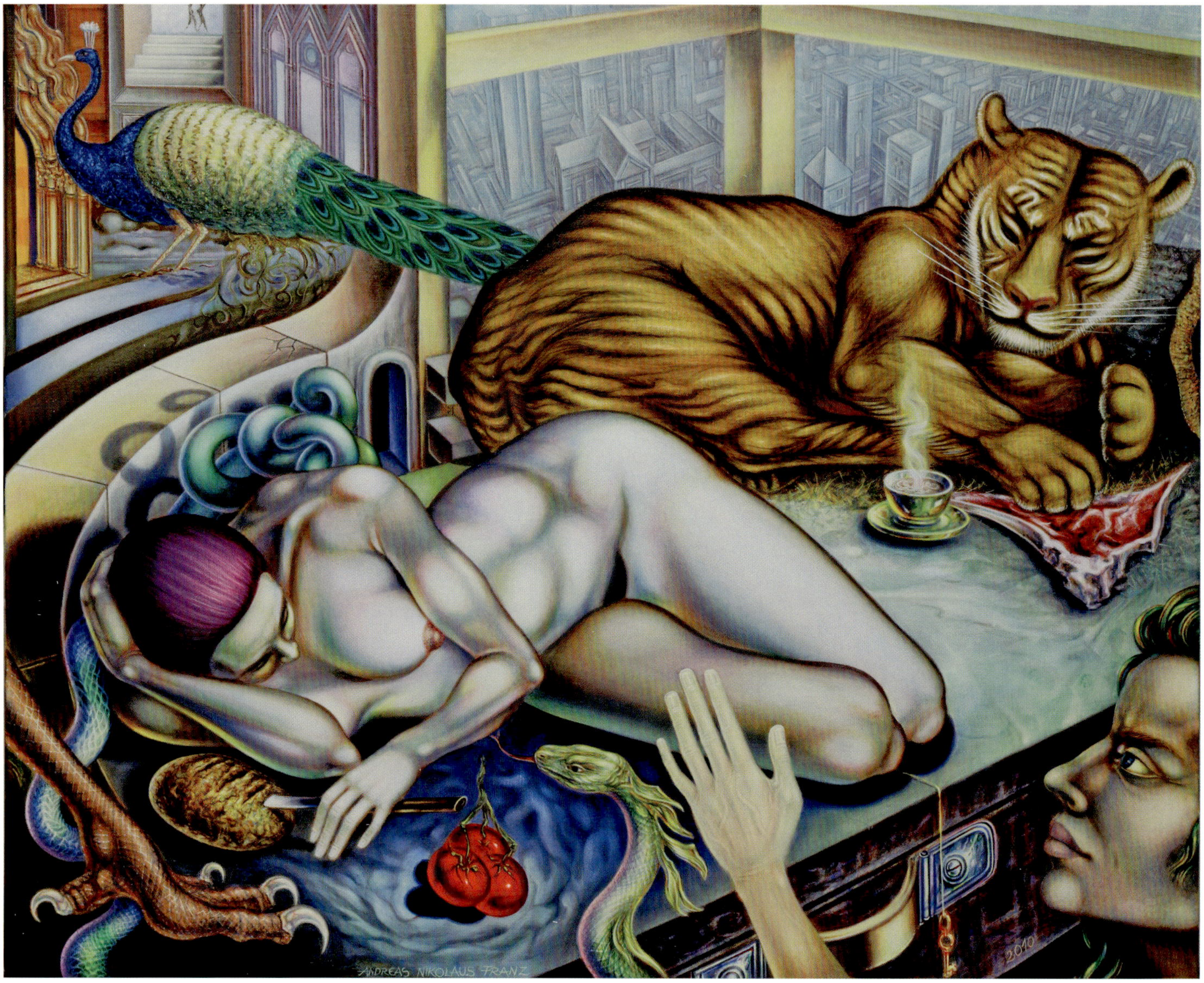

Peacock being · 100 x 120 cm · Oil / Caseintempera on canvas

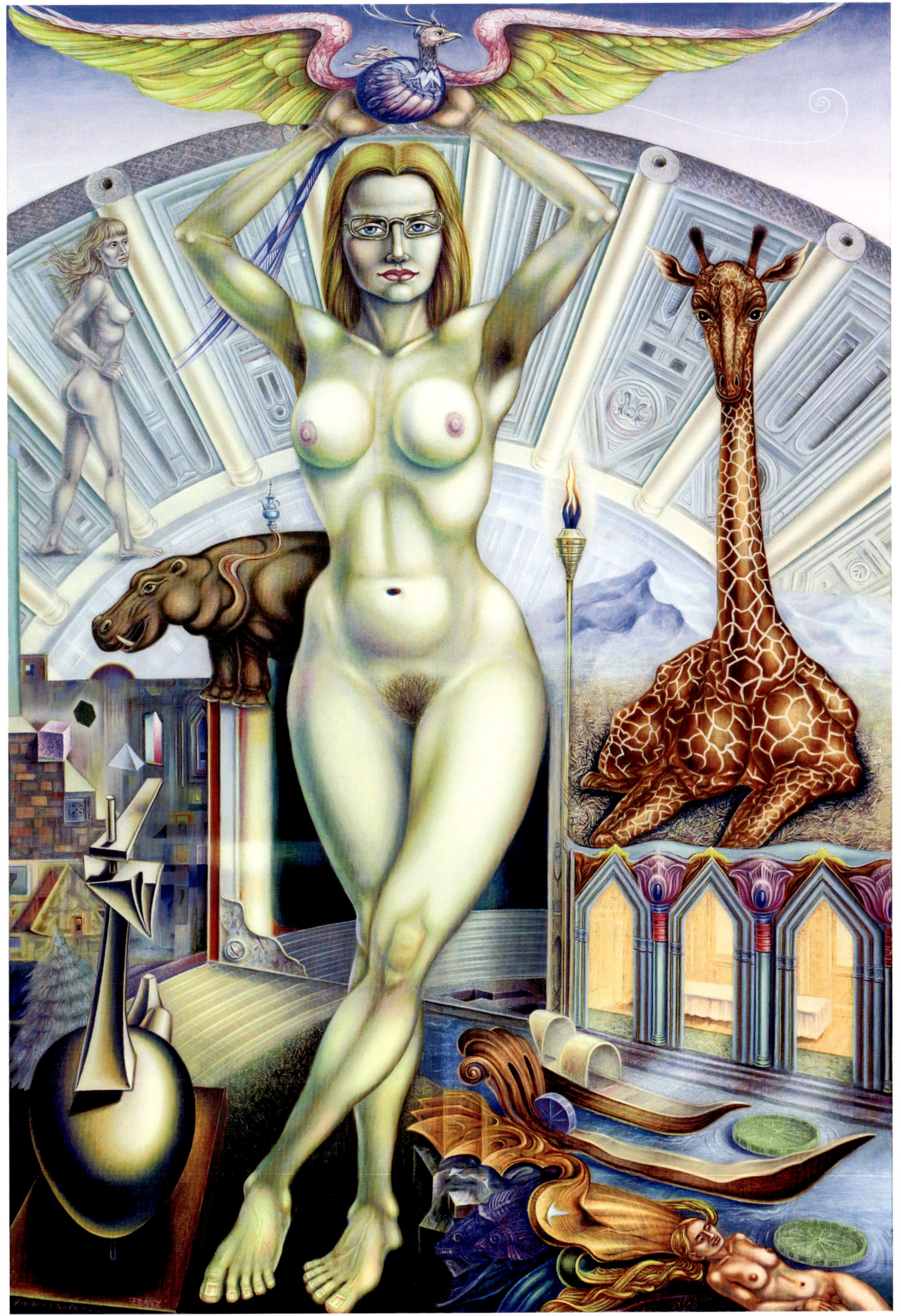

Leant back · 150 x 100 cm · Oil / Caseintempera on canvas

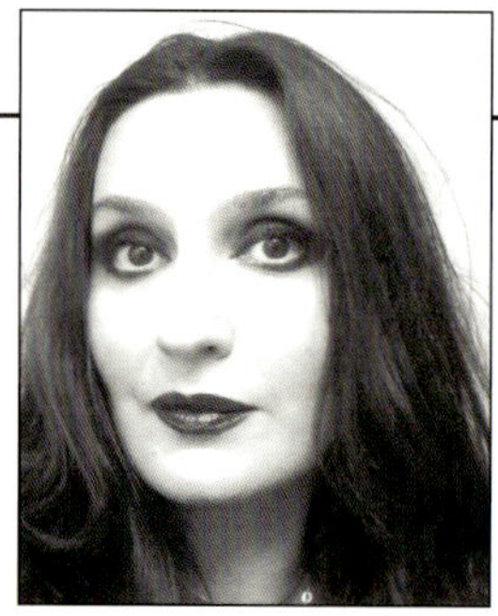

GABRIELA GARZA-PADILLA

1965 Mexico

www.gabrielagarzapadilla.com

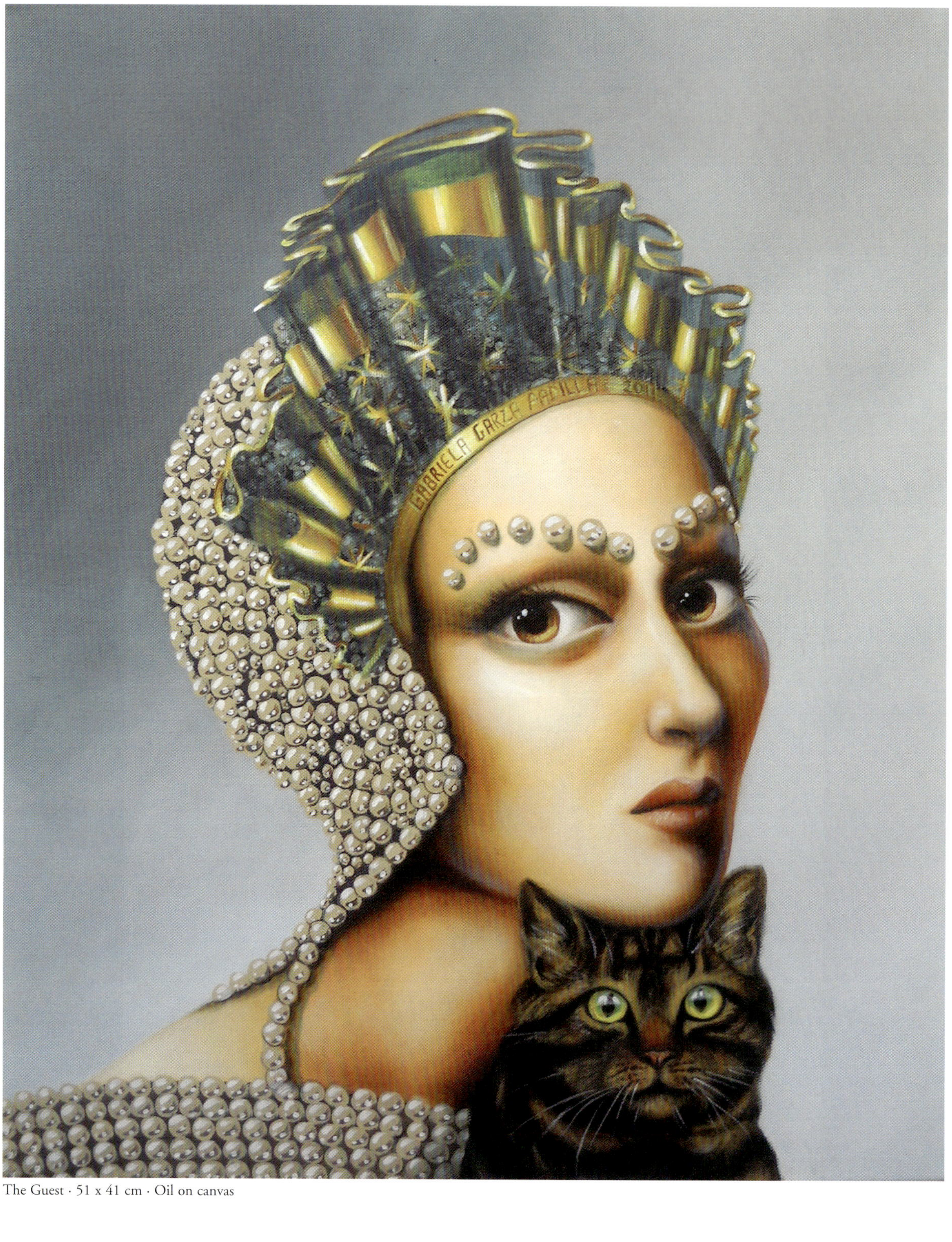

The Guest · 51 x 41 cm · Oil on canvas

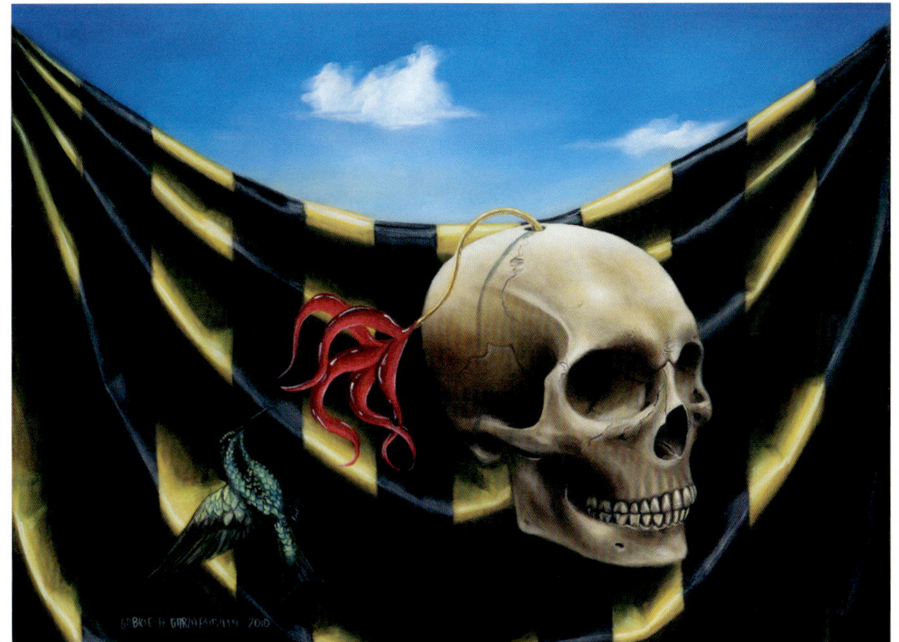

Thats Just the Way It Is · 46 x 61 cm · Oil on canvas

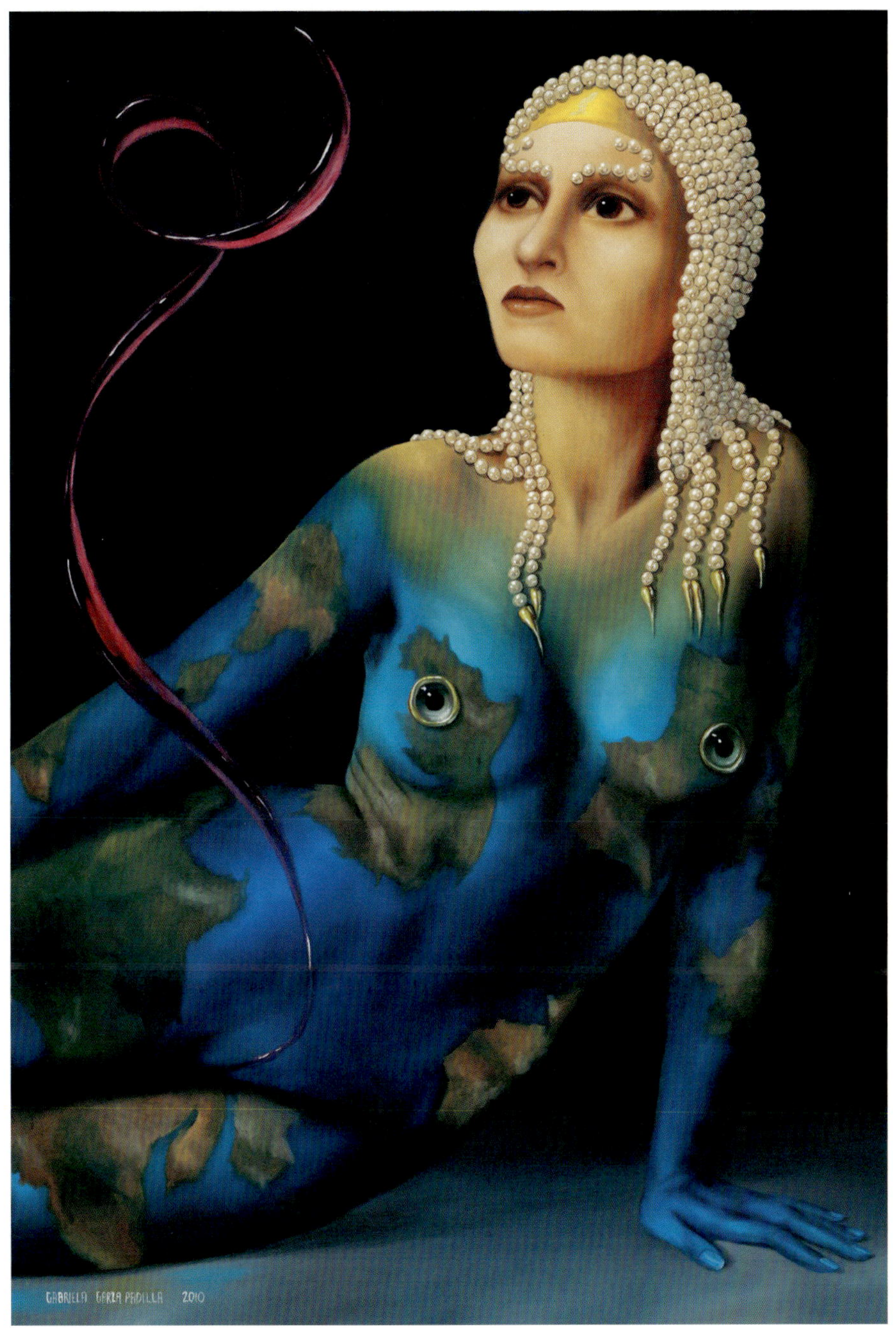

Nature Contains Nature · 92 x 61 cm · Oil on canvas

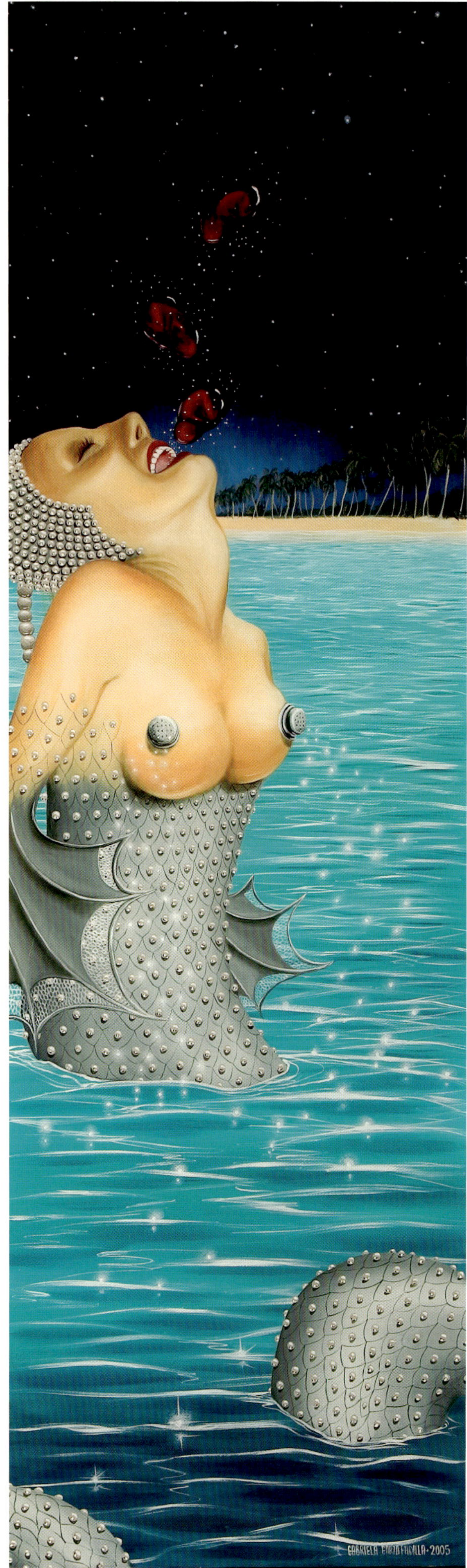

Salt Water · 51 x 41 cm · Oil on canvas

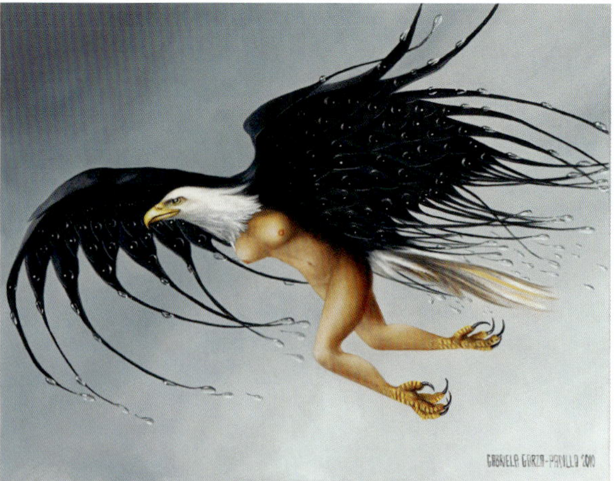

What is Next · 46 x 51 cm · Oil on canvas

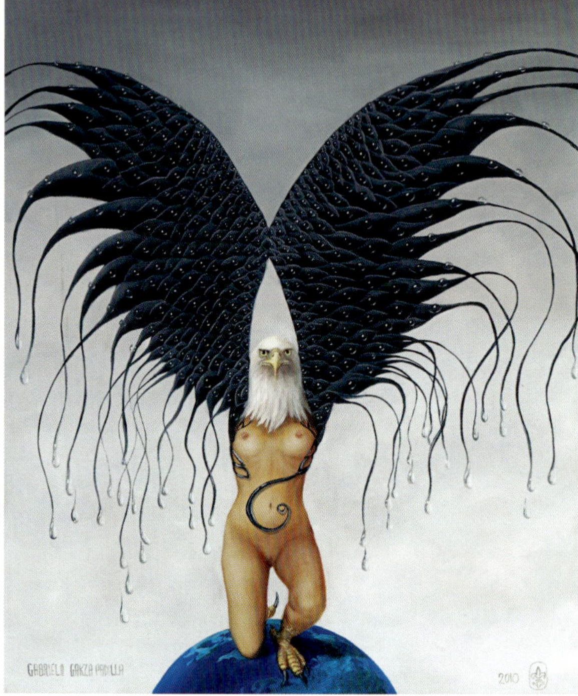

Prayers that are Answered · 51 x 41 cm · Oil on canvas

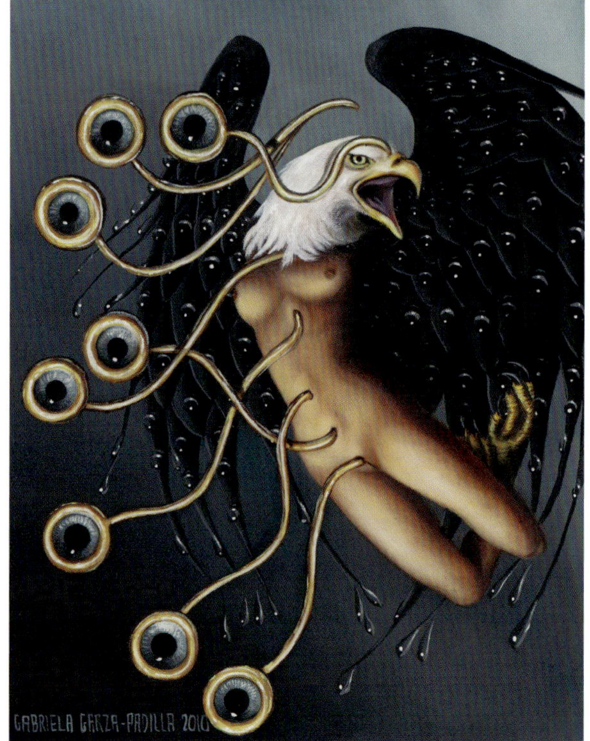

Into the Void · 36 x 28 cm · Oil on canvas

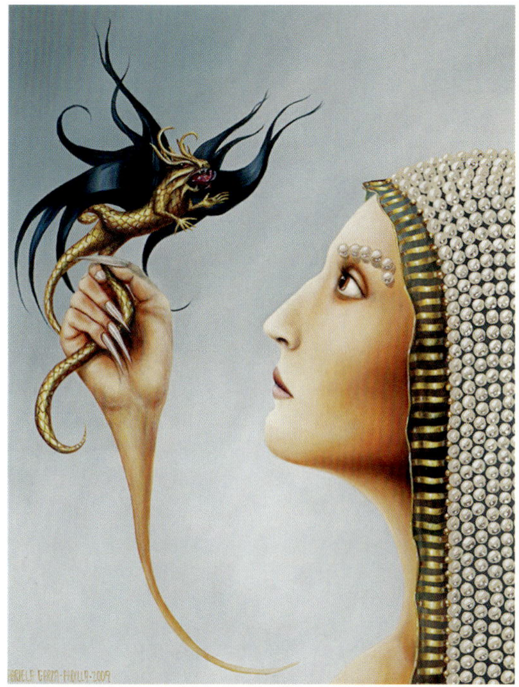
The Trap · 61 x 46 cm · Oil on canvas

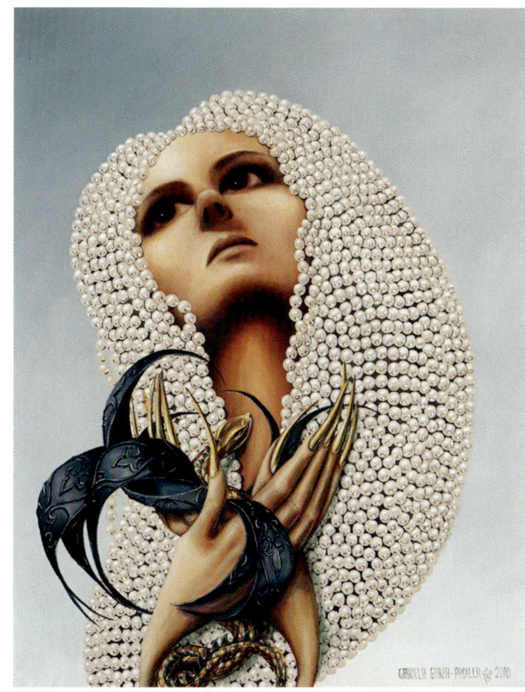
Sublime · 61 x 46 cm · Oil on canvas

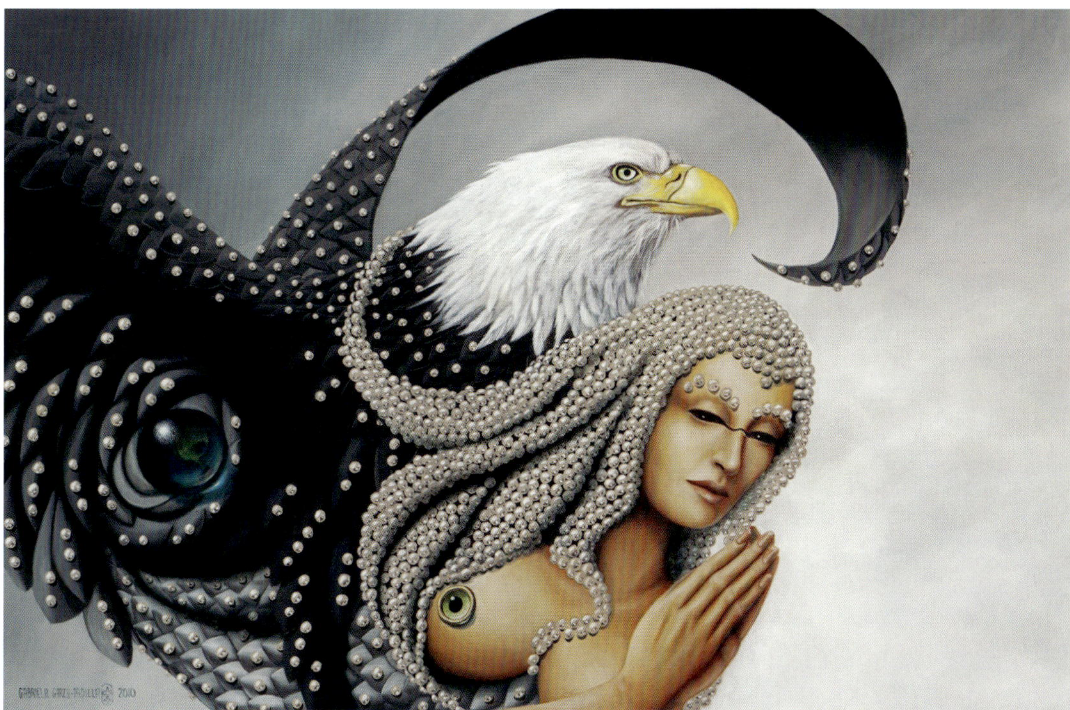
The Unavoidable Flight · 61 x 92 cm · Oil on canvas

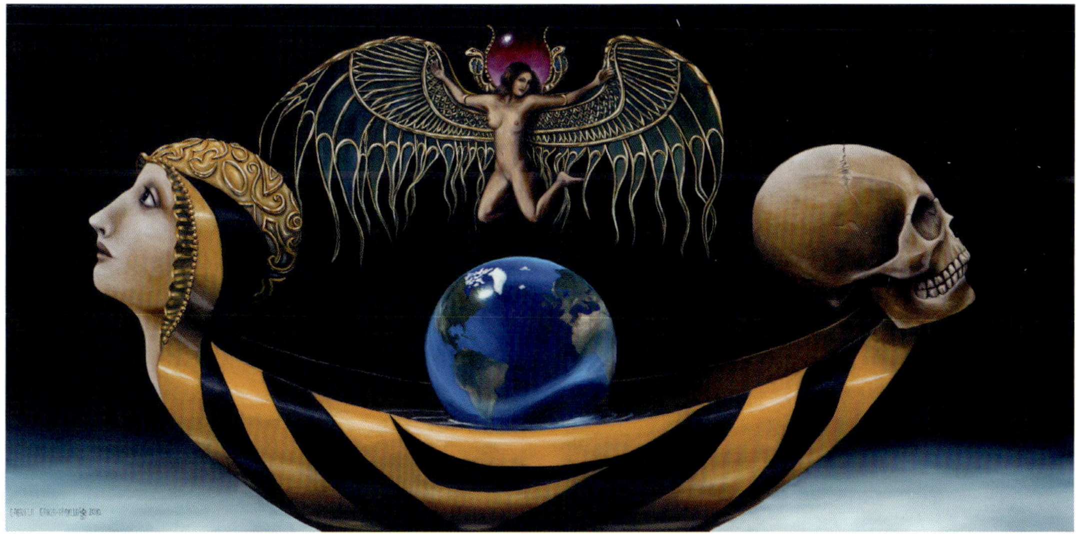
Fundamental Unity of Existence · 55 x 100 cm · Oil on canvas

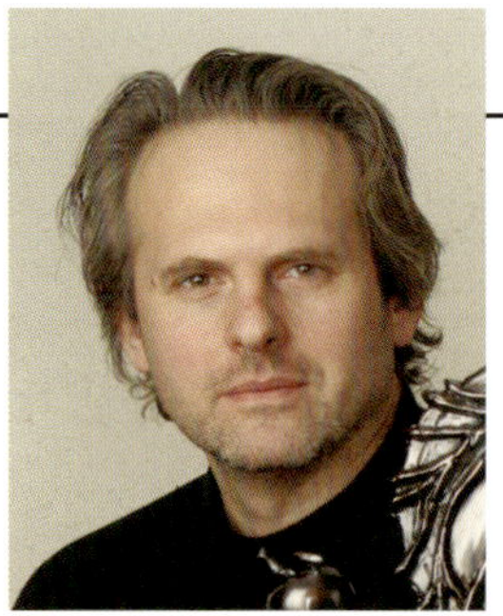

IGOR GRECHANYK

1960 Ukraine

www.grechanyk.com

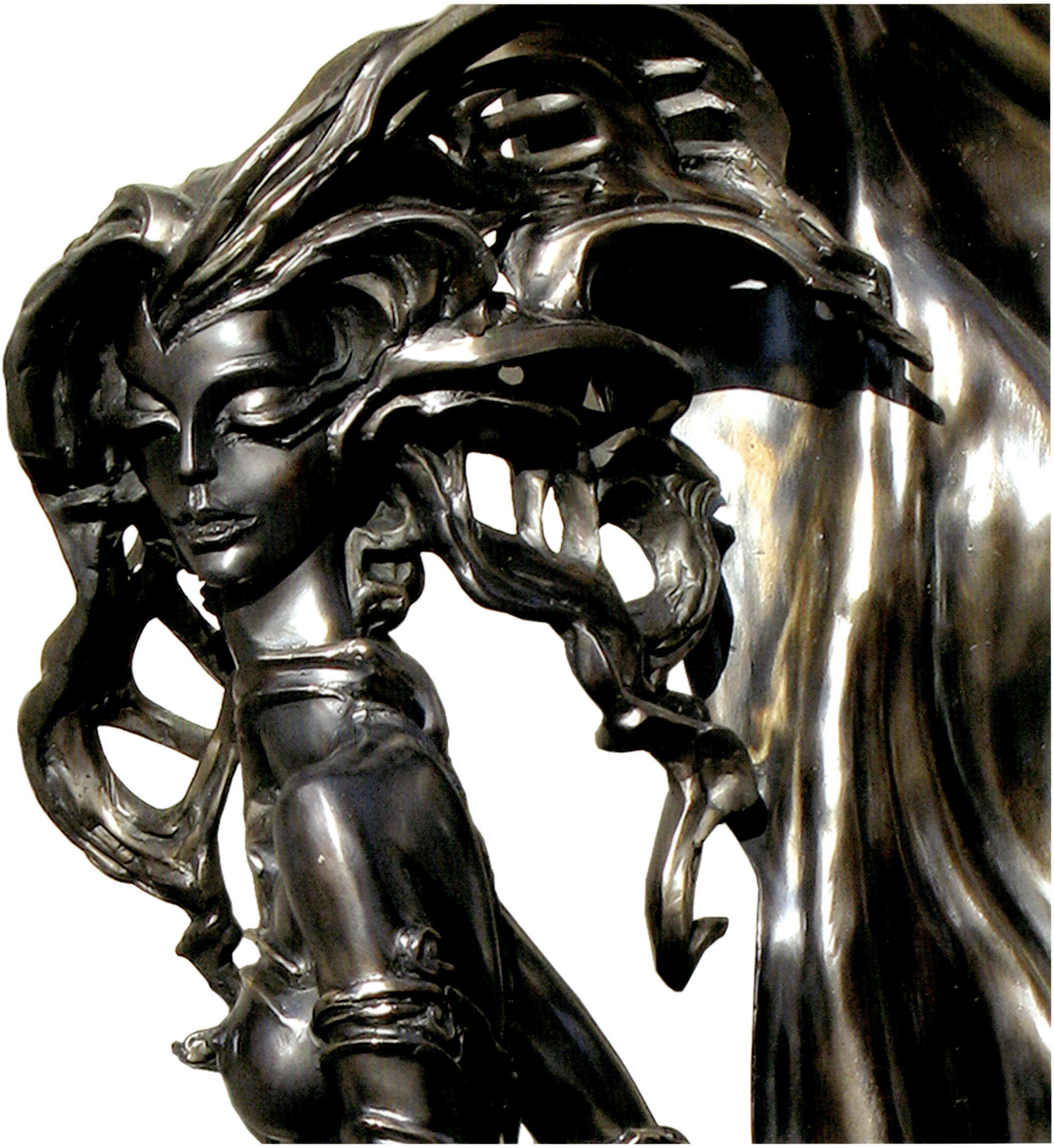

Midnight Window (fragment) · 130 cm H · Bronze

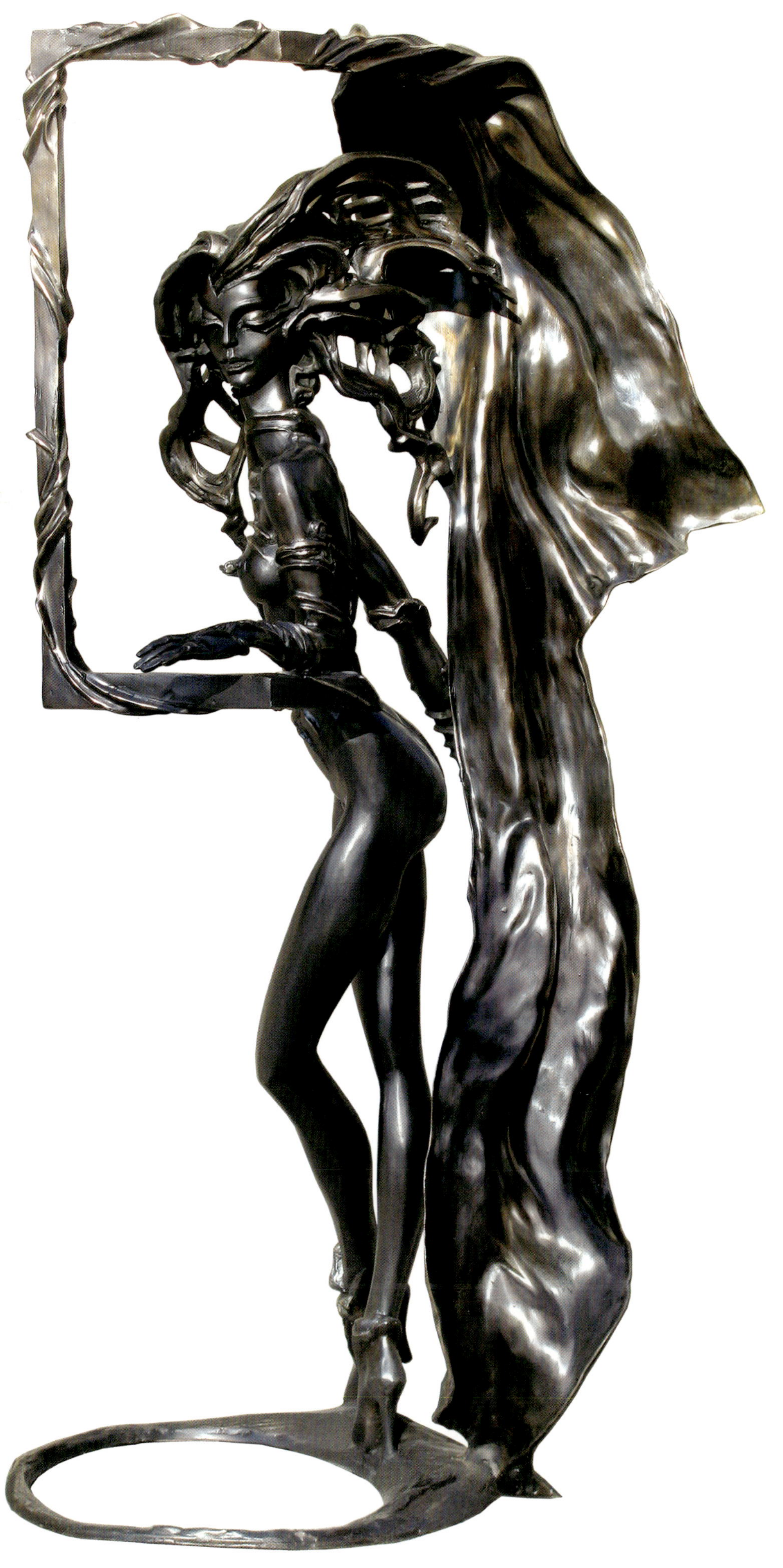

Midnight Window · 130 cm H · Bronze

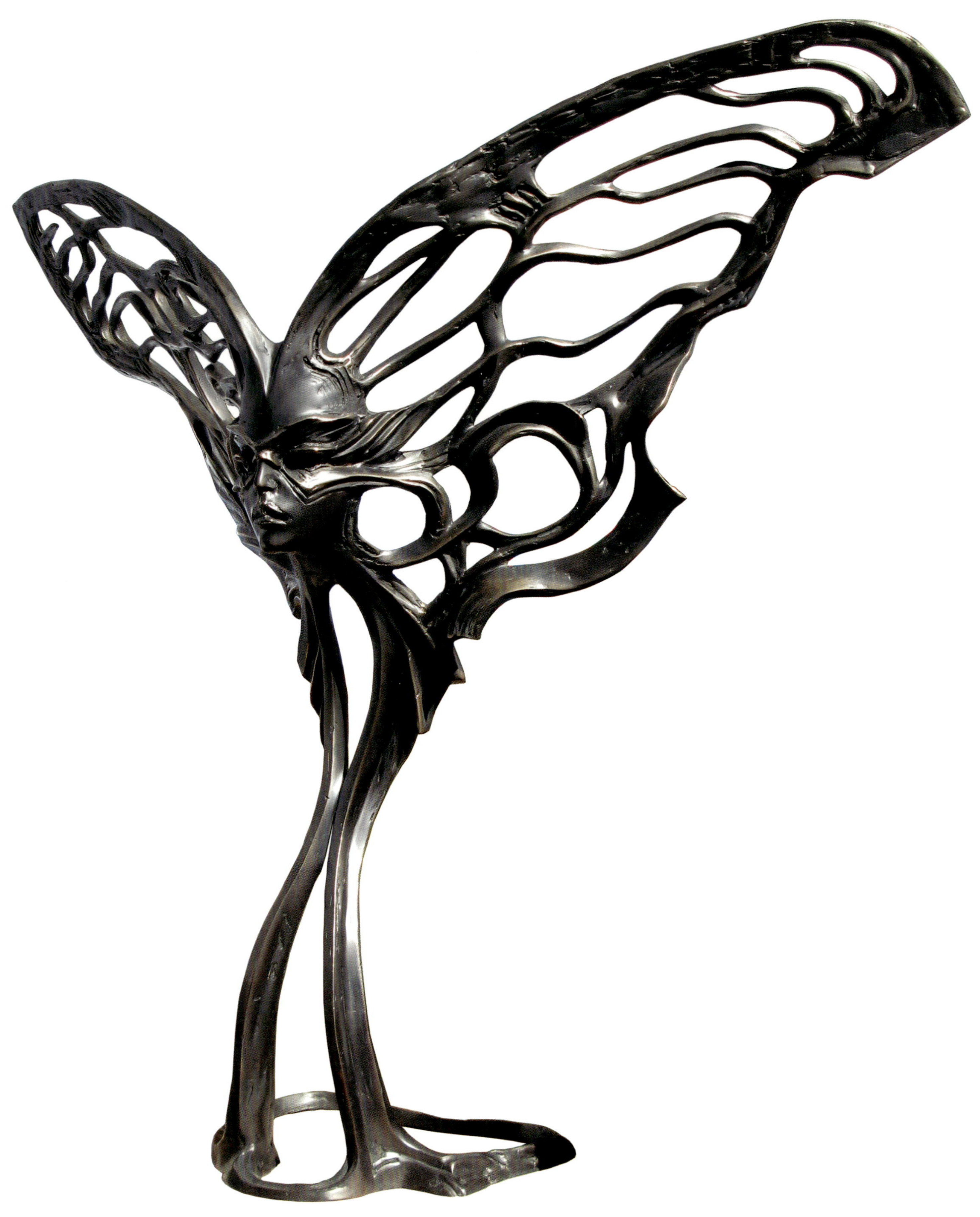

Night Flight · 77 cm H · Bronze

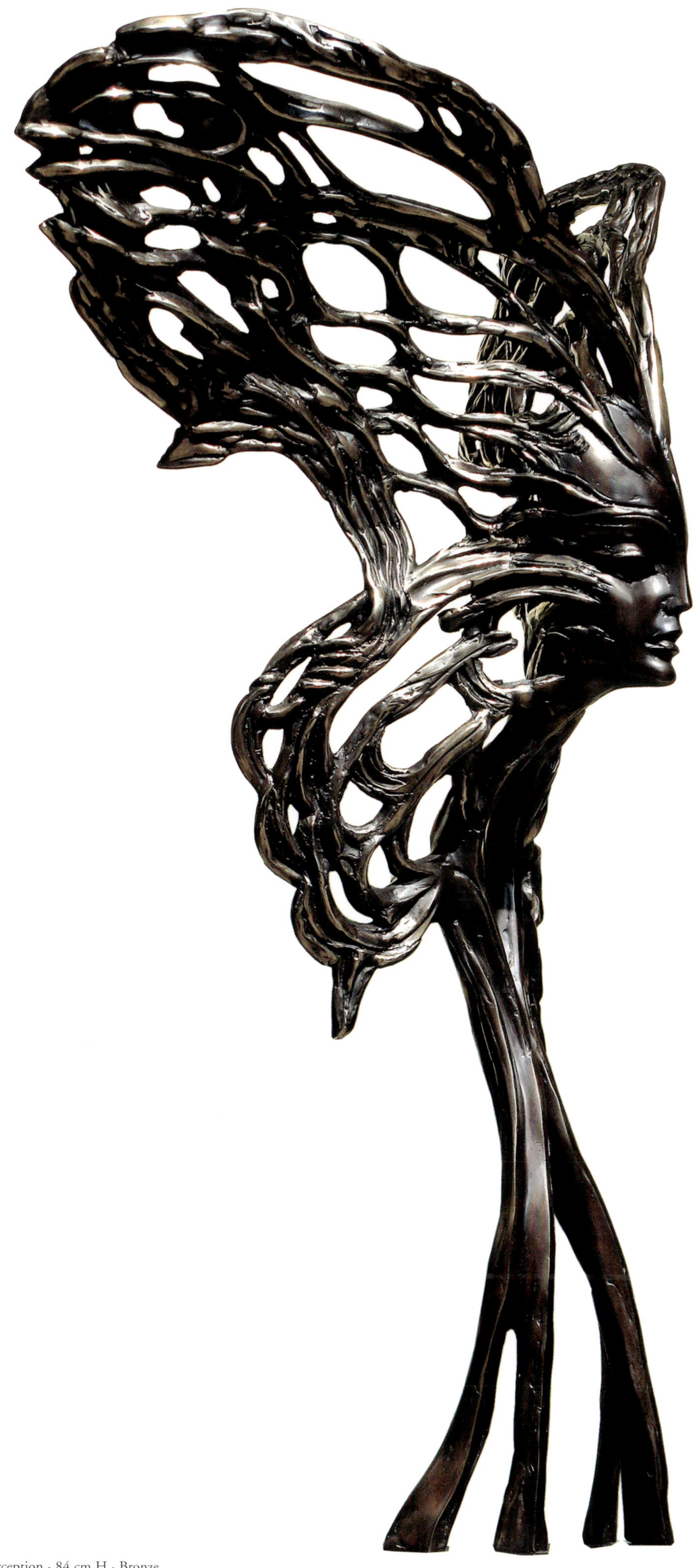

Wings of Perception · 84 cm H · Bronze

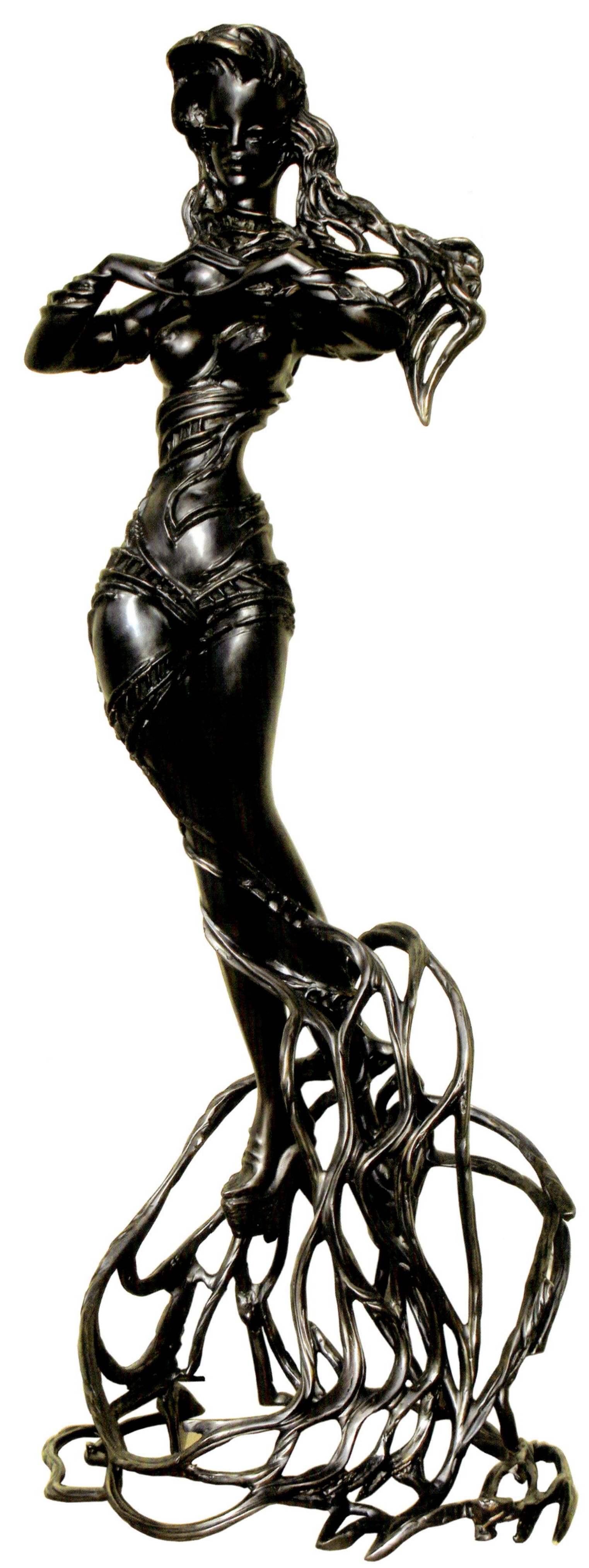

Violetta. Journey of Soul · 100 cm H · Bronze

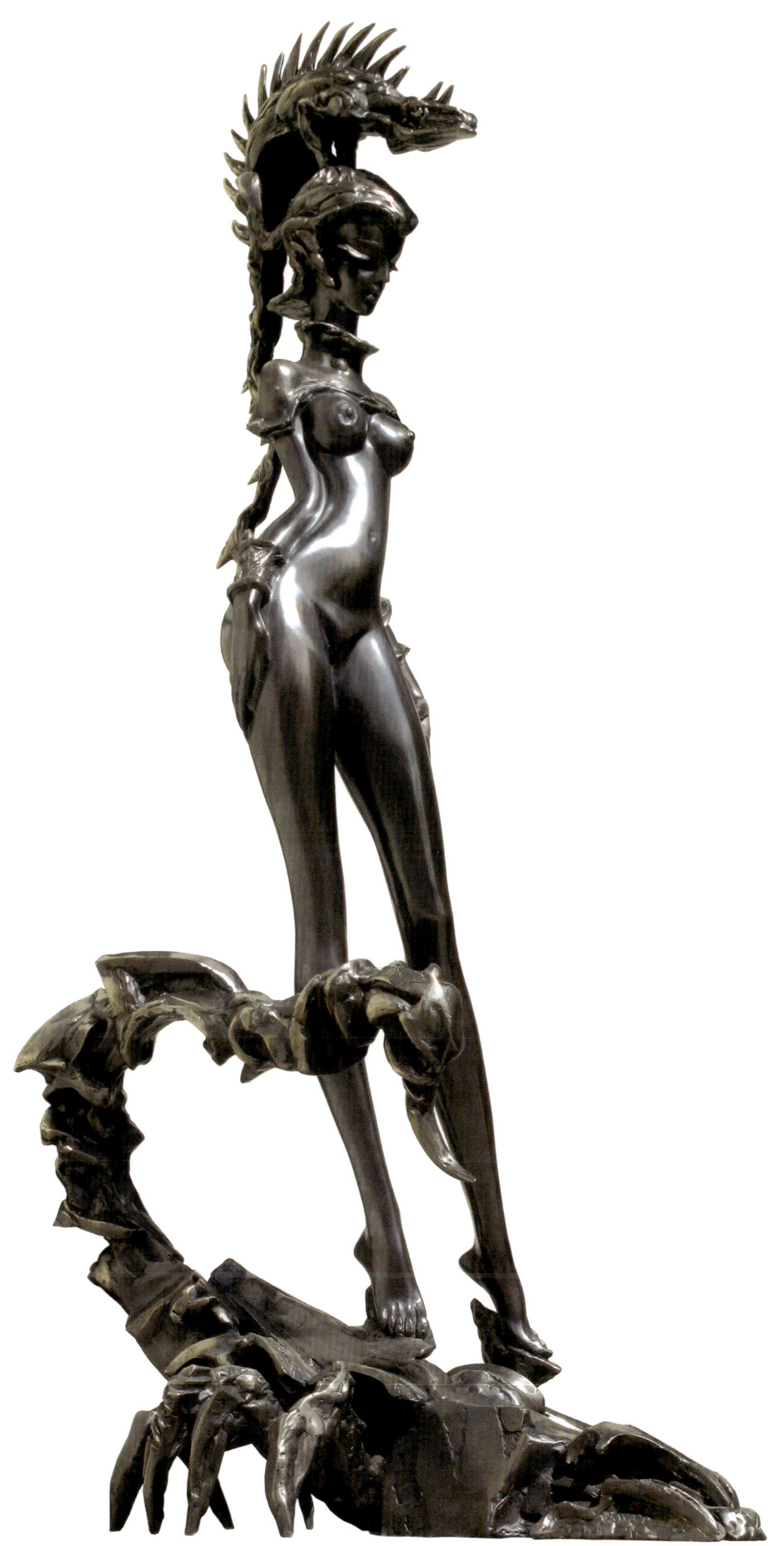

Time of Scorpio · 130 cm H · Bronze

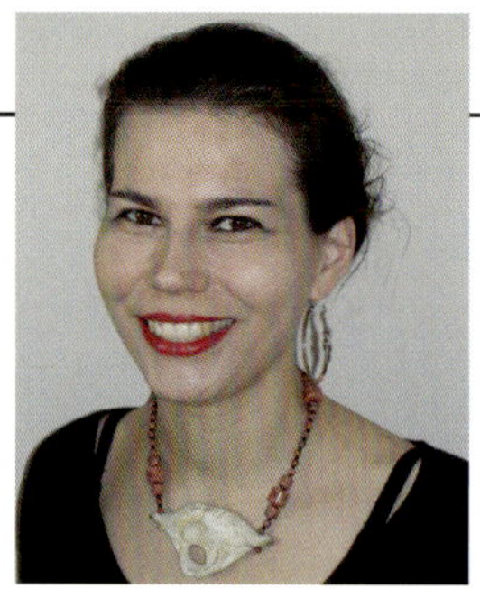

LINDA GROEN

1972 The Netherlands

www.lindagroen.nl

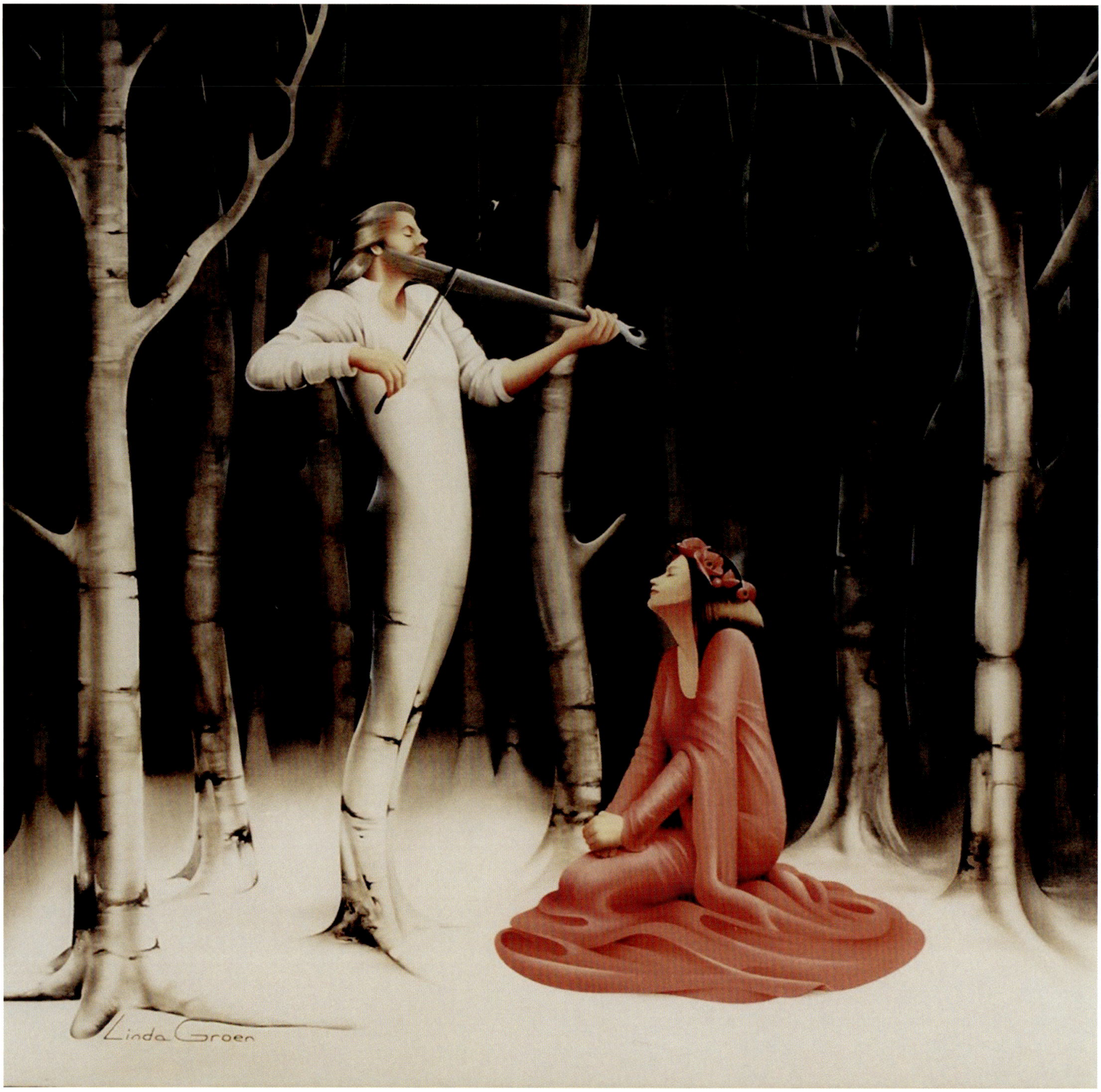

Fiddler in the Wood (a true story) · 41 x 41 cm · Oil on wood

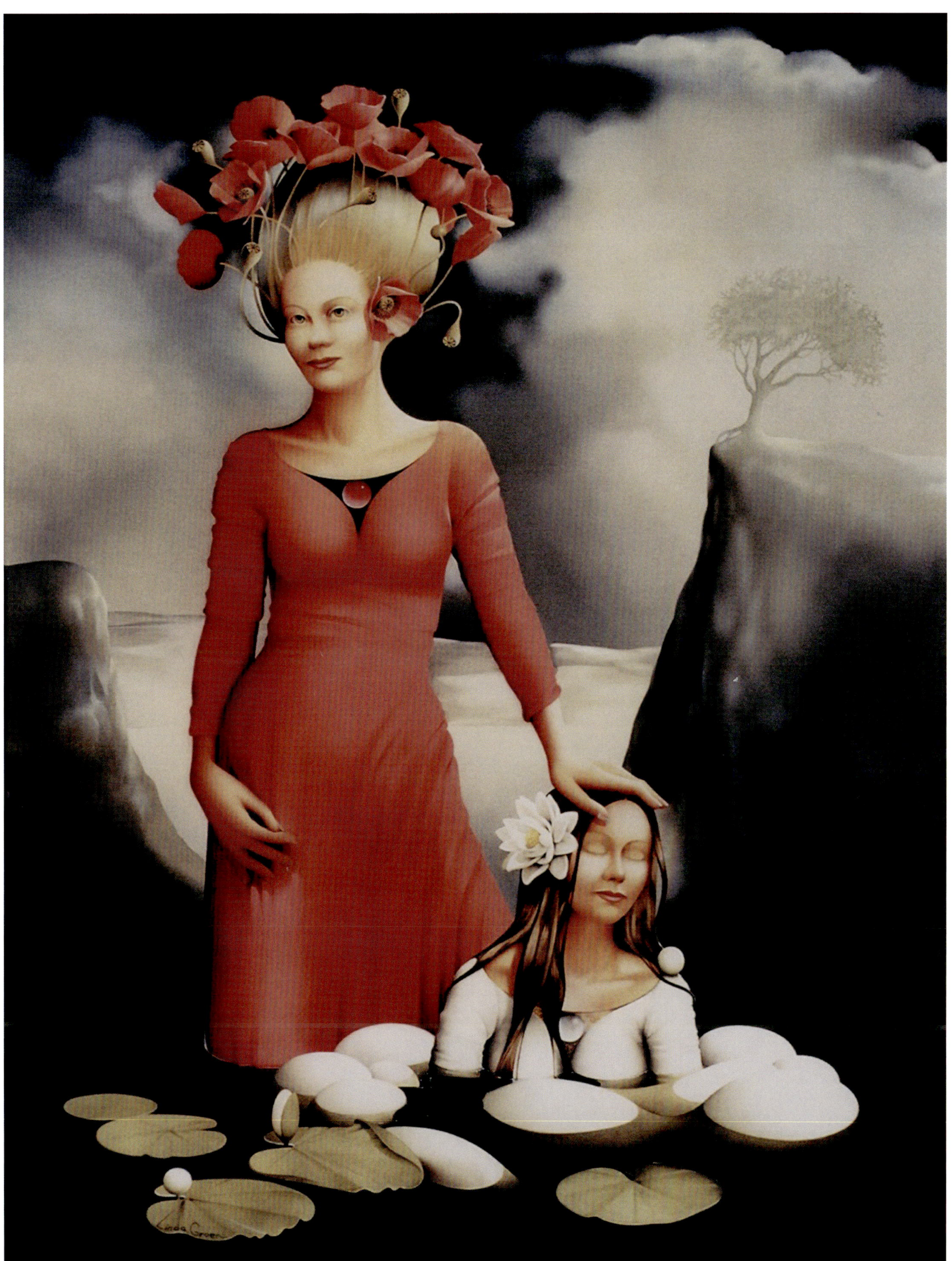

Present represses Past · 80 x 60 cm · Oil on canvas

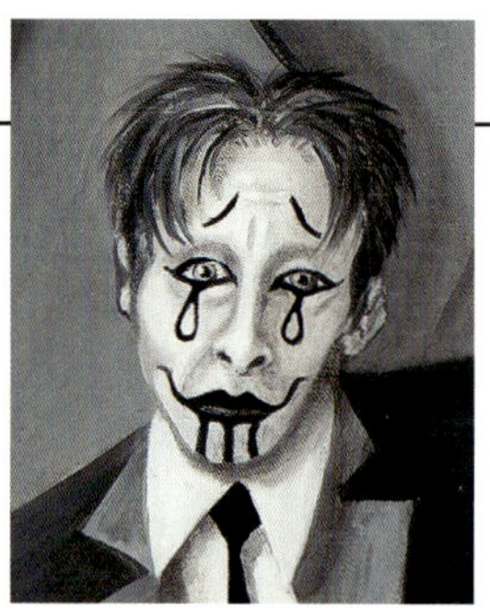

N. G. HAMMER

1964 Sweden

www.nghammer.com

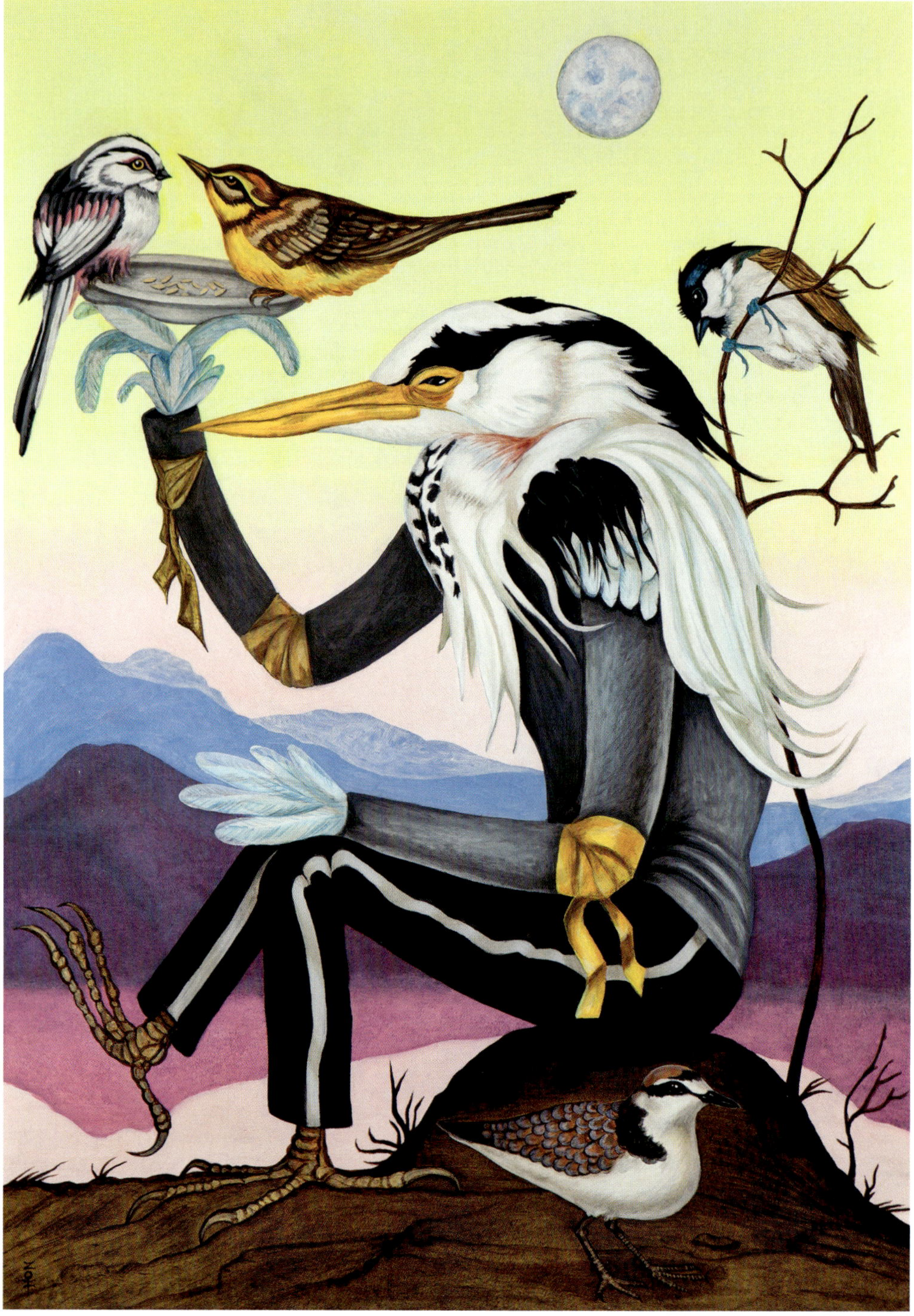

Scare Crow Patience · 100 x 70 cm · Oil on linen

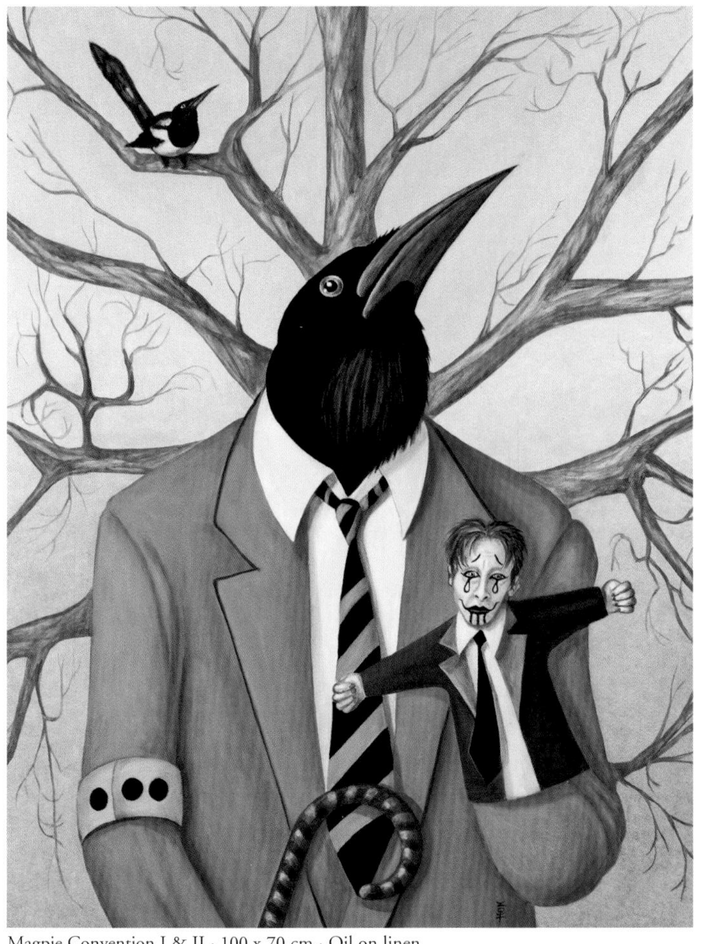

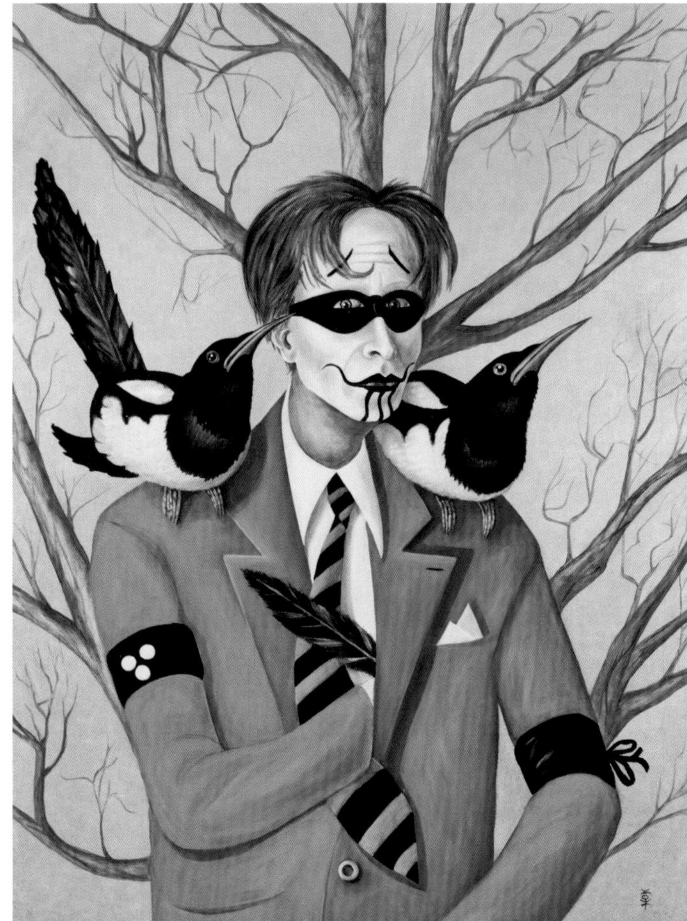

Magpie Convention I & II · 100 x 70 cm · Oil on linen

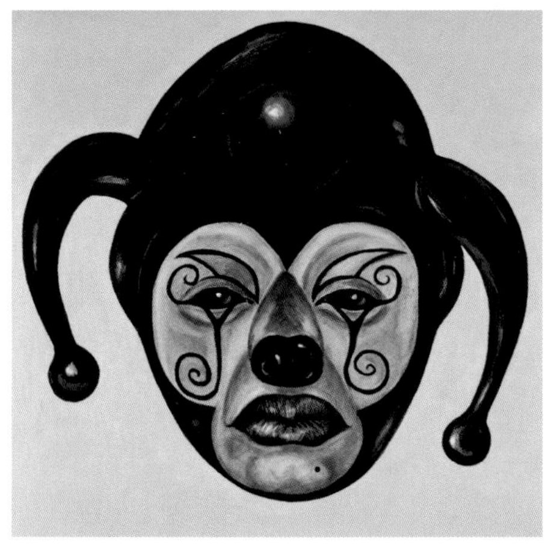

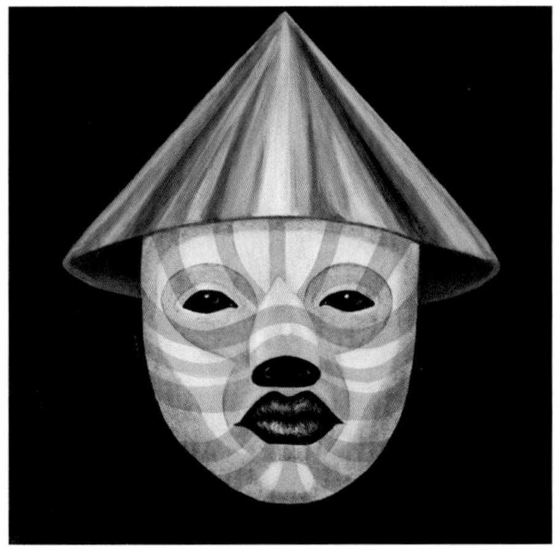

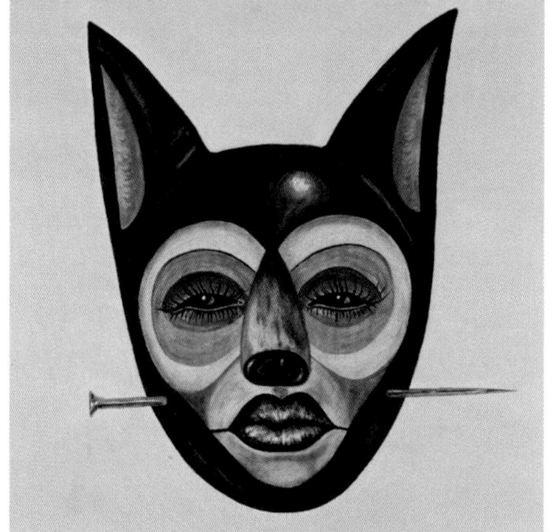

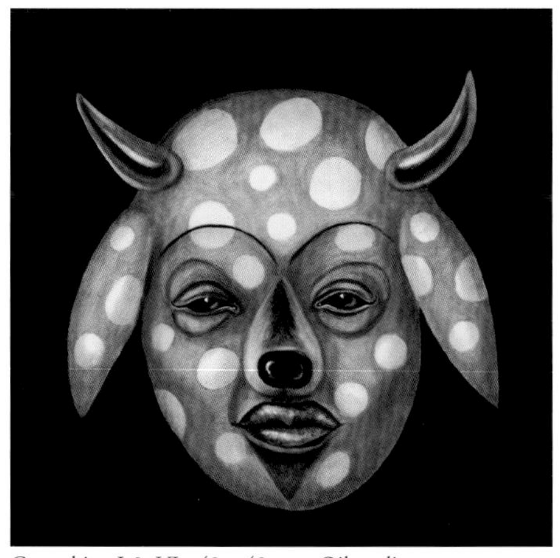

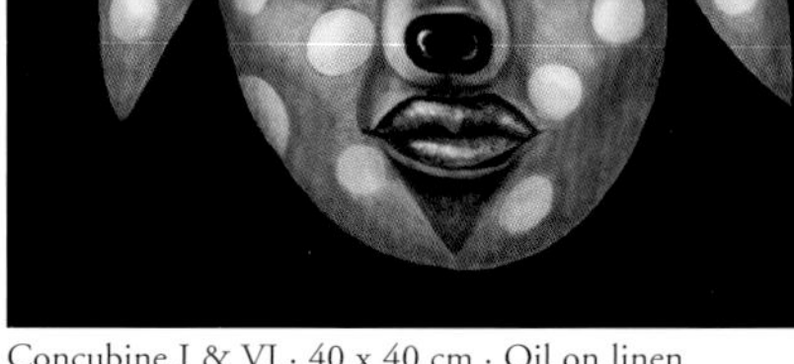

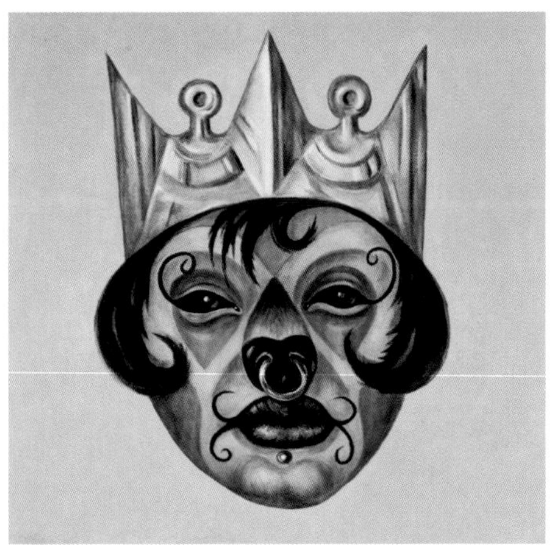

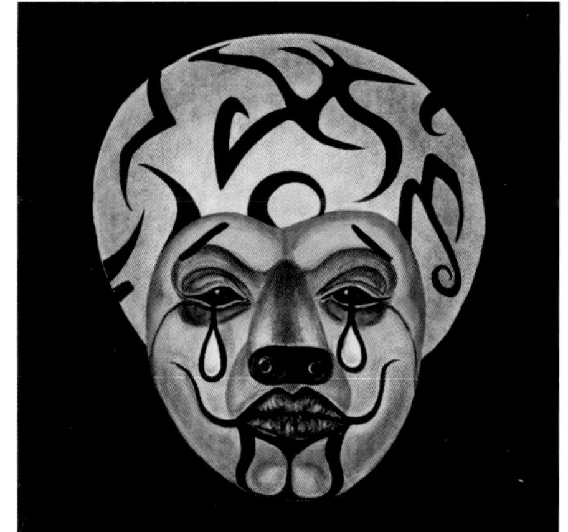

Concubine I & VI · 40 x 40 cm · Oil on linen

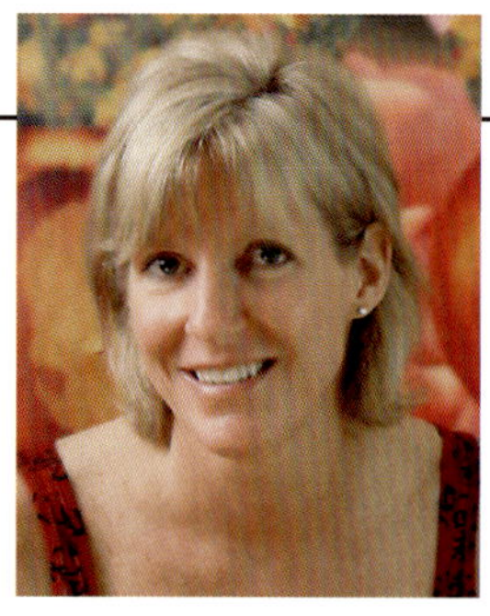

STEPHANIE HENDERSON

1959 USA

www.hendersonart.com

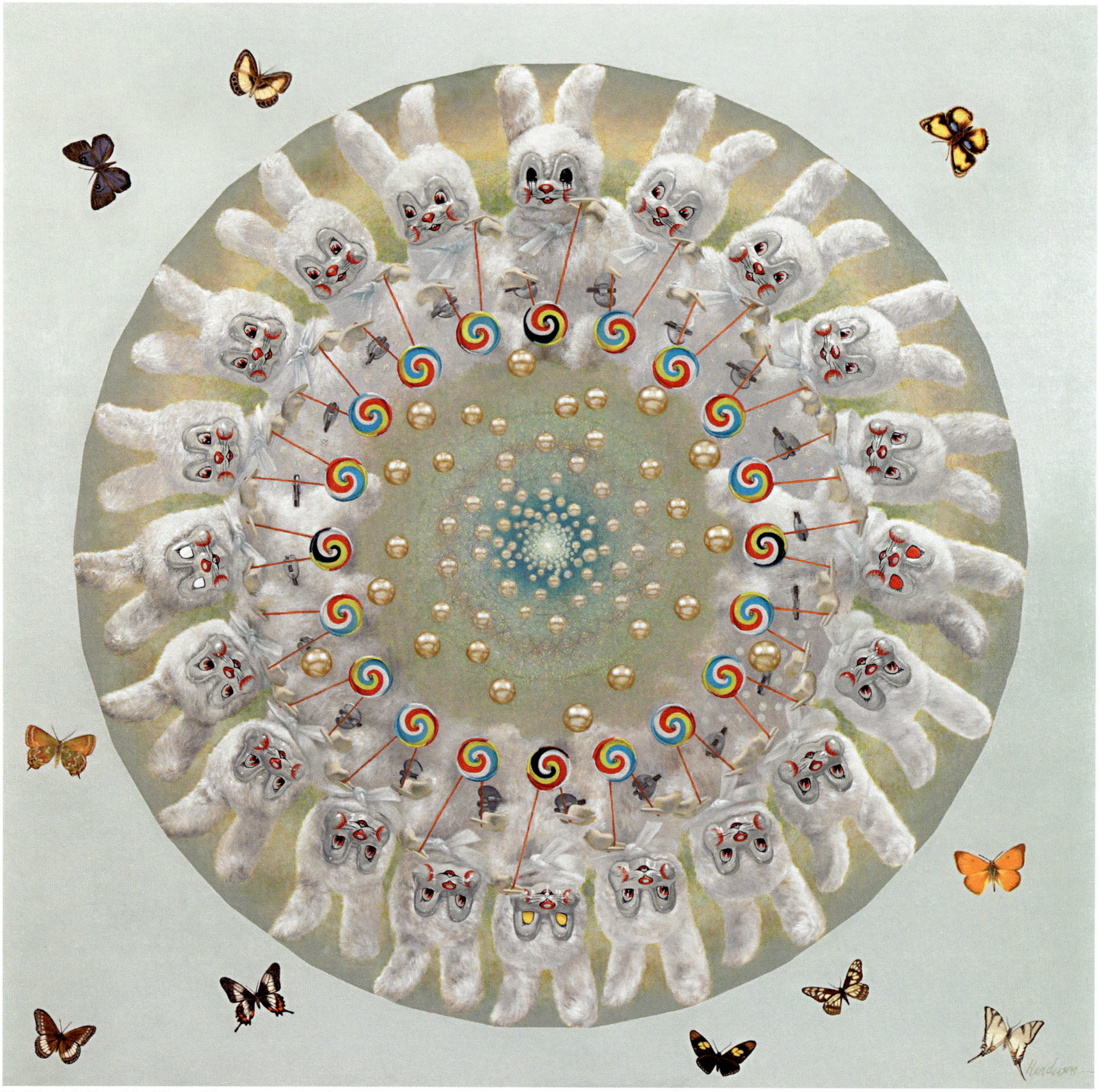

The Time Machine · 86 x 86 cm · Oil on canvas on board

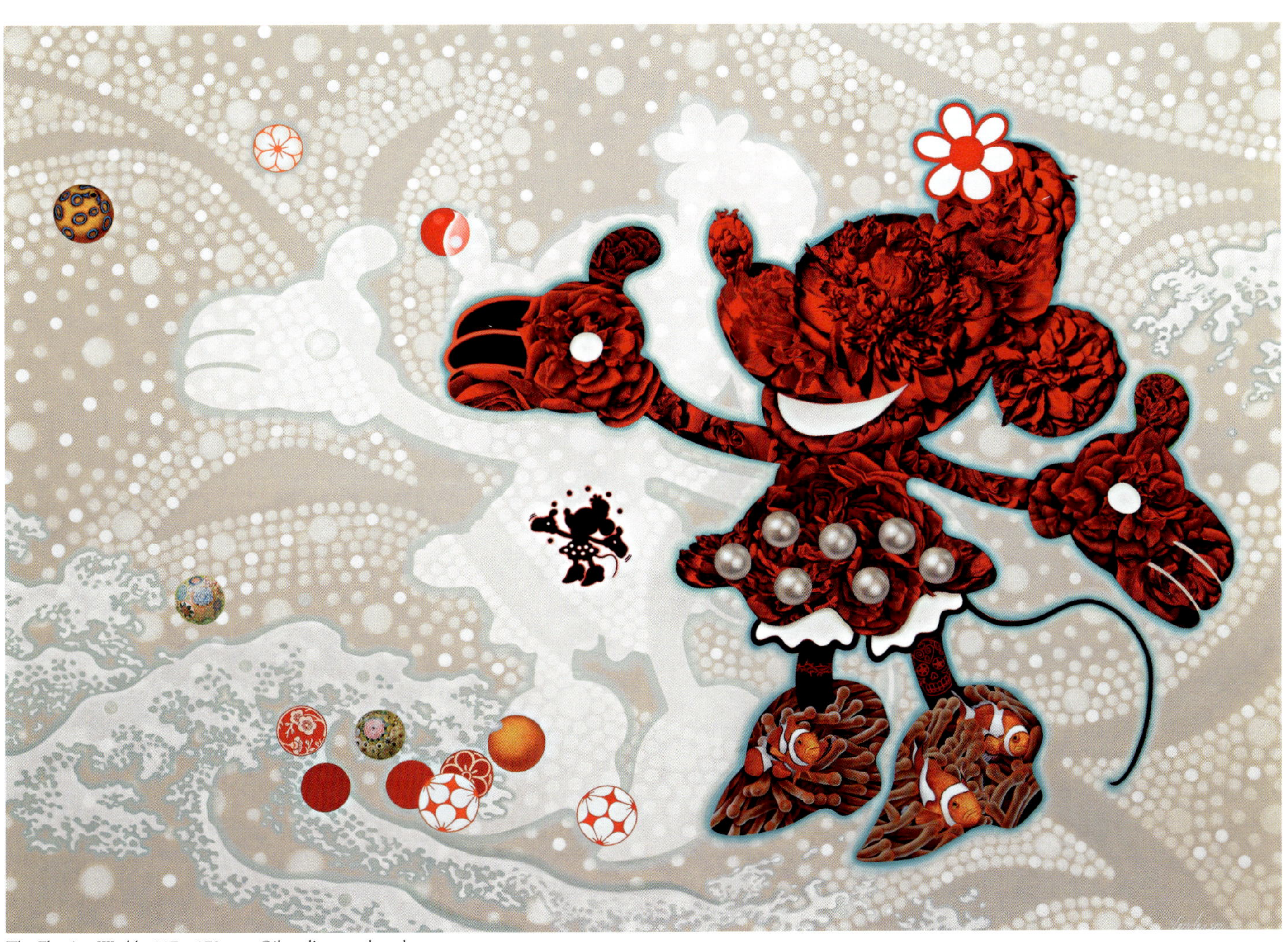

The Floating World · 117 x 170 cm · Oil on linen on board

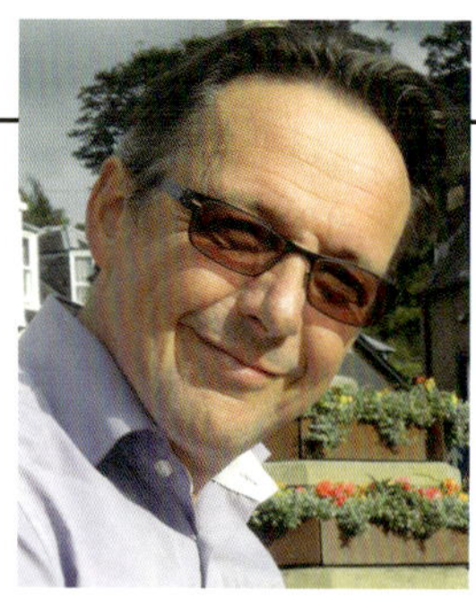

MICHAEL HIEP

1959 The Netherlands

www.michaelhiep.nl

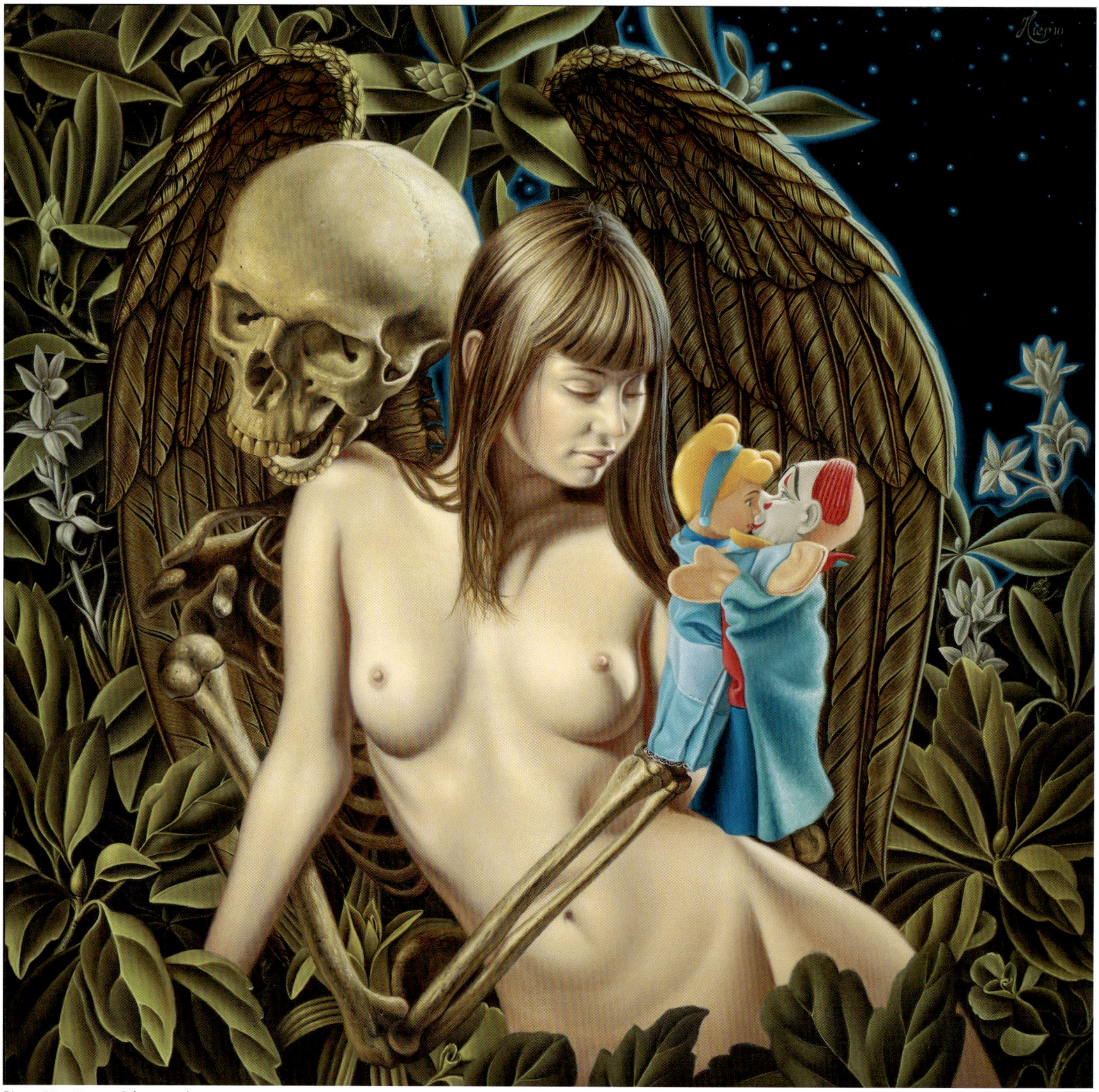

Pieta · 30 x 30 cm · Oil on panel

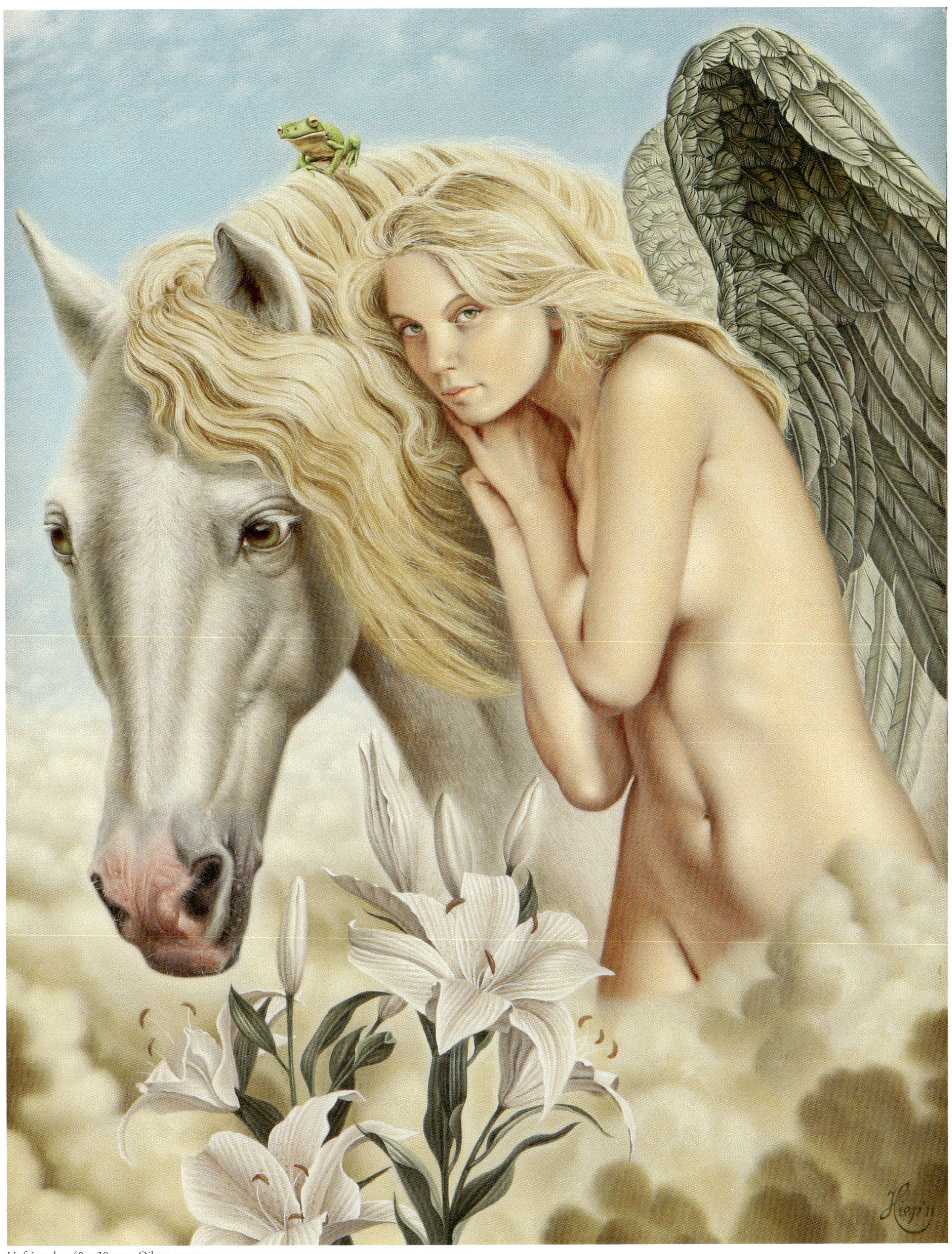

Unfairytale · 40 x 30 cm · Oil on canvas

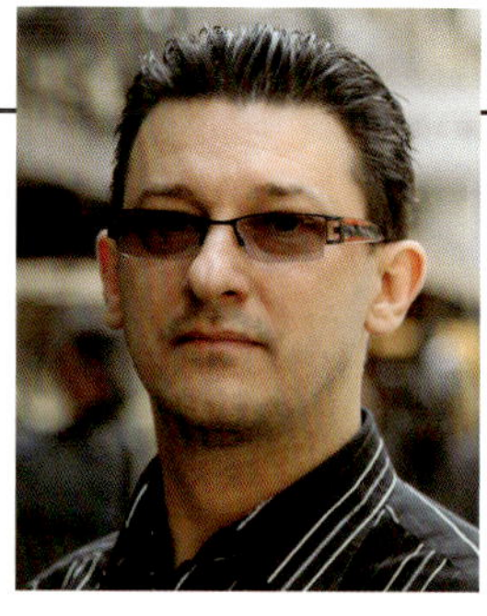

KRZYSZTOF IZDEBSKI-CRUZ

1966 Poland

www.izdebski.art.pl

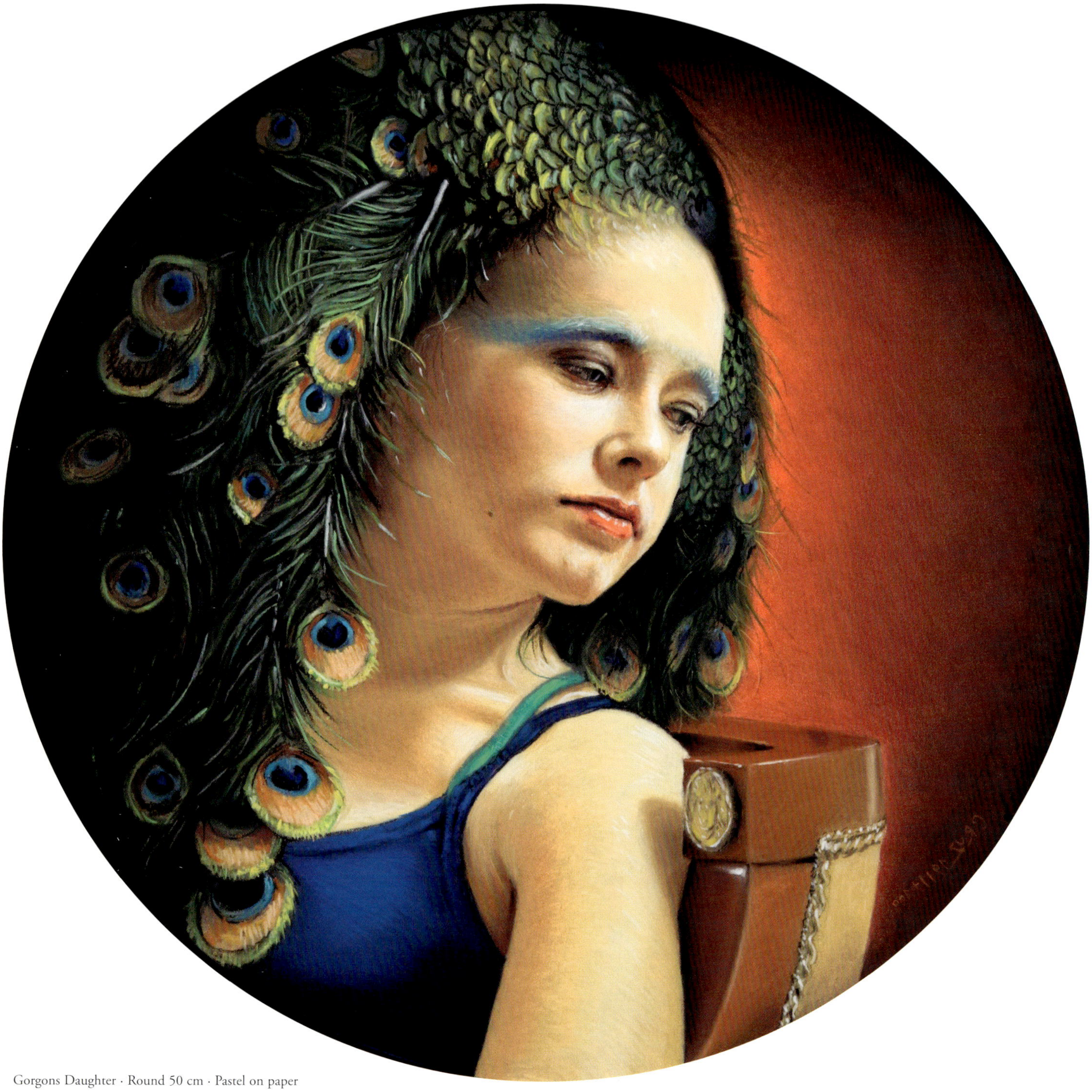

Gorgons Daughter · Round 50 cm · Pastel on paper

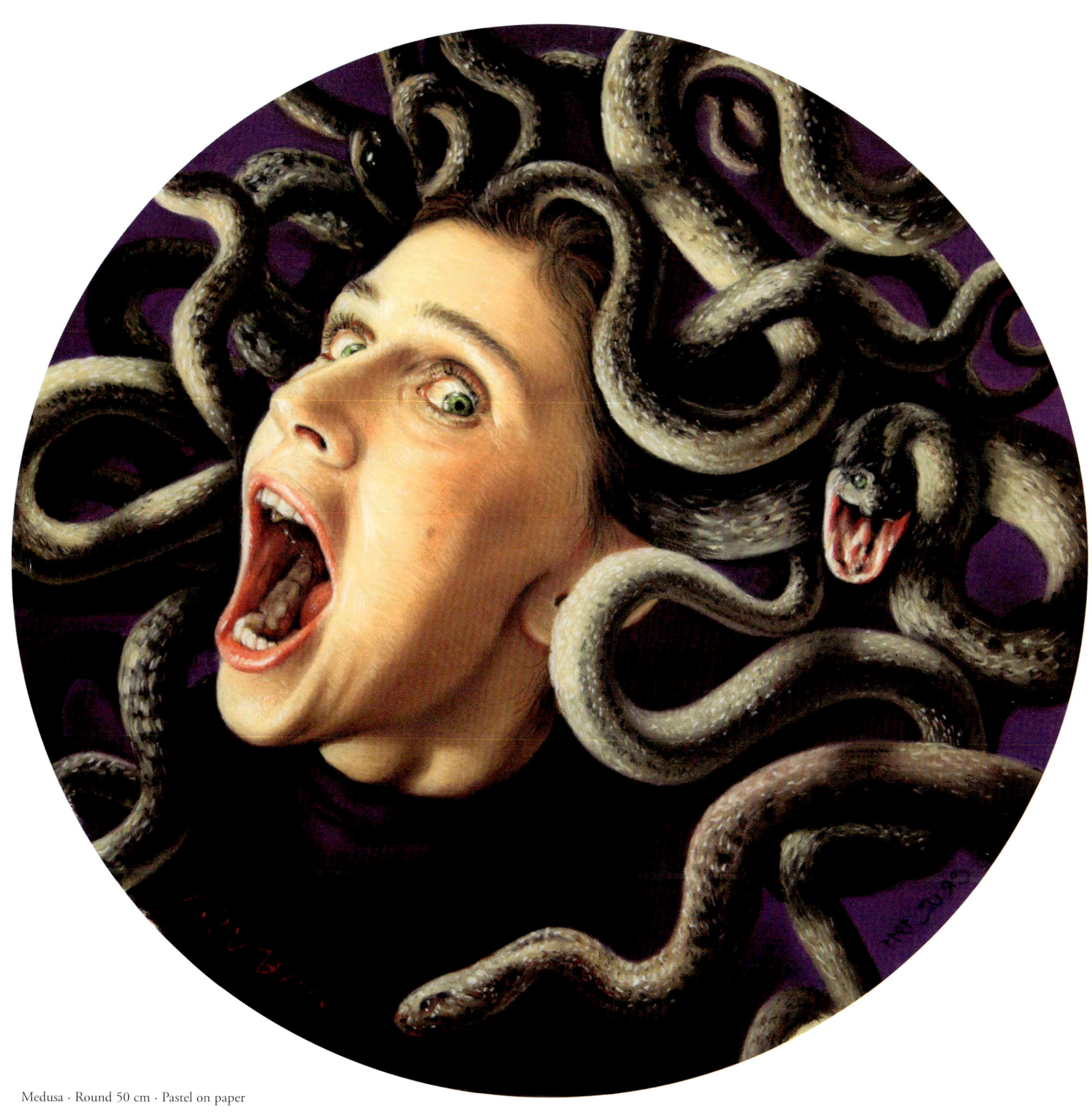

Medusa · Round 50 cm · Pastel on paper

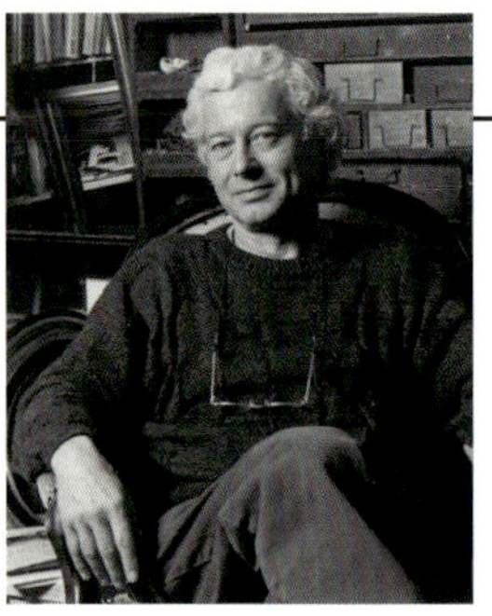

LUKÁŠ KÁNDL

1944 Czech Republic

www.kandl.net

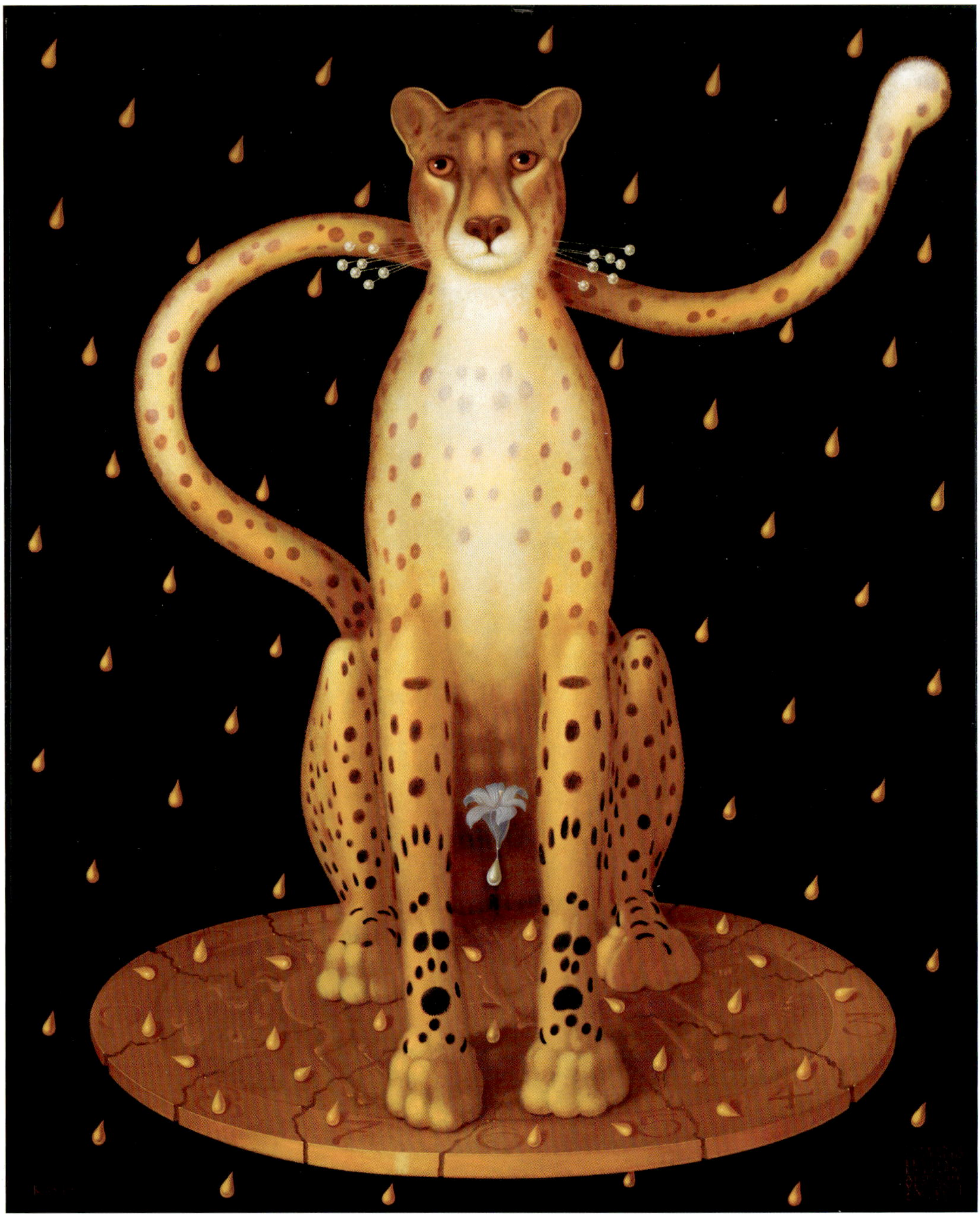

Il Pleut · 162 x 130 cm · Oil on canvas

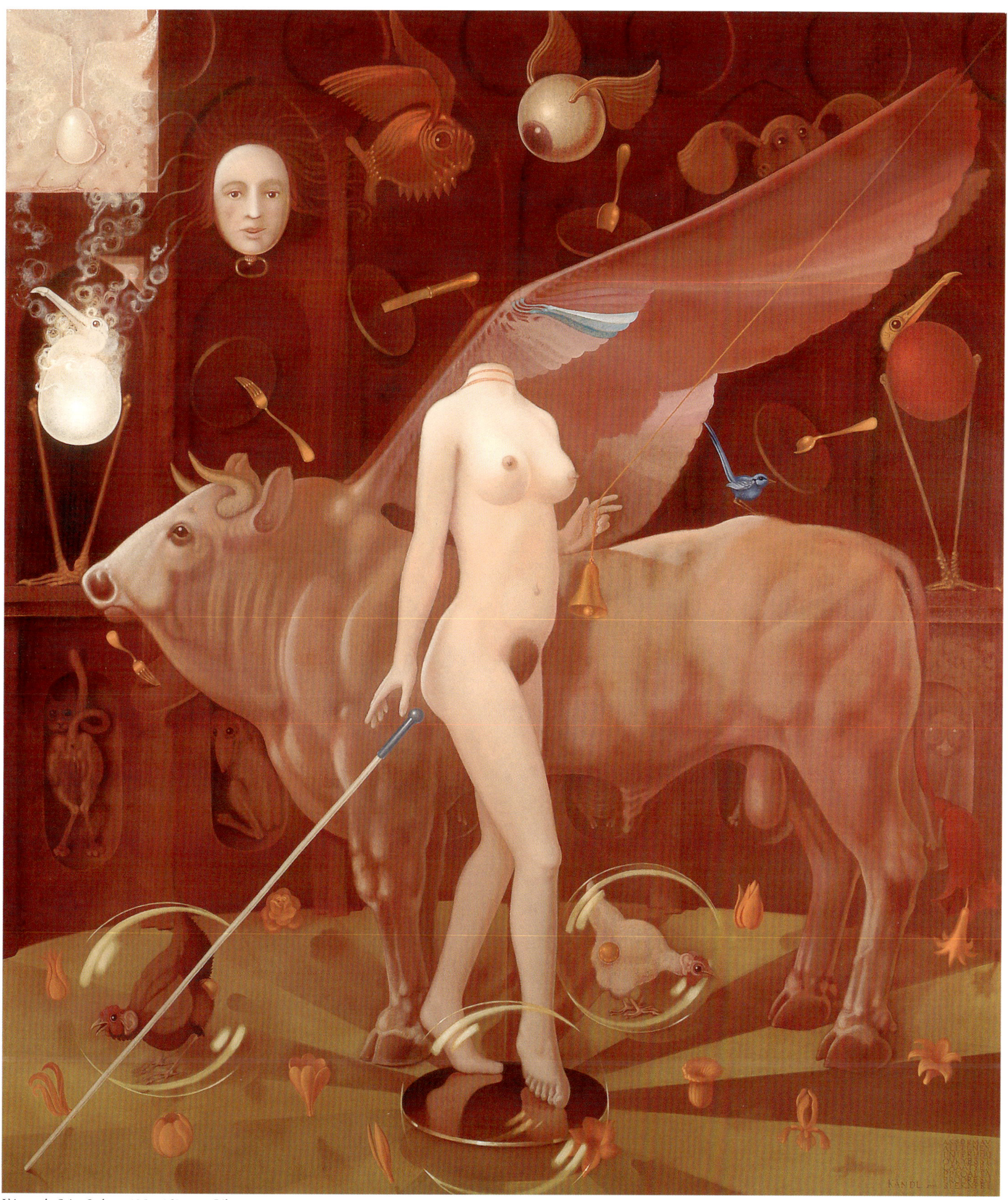

L'Ange de Saint Lukas · 195 x 162 cm · Oil on canvas

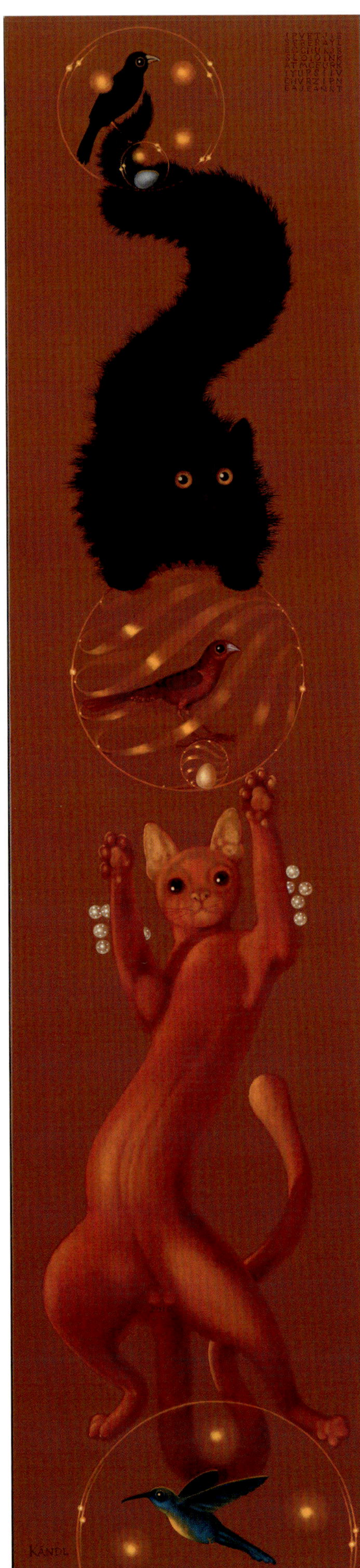

Les Chats Sourient I · 146 x 33 cm · Oil on canvas

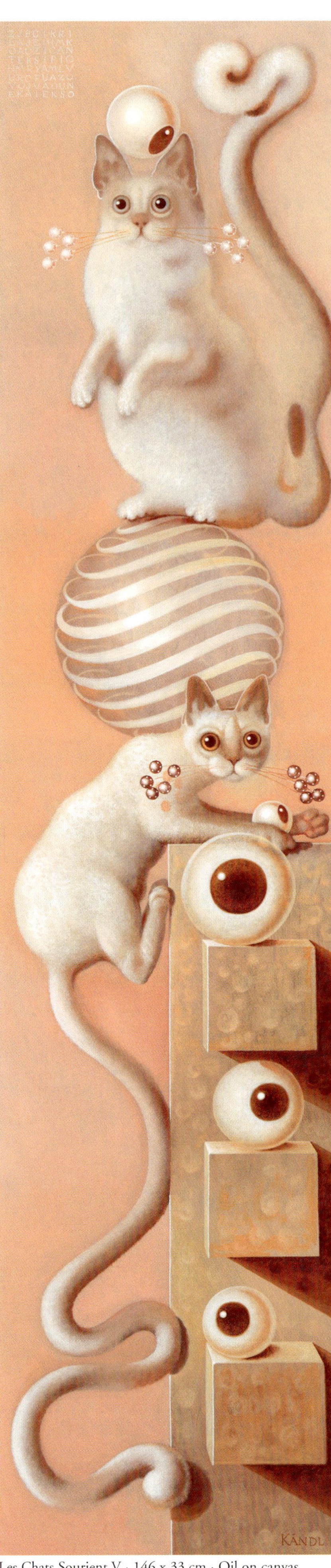

Les Chats Sourient V · 146 x 33 cm · Oil on canvas

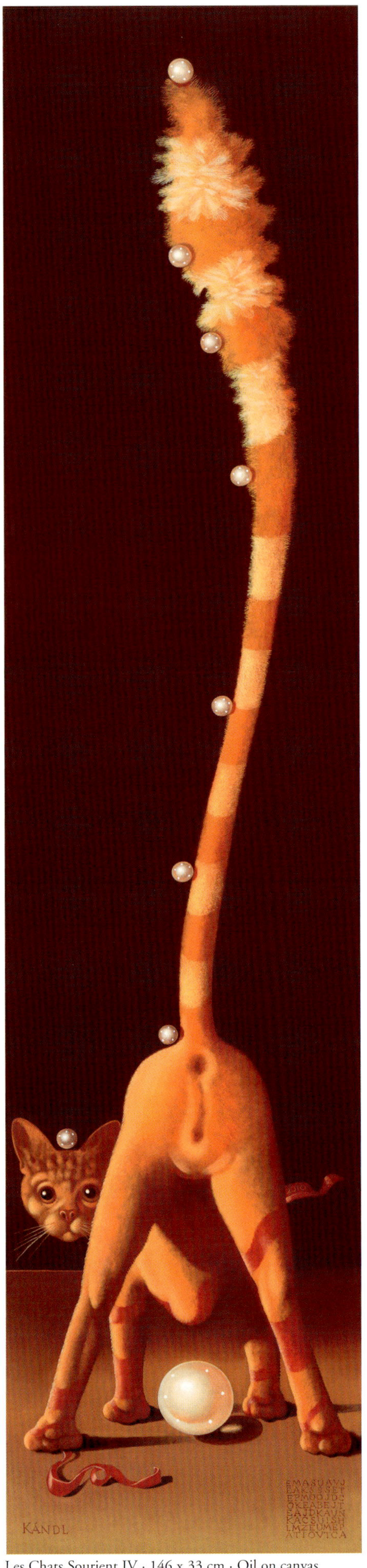

Les Chats Sourient IV · 146 x 33 cm · Oil on canvas

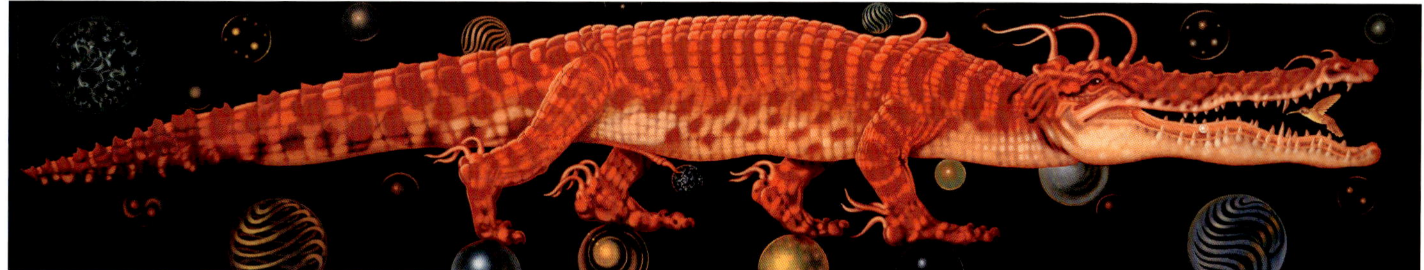
A la recherche de la Perle Perdue · 60 x 300 cm · Oil on canvas

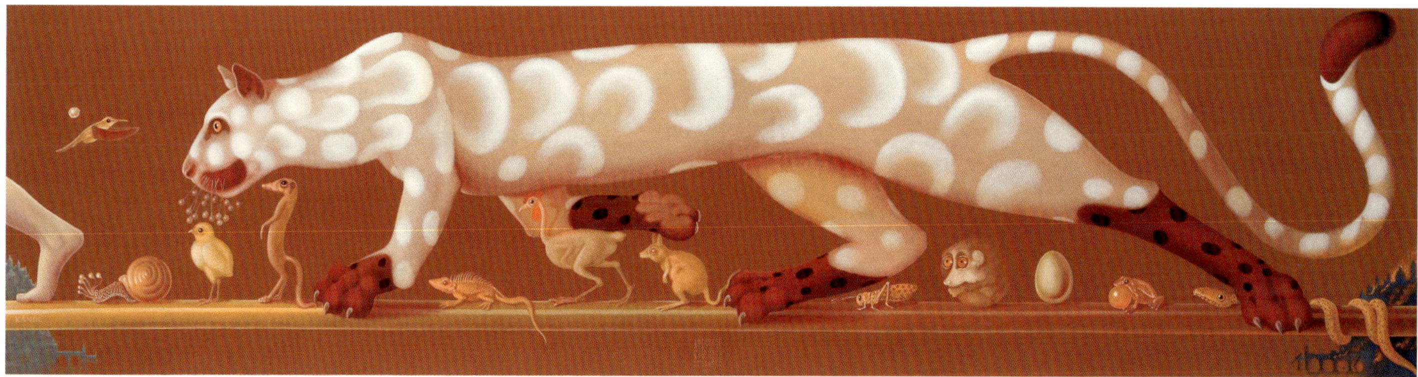
Passerelle Initiatique · 65 x 243 cm · Oil on canvas

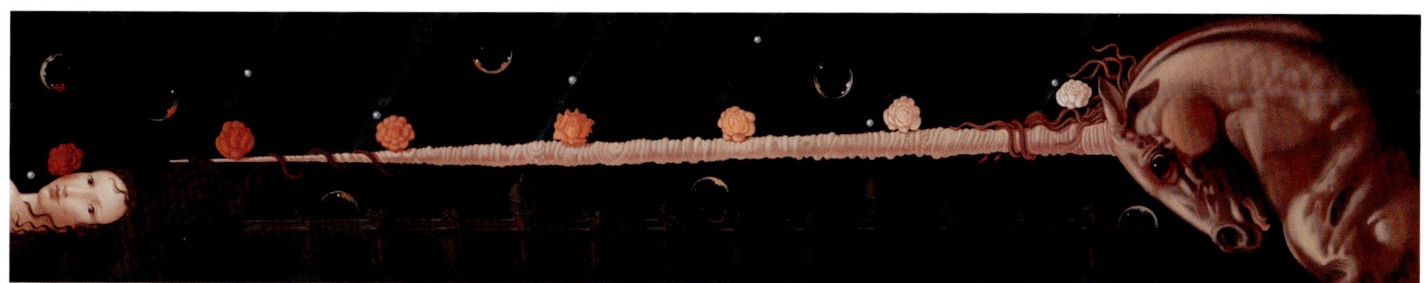
Rencontre Subliminale · 60 x 300 cm · Oil on canvas

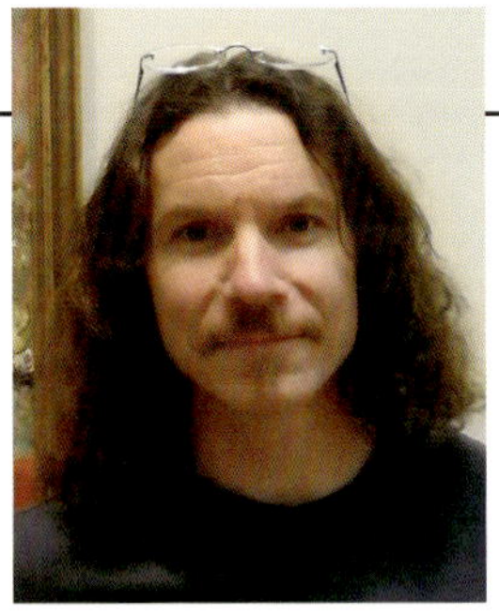

STEVEN KENNY

1962 USA

www.stevenkenny.com

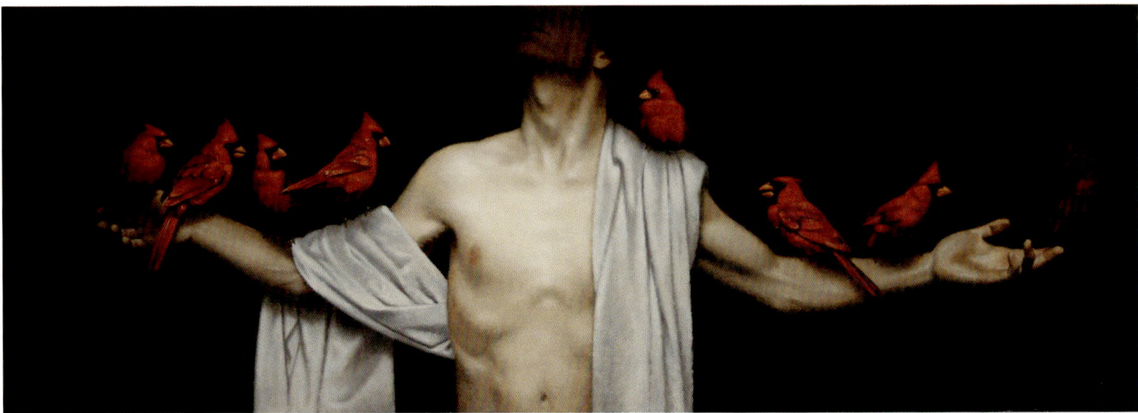

The Crux II · 56 x 152,5 cm · Oil on linen

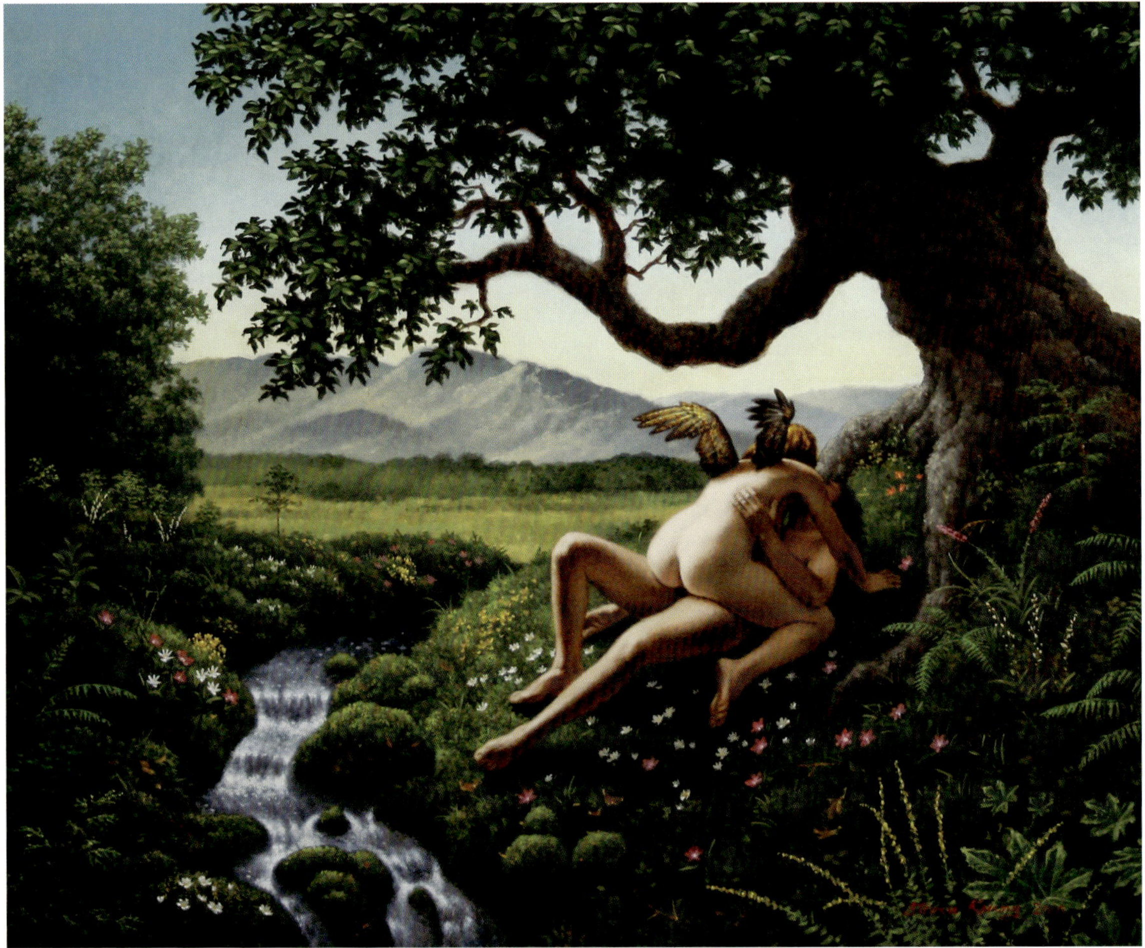

The Return to Eden · 51 x 63,5 cm · Oil on panel

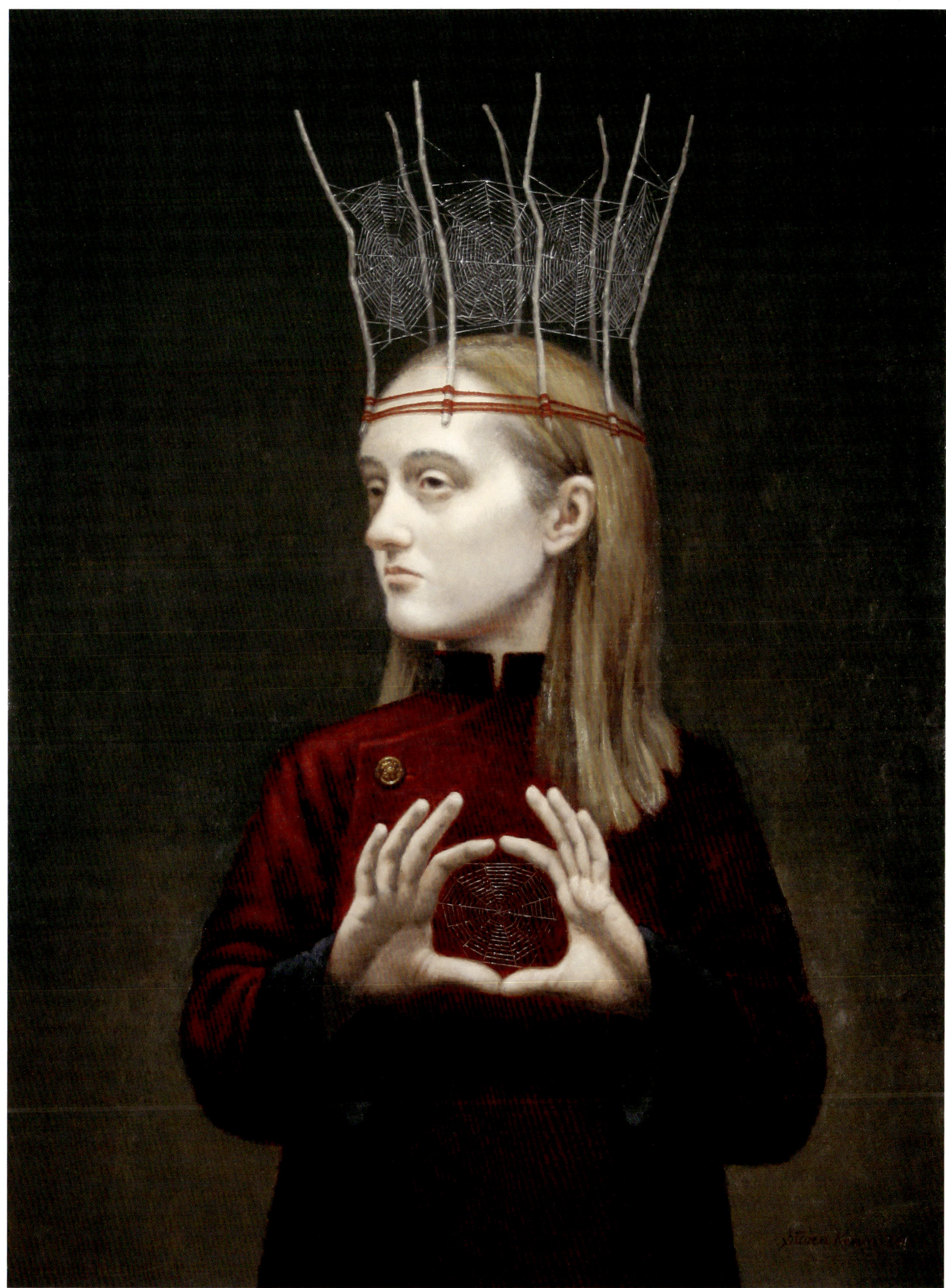

The Web · 76 x 56 cm · Oil on linen

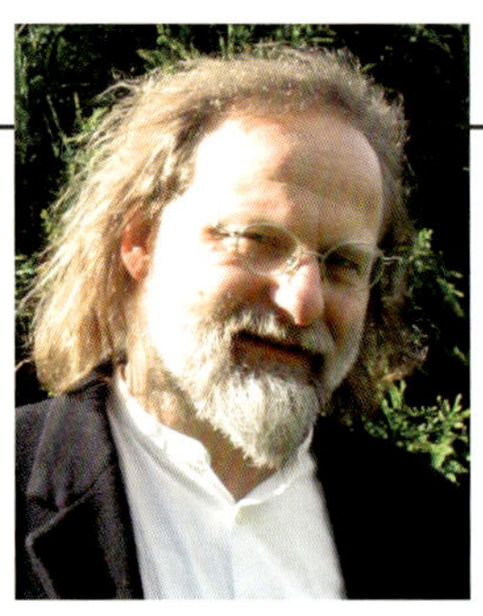

MARCIN KOLPANOWICZ

1963 Poland

www.marcin.kolpanowicz.art.pl

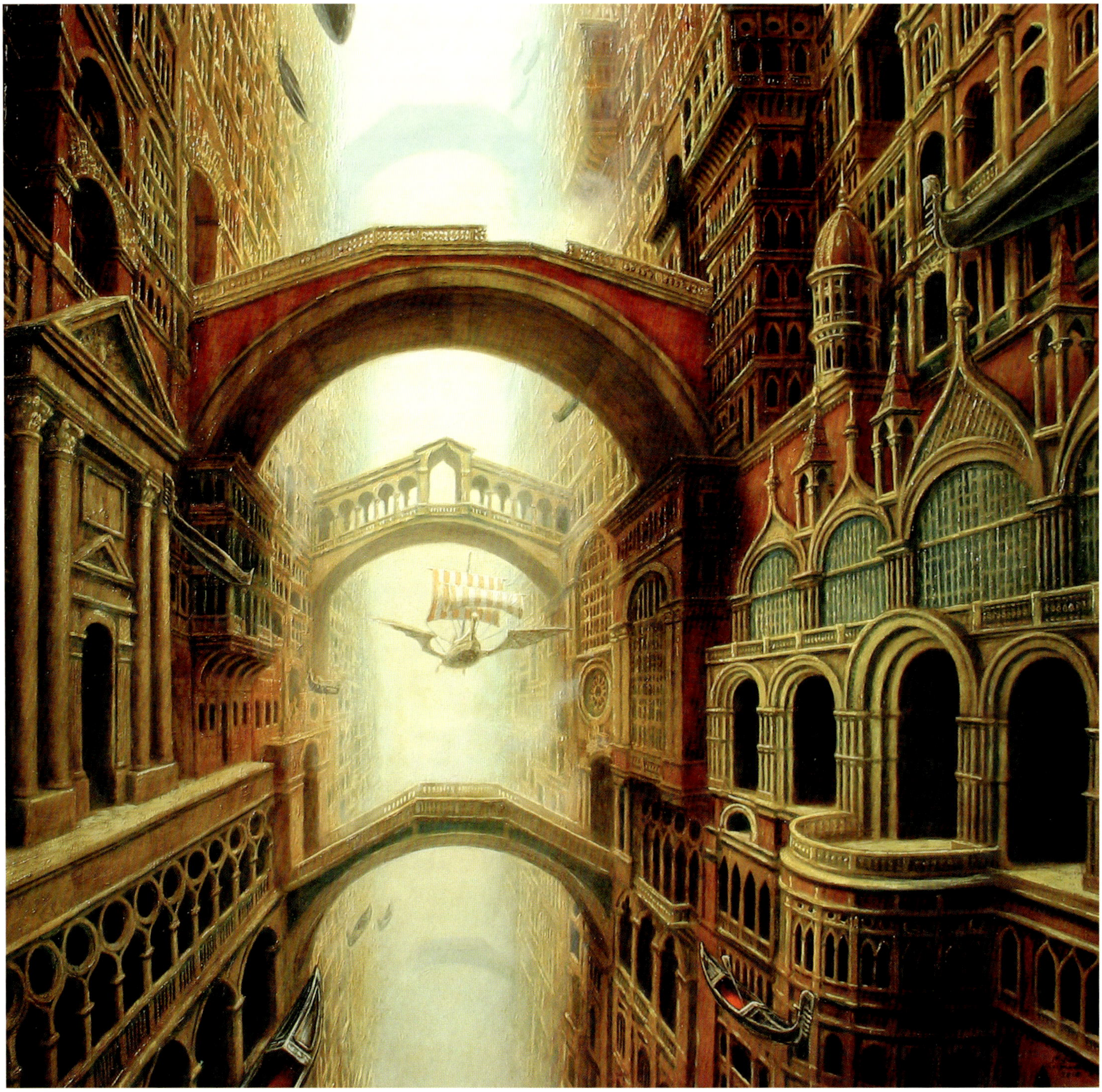

Venetian Caprice · 100 x 100 cm · Oil on canvas

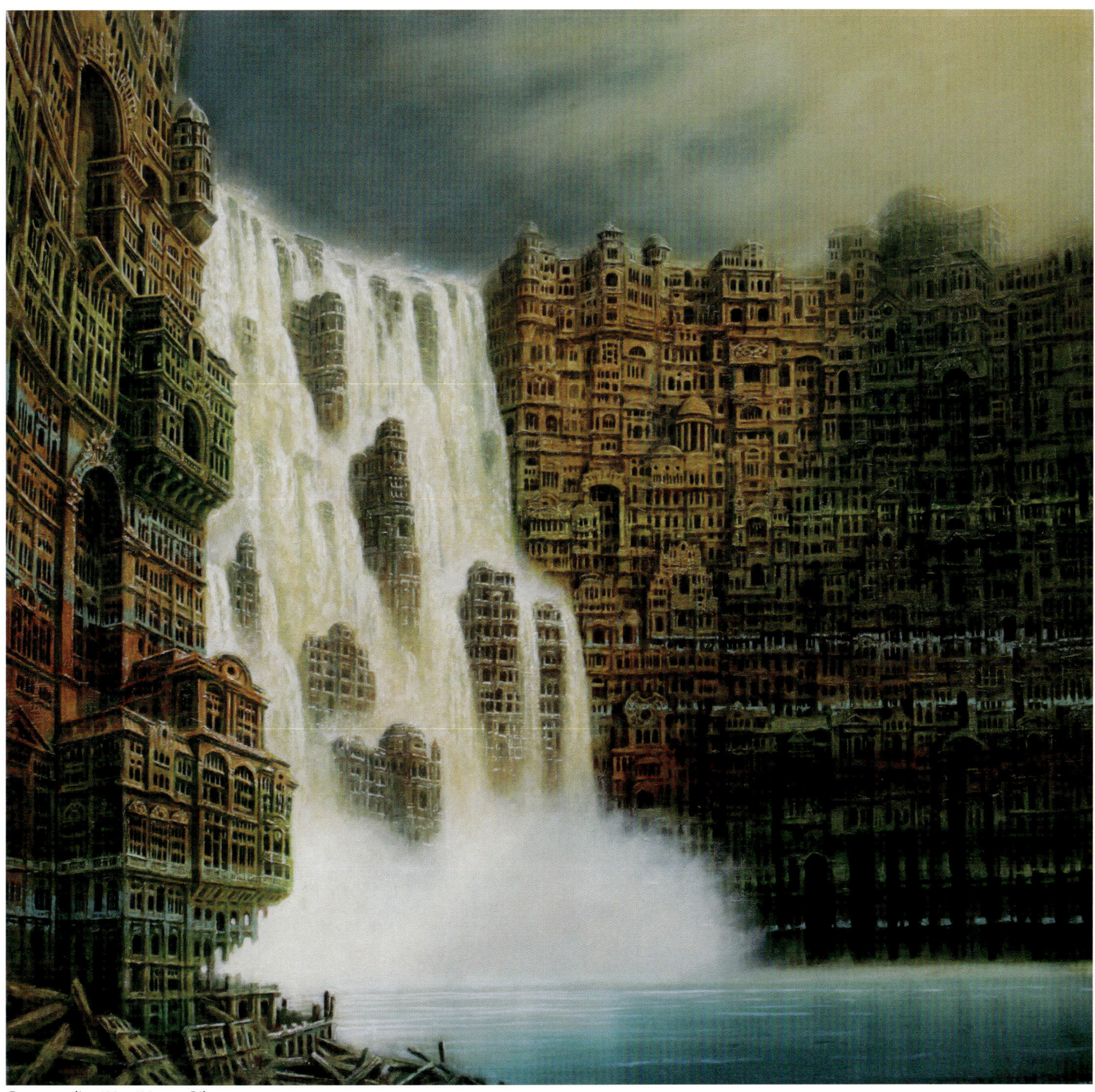

Cataractopolis · 100 x 100 cm · Oil on canvas

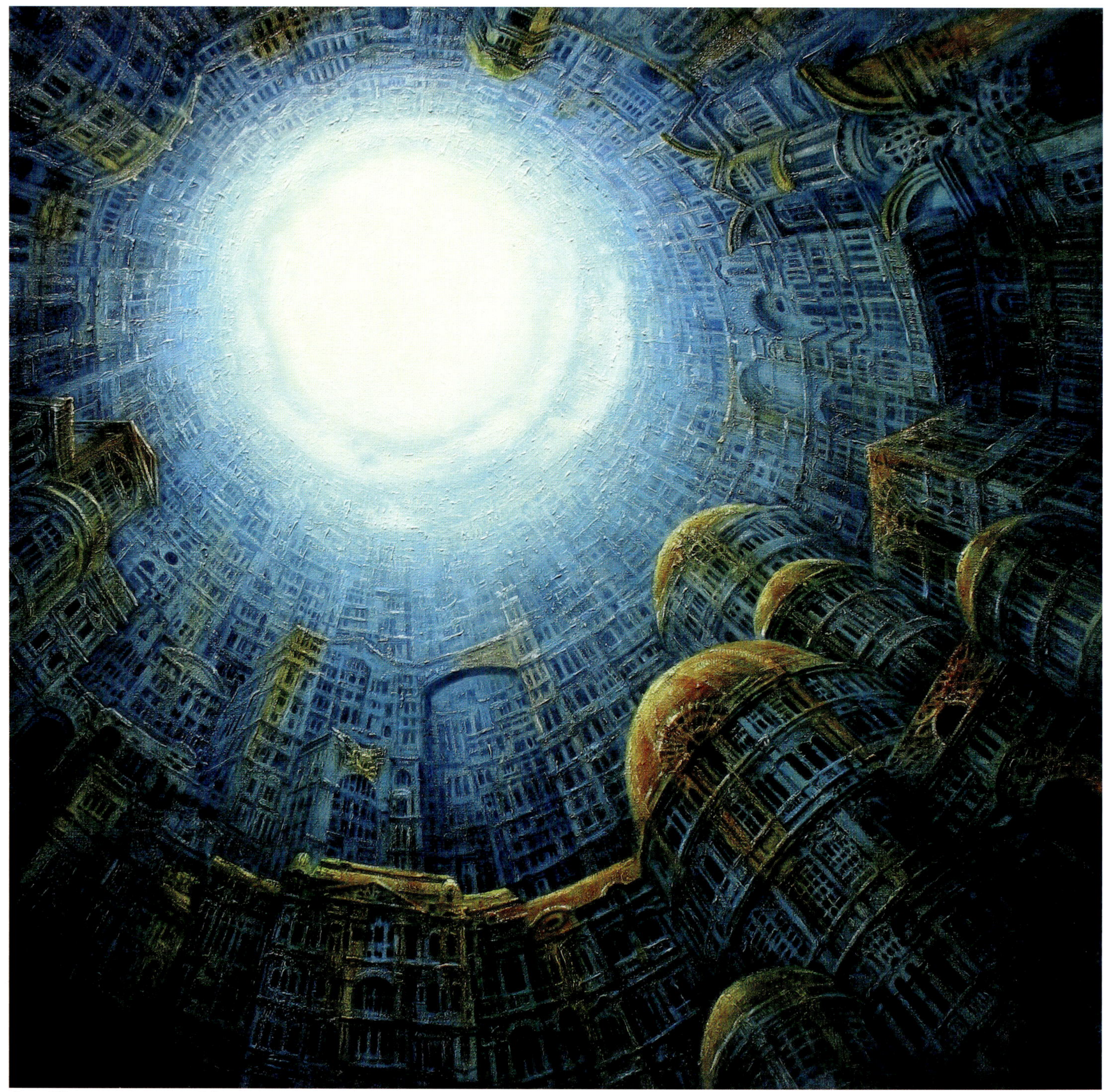
Gate of Heaven · 100 x 100 cm · Oil on canvas

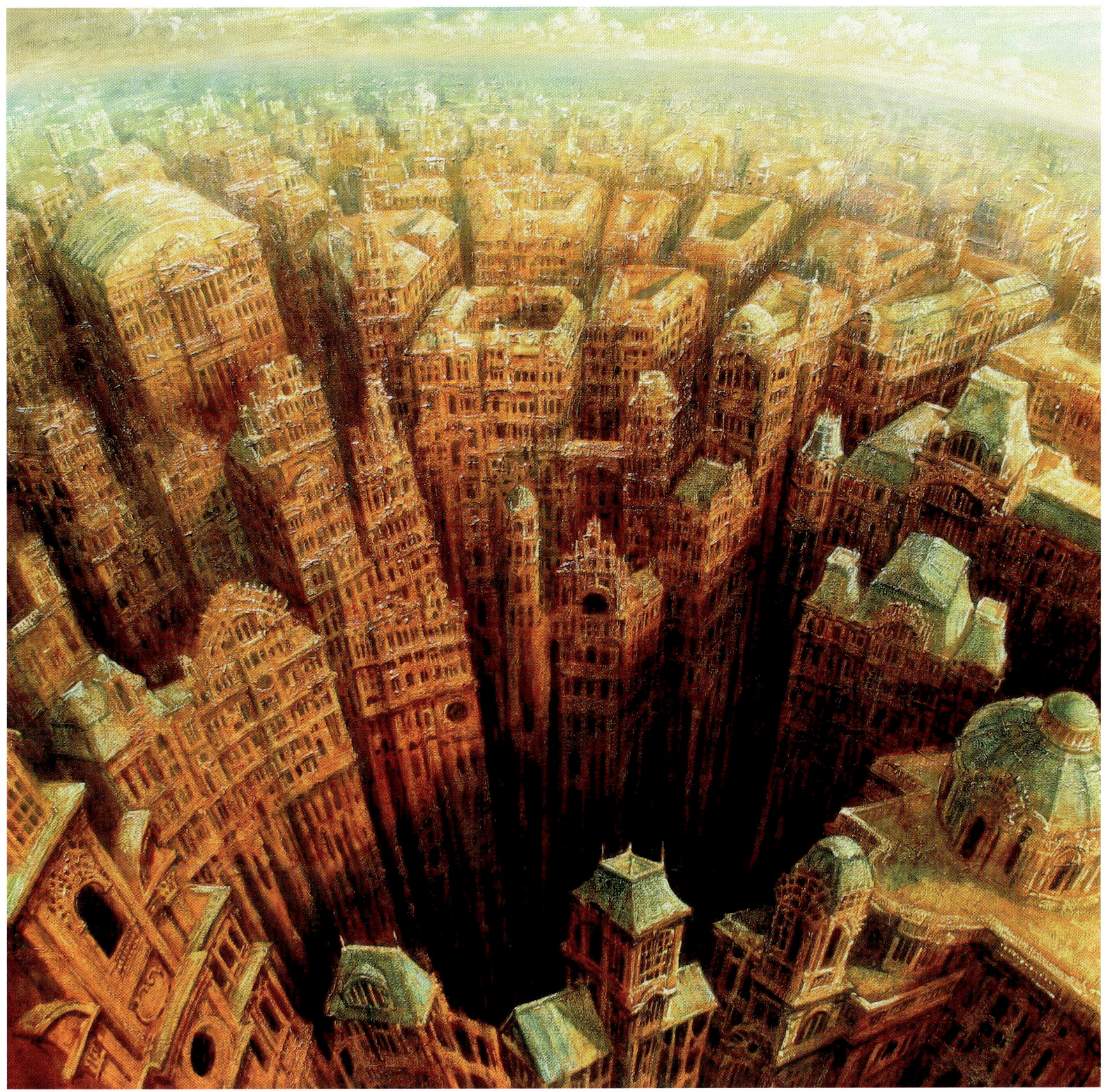
Gate of Hell · 100 x 100 cm · Oil on canvas

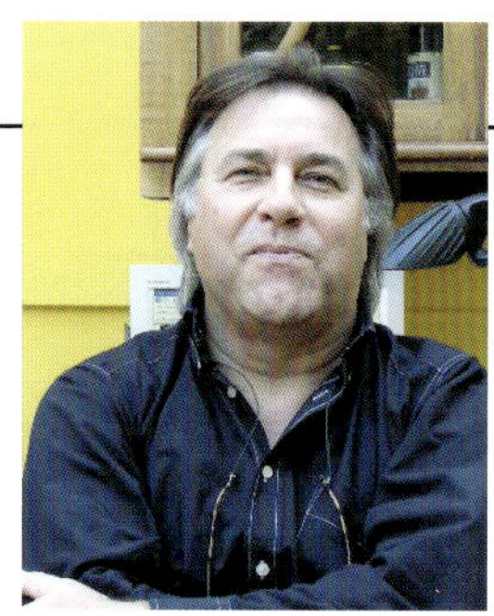

JACK LIPOWCZAN

1951 Poland/Germany

www.jacklipowczan.com

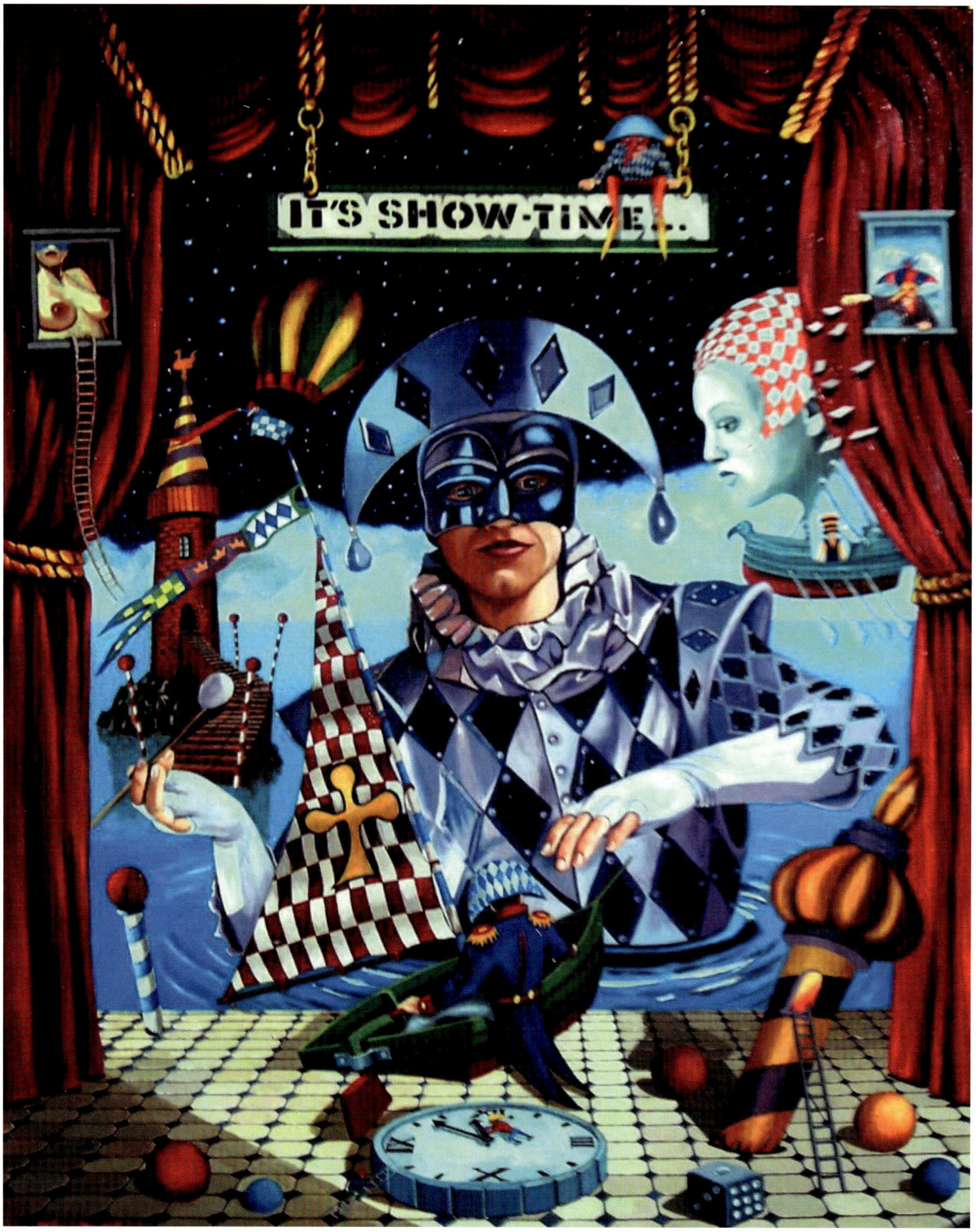

It's a Showtime... · 65 x 50 cm · Oil on wood

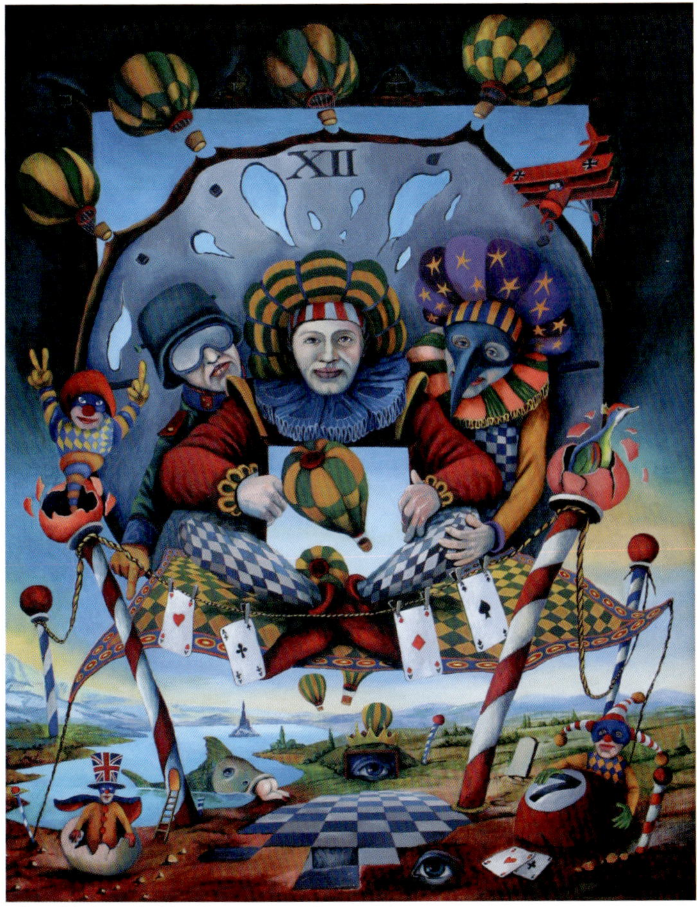

Tales of the Inexplicable · 65 x 50 cm · Oil on wood

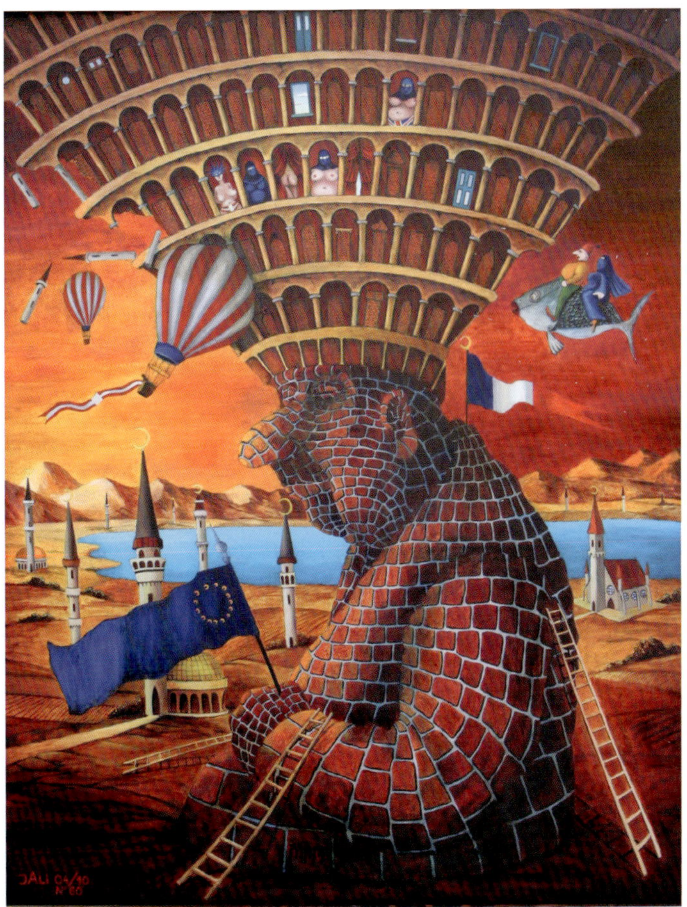

Europe? ....Europe! · 65 x 50 cm · Oil on wood

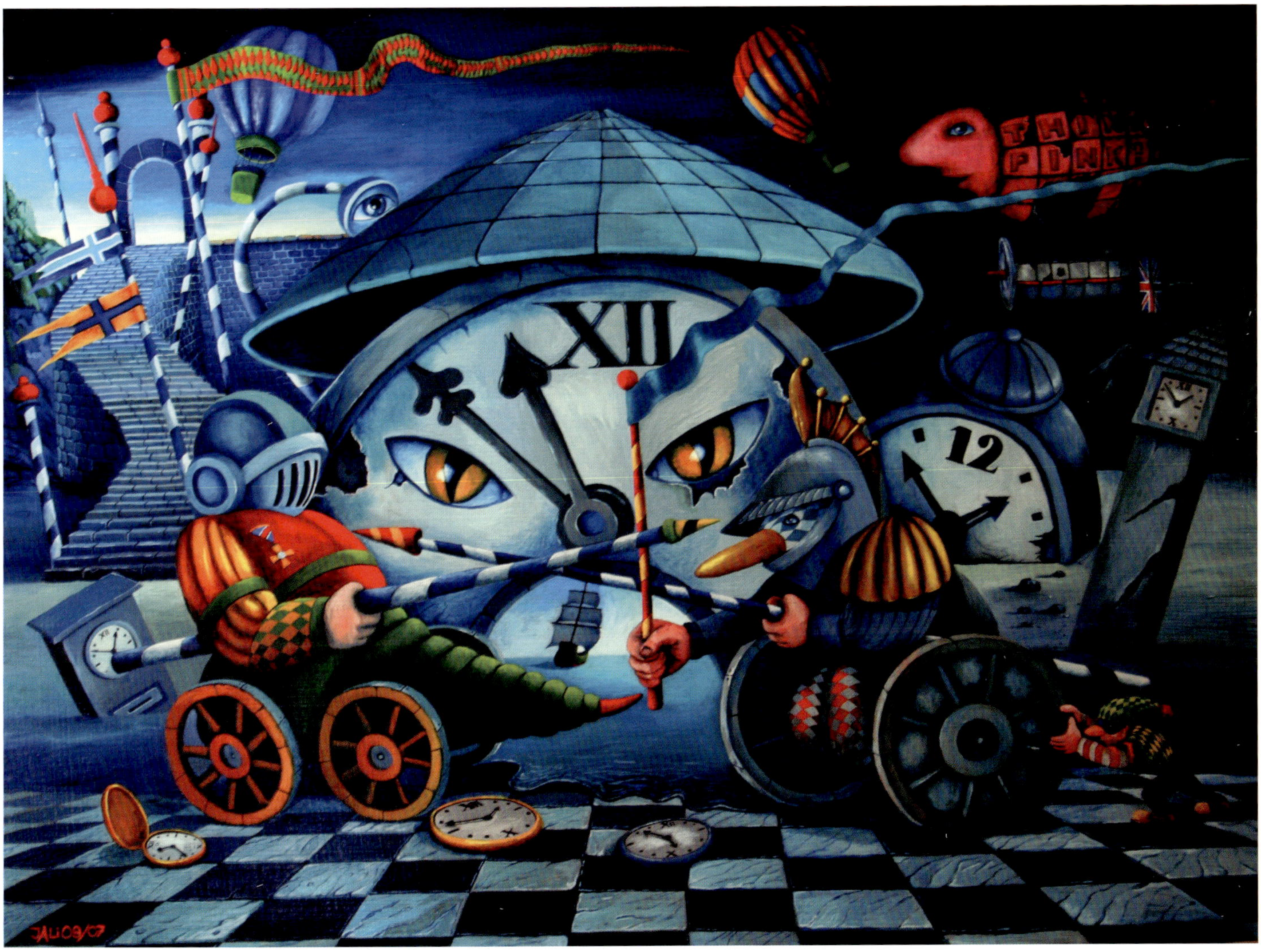

Think.... Pink · 50 x 65 cm · Oil on wood

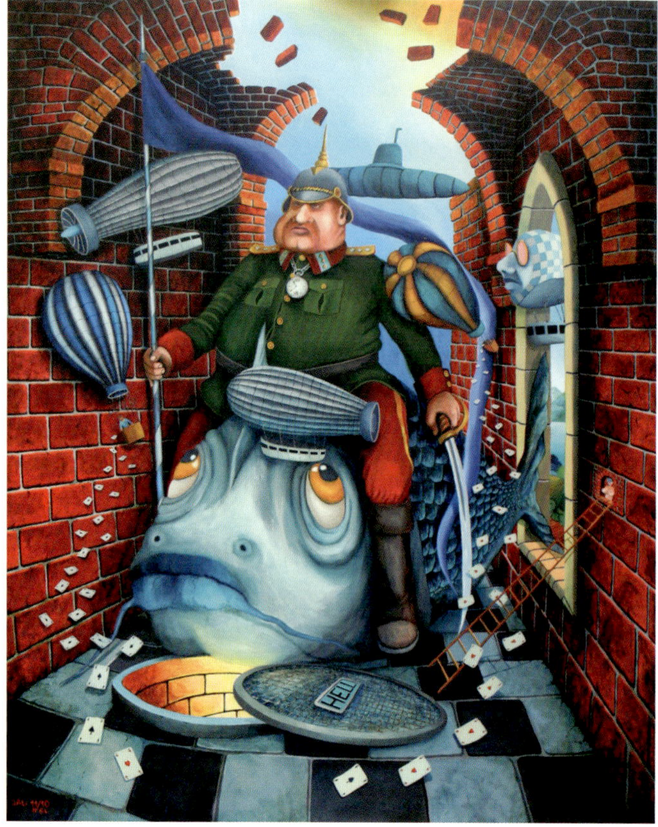

On Patrol.... · 92 x 72 cm · Oil on wood

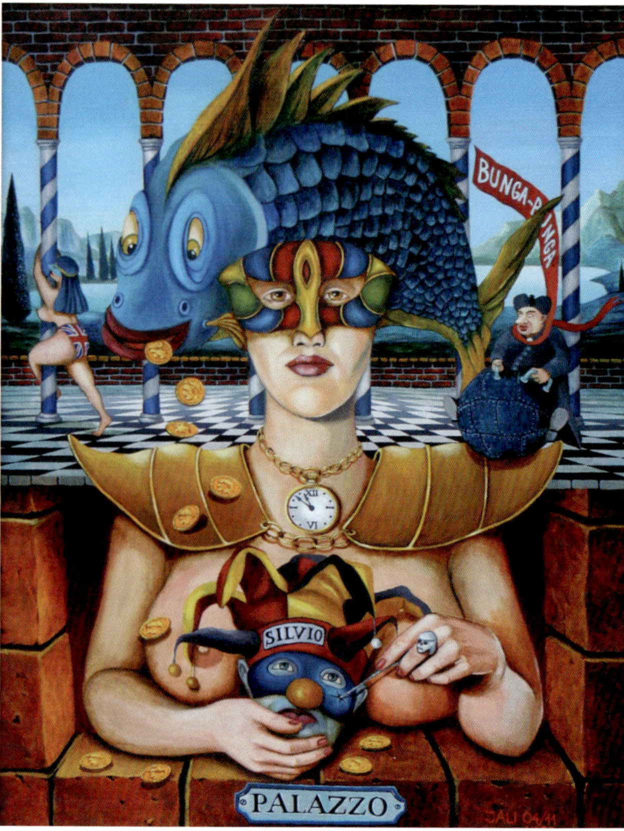

Bunga-Bunga Silvio! Silvio....only? · 55 x 40 cm · Oil on wood

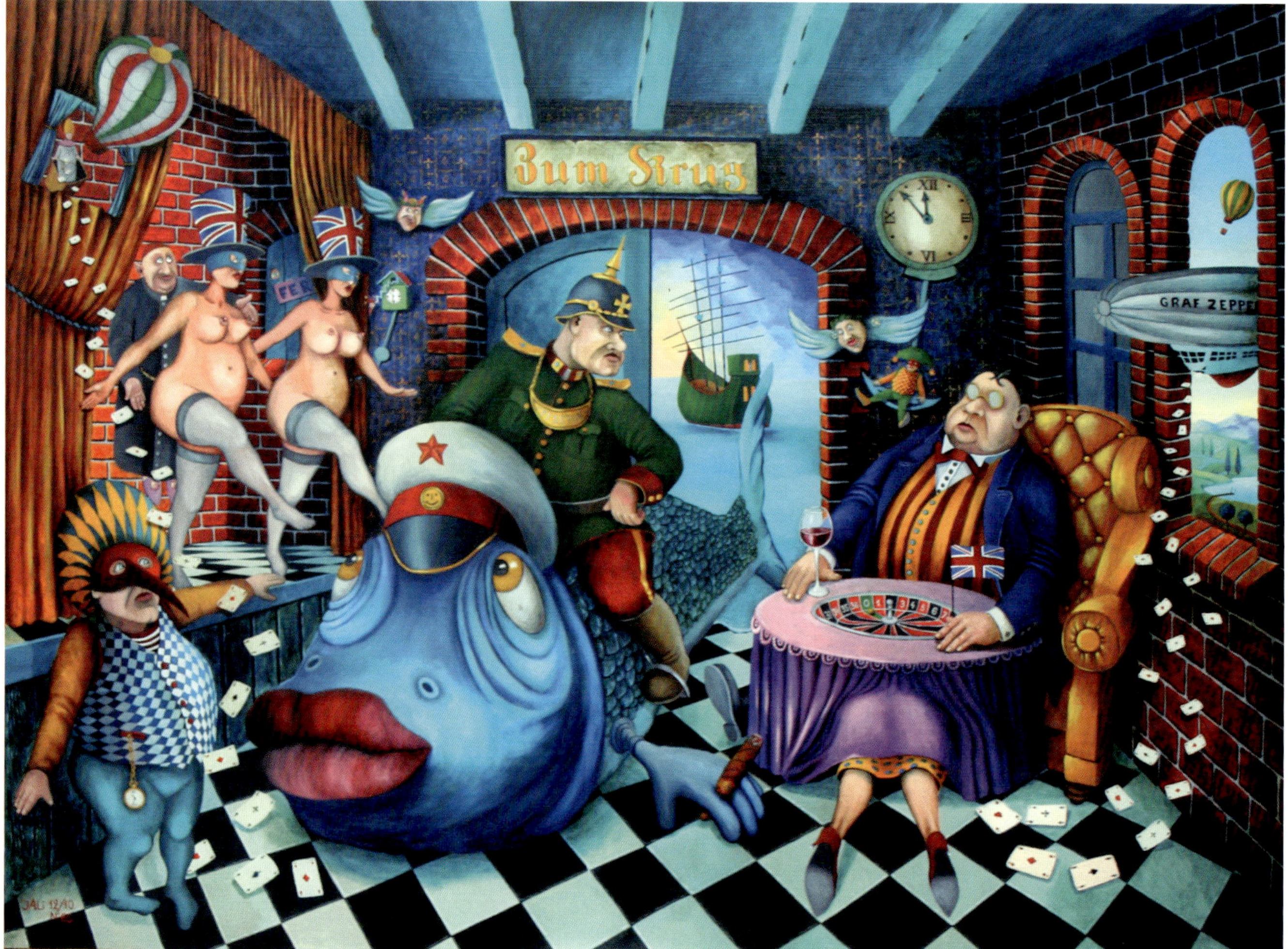

Everything can happen Tonight! · 81 x 92 cm · Oil on wood

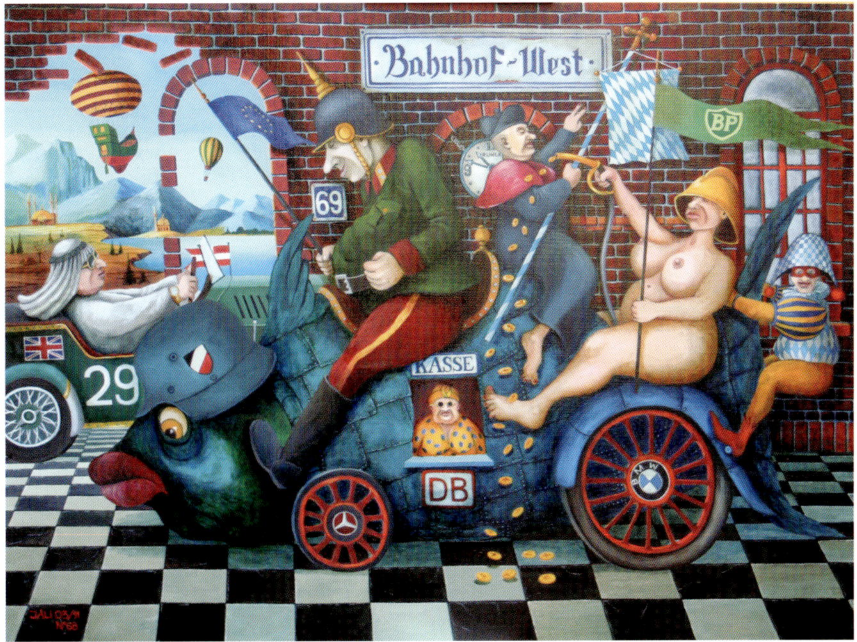

Checkpoint Westbahnhof · 75 x 92 cm · Oil on wood

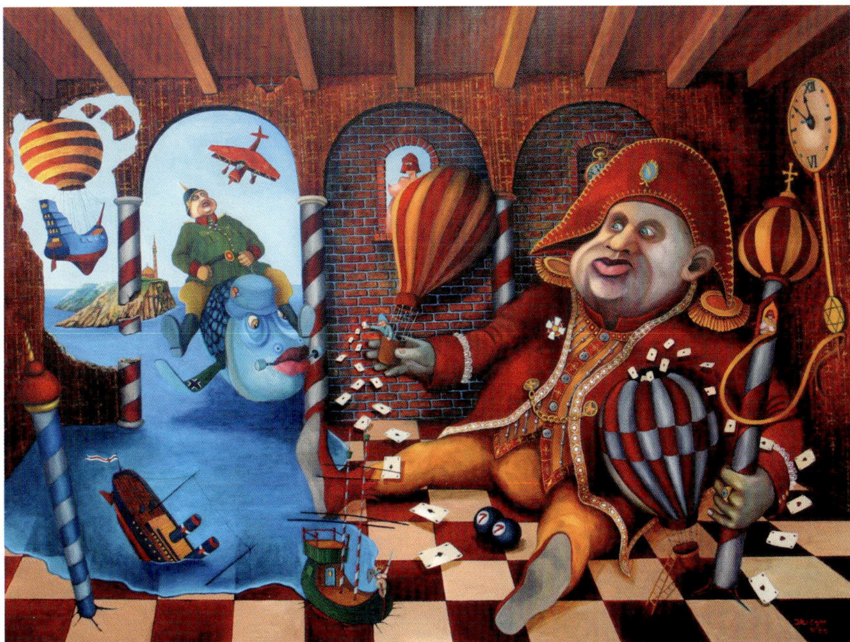
Interrupted snooze · 81 x 92 cm · Oil on wood

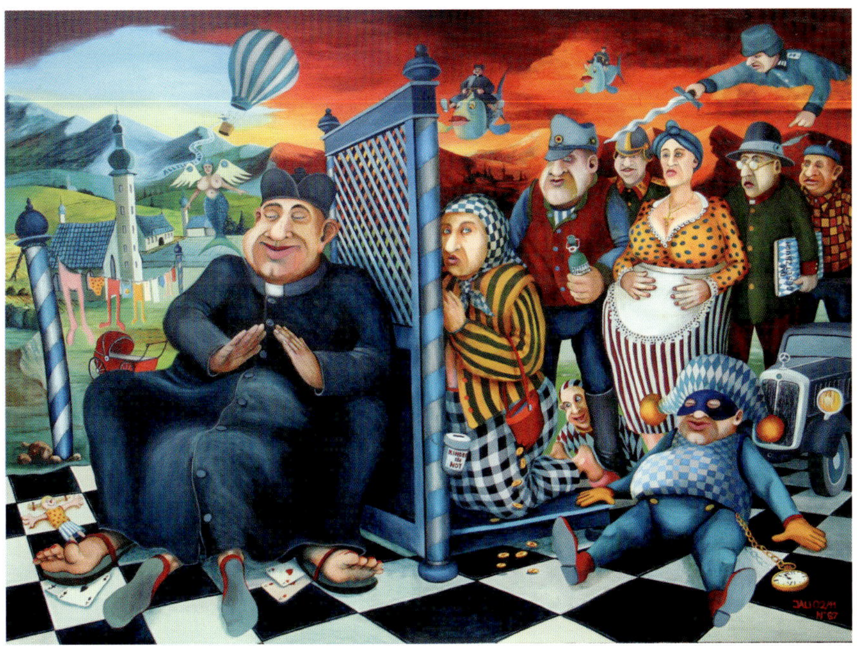
Bavarian Idyll or Seven Deadly Sins · 75 x 92 cm · Oil on wood

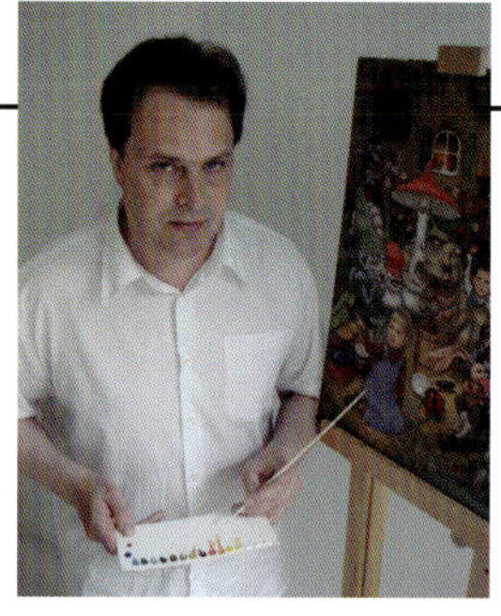

MICHA LOBI

1967 Sibiria

www.fantasmus-art.com • m.lobi@mail.ru

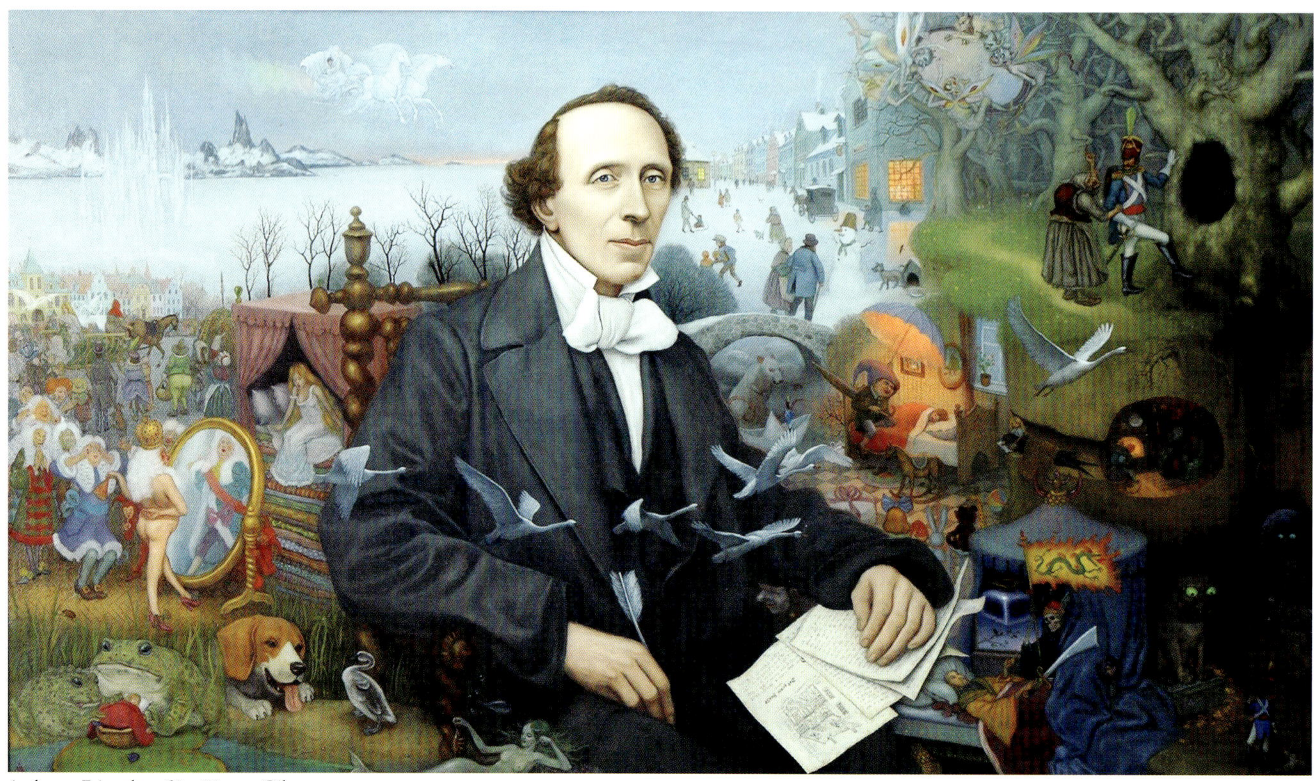

Andersen Fairytales · 60 x 98 cm · Oil on canvas

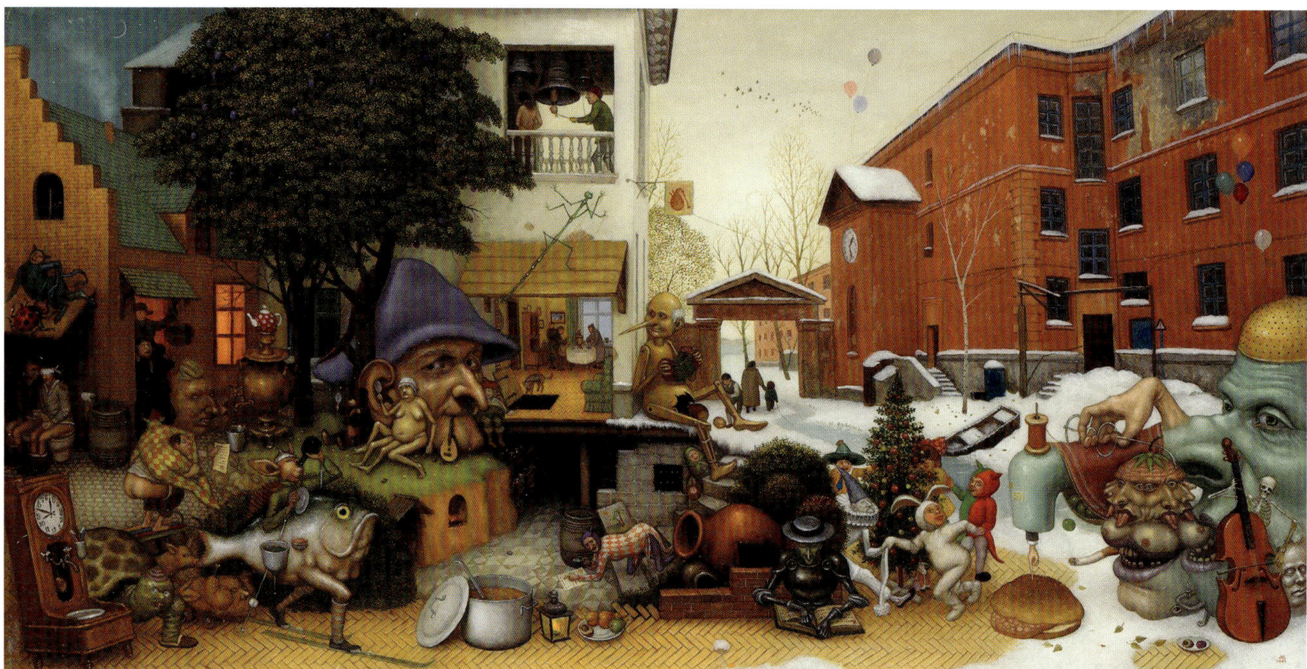

Aspects of Life · 22 x47 · Oil on panel

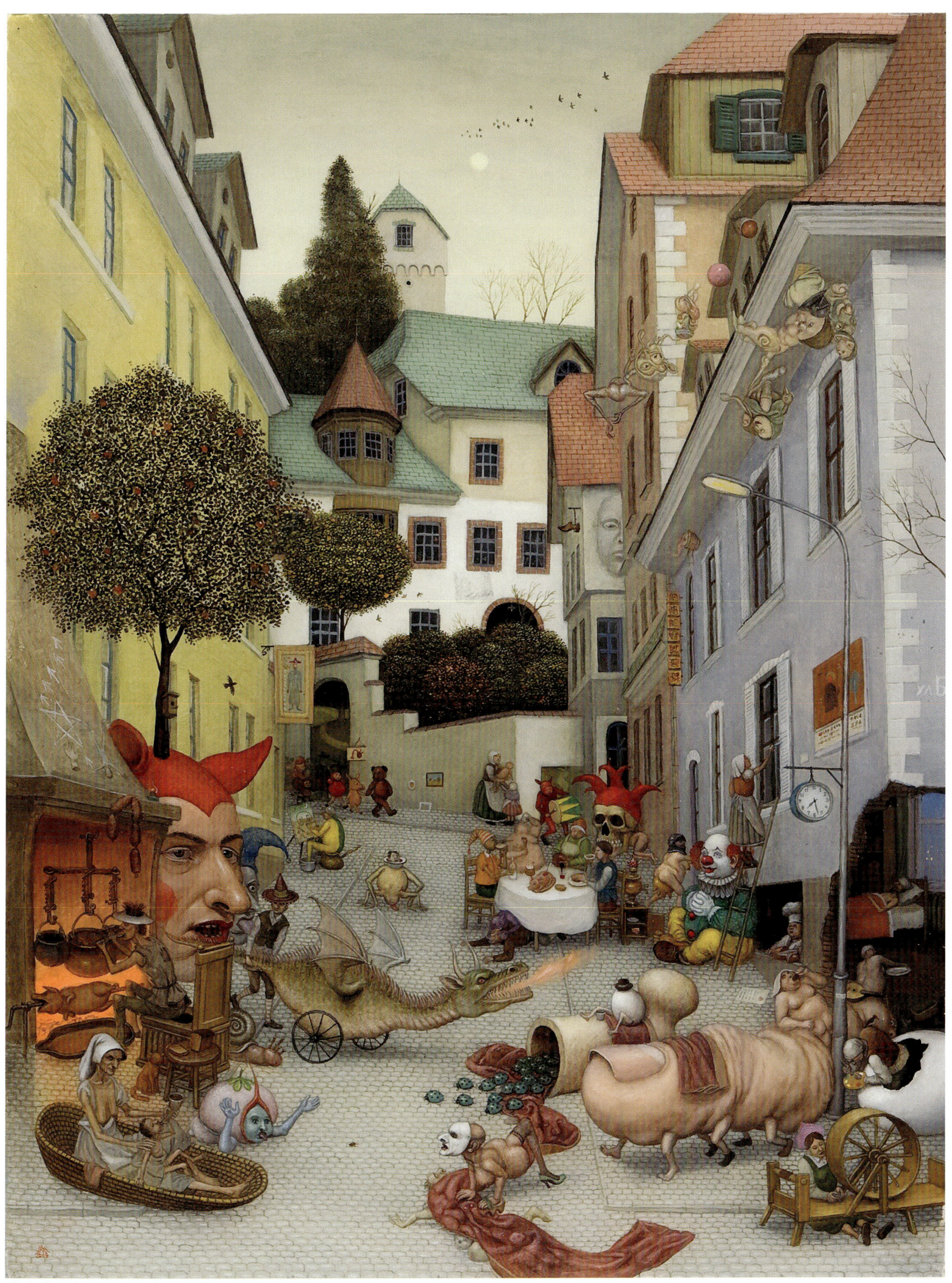

Blind Alley · 40 x 30 cm · Oil on panel

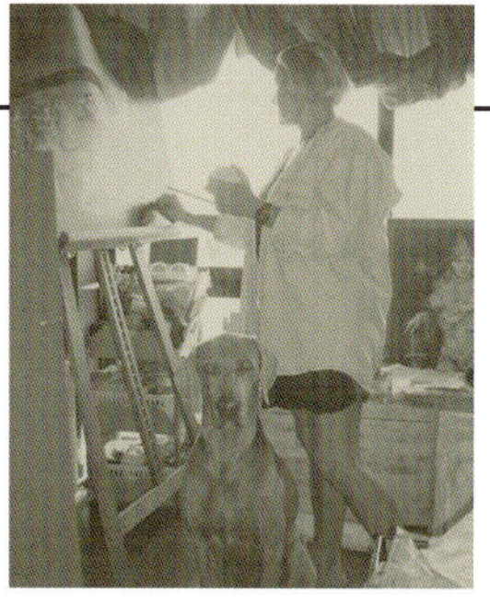

LUDMILA

1958 Russia / Portugal

www.ludmila-fantasticart.blogspot.com

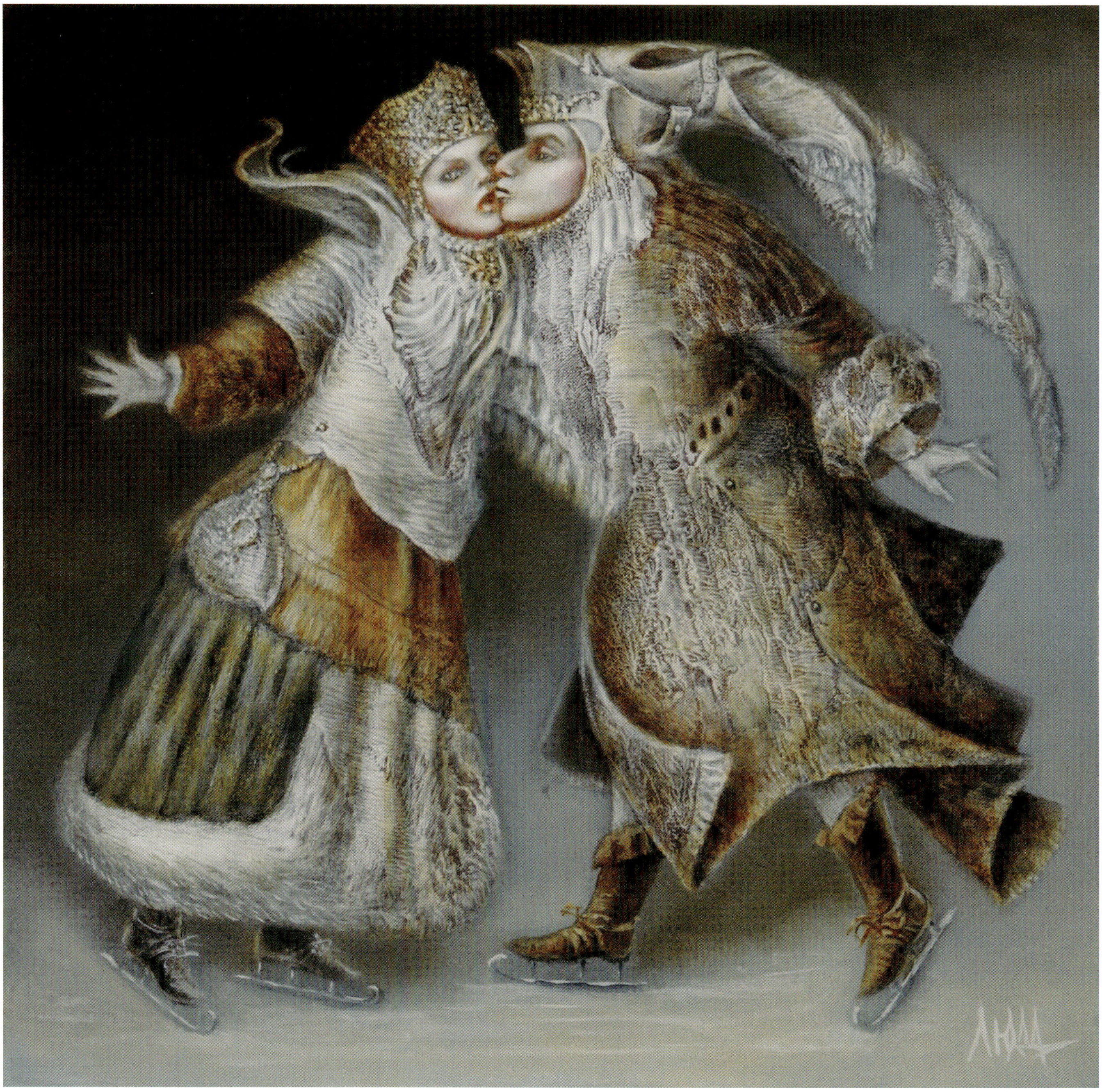

Accidental Kiss · 30 x 30 cm · Oil on board.

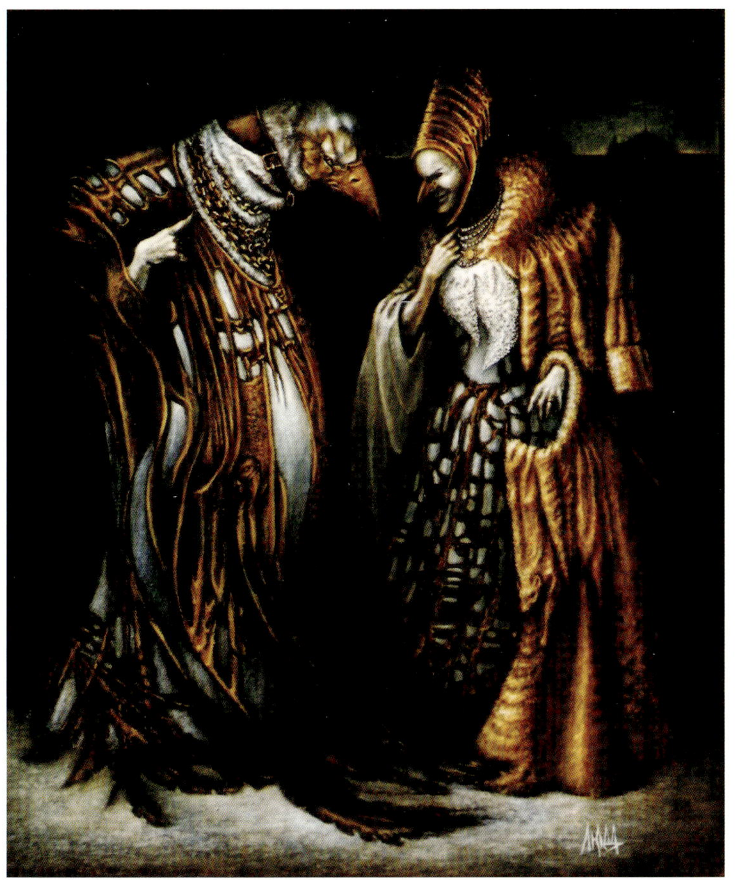

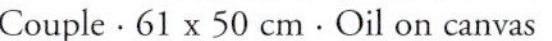

Couple · 61 x 50 cm · Oil on canvas

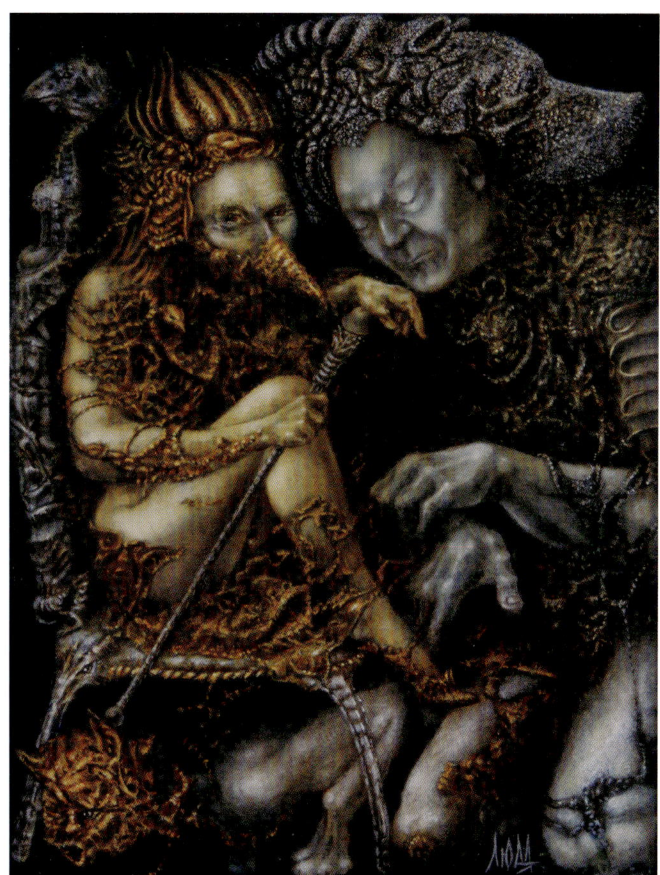

Cena Familiar · 24 x 18 cm · Oil on canvas

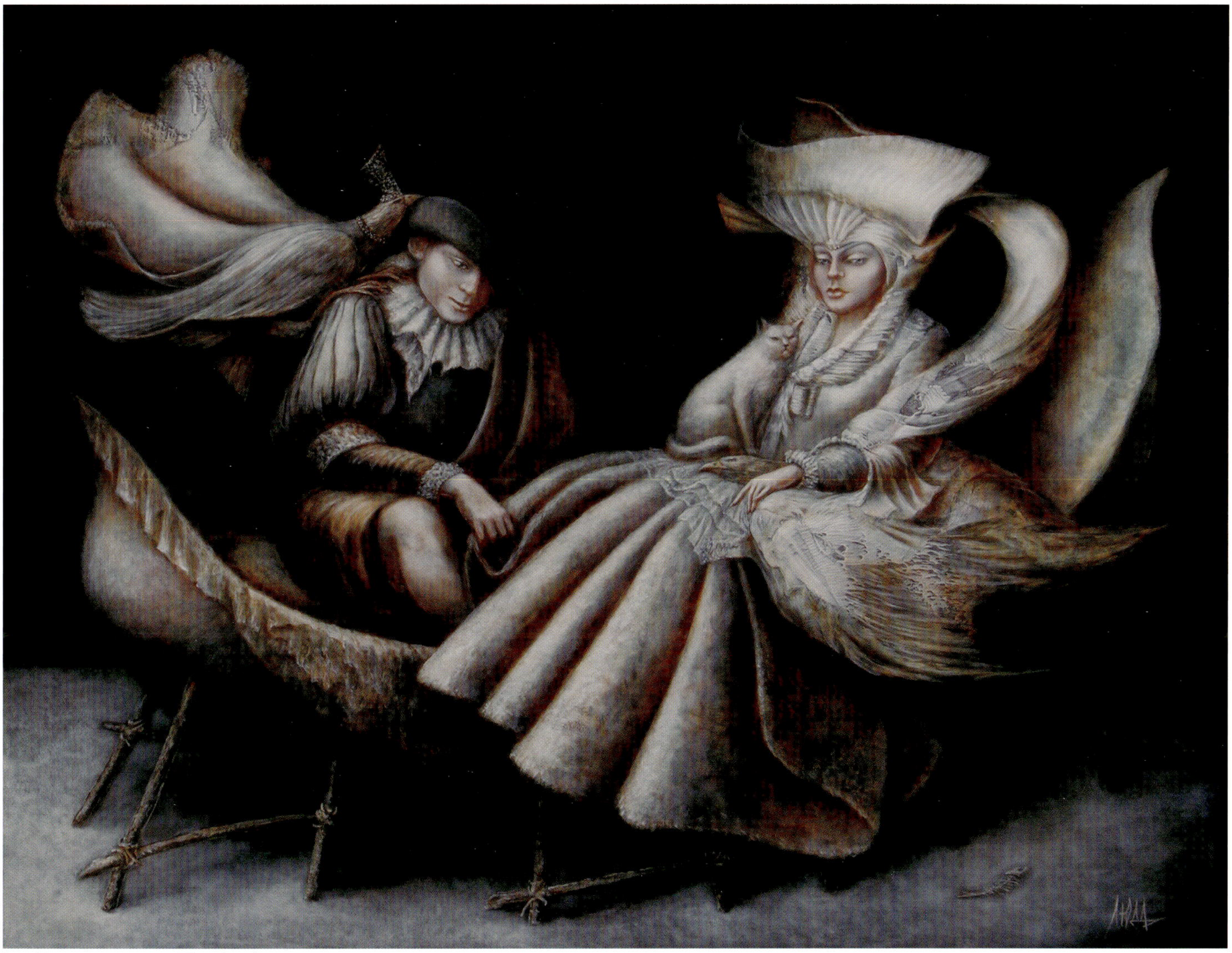

Love Boat · 80 x 100 cm · Oil on board

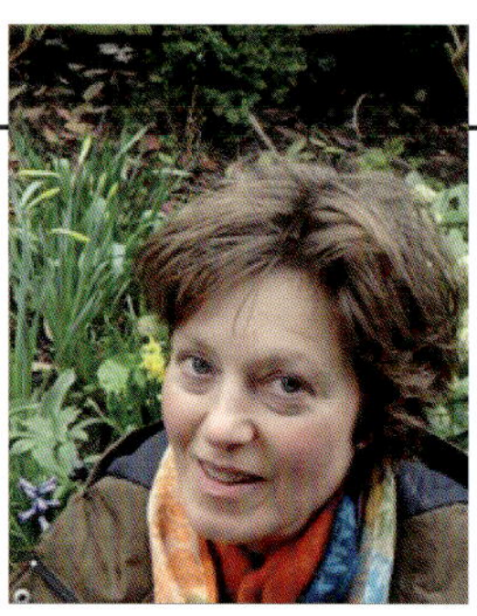

NANNY LUIJSTERBURG

1967 Netherlands

www.luysterburg.com

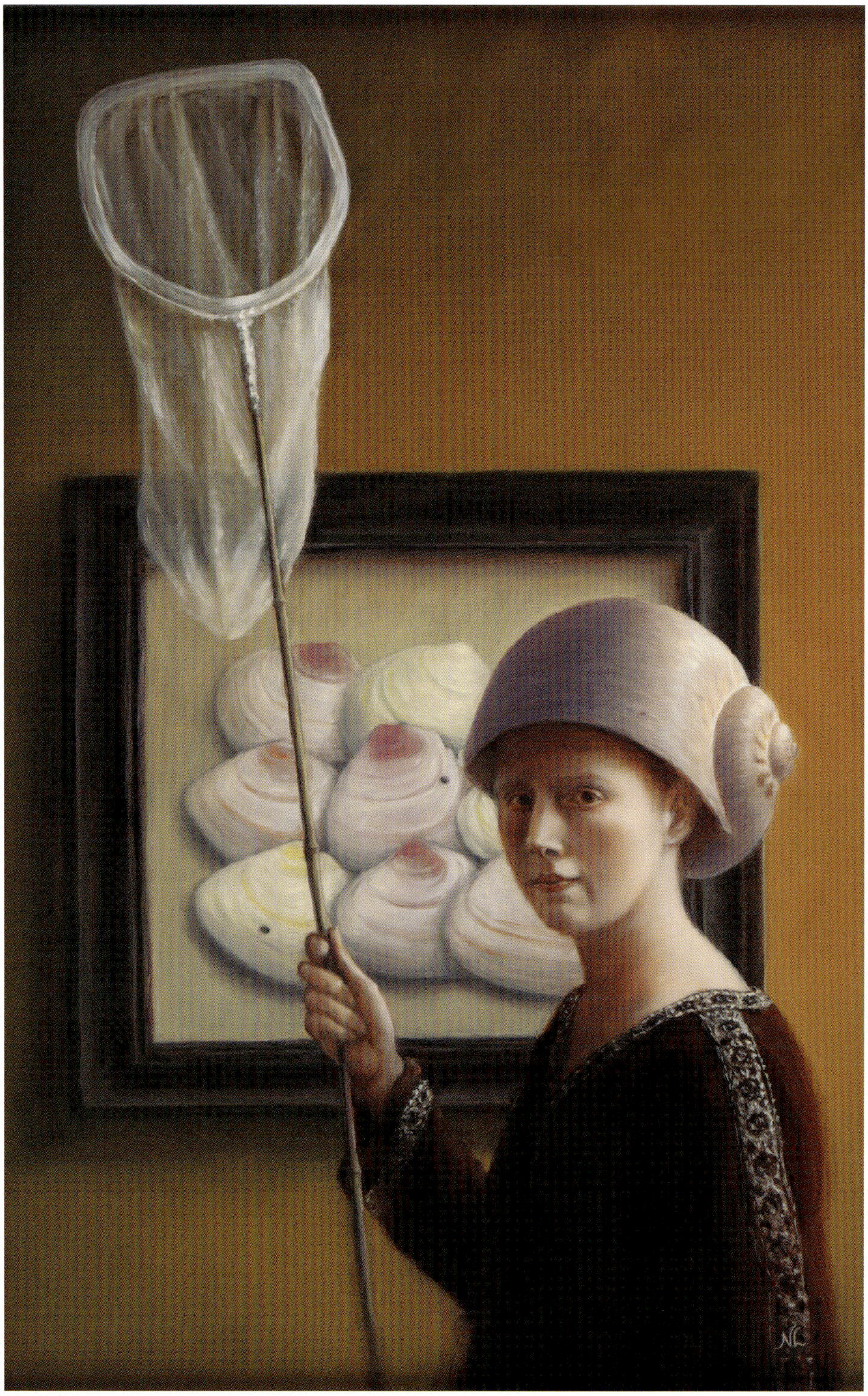

The Collector · 35 x 22 cm · Oil on panel

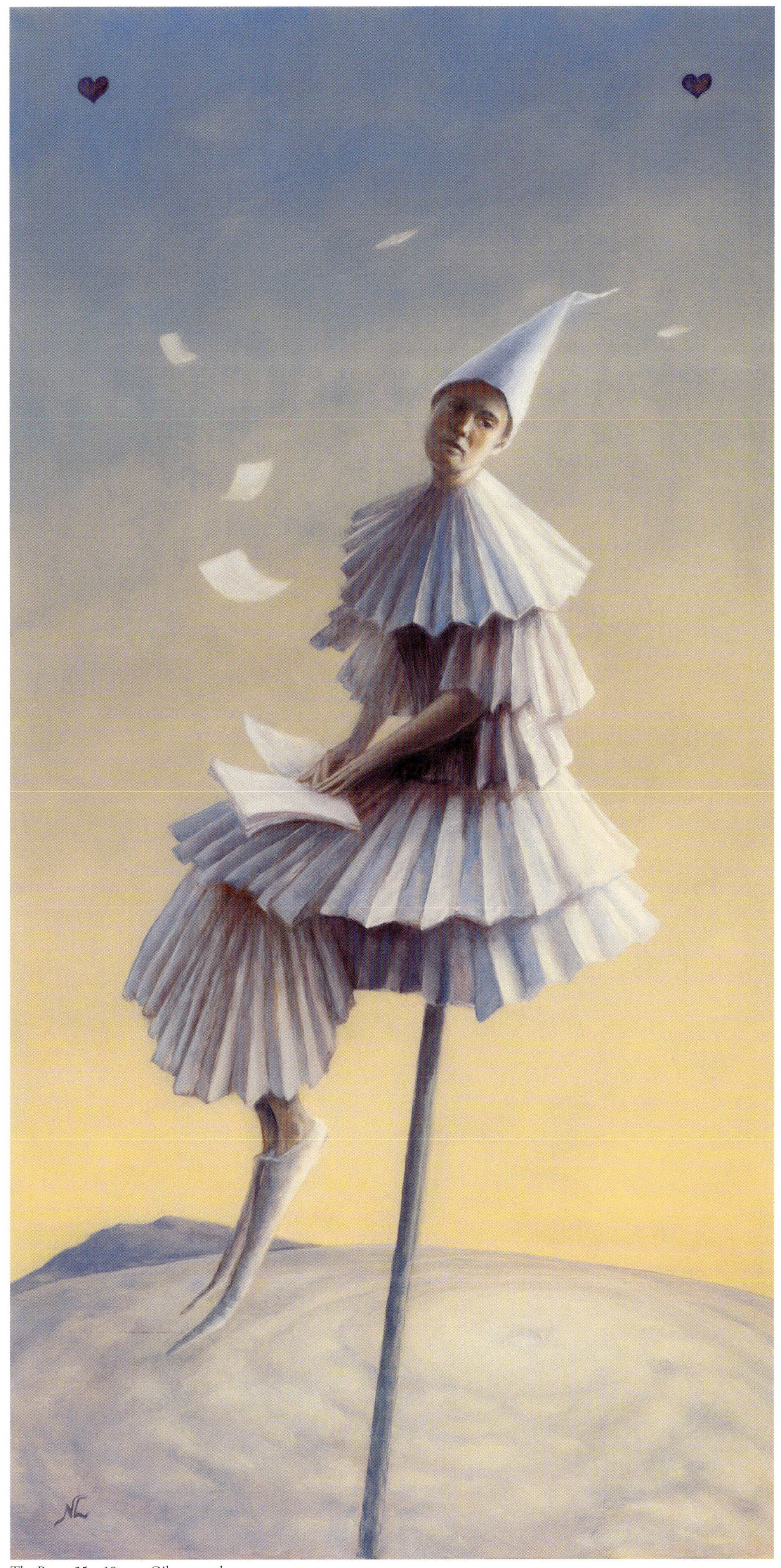

The Poet · 35 x 18 cm · Oil on panel

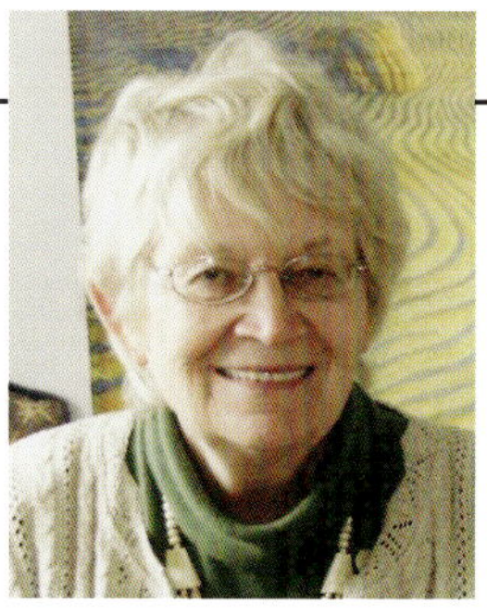

BRIGID MARLIN

USA

www.brigidmarlin.com

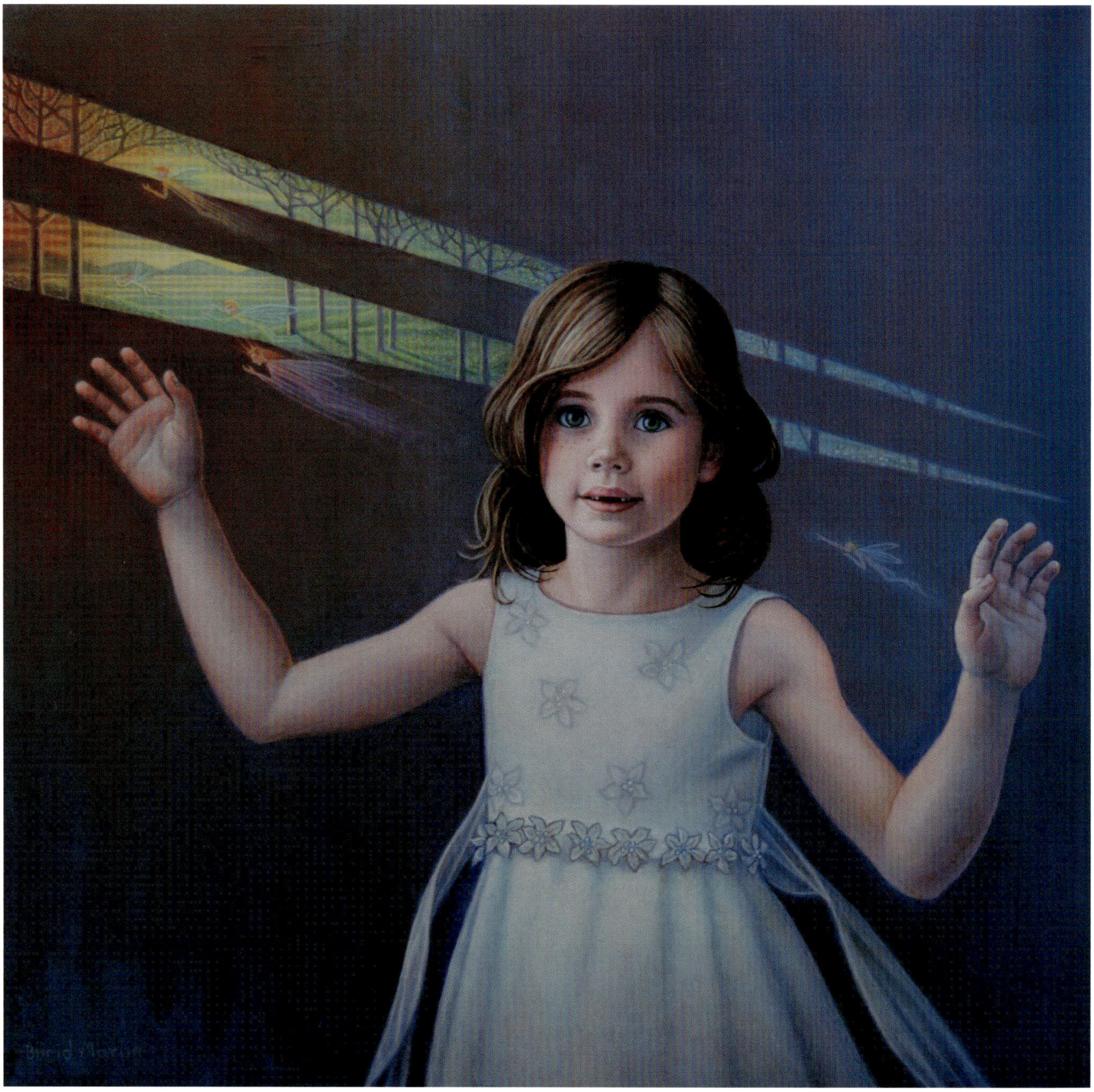

Sophie's other World · 60 x 75 cm · Mische technique

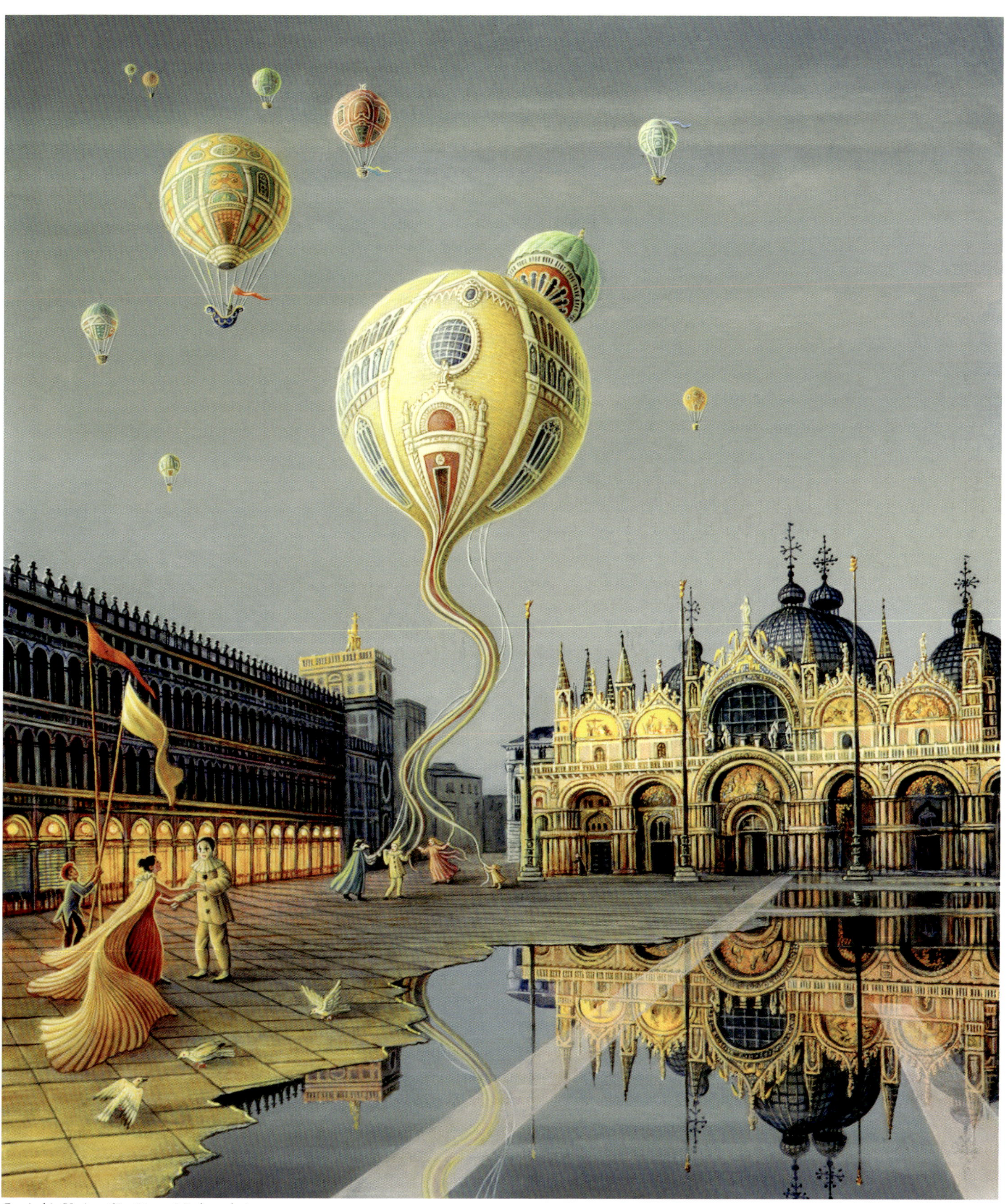

Carnival in Venice · 65 x 95cm · Mische technique

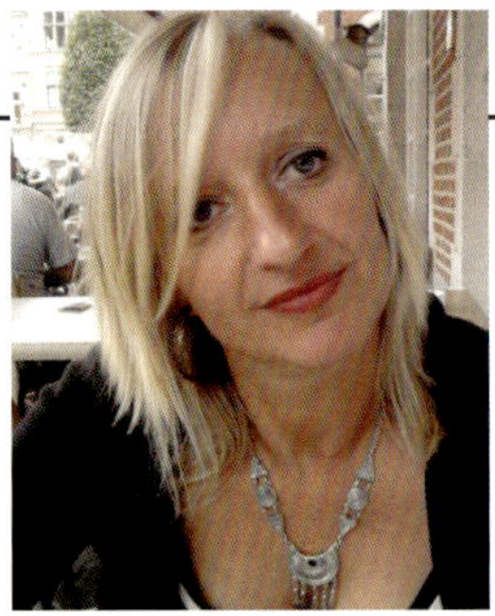

CHRISTINE MORREN

1966 Belgium

www.christinemorren.com

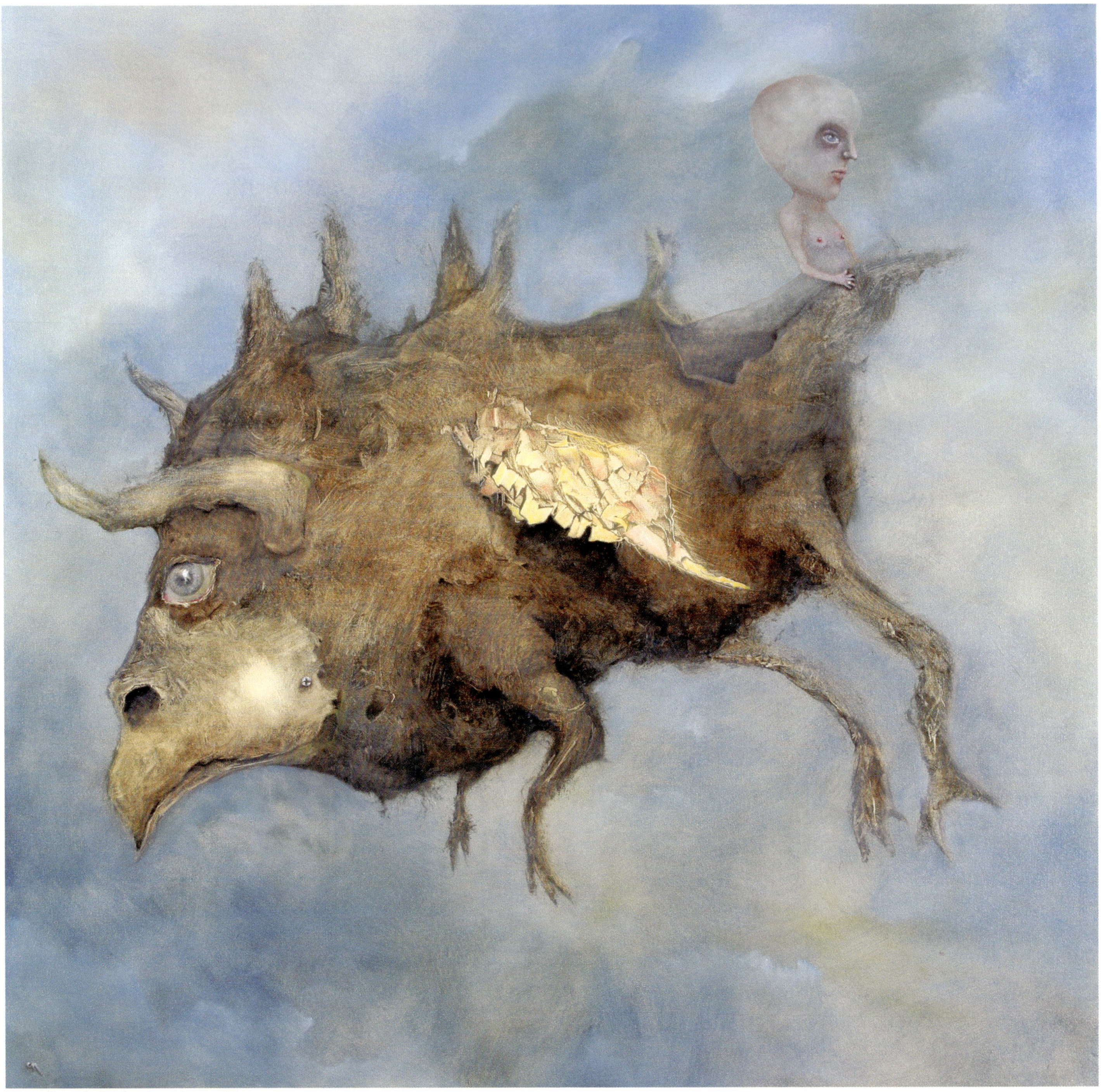

Escape from the Myth · 70 x 70 cm · Oil on canvas

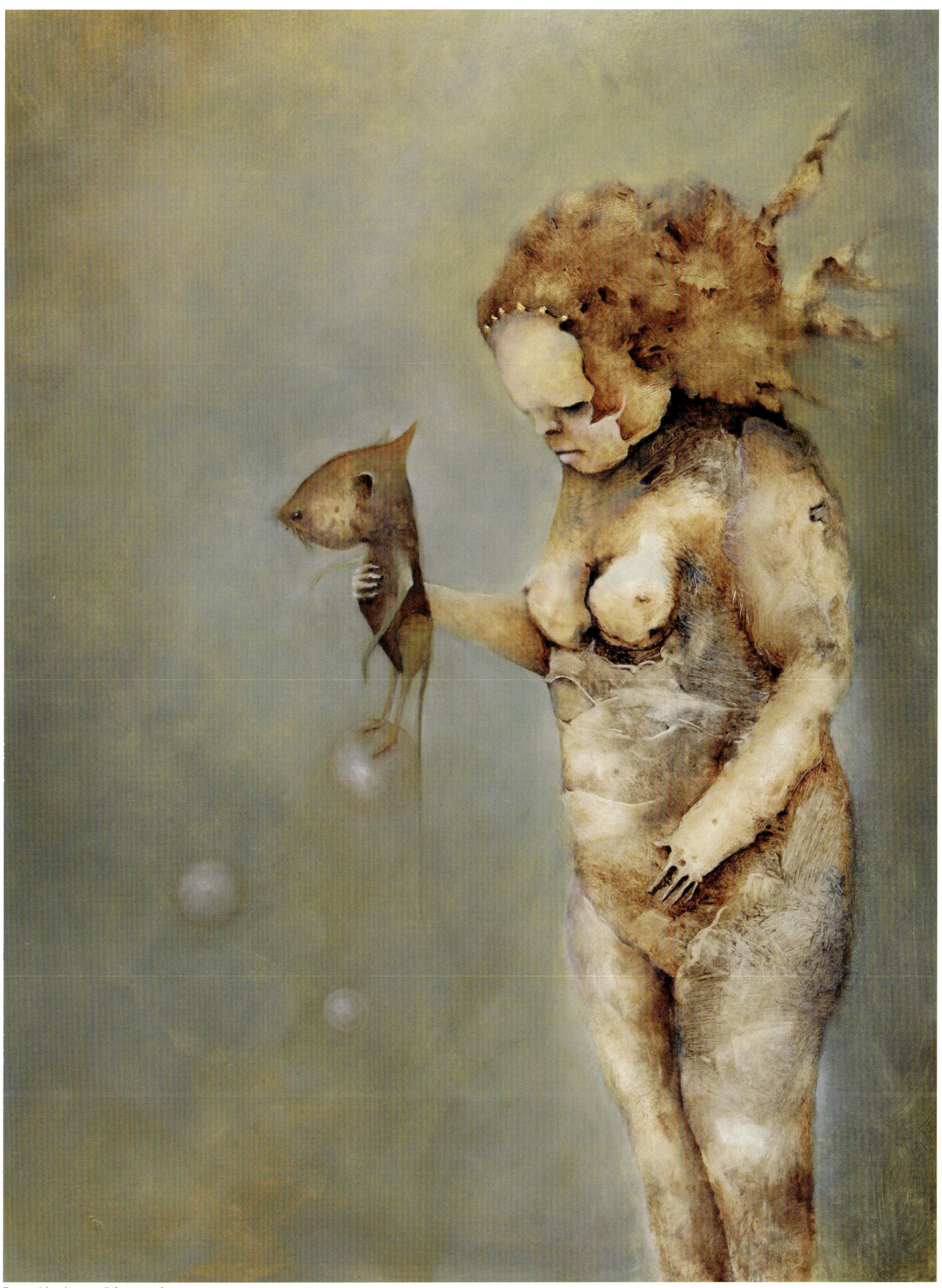

Rosa · 54 x 40 cm · Oil on panel

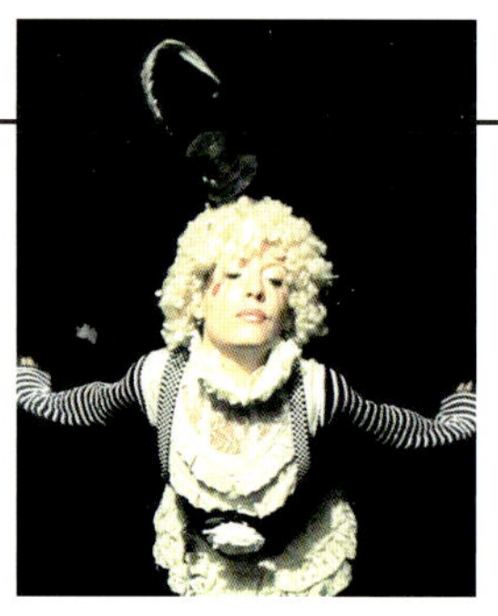

AUTUMN SKYE MORRISON

1983 Canada

www.autumnskyemorrison.com

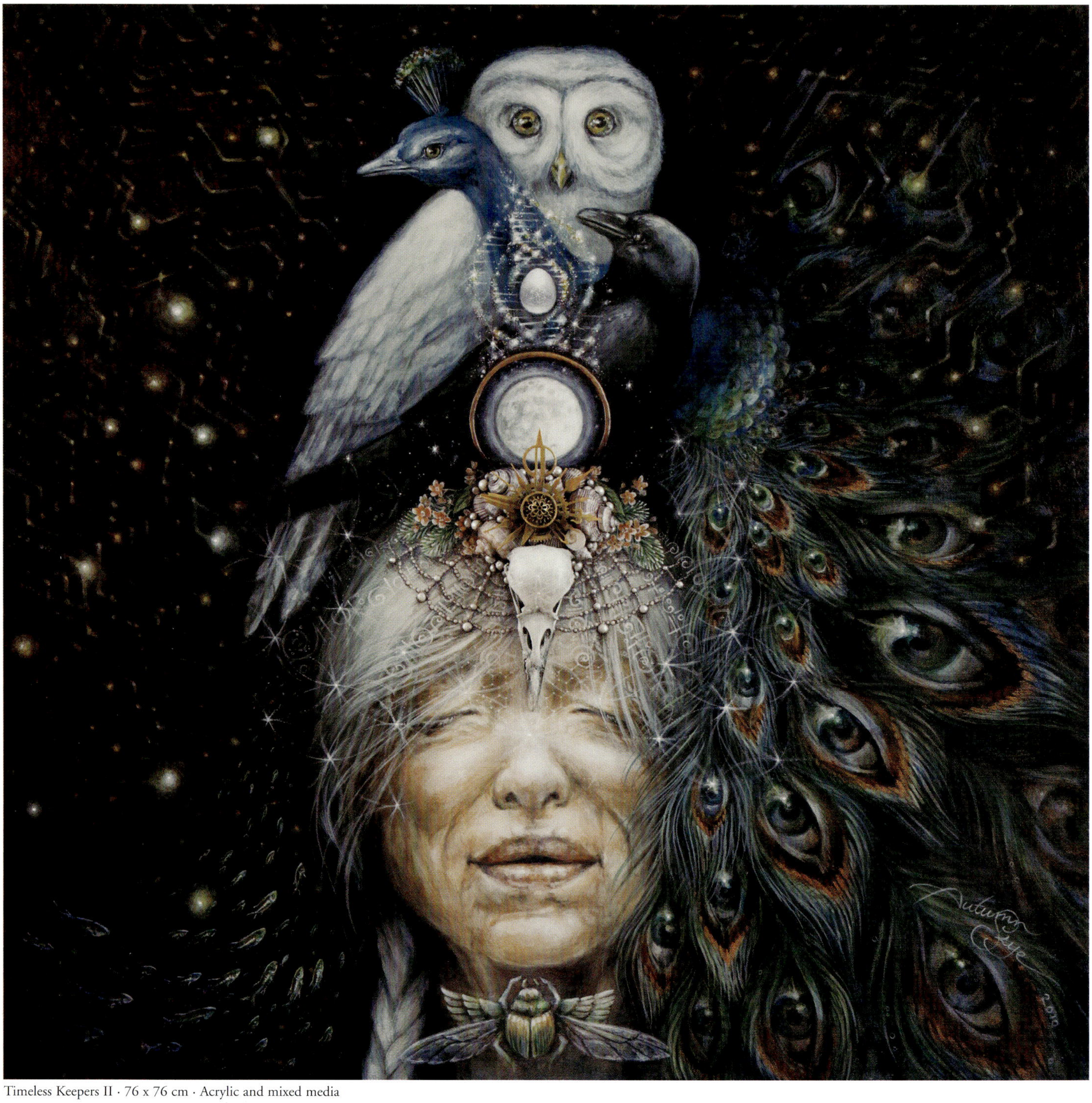

Timeless Keepers II · 76 x 76 cm · Acrylic and mixed media

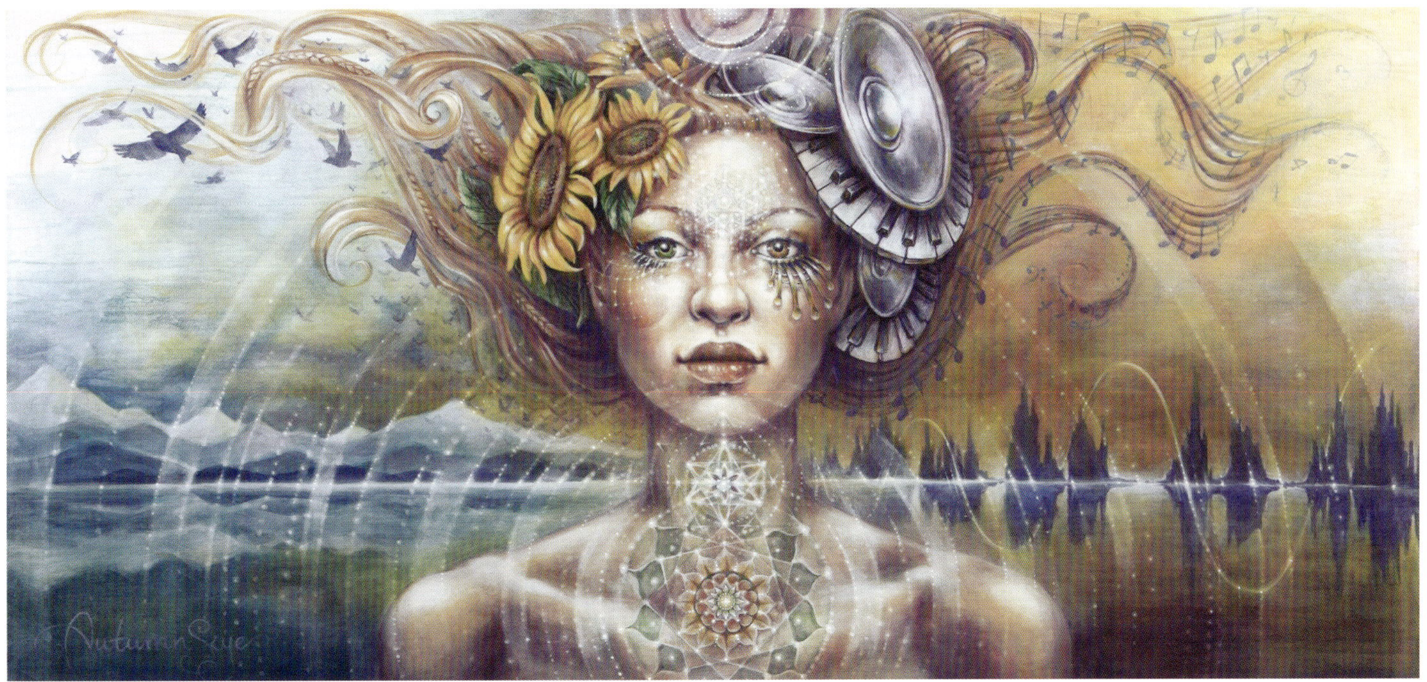

Harmonic Transformation · 61 x 122 cm · Acrylic on canvas

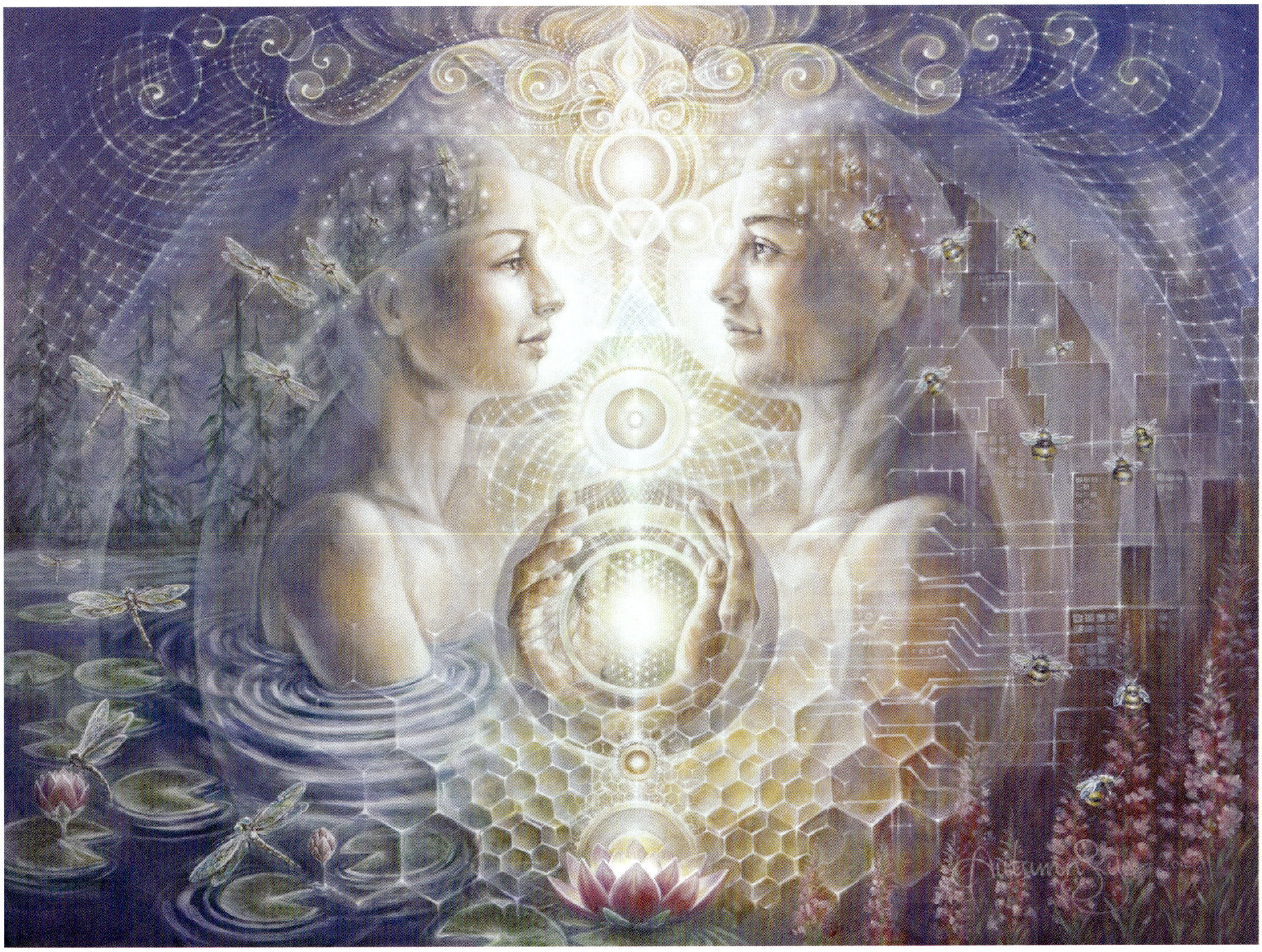

Beloved Medium · 91,5 x 122 cm · Acrylic on canvas

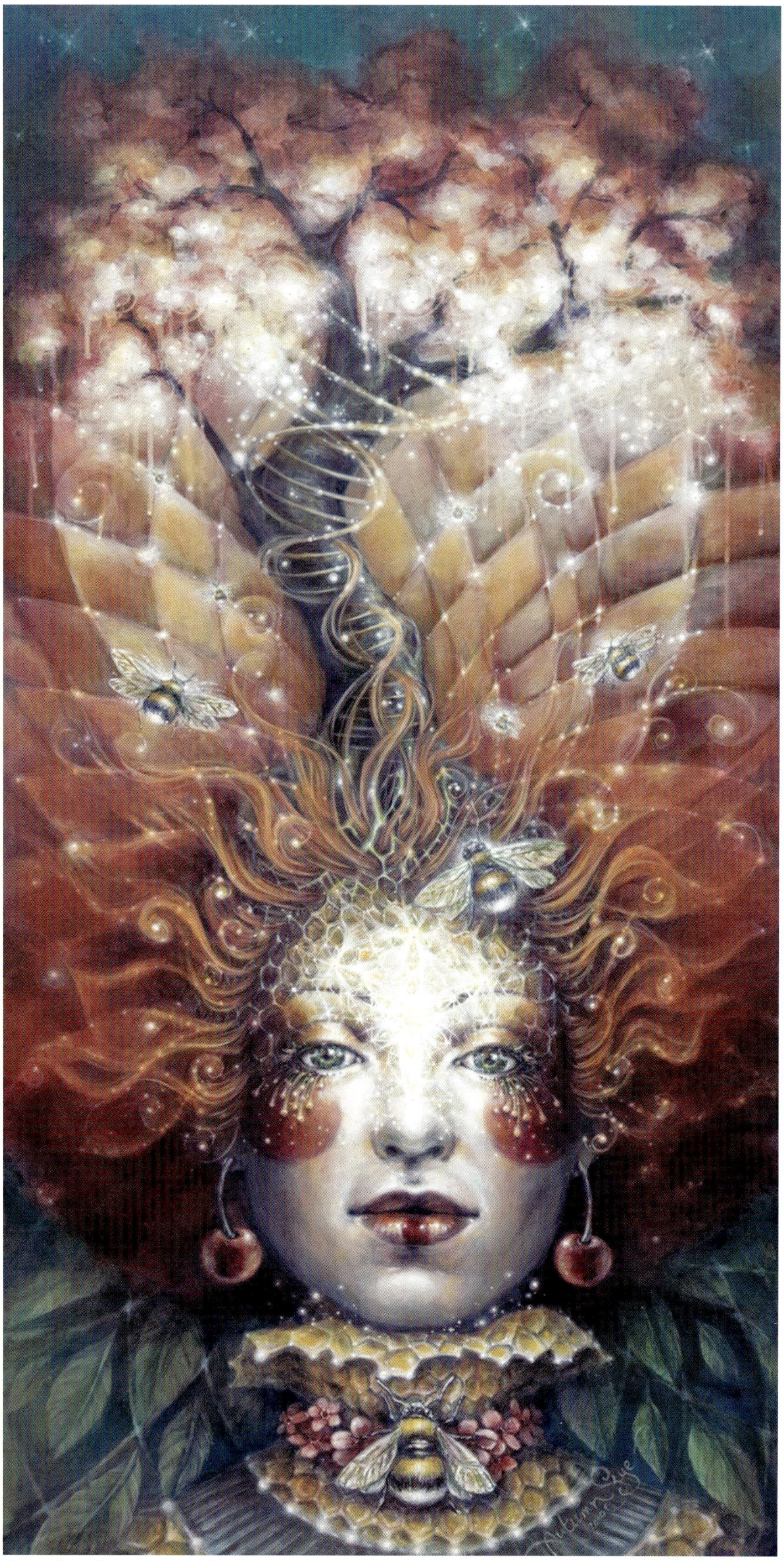

Queen Be · 122 x 61 cm · Acrylic on canvas

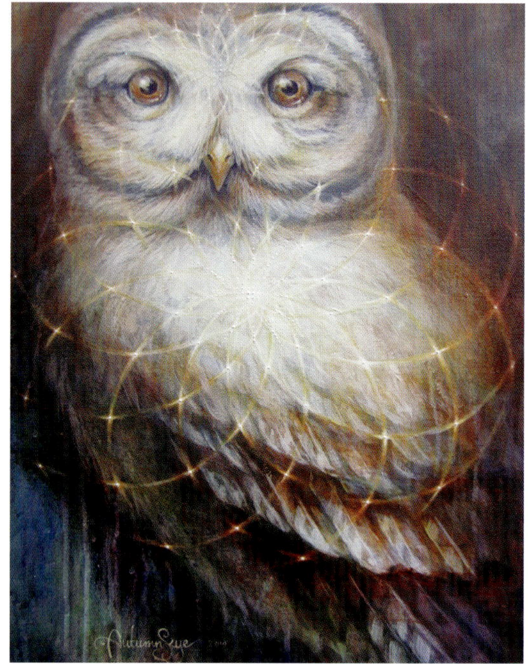

The Seer · 61 x 46 cm · Acrylic on canvas

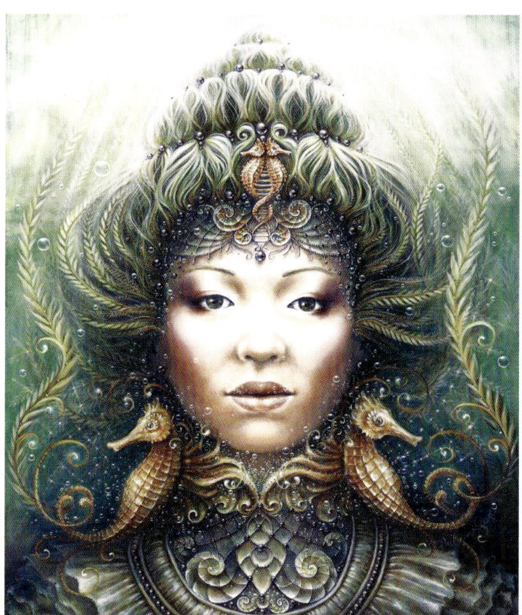

The Grace of Mer · 91,5 x 76 cm · Acrylic and mixed media

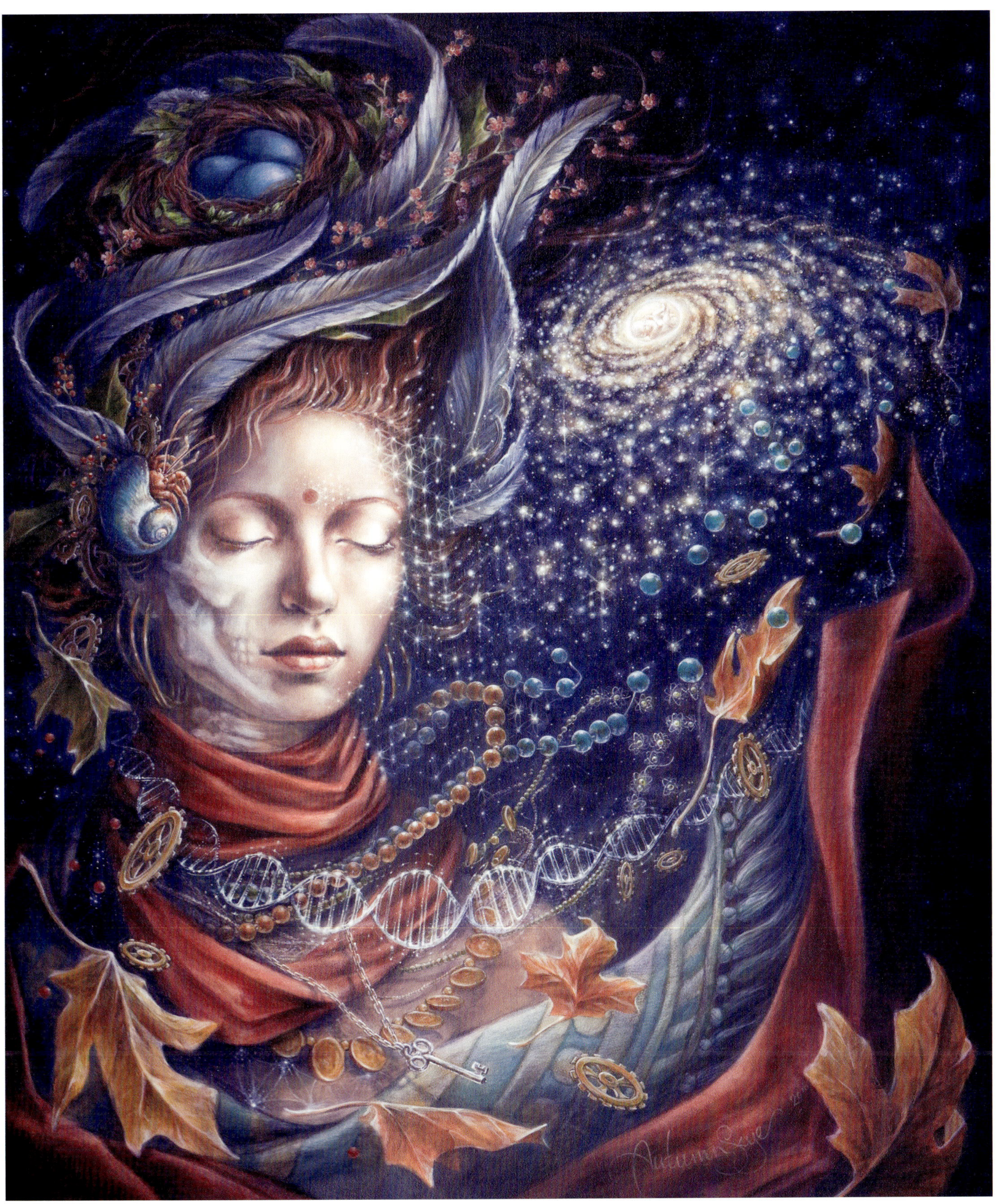

Remembering Eternity · 91,5 x 76 cm · Acrylic on canvas

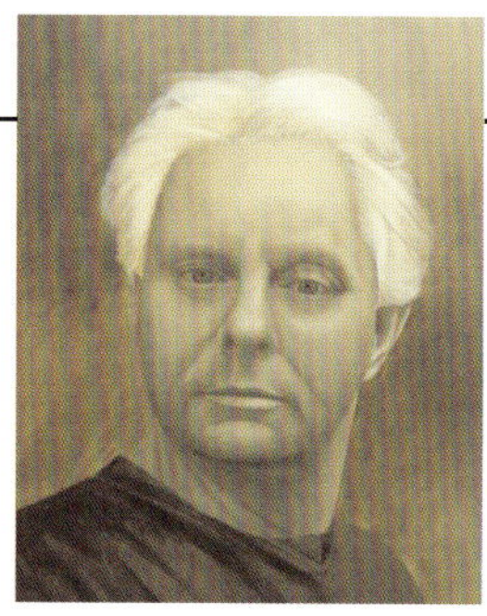

PETER VAN OOSTZANEN

1962 The Netherlands

www.vanoostzanen.com

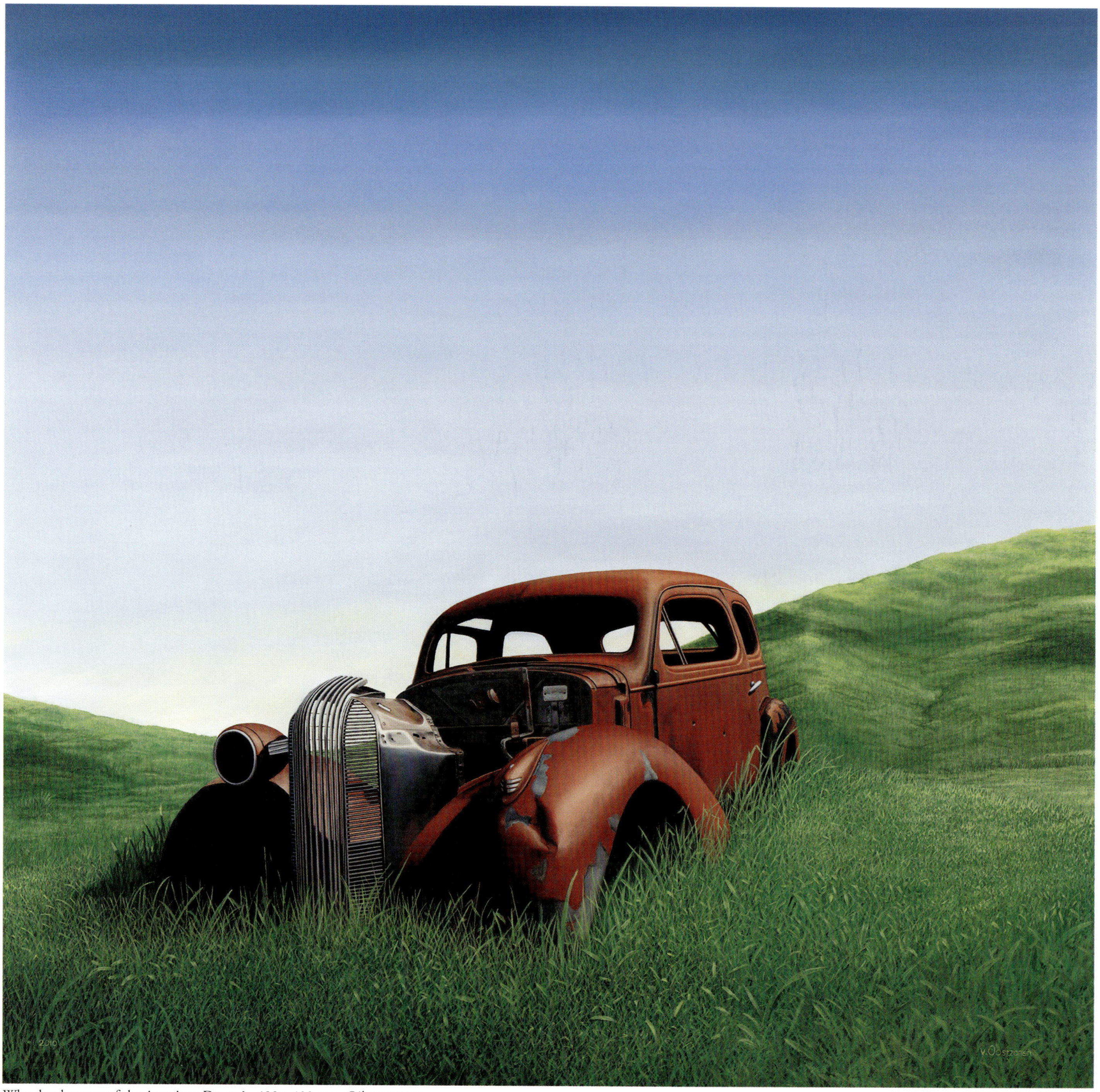

What has become of the American Dream? · 100 x 100 cm · Oil on canvas

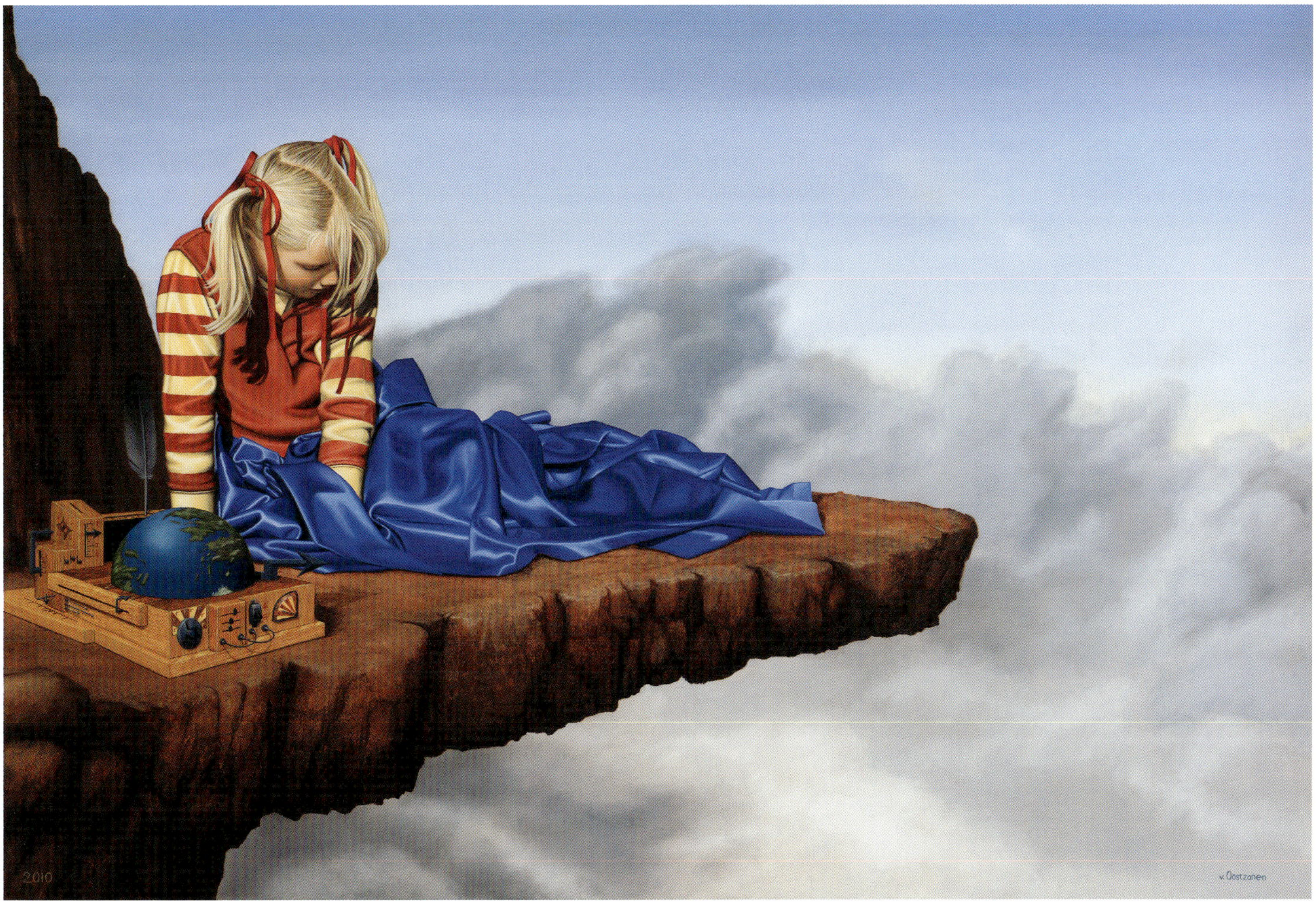

Try to Navigate by the Machine · 70 x 100 cm · Oil on canvas

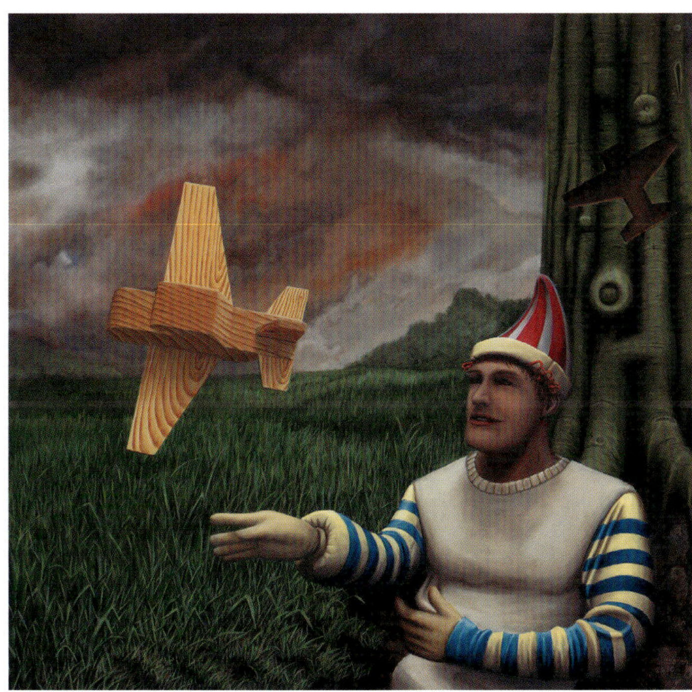

The Plain Baron · 30 x 30 cm · Oil on panel

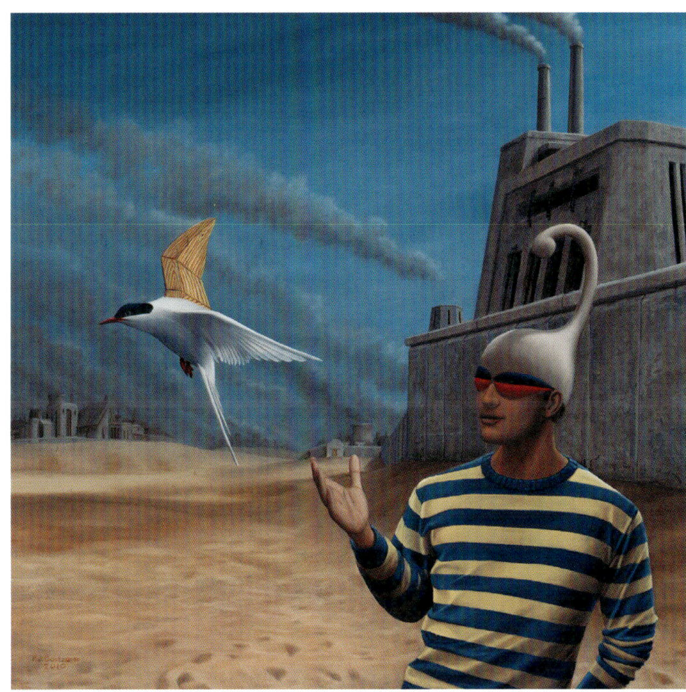

The Bird Repair · 30 x 30 cm · Oil on panel

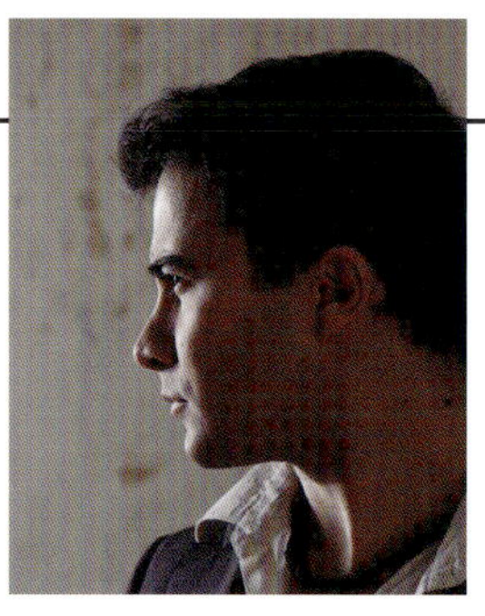

JOSÉ PARRA

1975 Mexico

www.joseparra.com

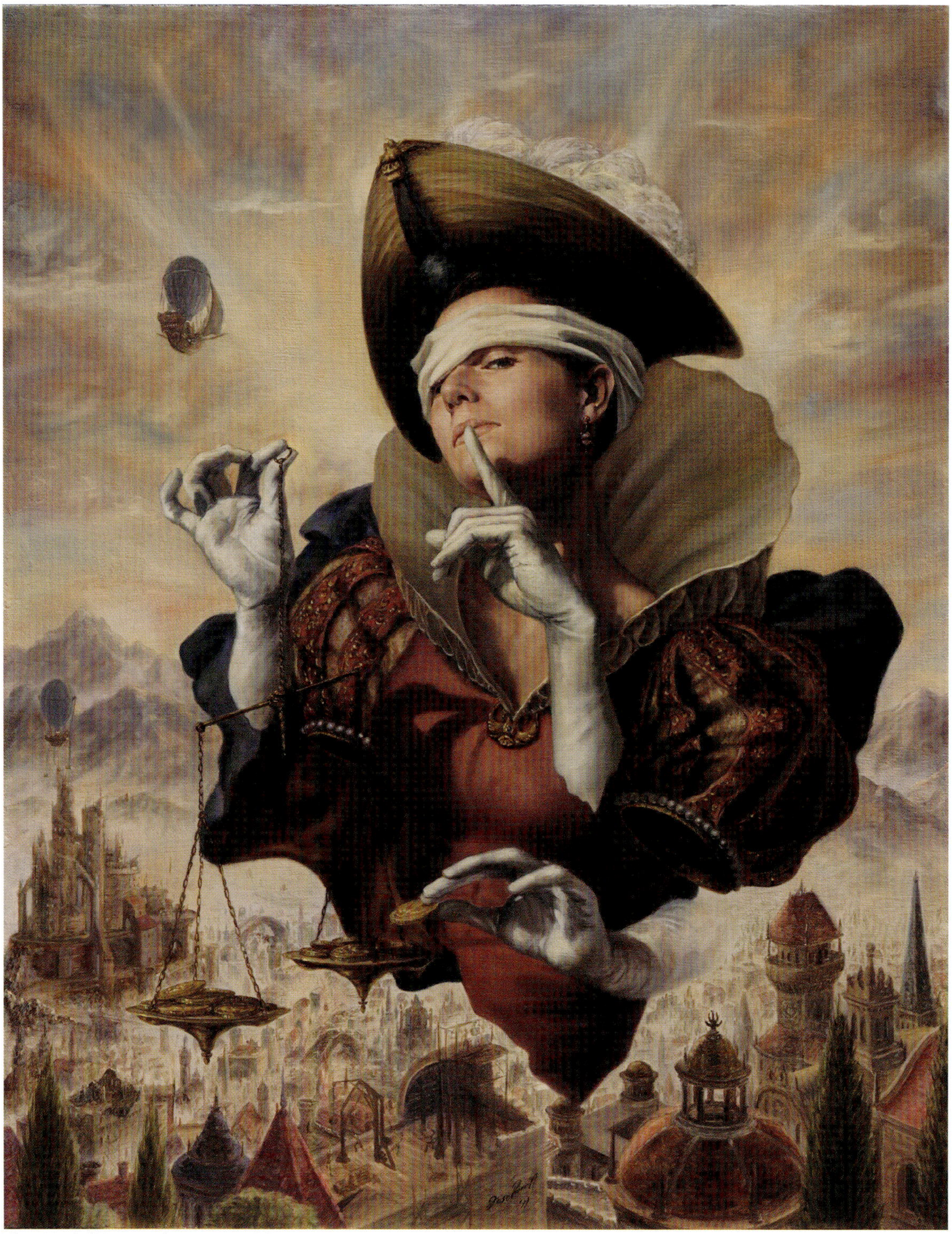

Three Handed Fortune · 68.5 x 89 cm · Oil on canvas

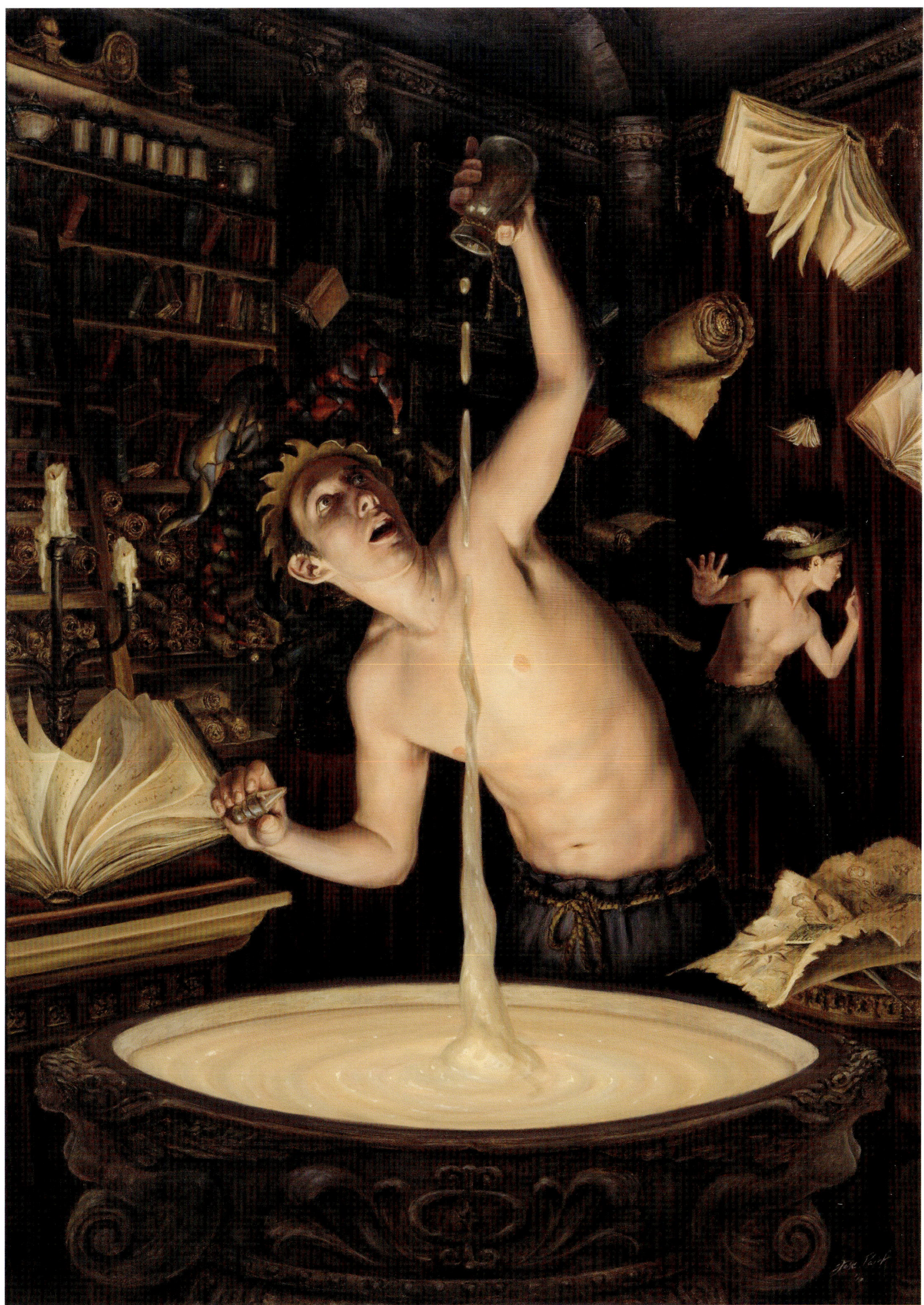

The Source of Miracles · 95 x 65 cm · Oil on canvas

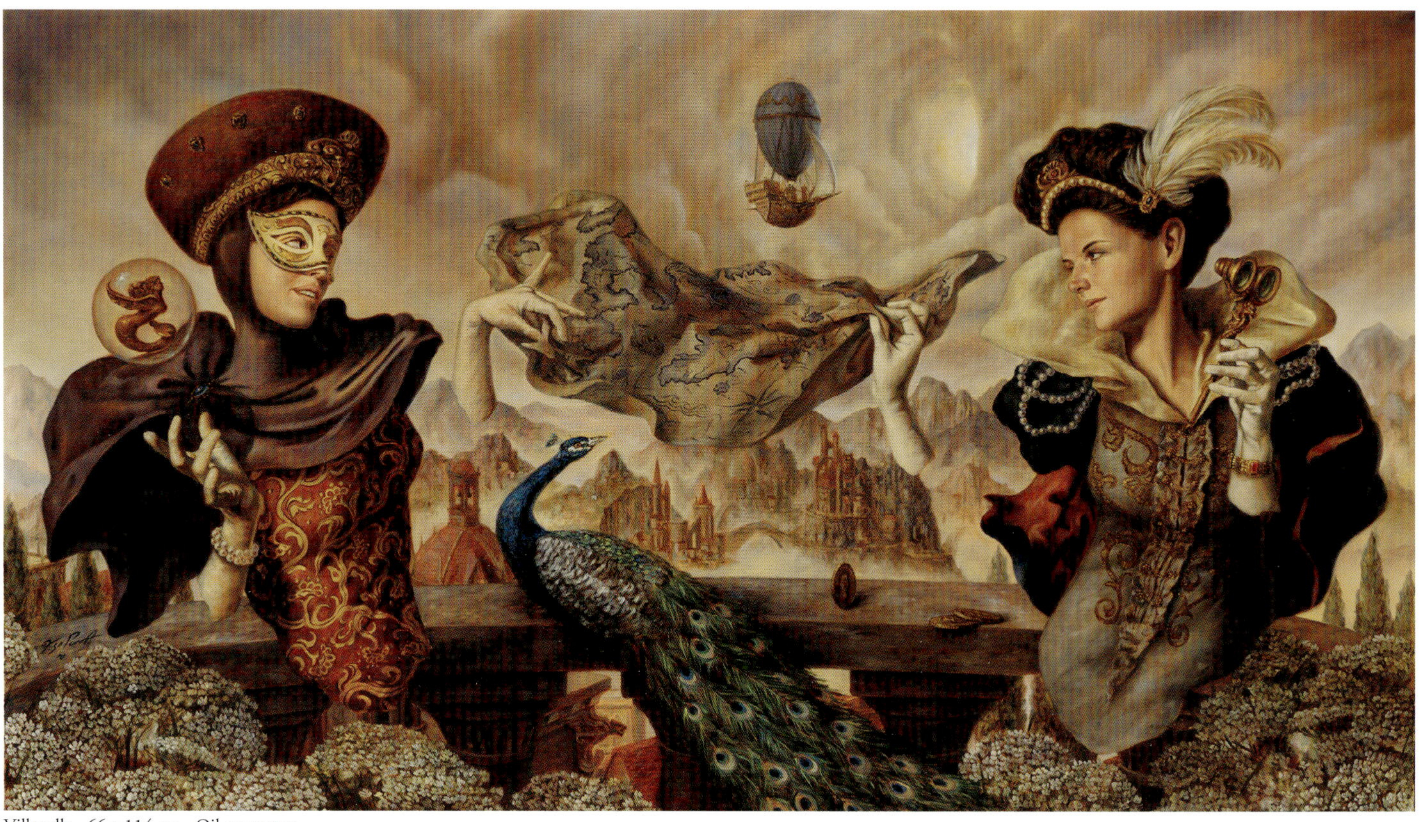

Villanelle · 66 x 114 cm · Oil on canvas

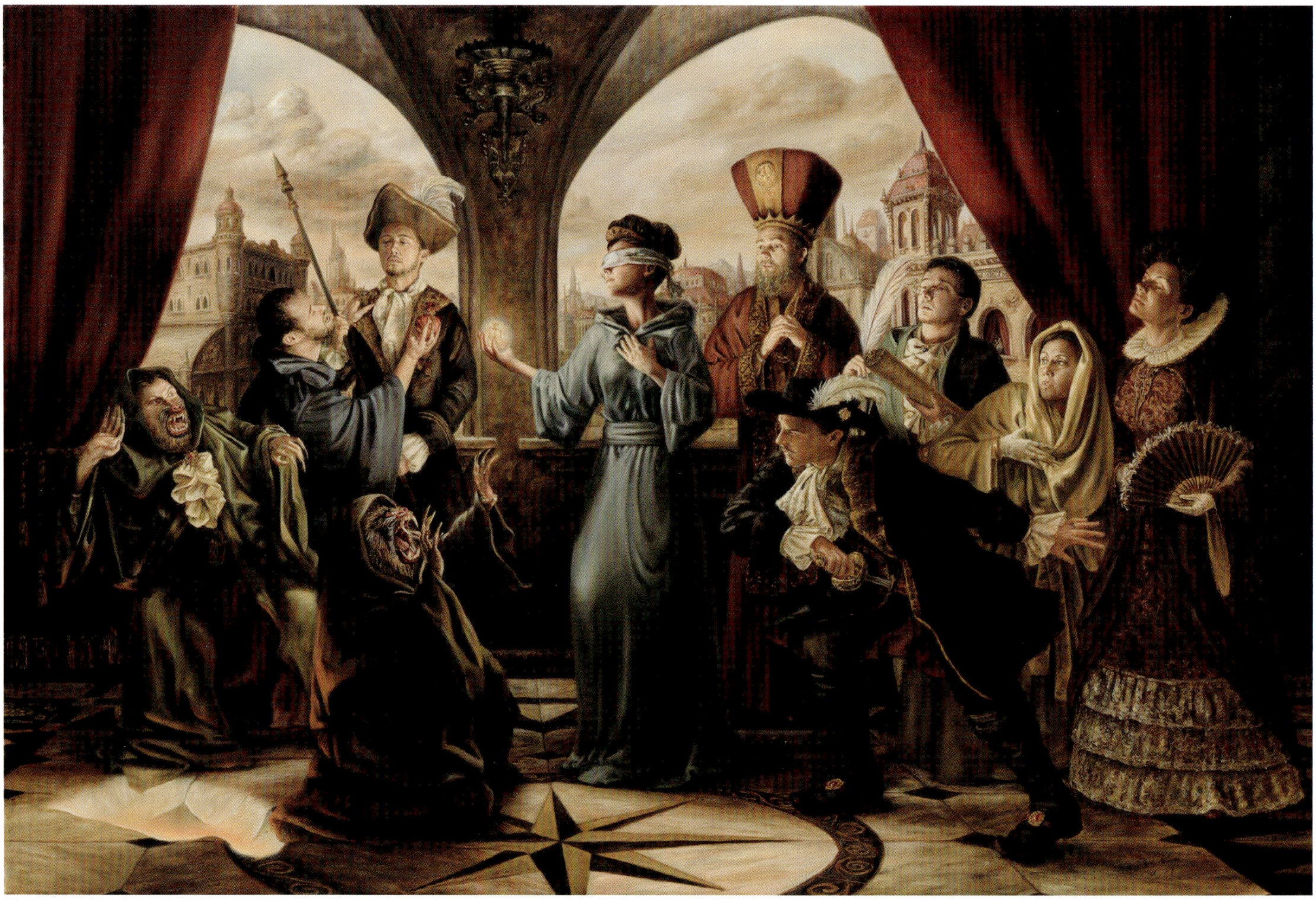

The Hall of Truth · 100 x 145 cm · Oil on canvas

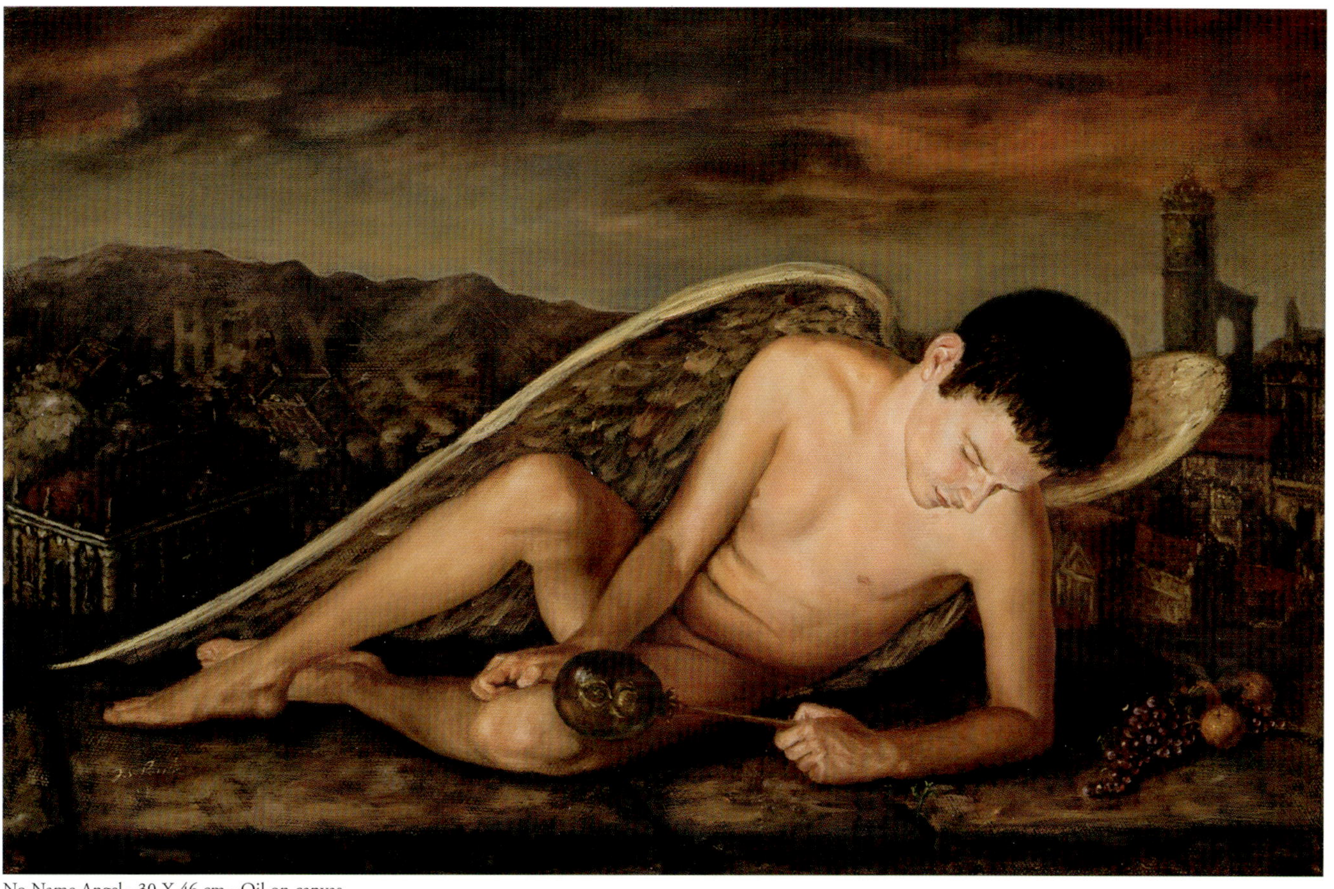
No Name Angel · 30 X 46 cm · Oil on canvas

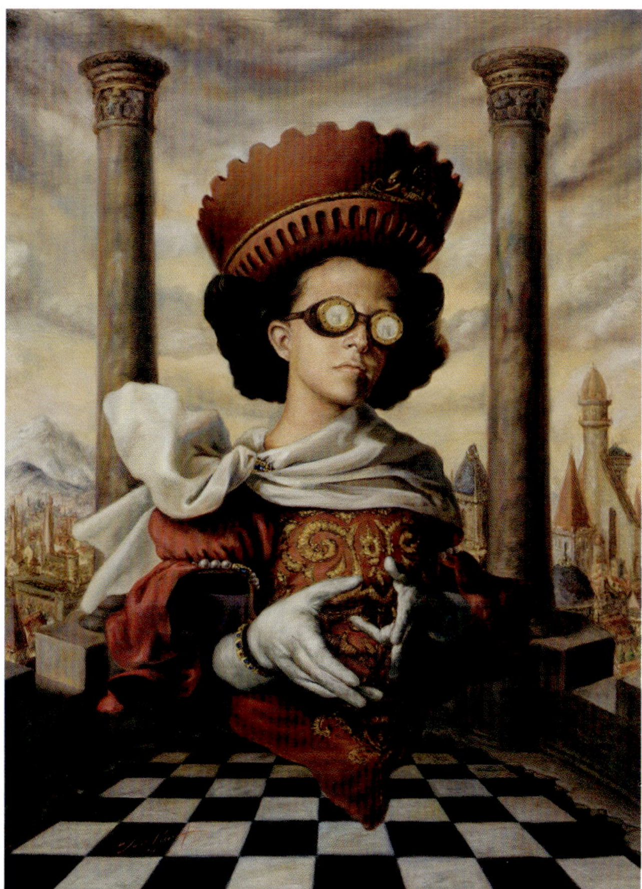
Red Tower (From the Chess series) · 61 x 43 cm · Oil on canvas

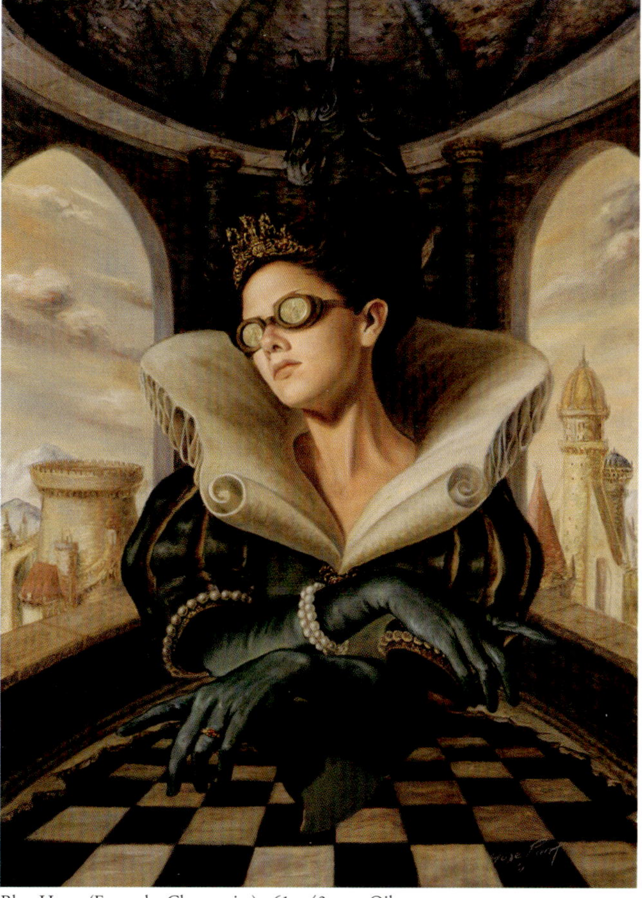
Blue Horse (From the Chess series) · 61 x 43 cm · Oil on canvas

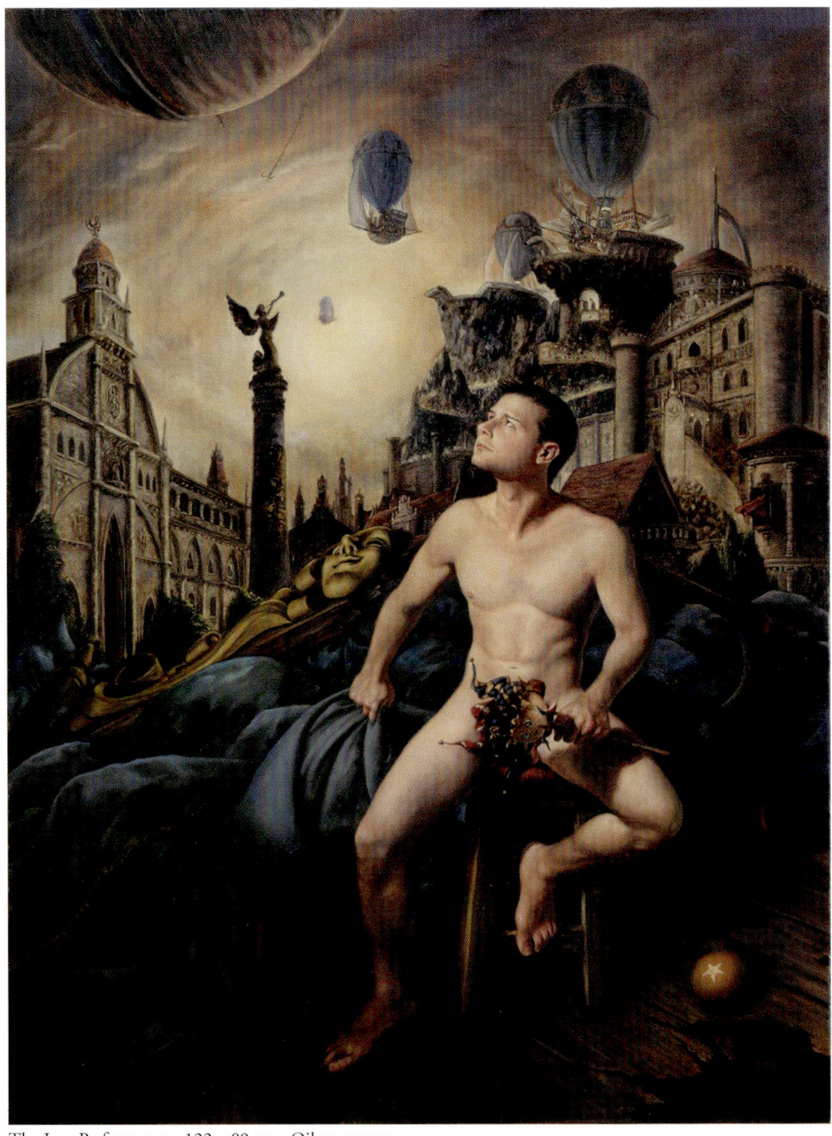

The Last Performance · 122 x 89 cm · Oil on canvas

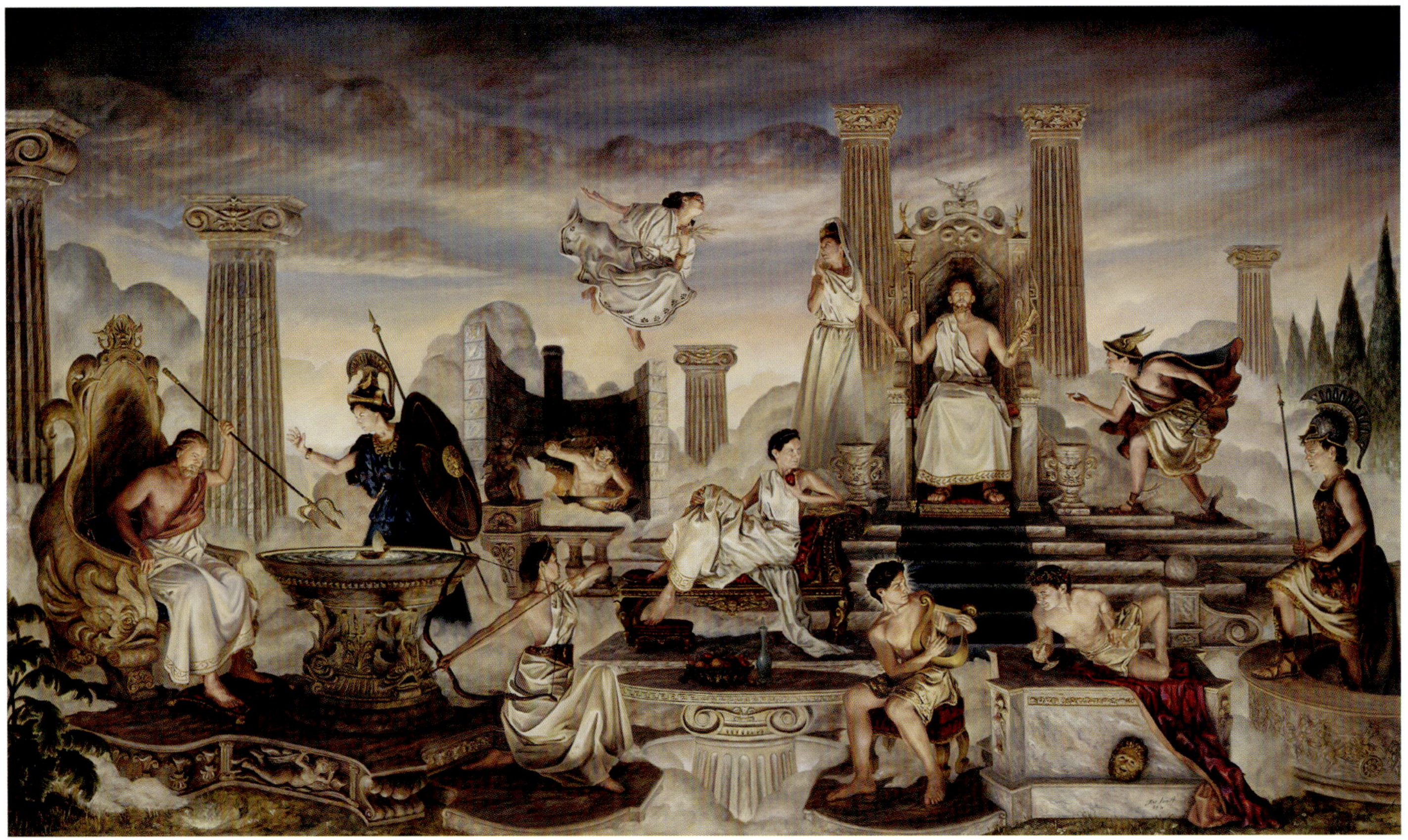

Olympus · 152 x 241cm · Oil on canvas

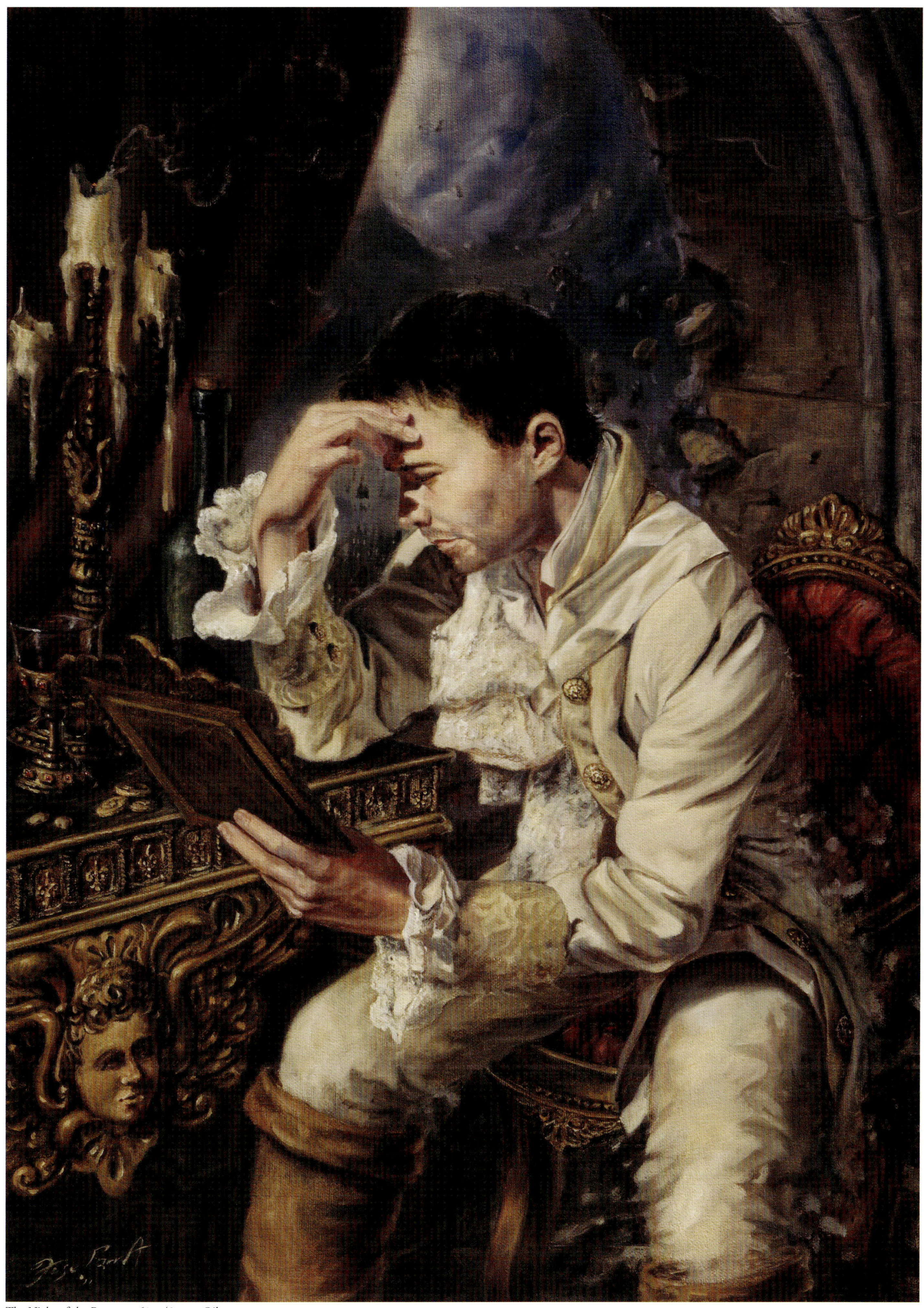
The Night of the Rapture · 61 x 43 cm · Oil on canvas

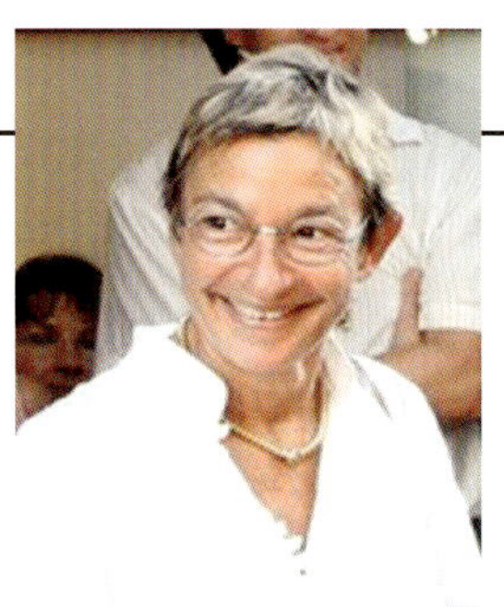

ISABELLE PLANTÉ

1949 France

www.isabelleplante.com

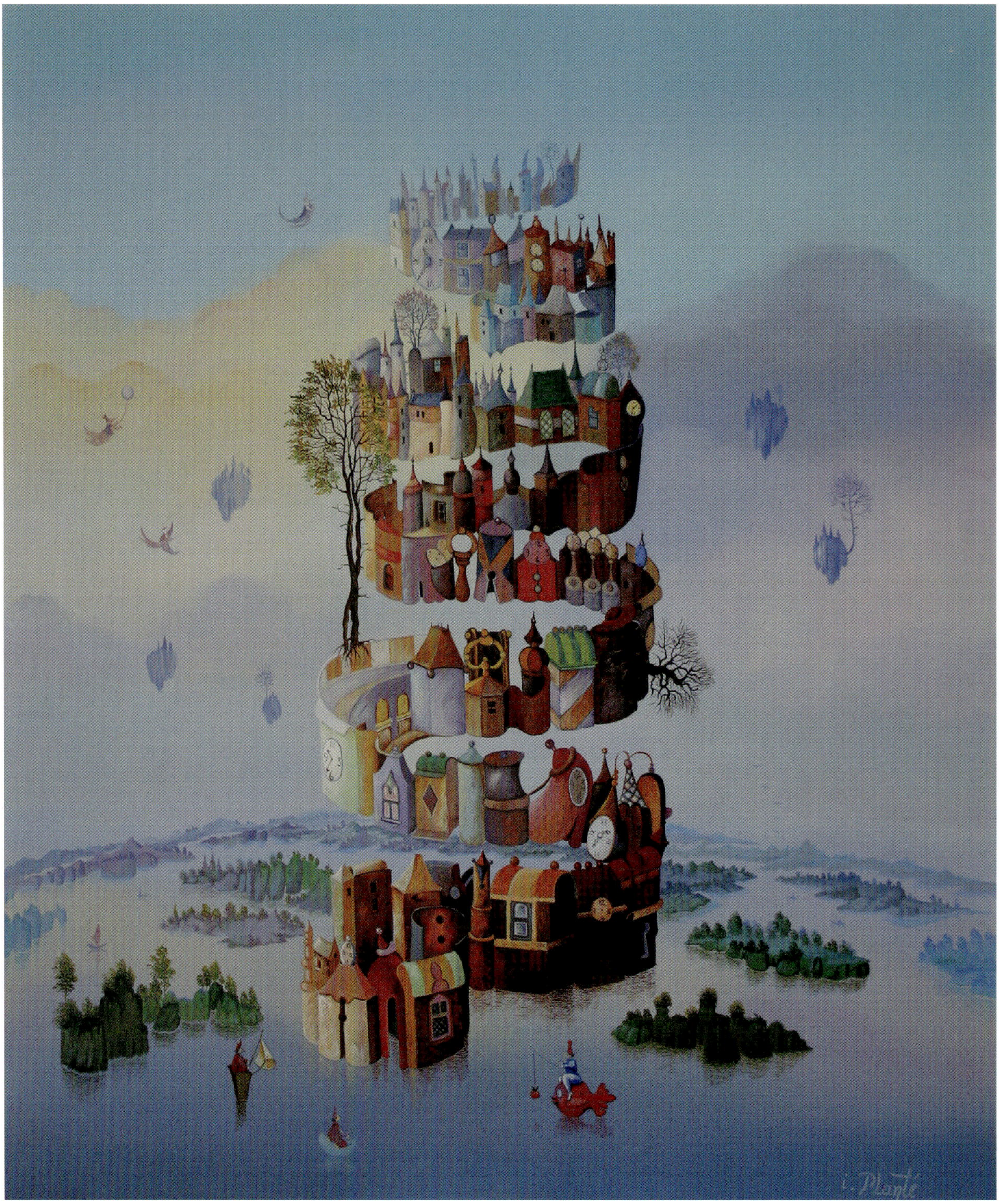

Audace · 61 x 50 cm · Oil on canvas

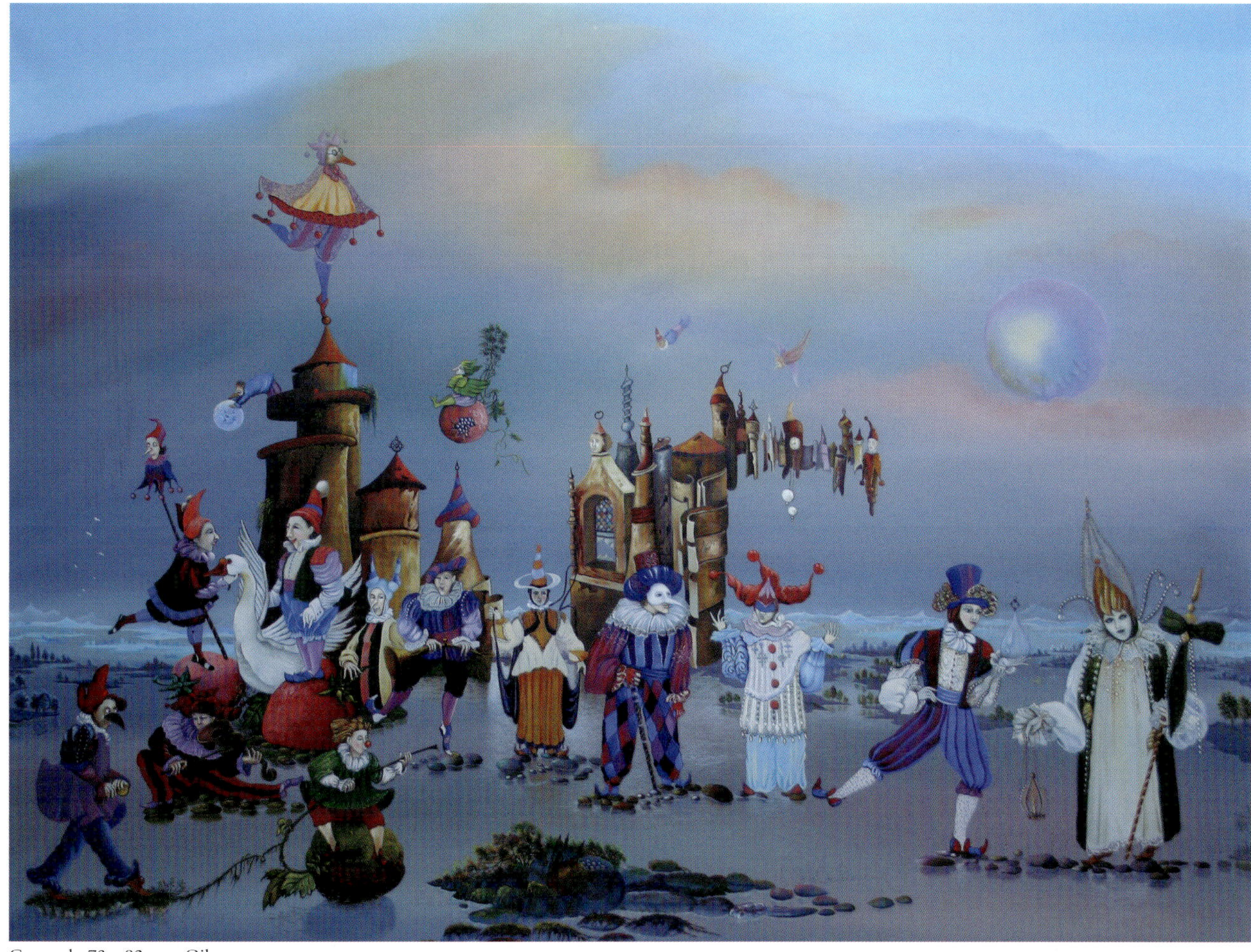

Carnaval · 73 x 92 cm · Oil on canvas

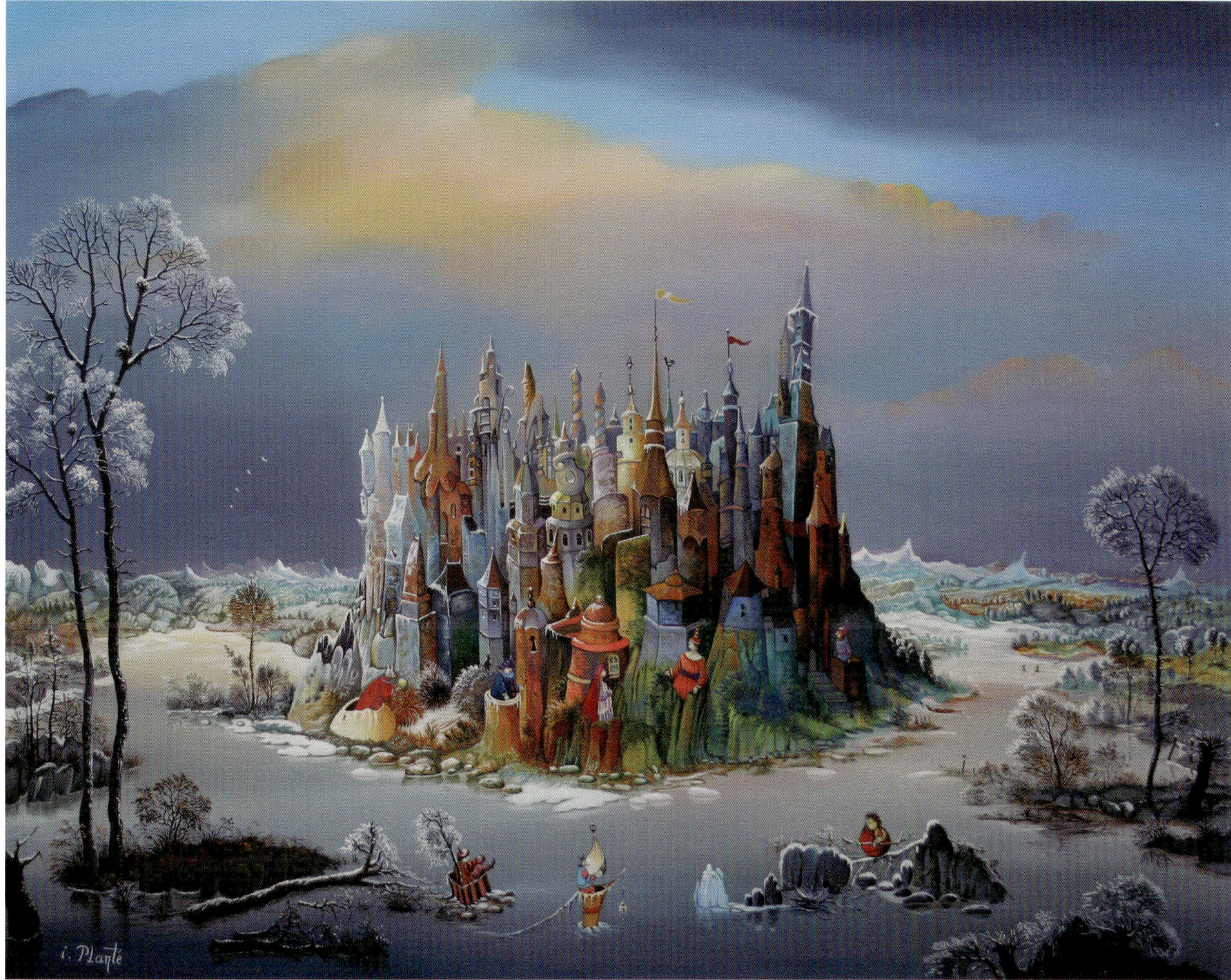

Emergitur · 65 x 81 cm · Oil on canvas

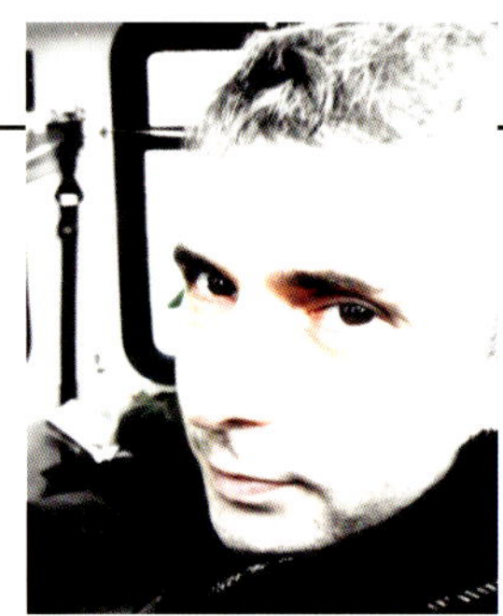

T.B. RATHBUN

1966 Denmark / USA

http://messart.gallerisider.dk

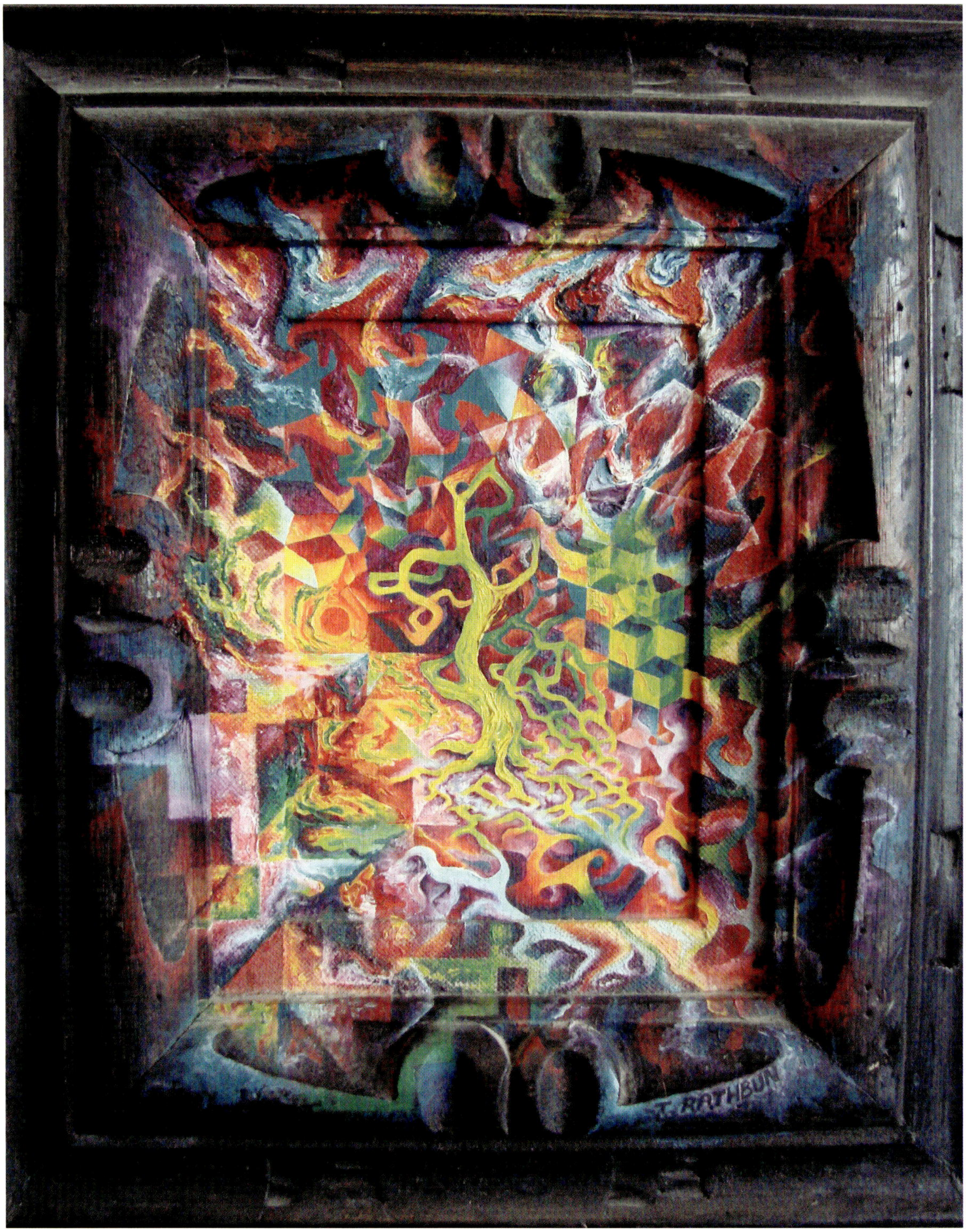

Tree · 28 x 23 cm · Oil on canvas board and frame

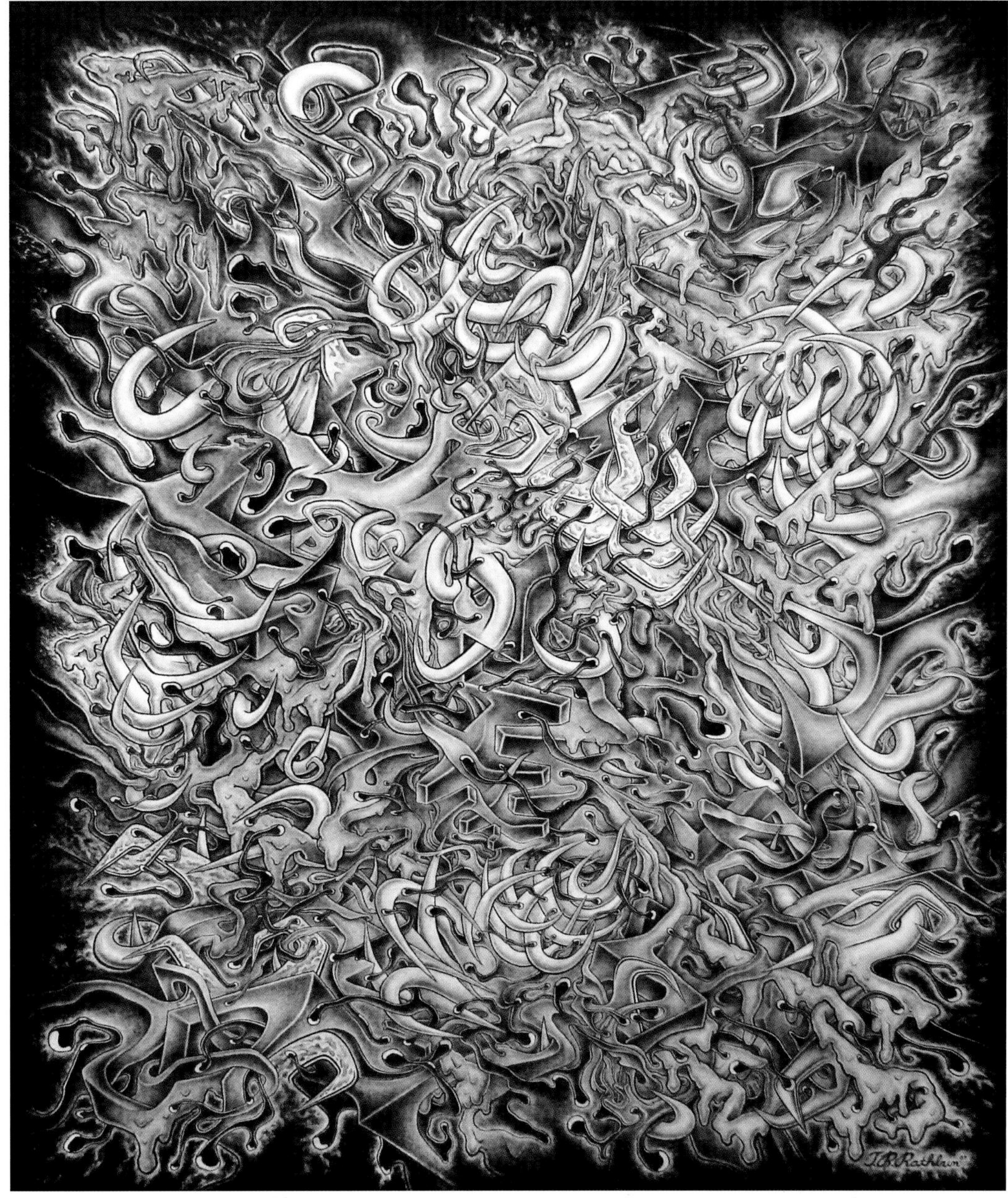

Intraicate Maddness · 60 x 50 cm · Oil on canvas

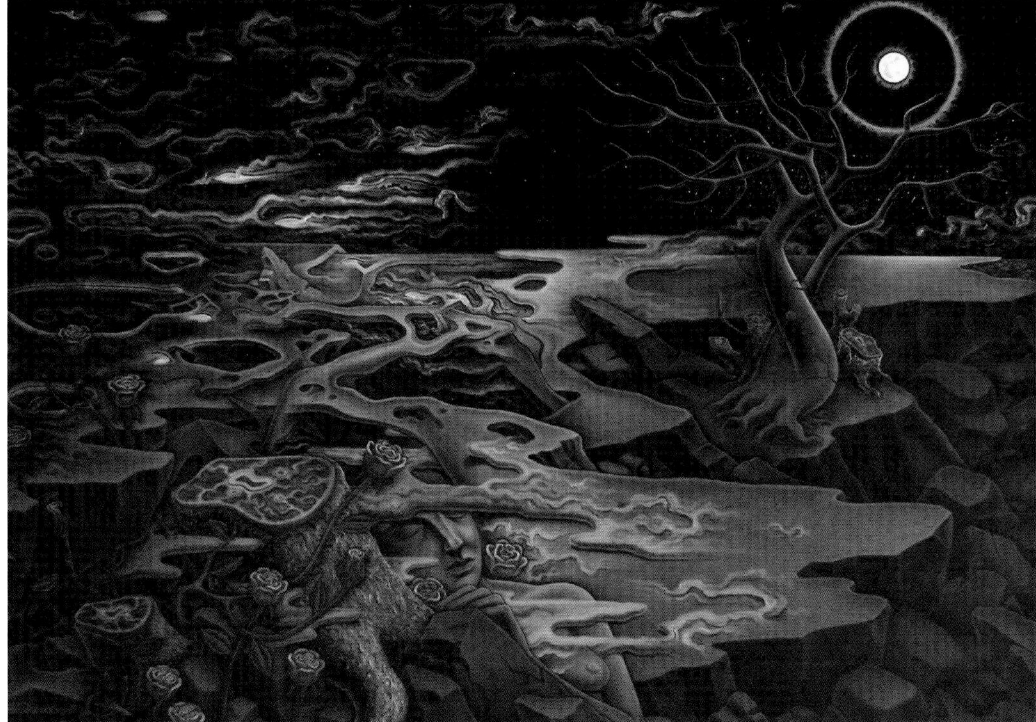

Asleep with Stumps · 70 x 100 cm · Oil on canvas

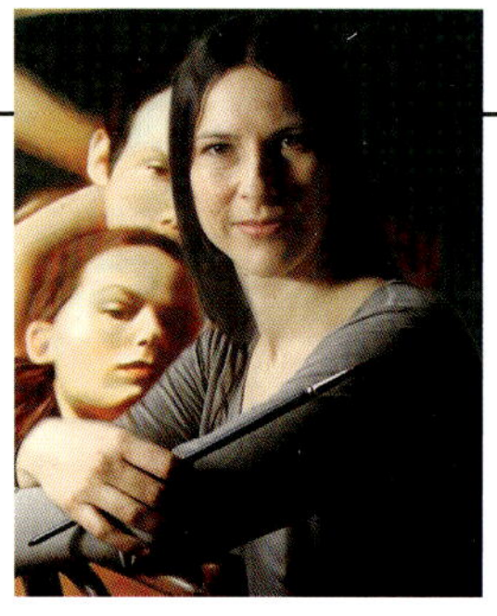

JOLANDA RICHTER

1971 Austria

www.jolanda.at

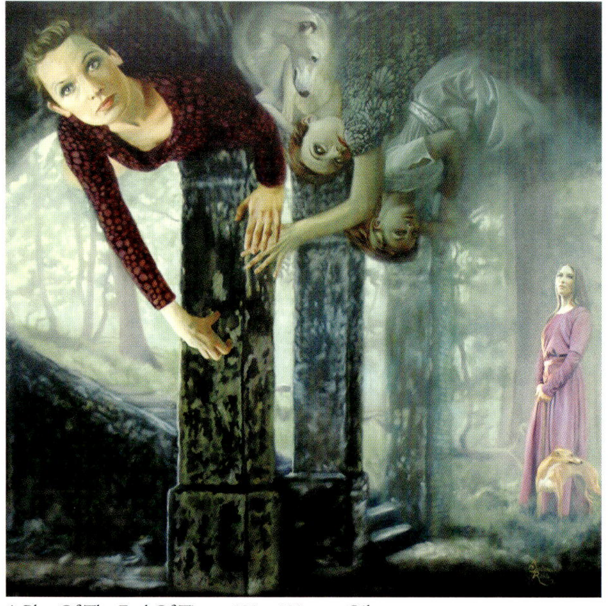

A Play Of The End Of Time · 100 x 100 cm · Oil on canvas

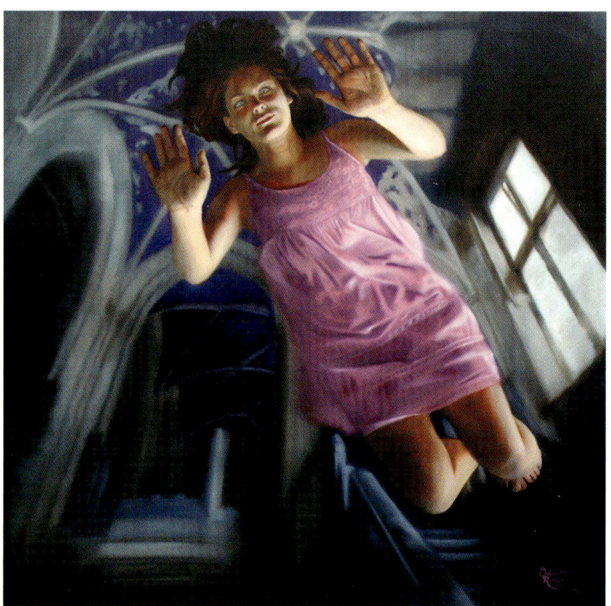

Lucid Dream · 100 x 100 cm · Oil on canvas

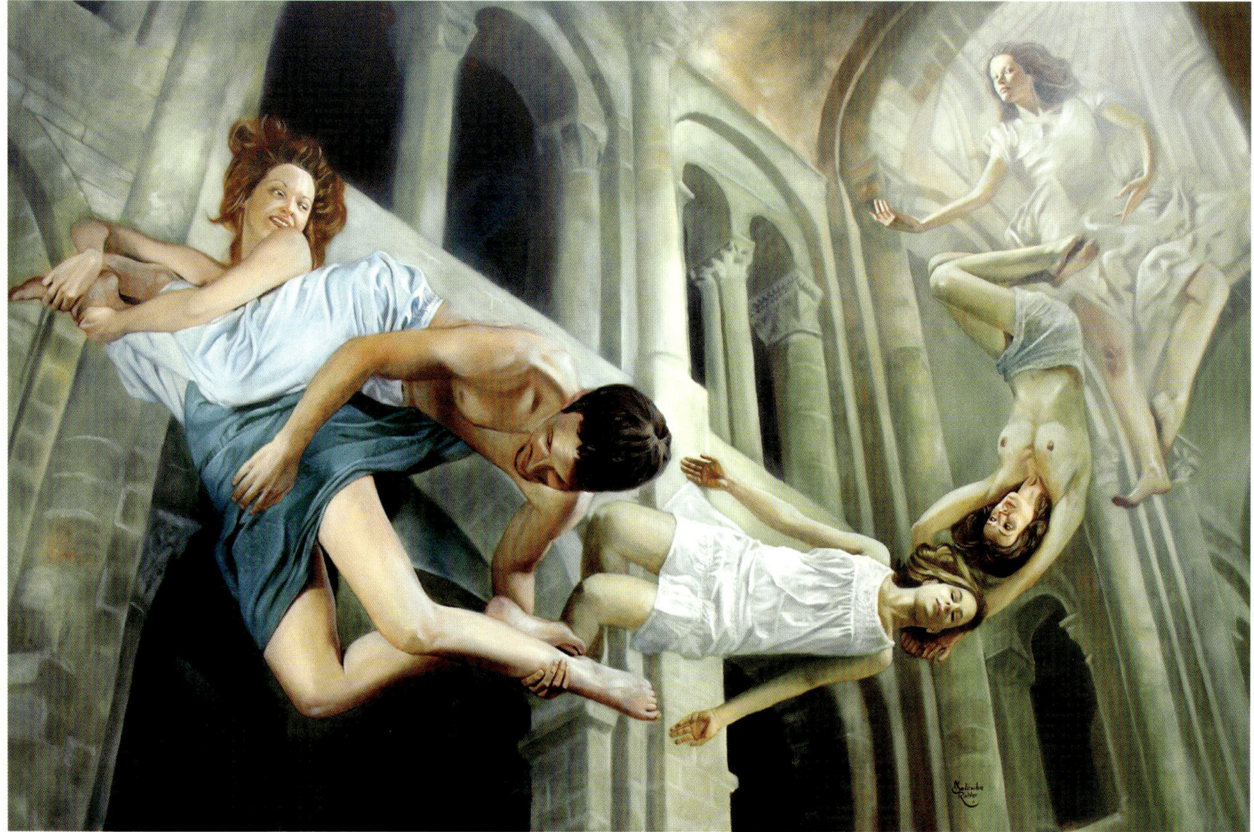

Veni Creator Spiritus · 120 x 180 cm · Oil on canvas

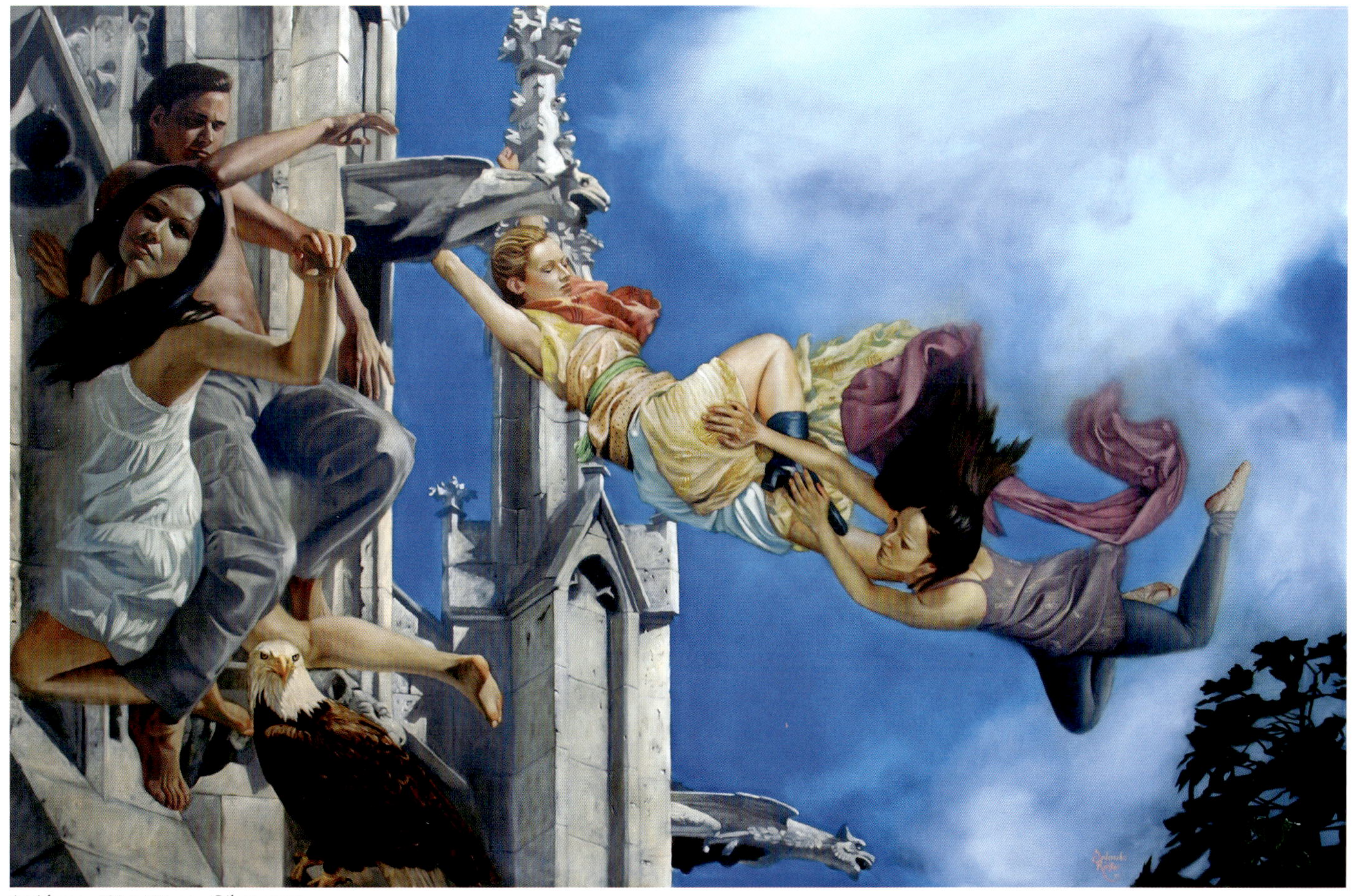

Antitheses · 120 x 180 cm · Oil on canvas

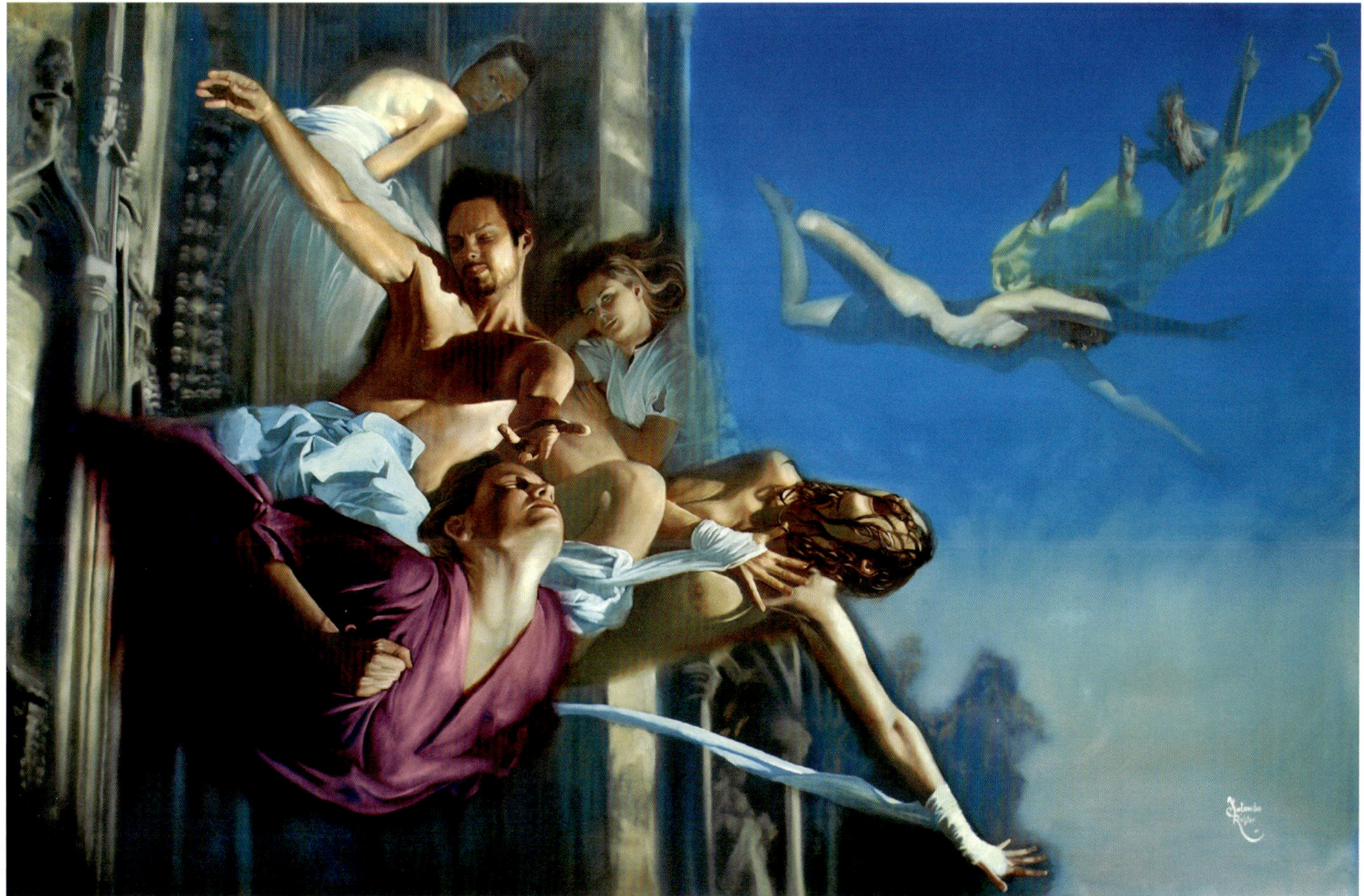

Dies Irae · 140 x 210 cm · Oil on canvas

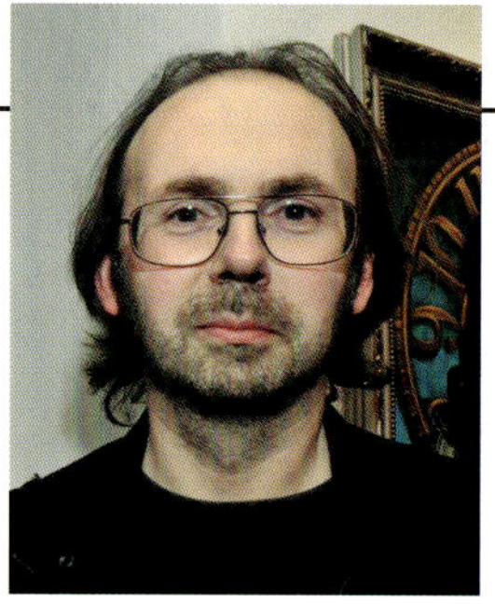

TIM ROOSEN

1972 Belgium

www.novabelgica.com

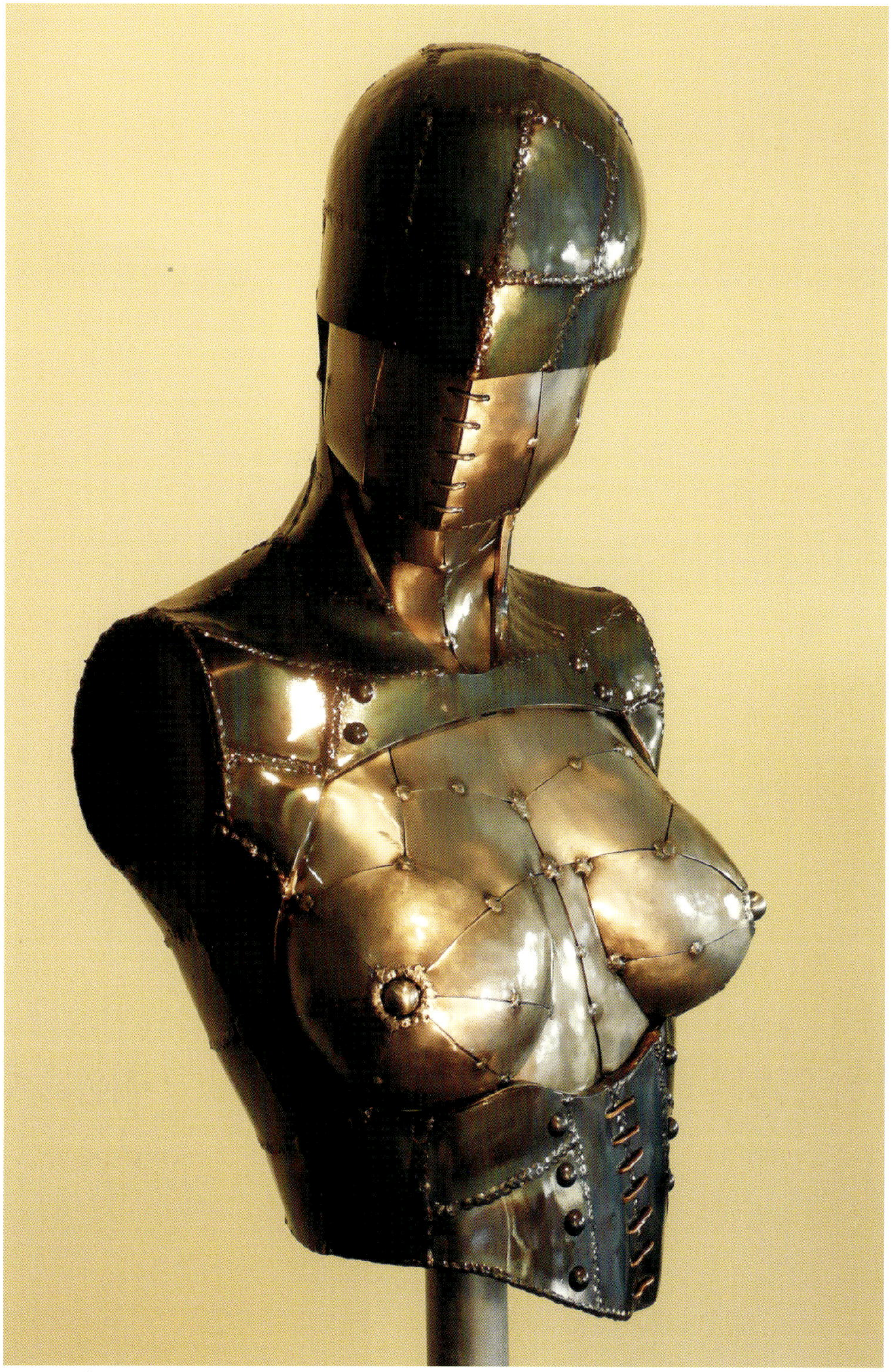

Luxuria · Life size · Mild steel

Photos by
Ansgar Noeth
www.ansgarnoeth.de

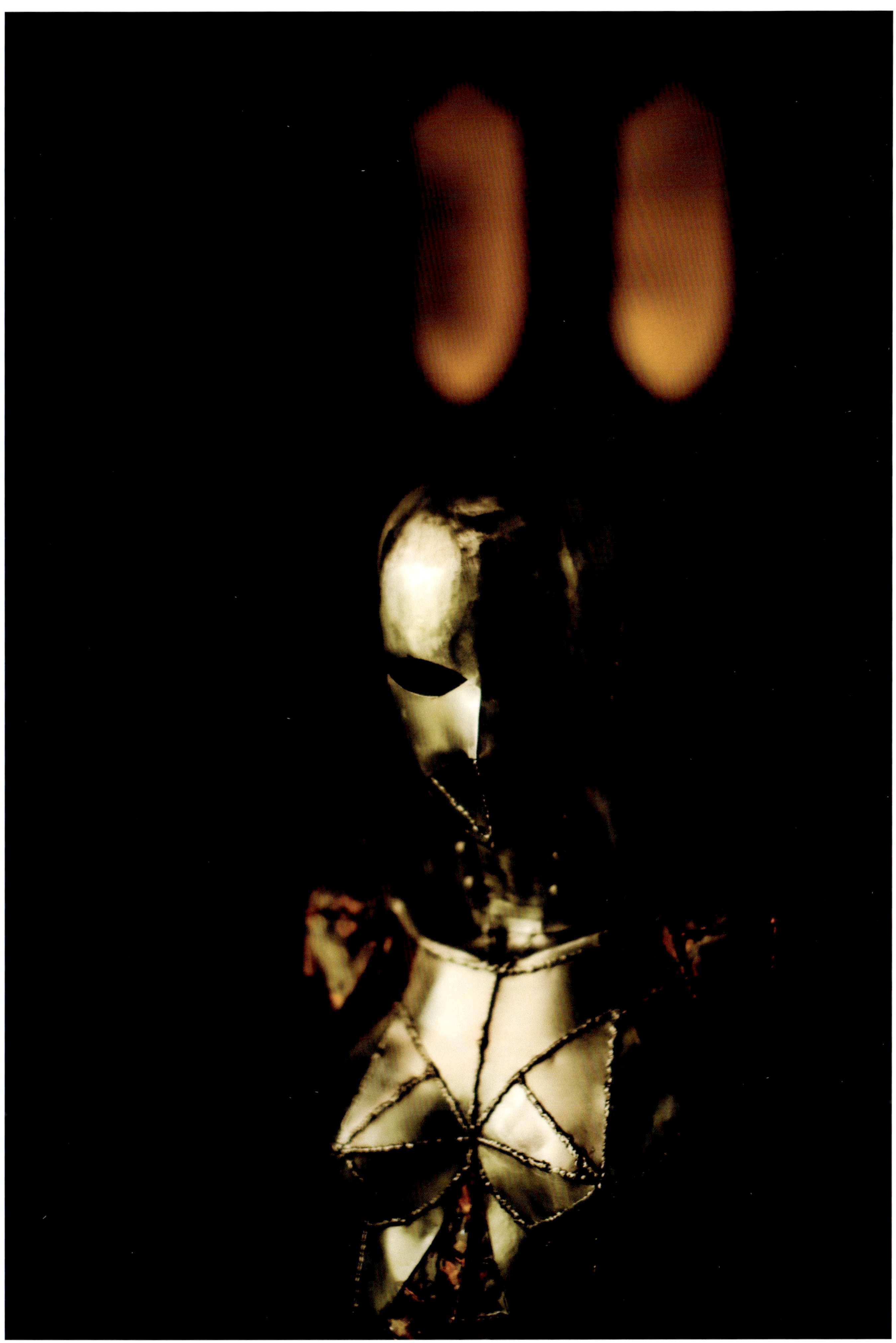

Callisto · Life size · Mild steel and copper

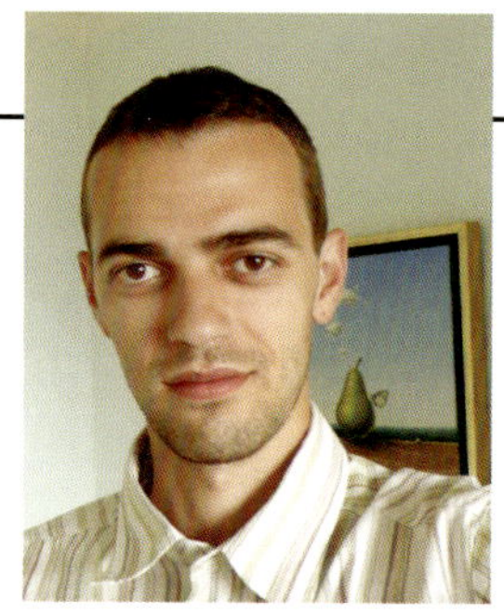

ISKREN SEMKOV

1984 Bulgaria

www.my.awenart.info/iskren

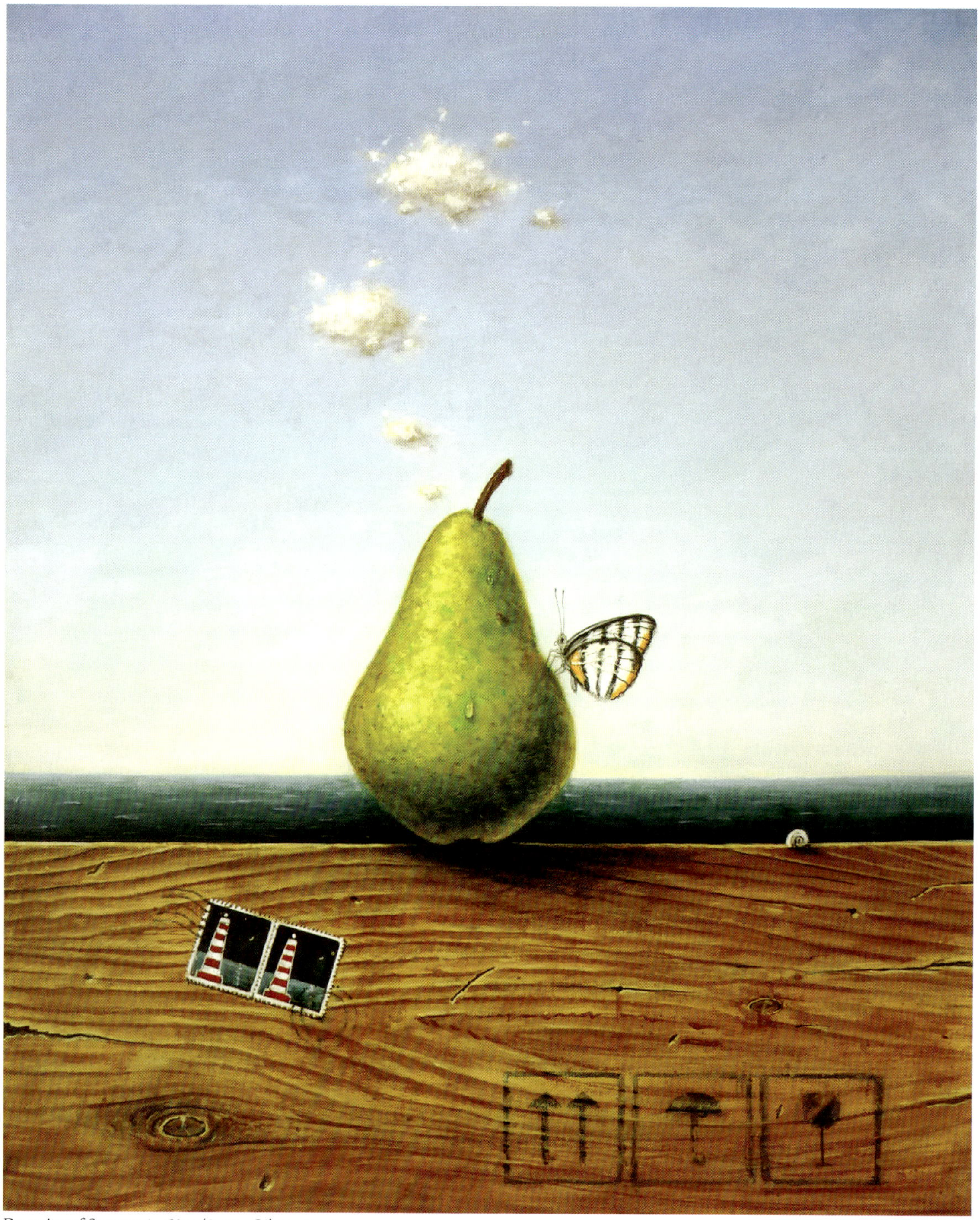

Dreaming of Summer 1 · 50 x 40 cm · Oil on canvas

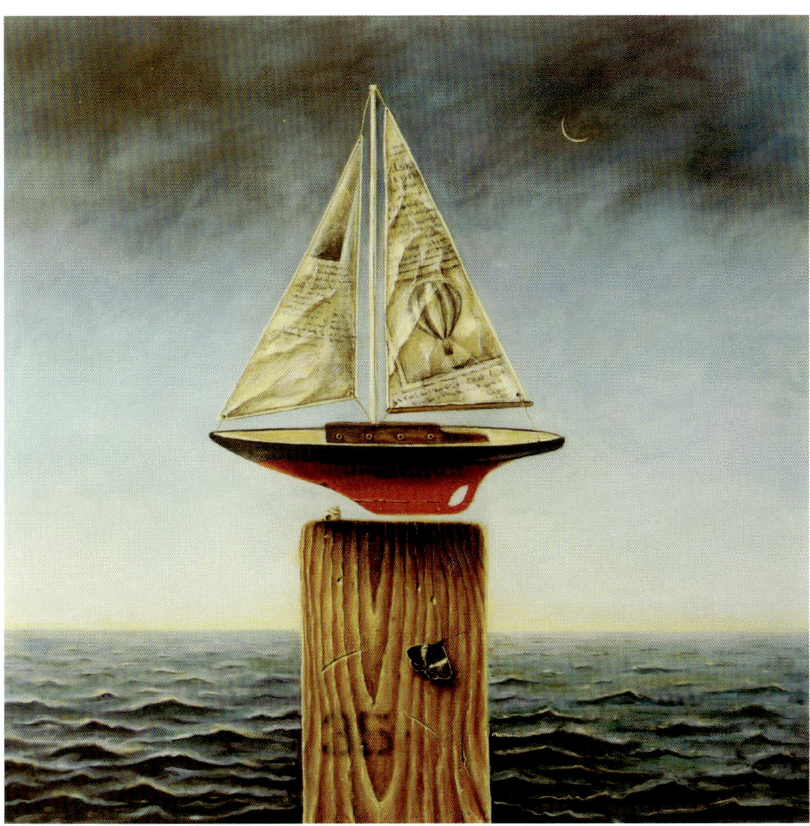
Mental Journey · 70 x 70 cm · Oil on canvas

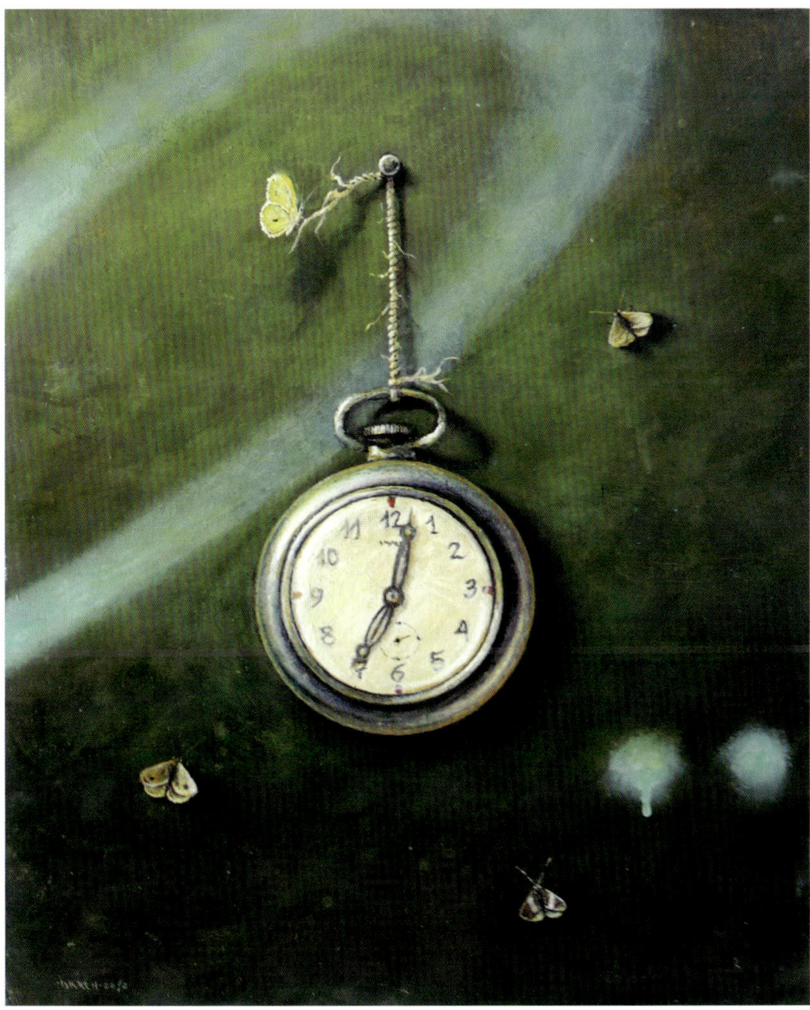
Time Travelers · 25 x 20 cm · Oil on panel

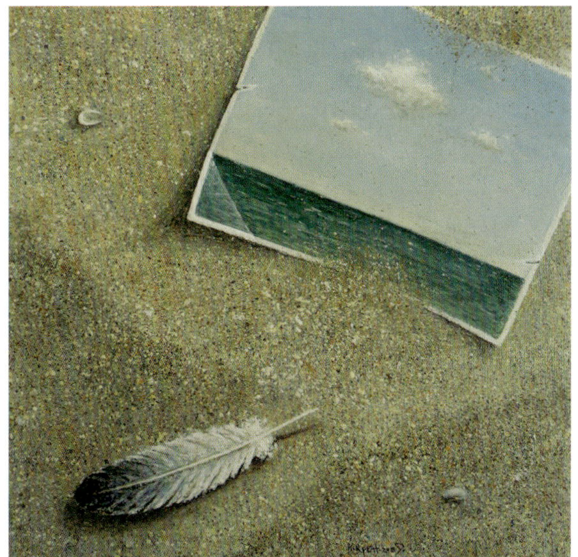
Sea Memory 1 · 30 x 30 cm · Oil on canvas

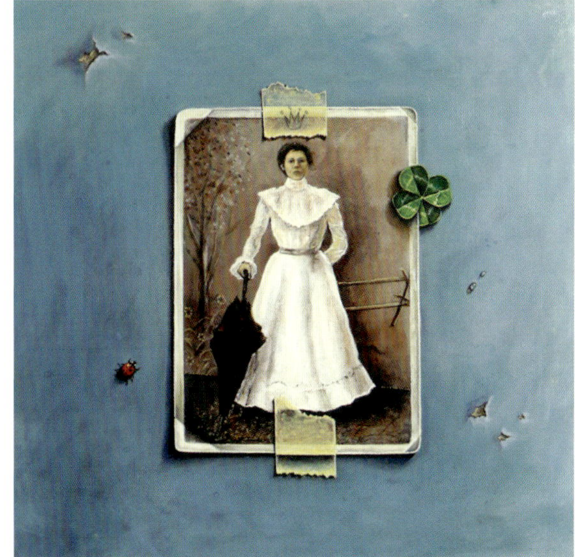
The New Princess · 30 x 30 cm · Oil on canvas

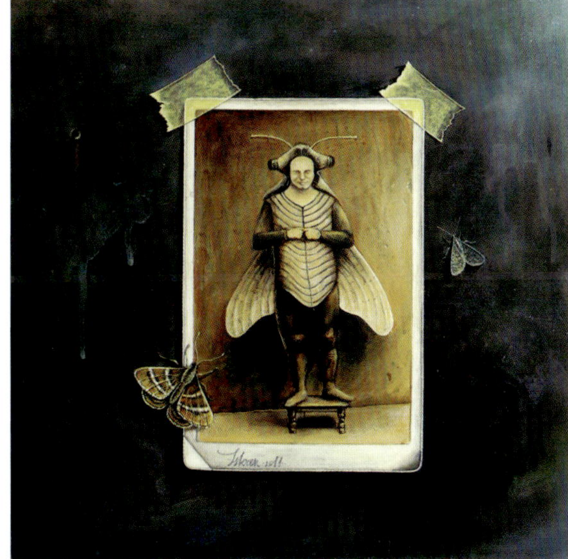
The Father of Butterflies · 30 x 30 cm · Oil on canvas

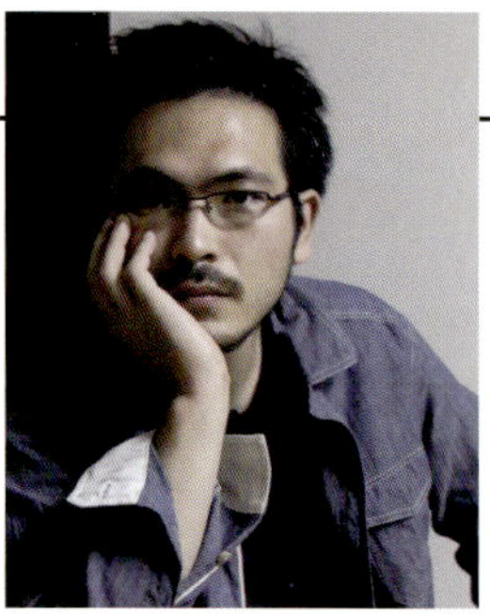

YU SUGAWARA

1977 Japan

http://homepage2.nifty.com/yakeiban/index.html

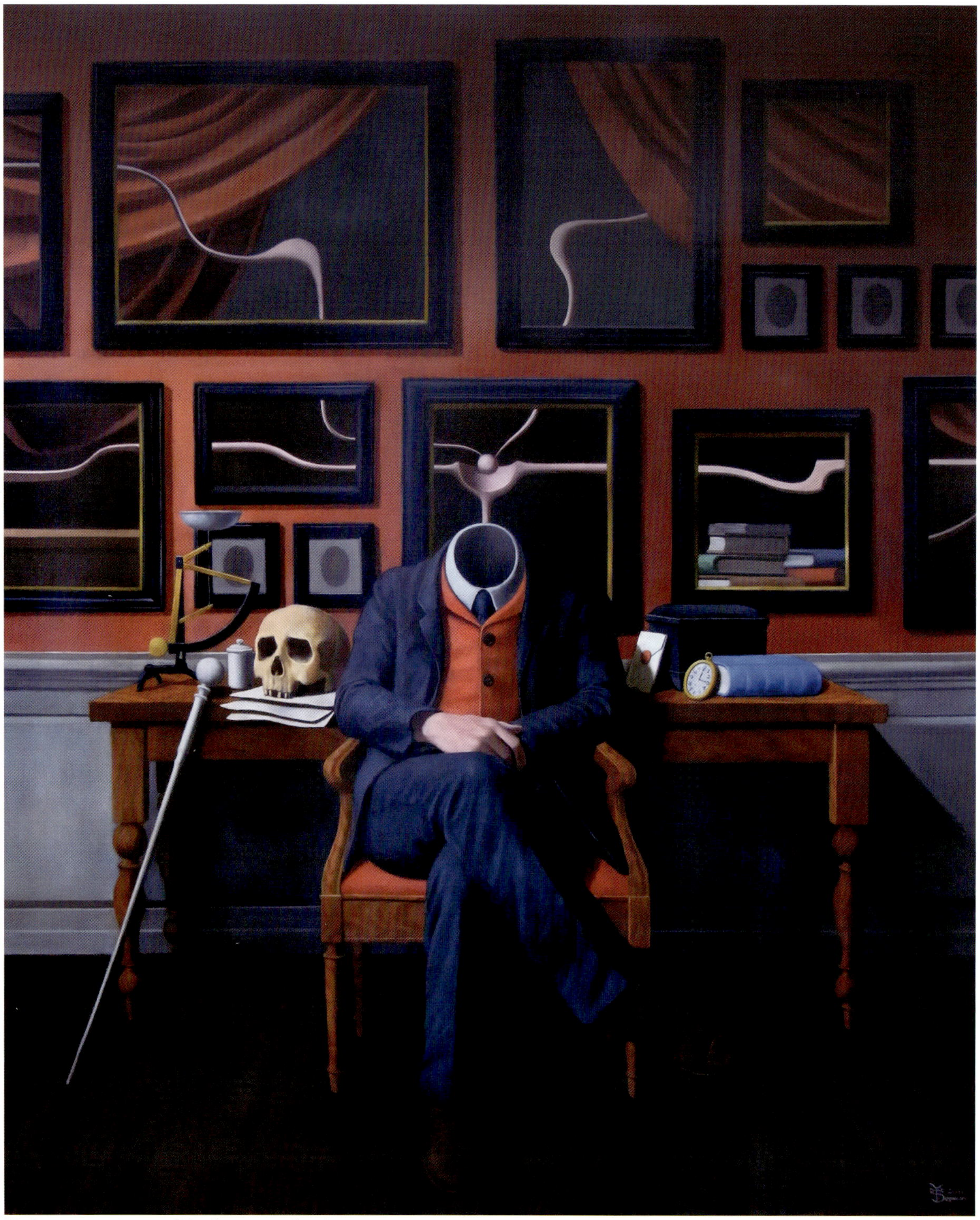

His Room · 91 x 72,7 cm · Oil and tempera on board

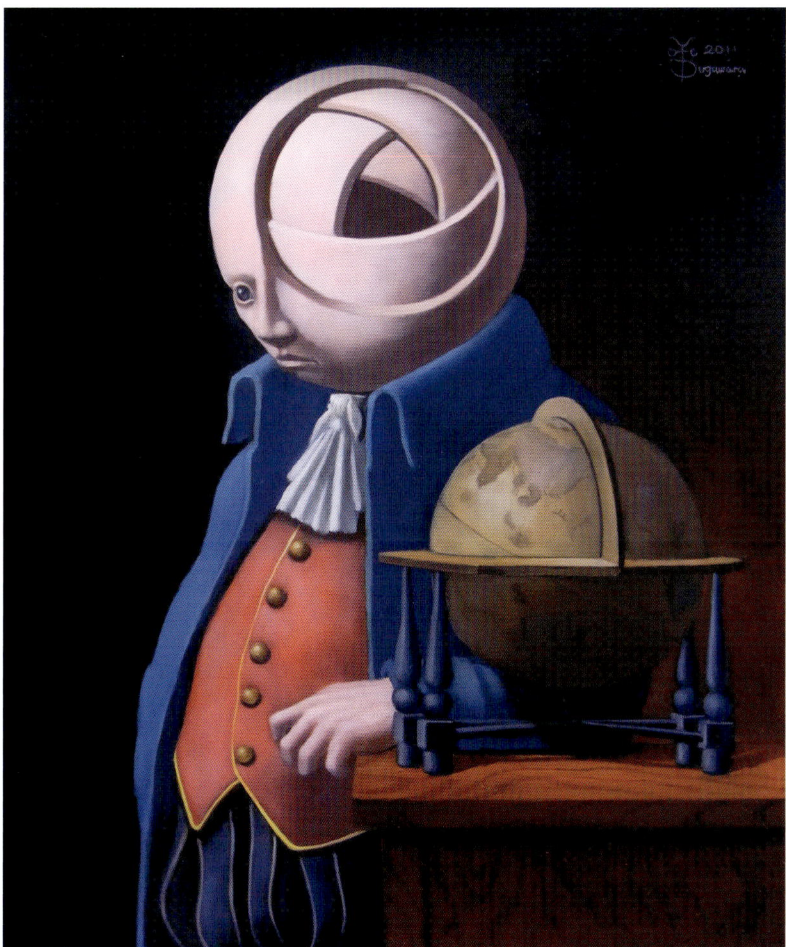

Geographer · 27,3 x 22 cm · Oil and tempera on board

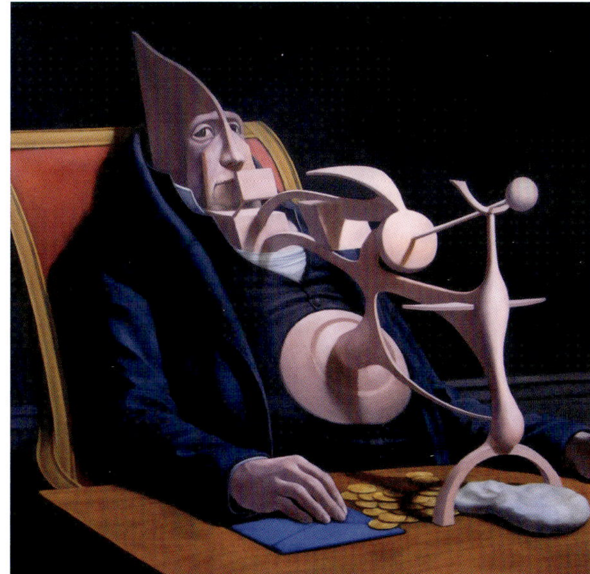

Rich man · 50 x 50 cm · Oil and tempera on board

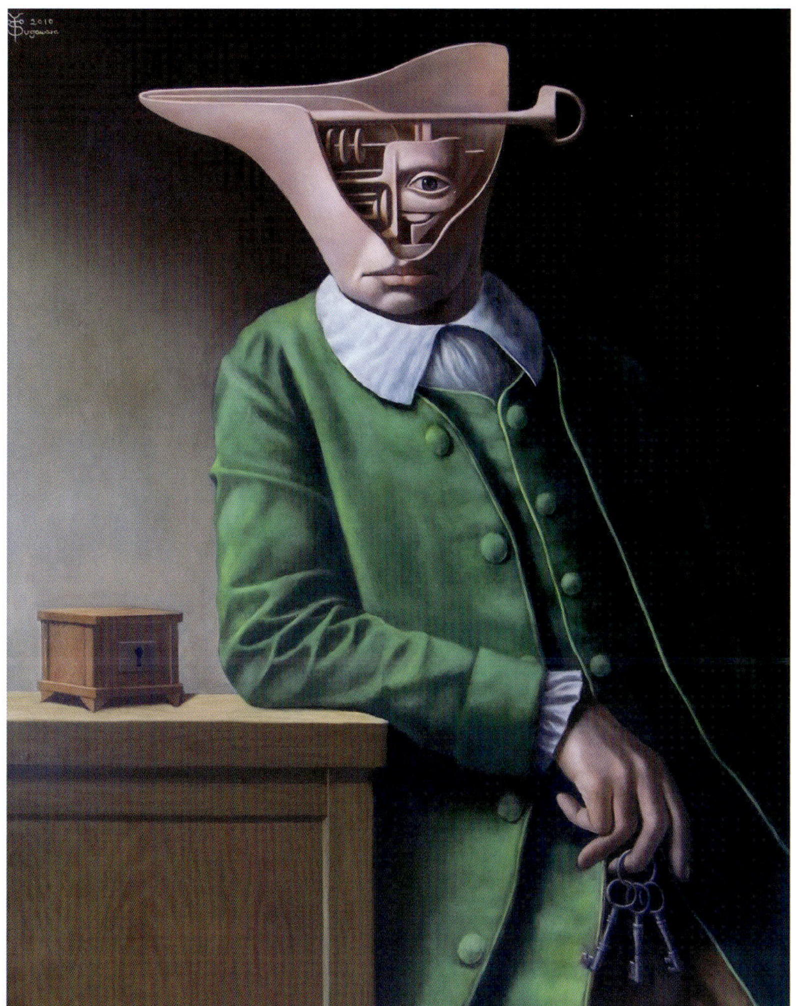

Key Smith · 53 x 41 cm · Oil and tempera on board

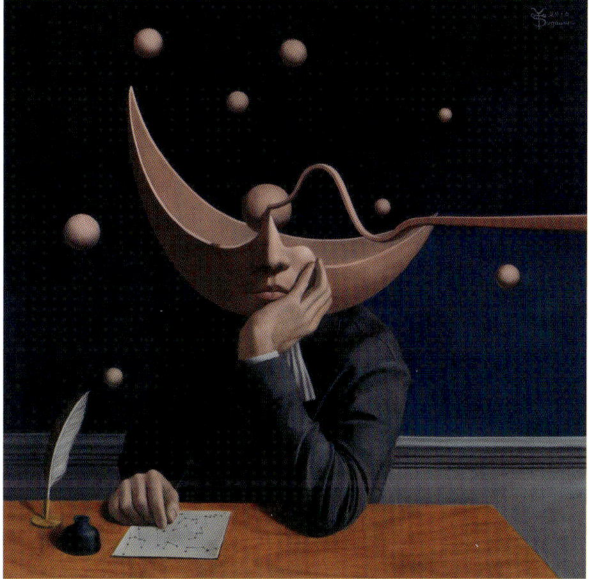

Astronomer · 38 x 38 cm · Oil and tempera on board

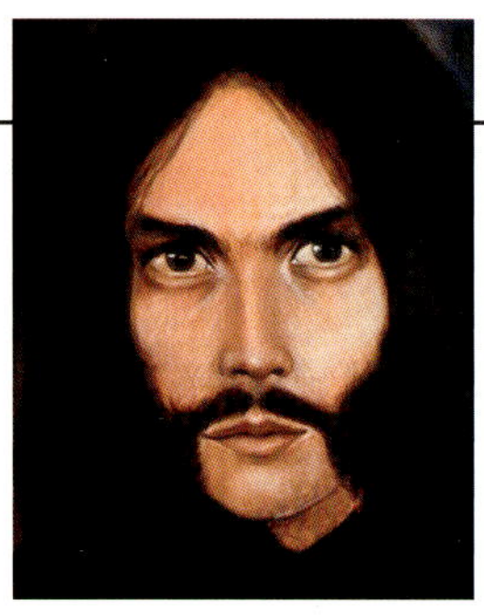

JEAN THOMASSEN

1949 The Netherlands

www.jeanthomassen.nl

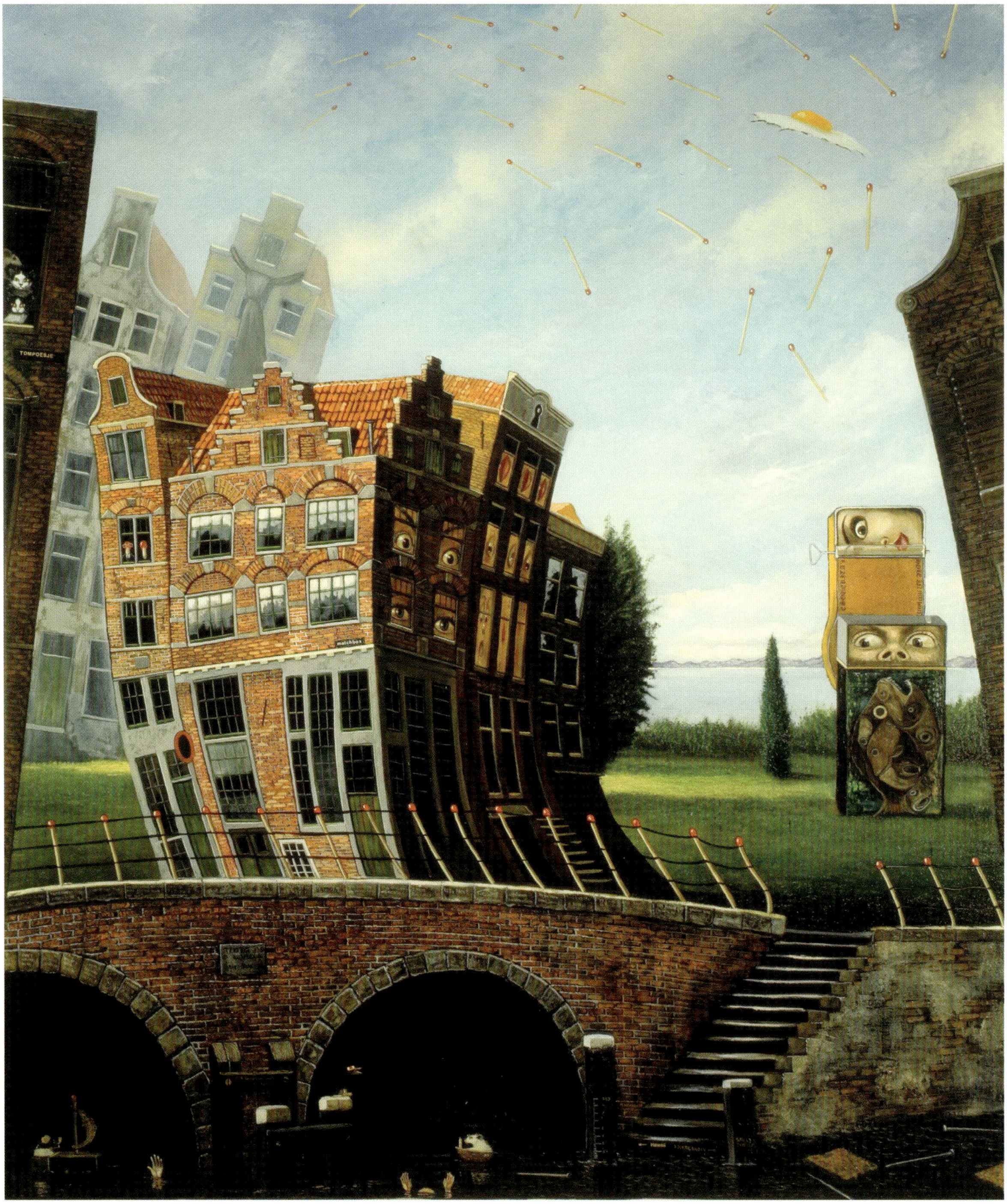

Matchbox over Amsterdam · 100 x 80 cm · Oil on canvas

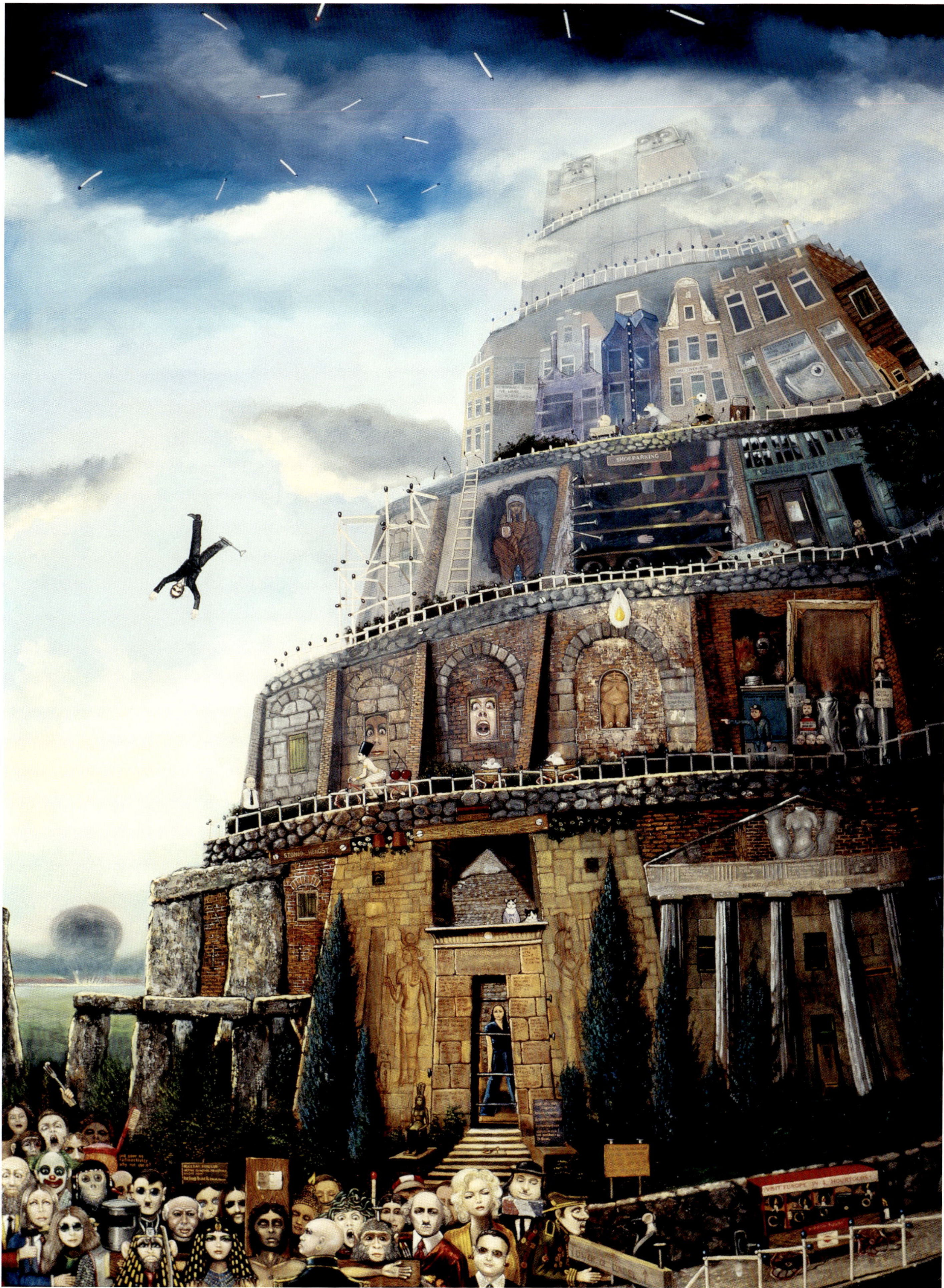

Tower of Babel · 150 x 100 cm · Oil on canvas

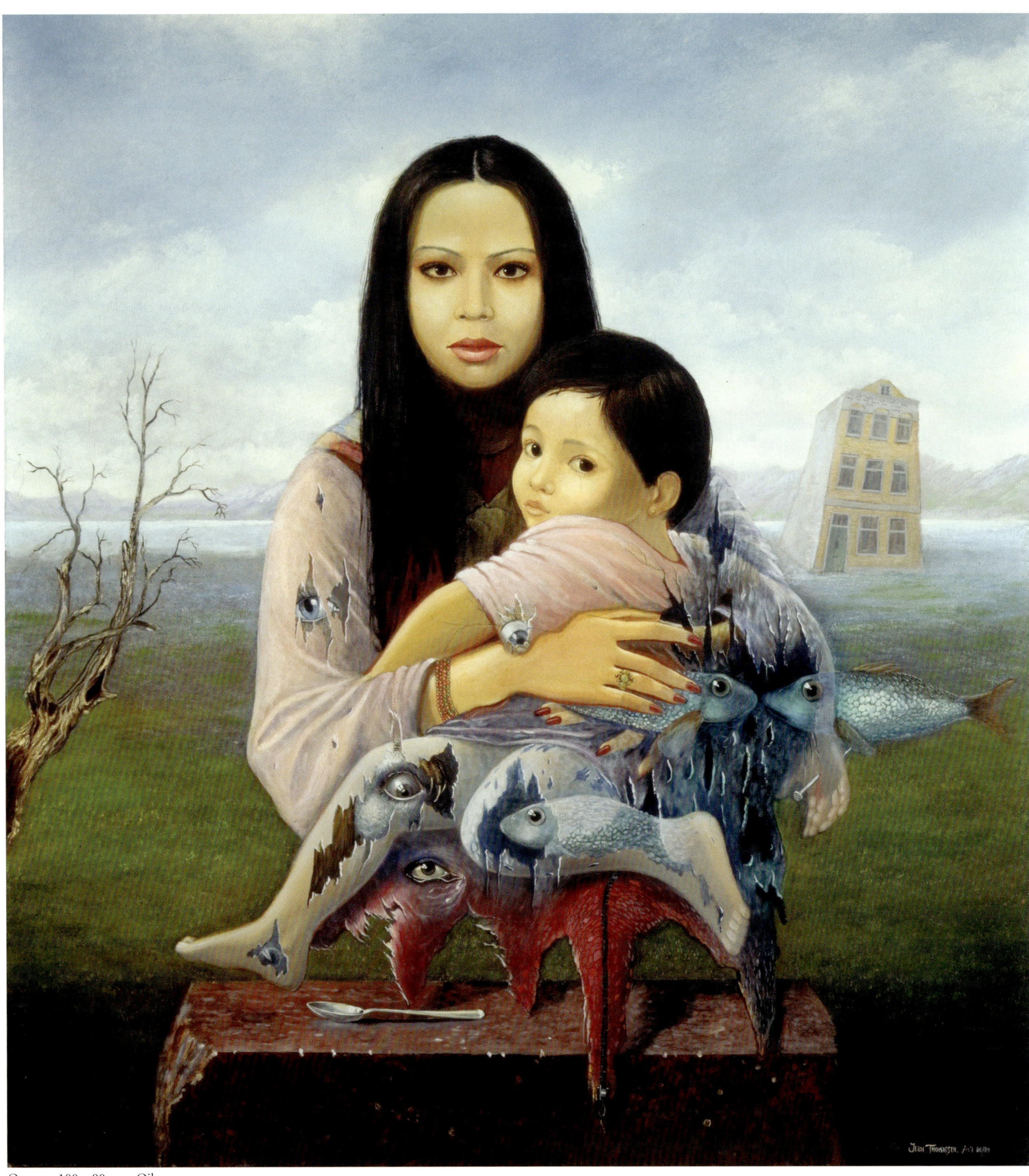

Once... · 100 x 80 cm · Oil on canvas

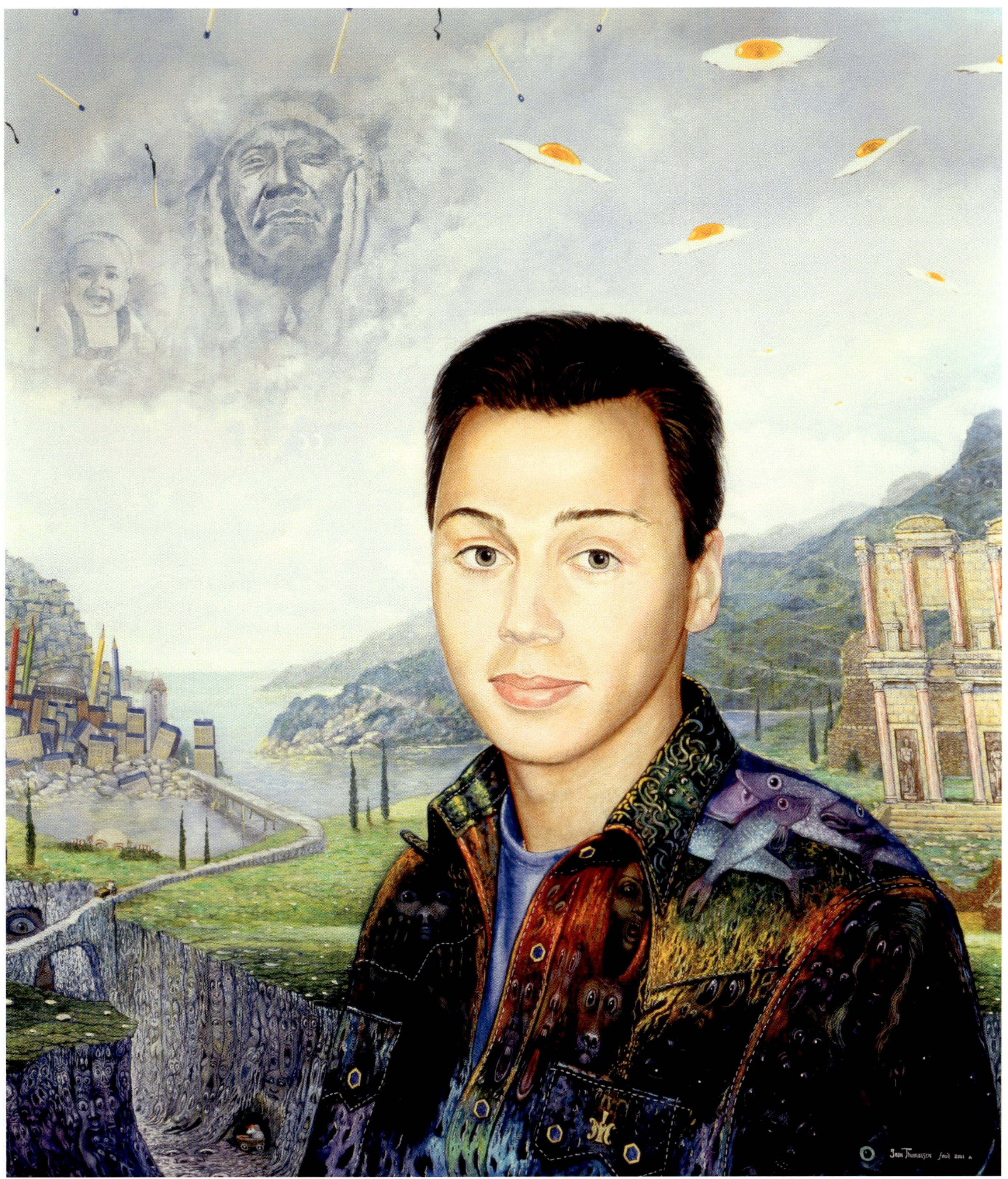

Marc van den Berg · 90 x 80 cm · Oil on canvas

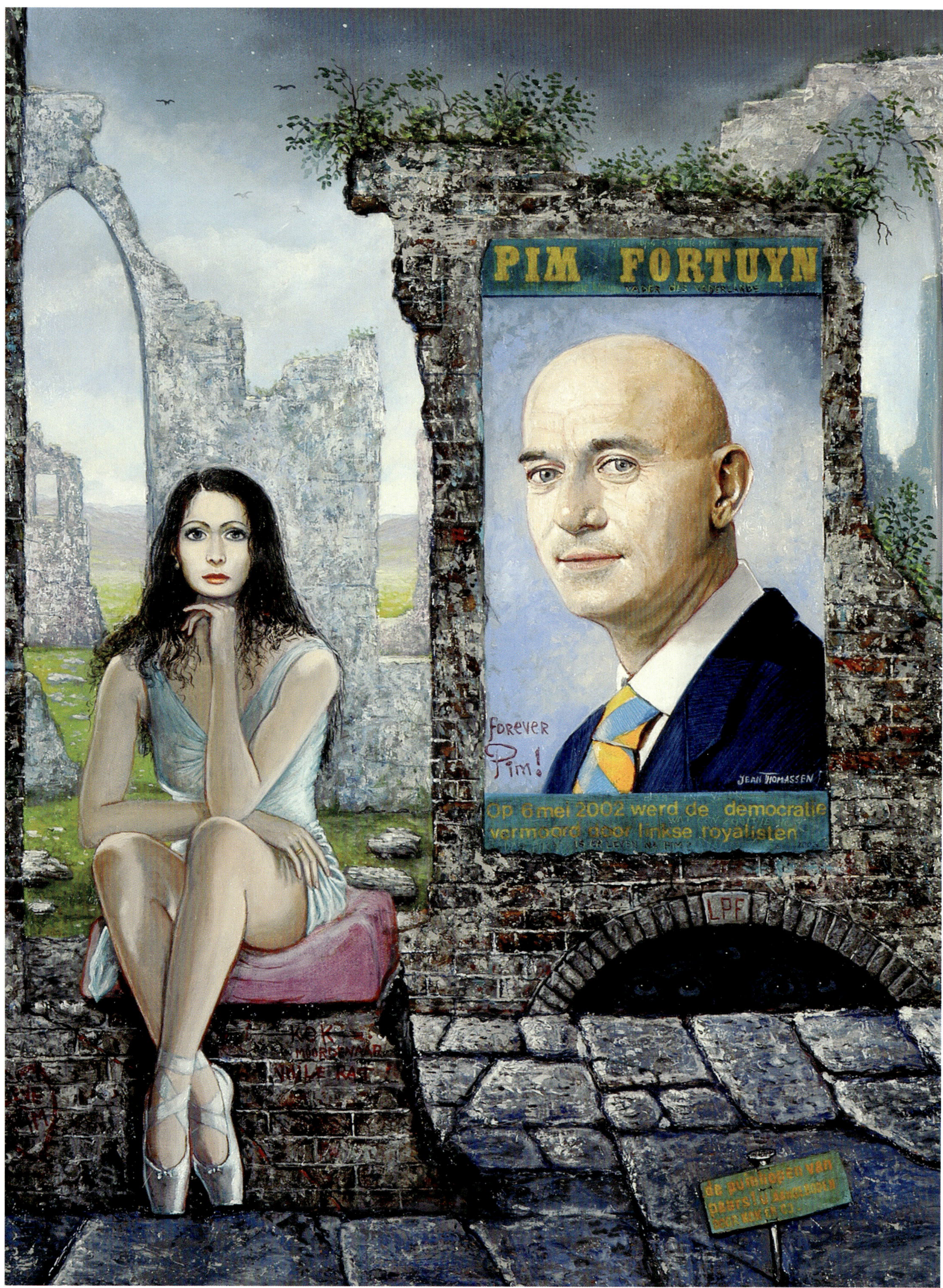

Murder according to the Crown · 40 x 30 cm · Oil on canvas

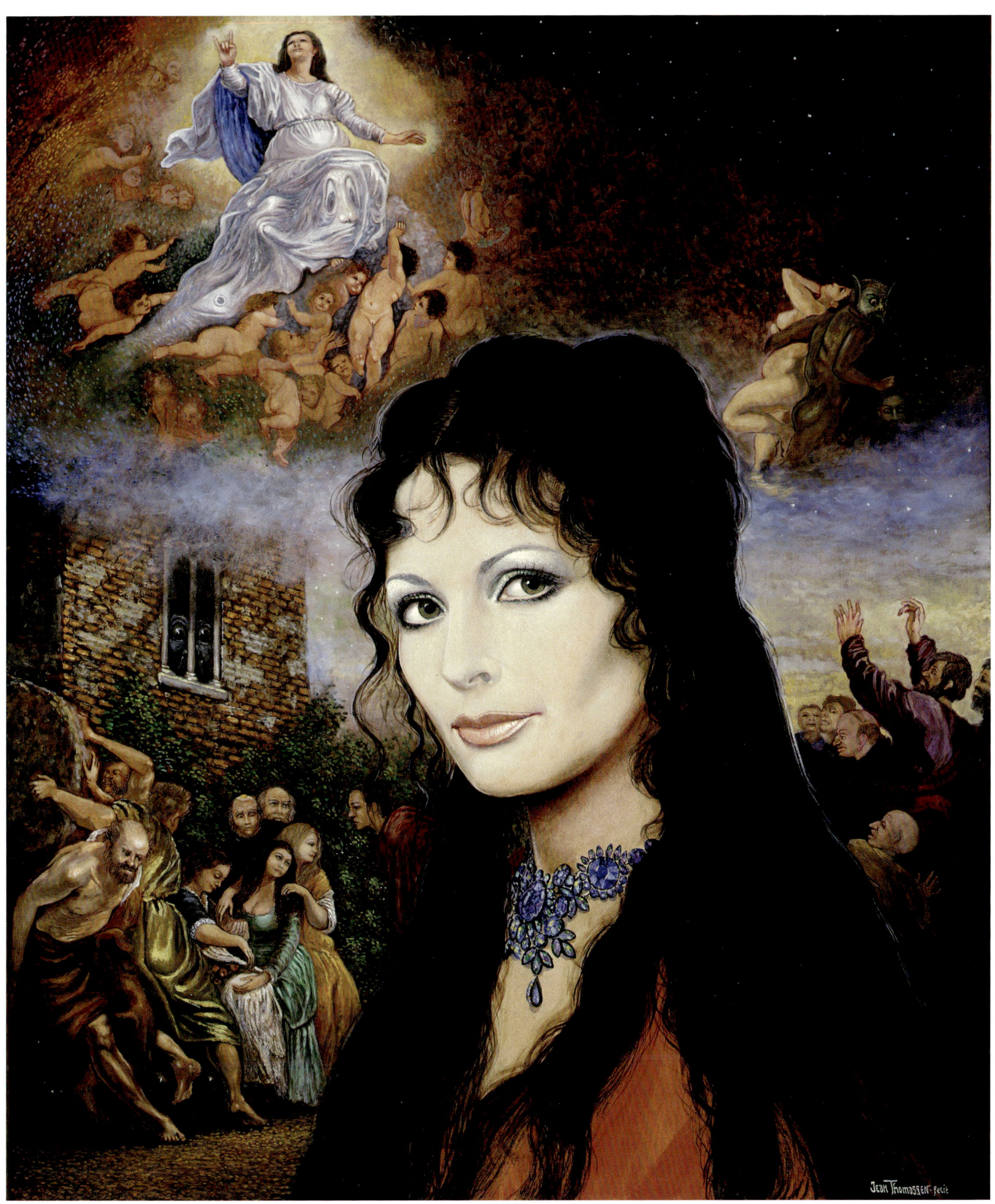

Souvenirs de Venise, portrait of the actress Ine Veen · 90 x 80 cm · Oil on canvas

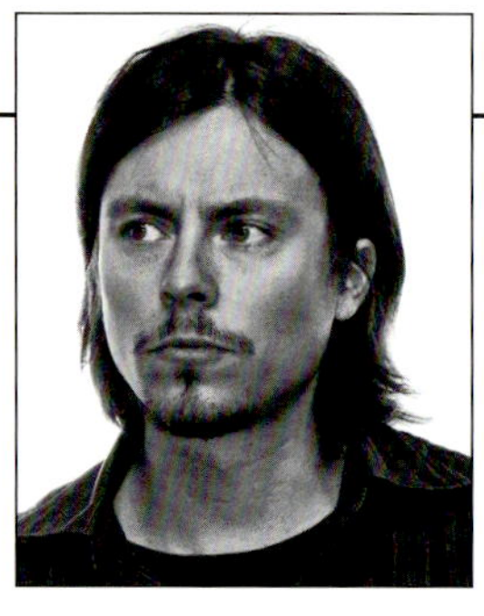

TOMMAS

1980 Denmark

www.tommas.dk

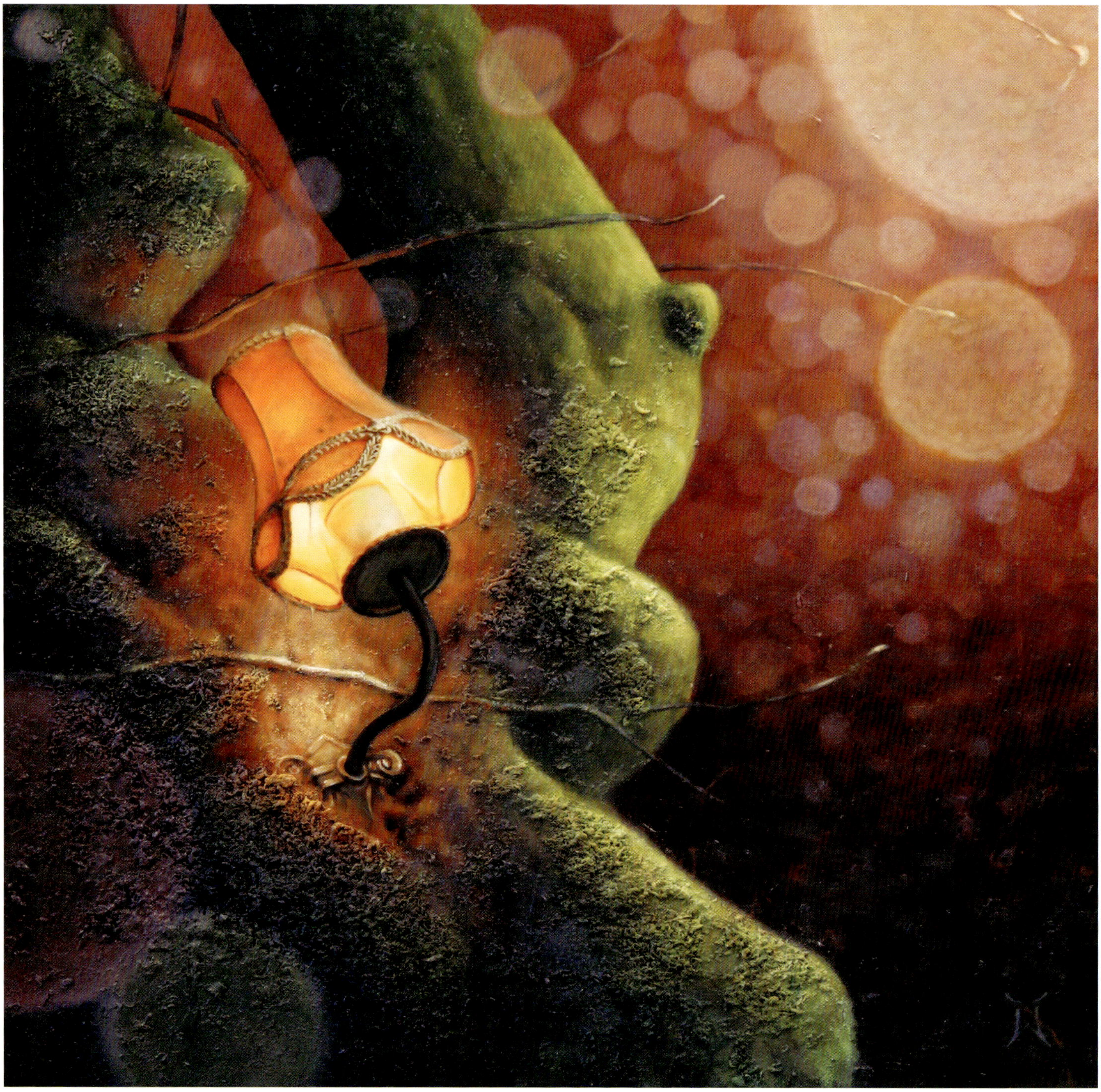

Glowing Remains · 100 x 100 cm · Oil on canvas

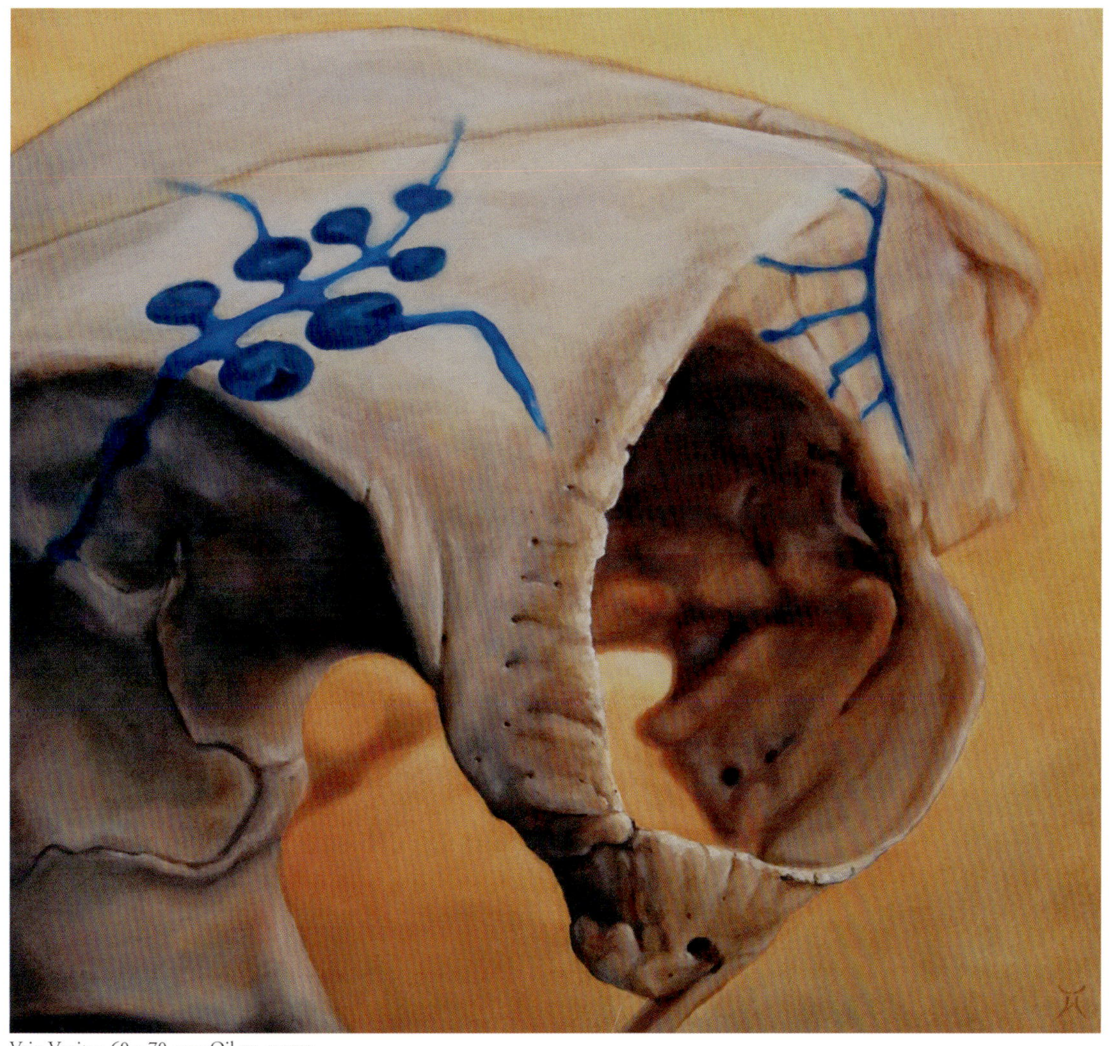

Vain Vanity · 60 x 70 cm · Oil on canvas

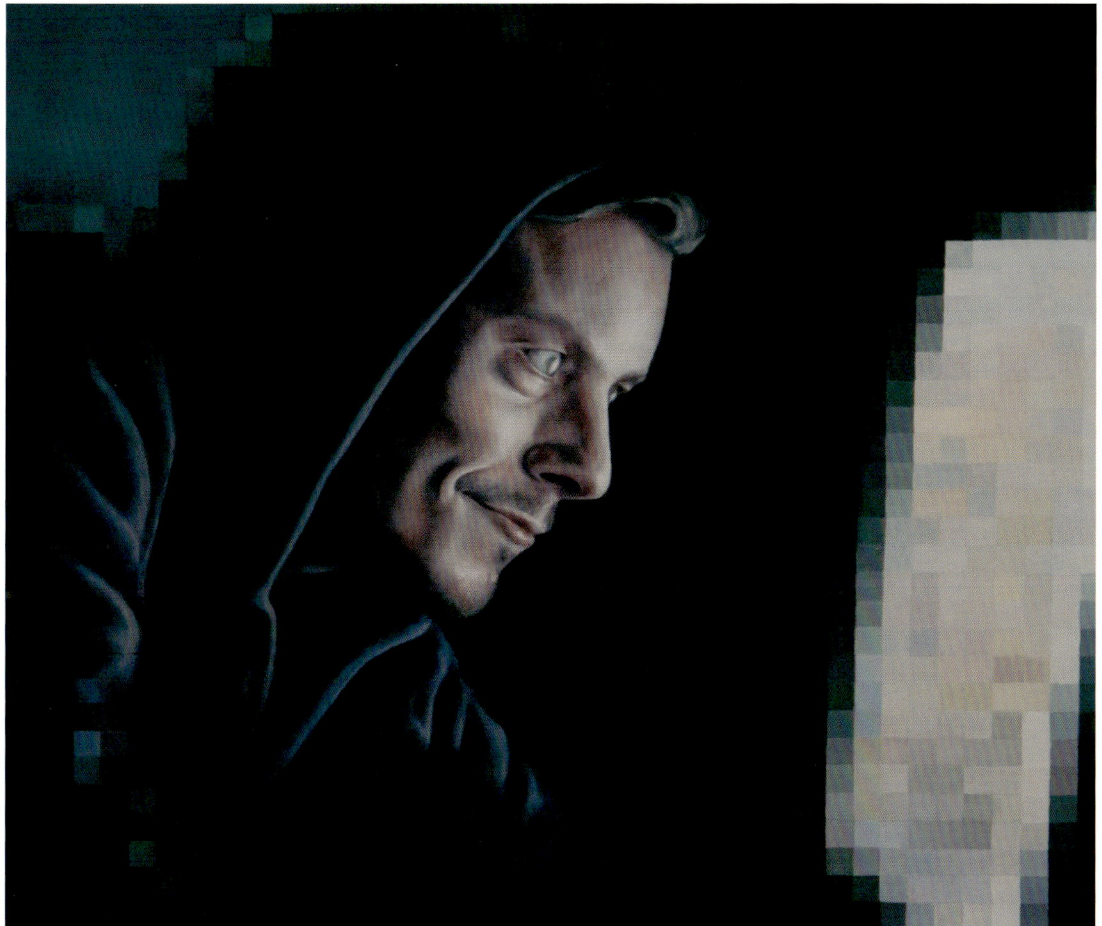

Inappropriate Surfing · 70 x 80 cm · Oil on canvas

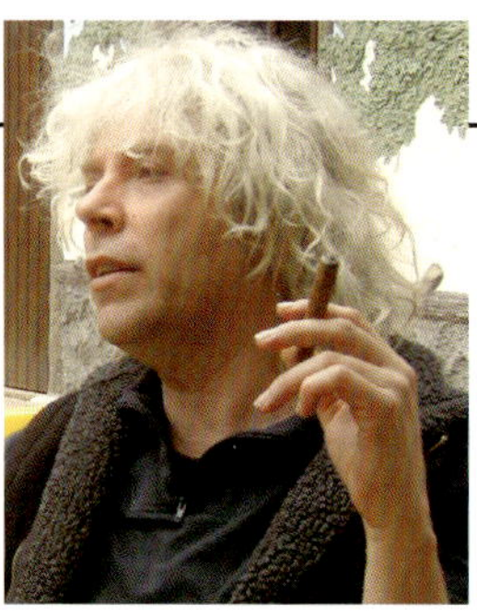

CAS WATERMAN

1958 The Netherlands

www.caswaterman.com

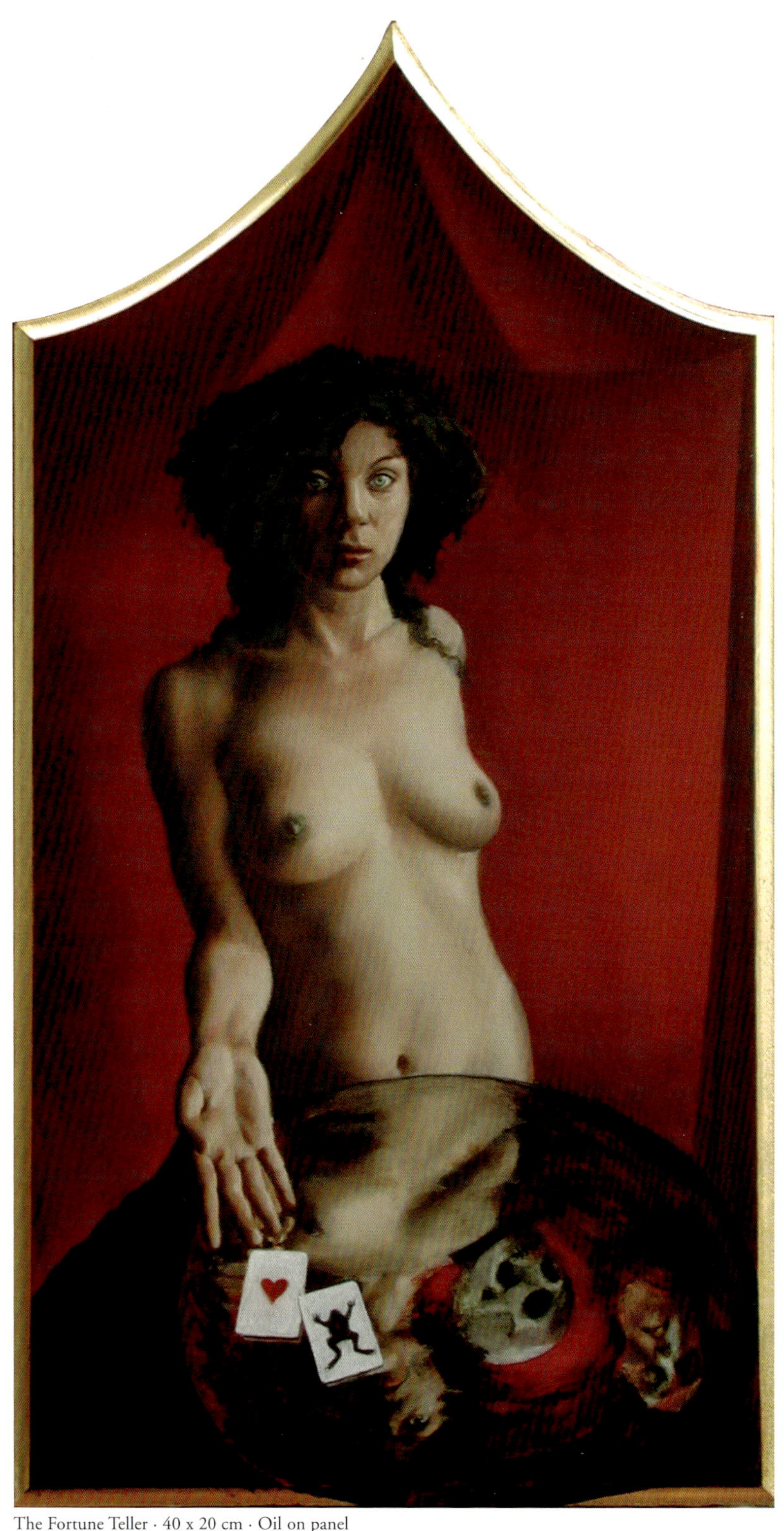

The Fortune Teller · 40 x 20 cm · Oil on panel

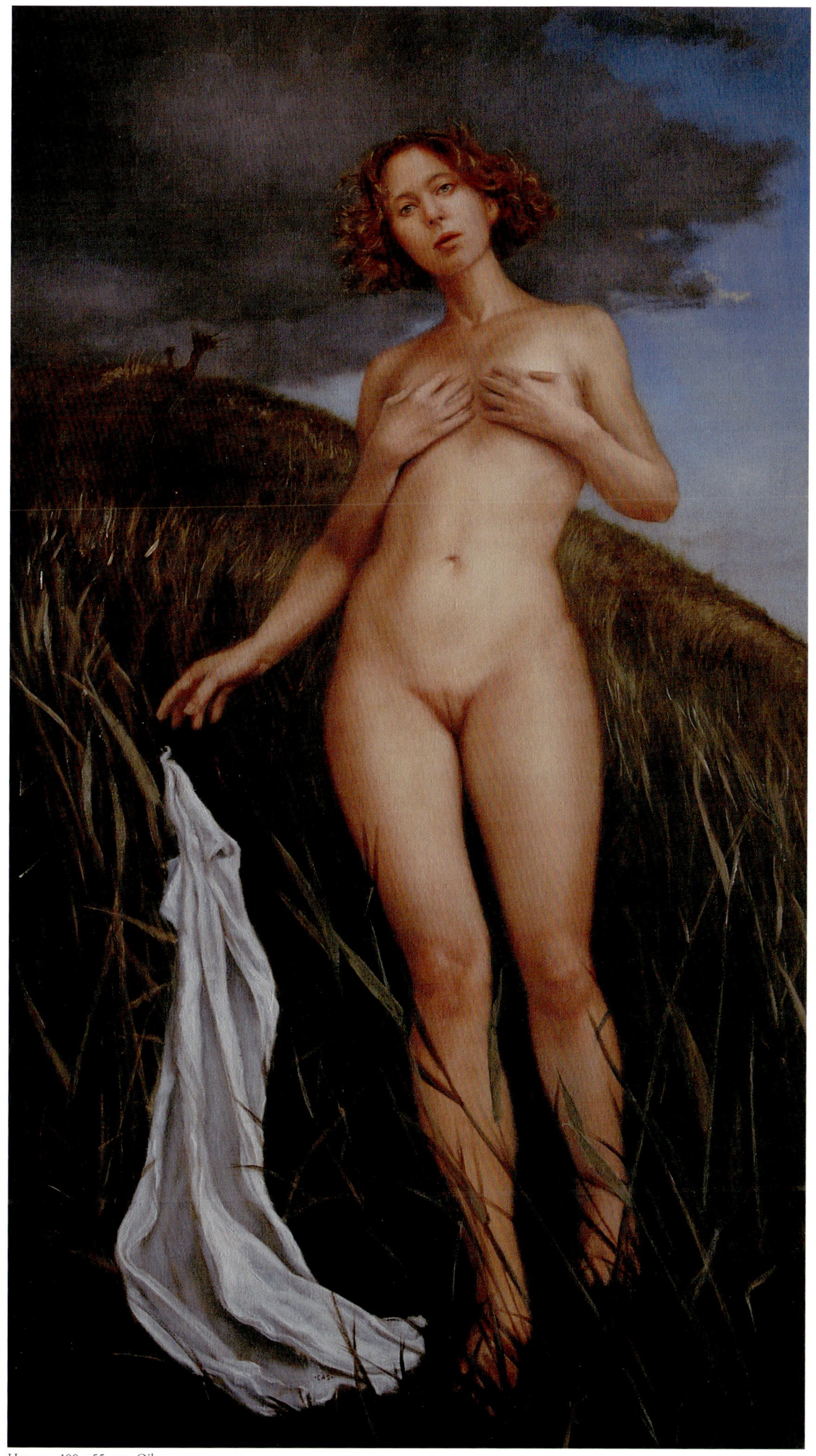

Hergest · 100 x 55 cm · Oil on canvas

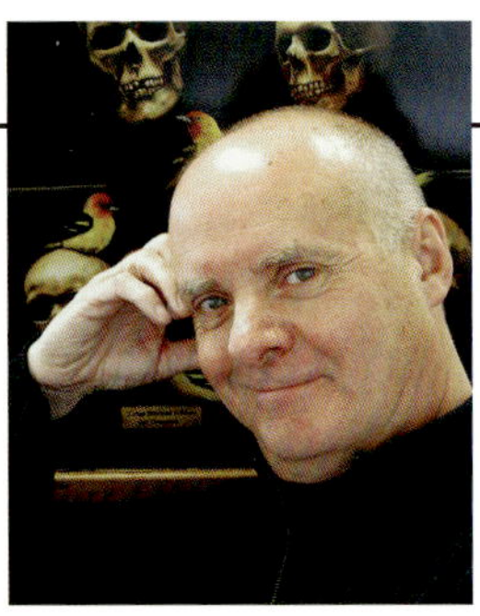

RODNEY WOOD

1951 USA

www.rodneywood.com

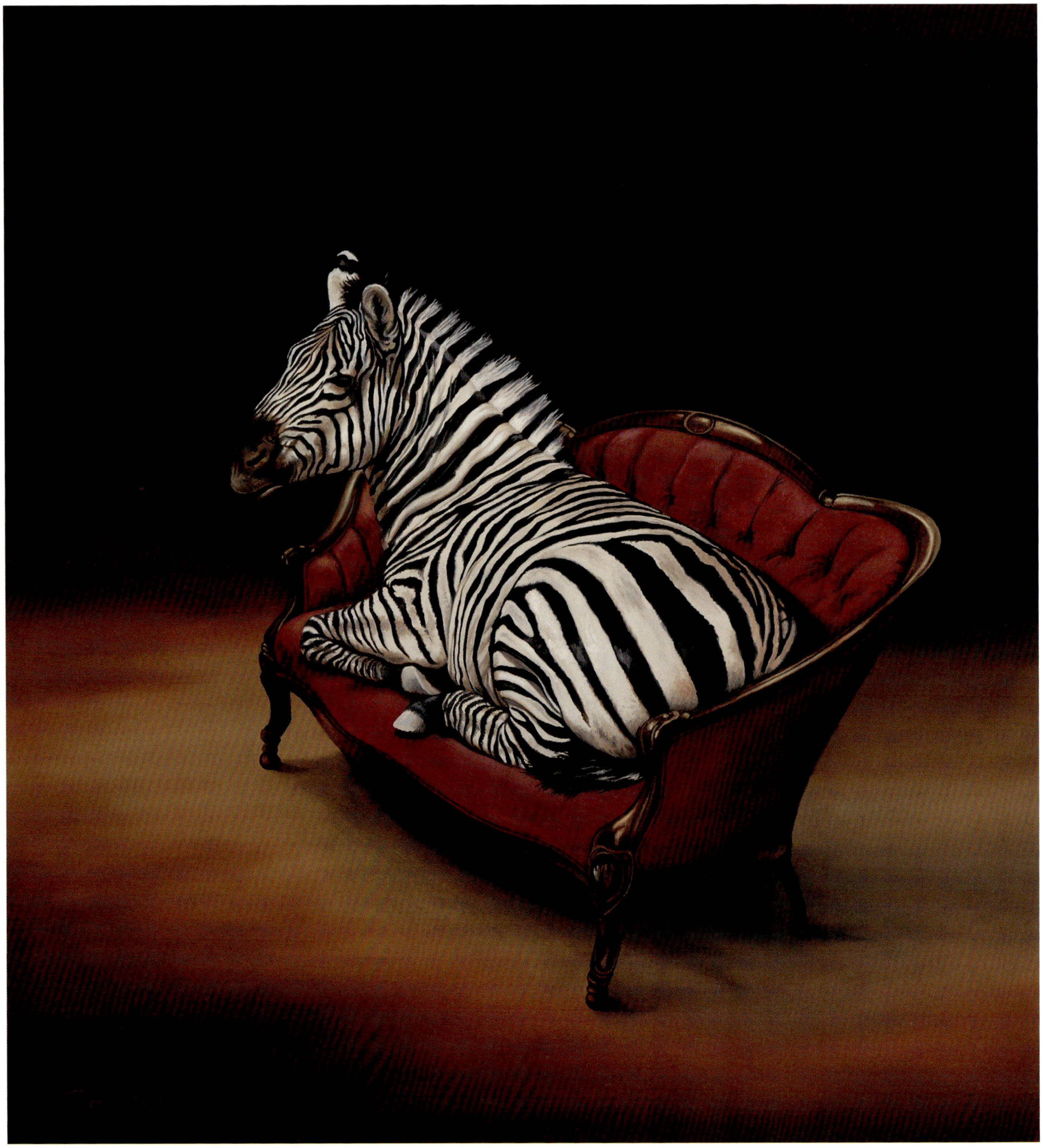

Paramour · 43 x 38 cm · Oil on panel

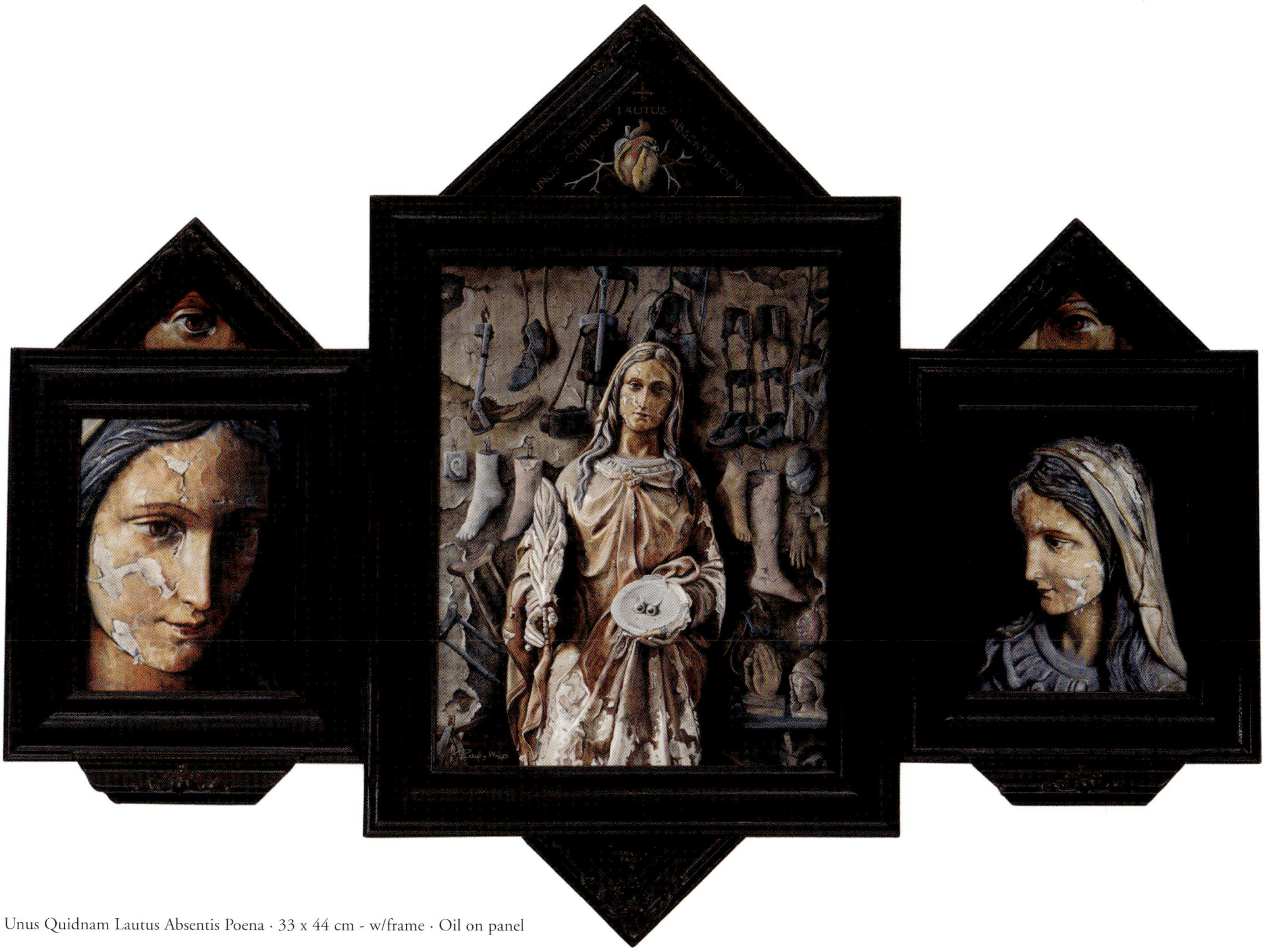

Unus Quidnam Lautus Absentis Poena · 33 x 44 cm - w/frame · Oil on panel

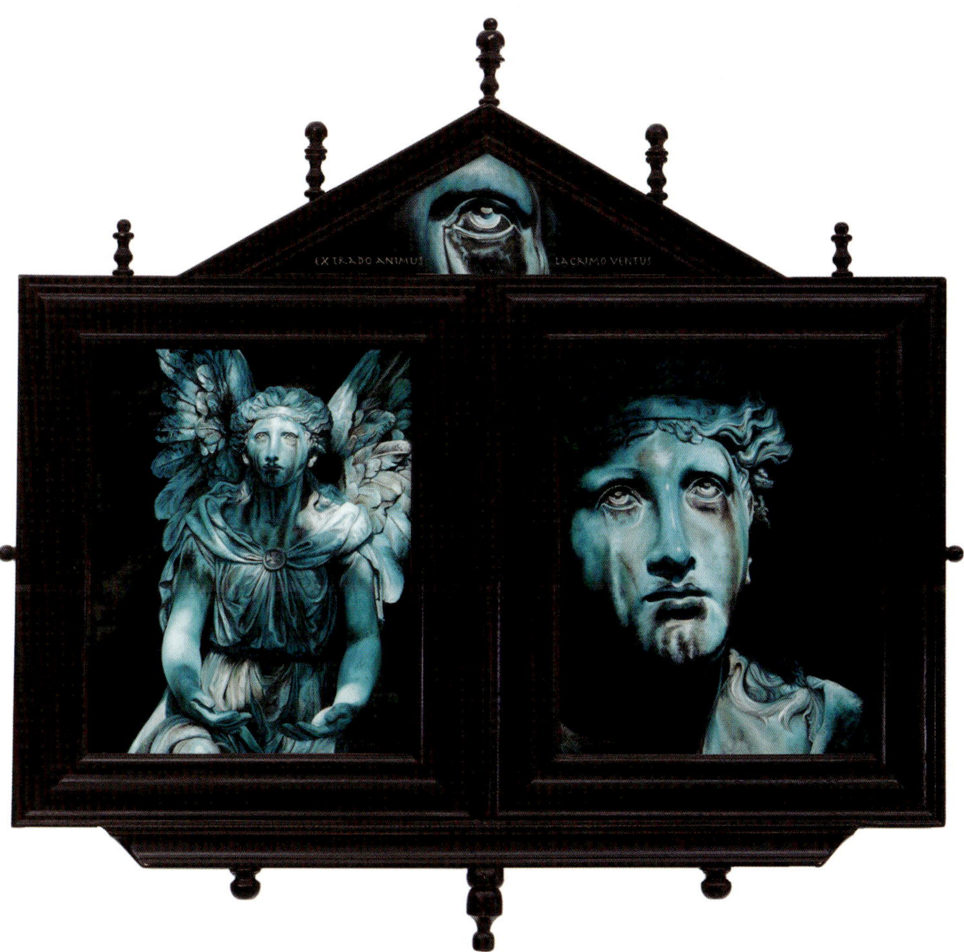

Ex Trado Animus Lacrimo Ventus · 84 x 82cm - w/frame · Oil on panel

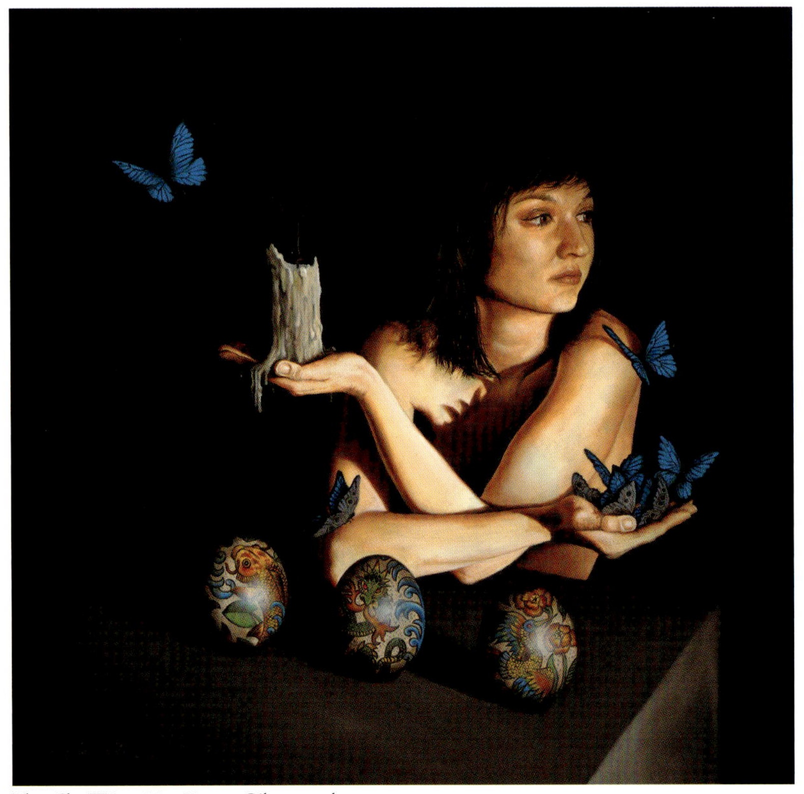
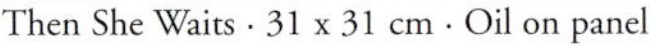
Then She Waits · 31 x 31 cm · Oil on panel

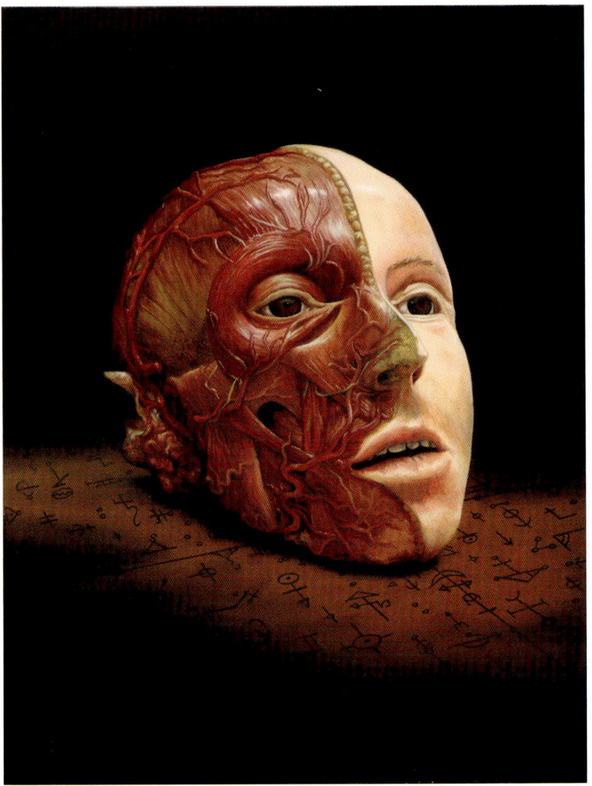
Testimonial · 41 x 31 cm · Oil on panel

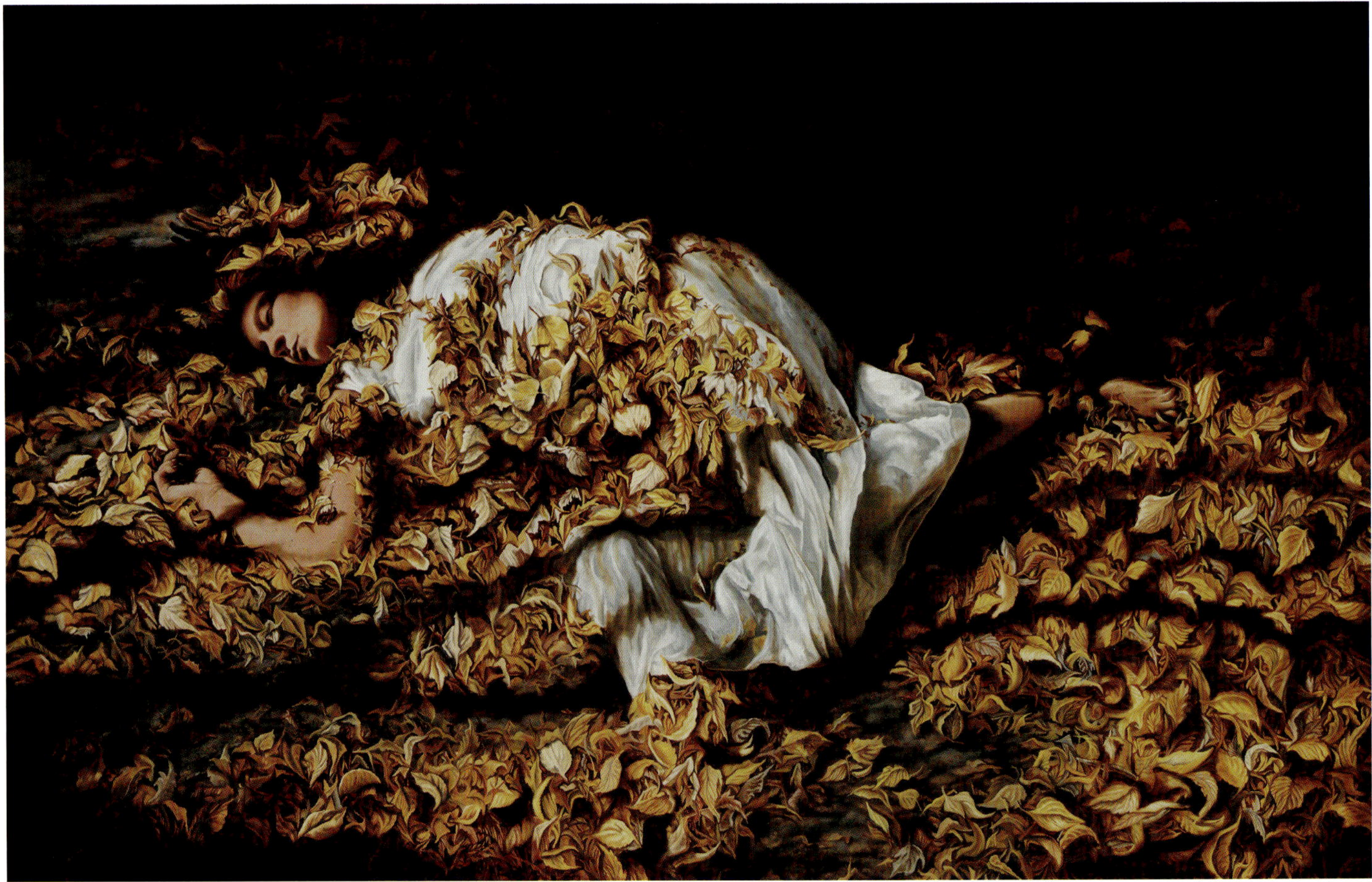
In the Arms of Morpheus · 66 x 102 cm - w/frame · Oil on panel

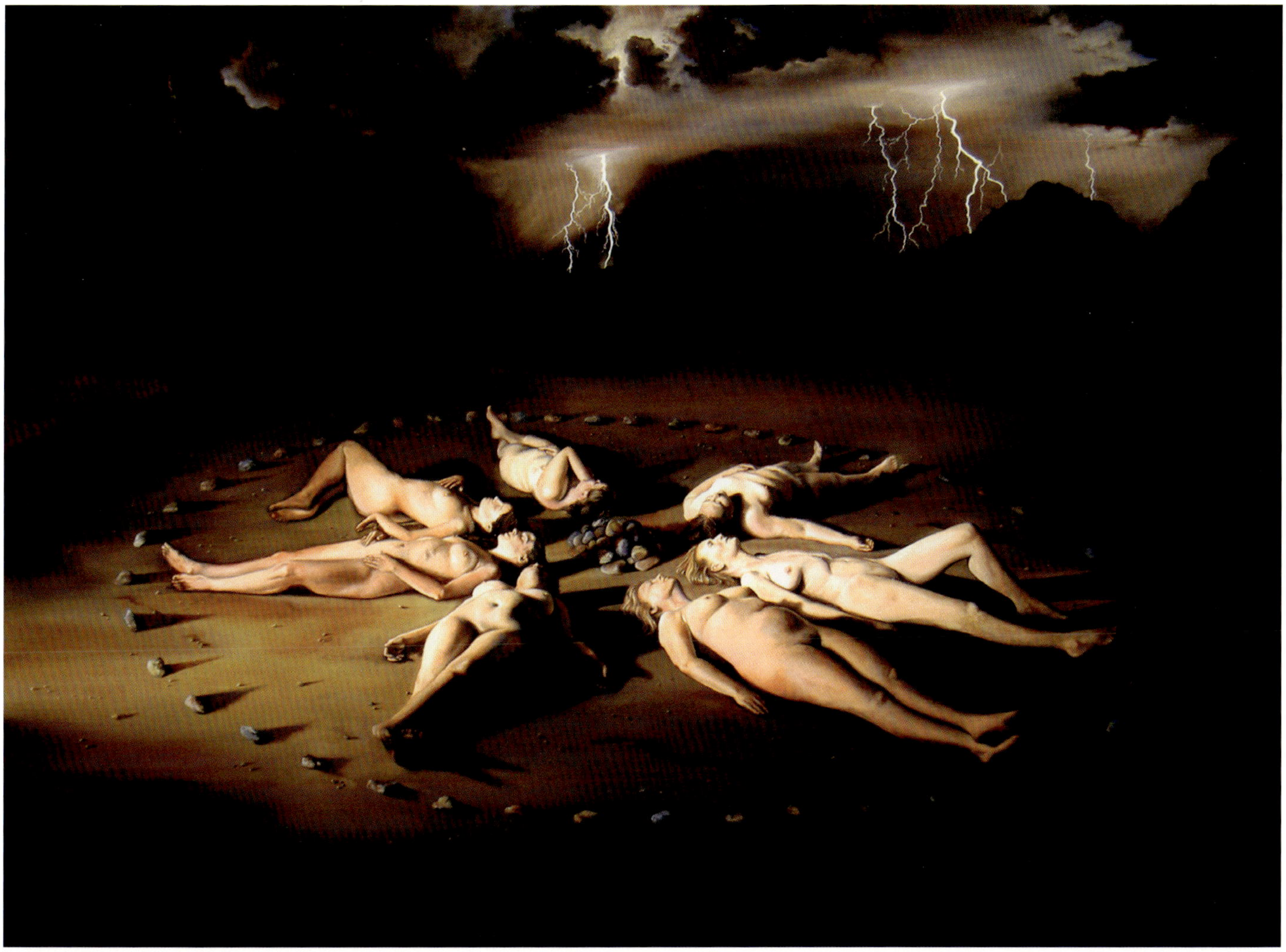

Faith · 61 x 82 cm · Oil on panel

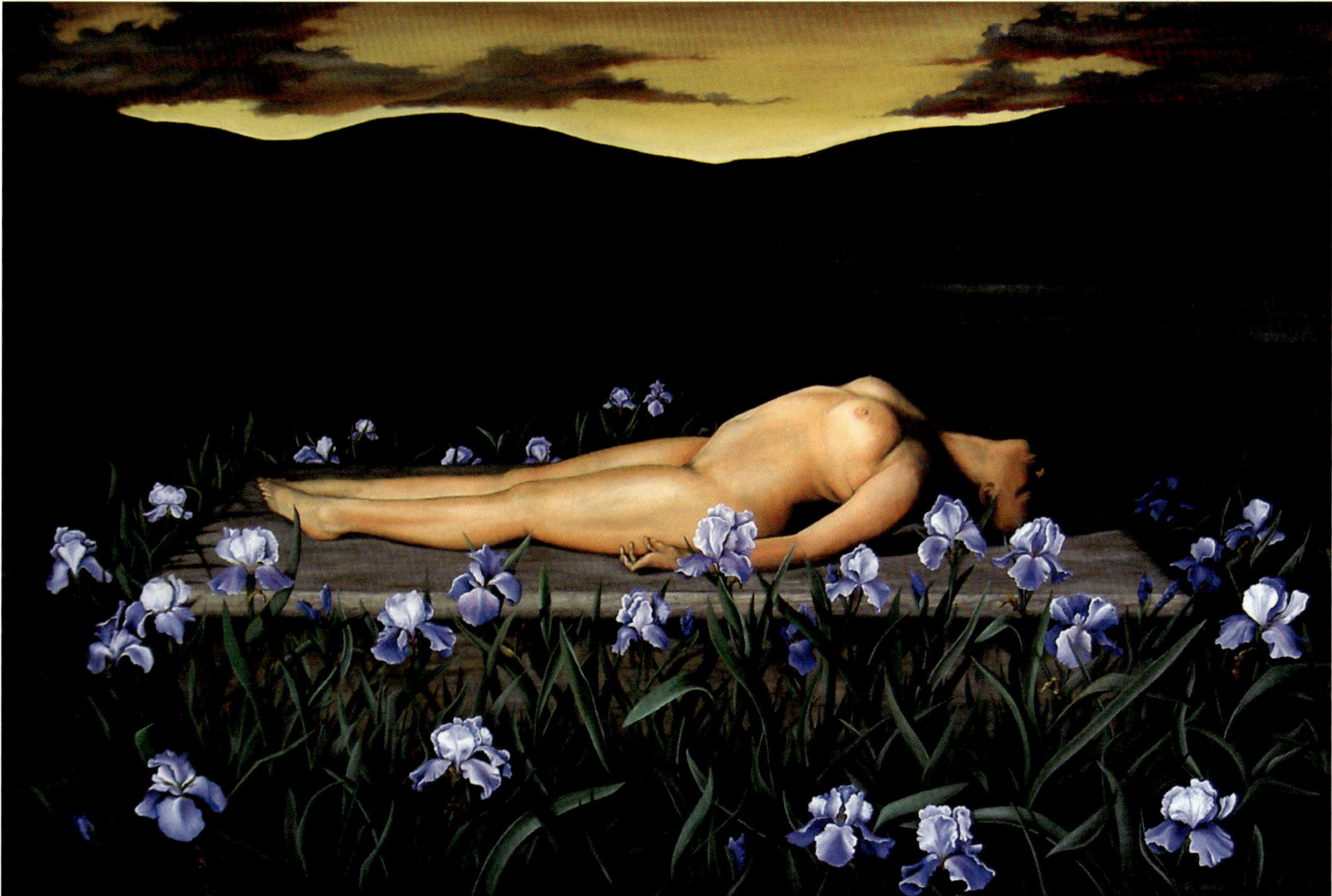

Flora · 61 x 92 cm · Oil on panel

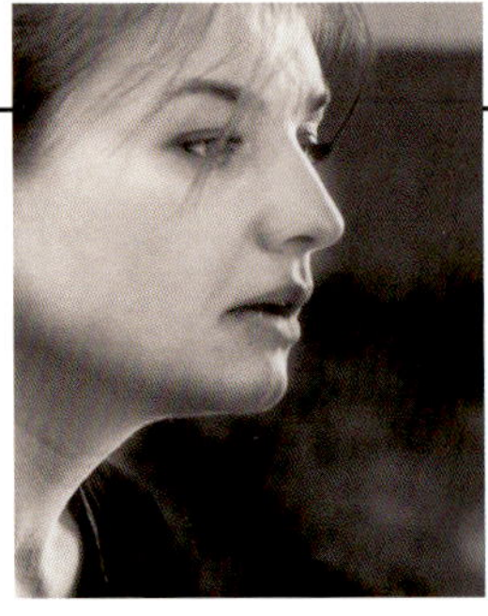

OXANA YAMBYKH

1966 Ukraine

www.yambykh.com

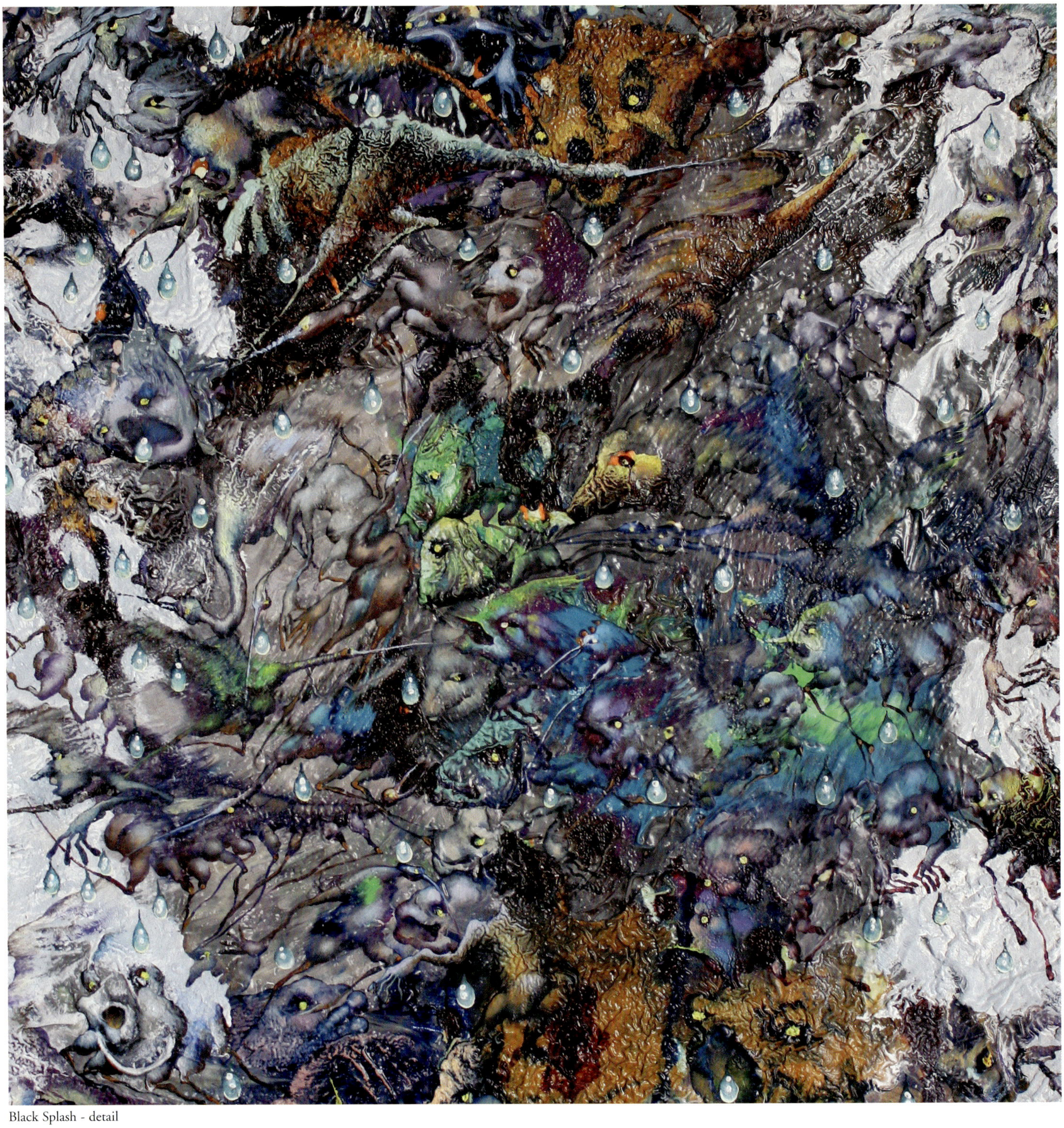

Black Splash - detail

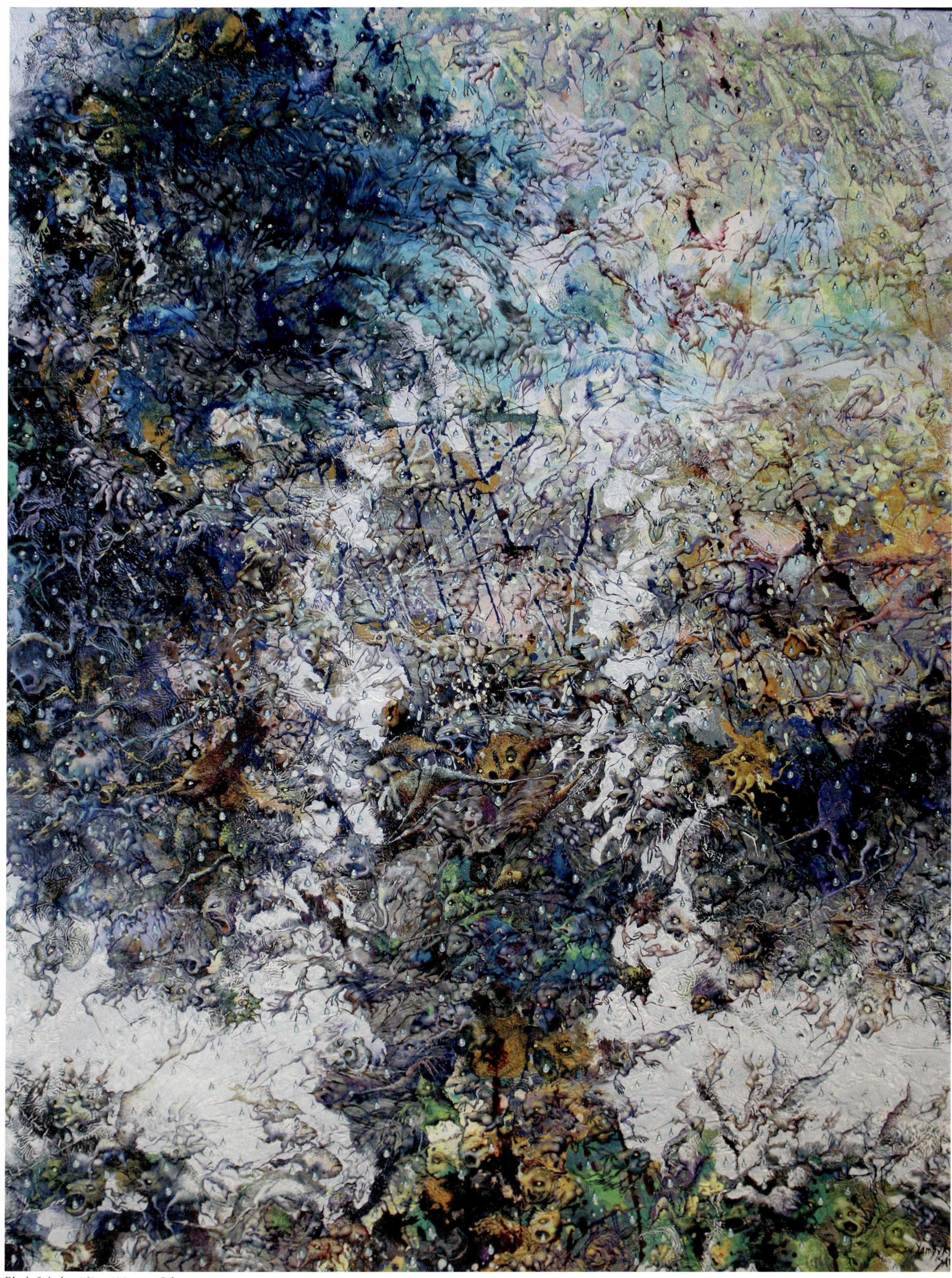
Black Splash · 160 x 120 cm · Oil on canvas

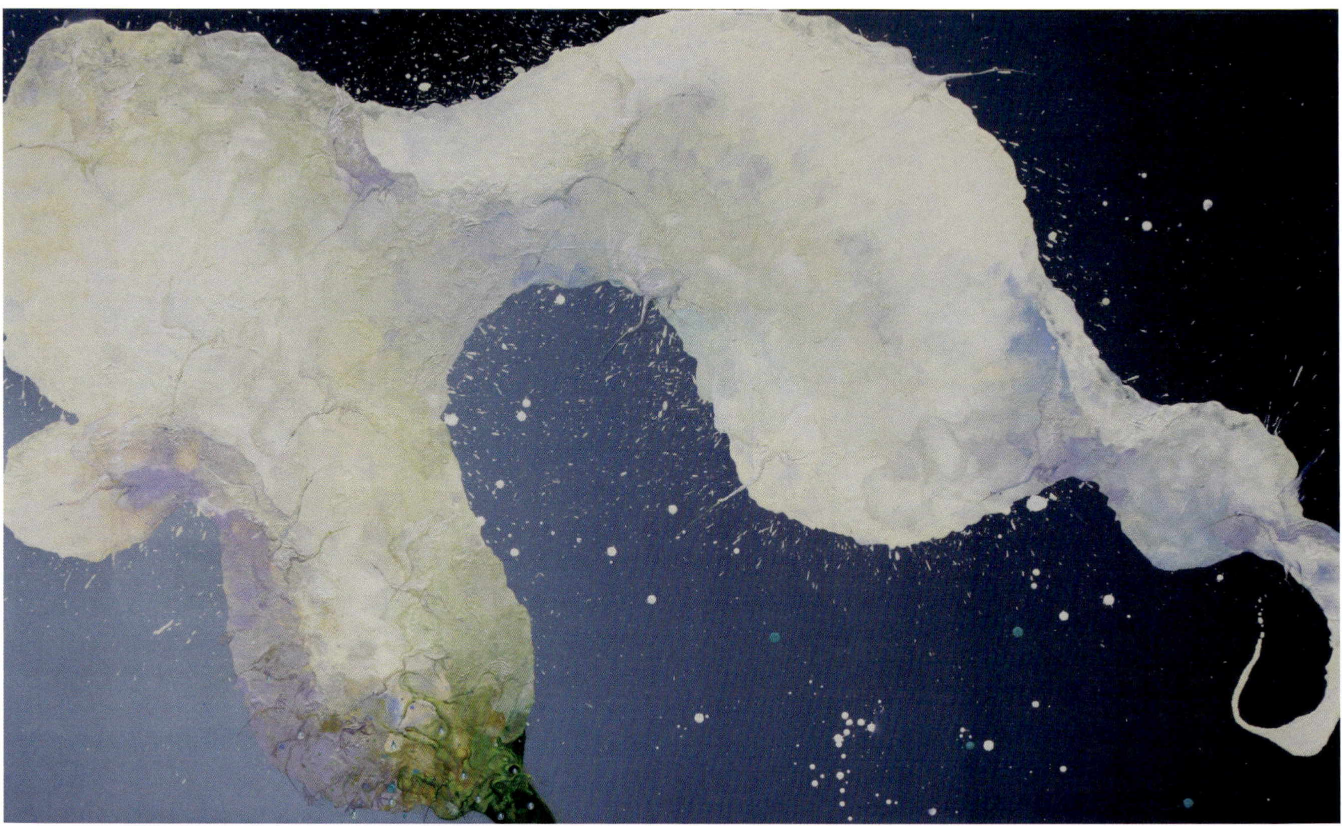

White Flight · 89 x 146 cm · Oil on canvas

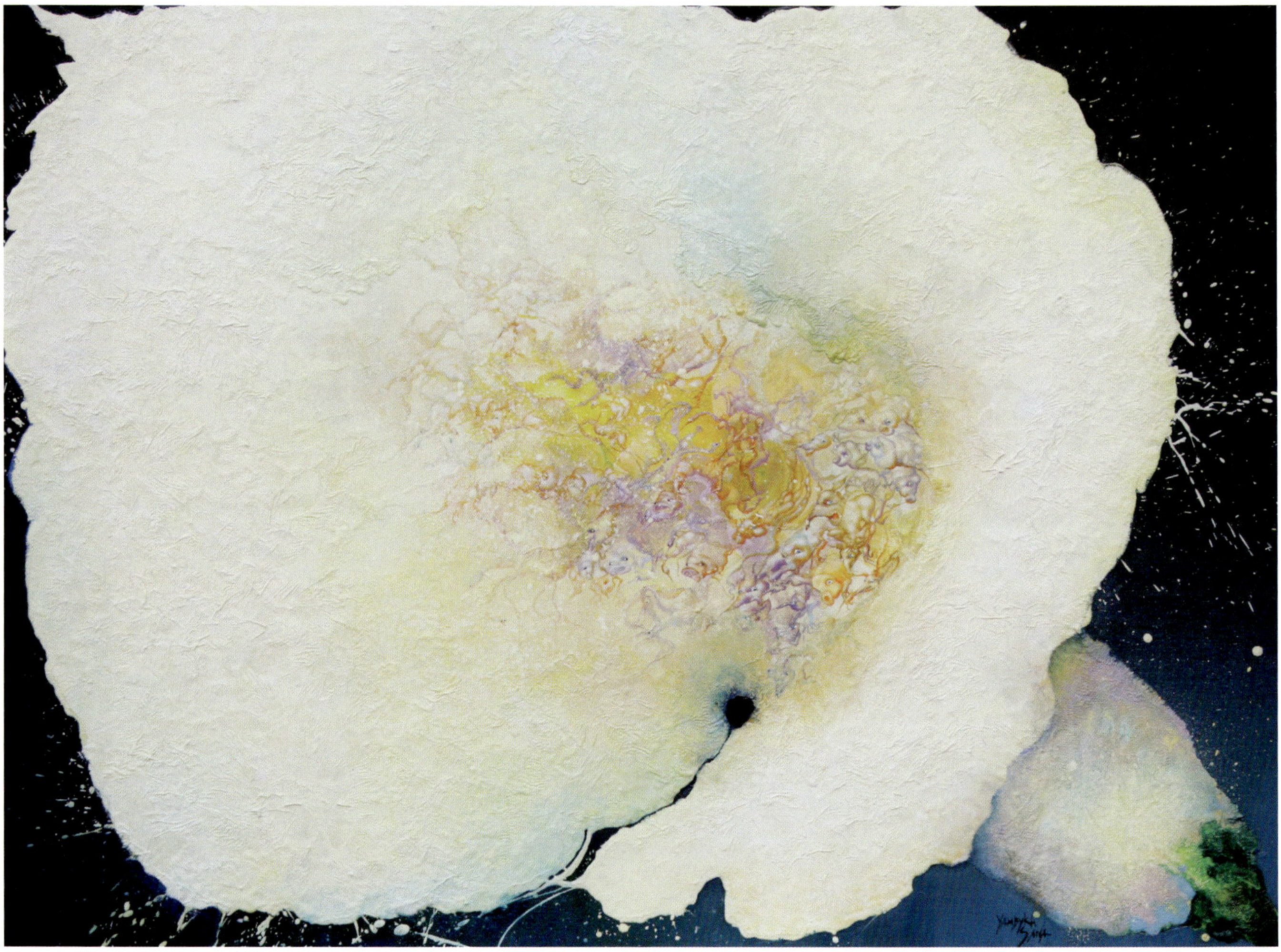

Dream in White · 97 x 130 cm · Oil on canvas

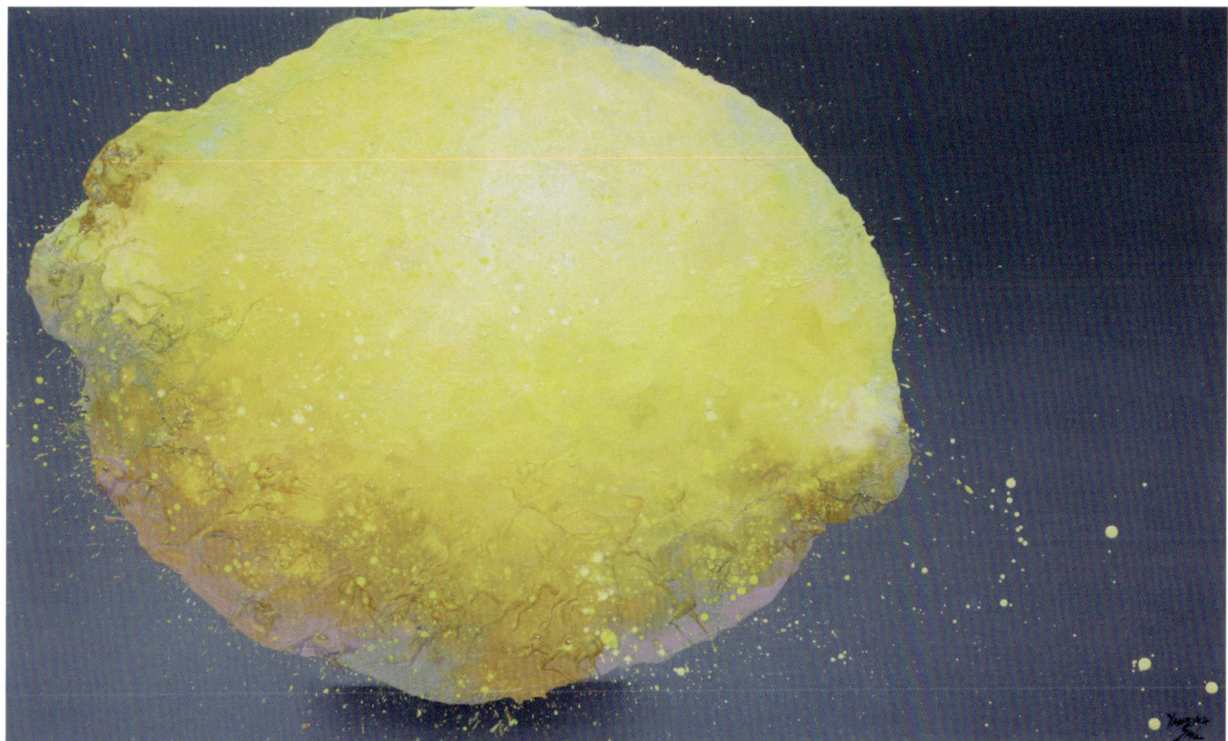

Lemon · 81 x 130 cm · Oil on canvas

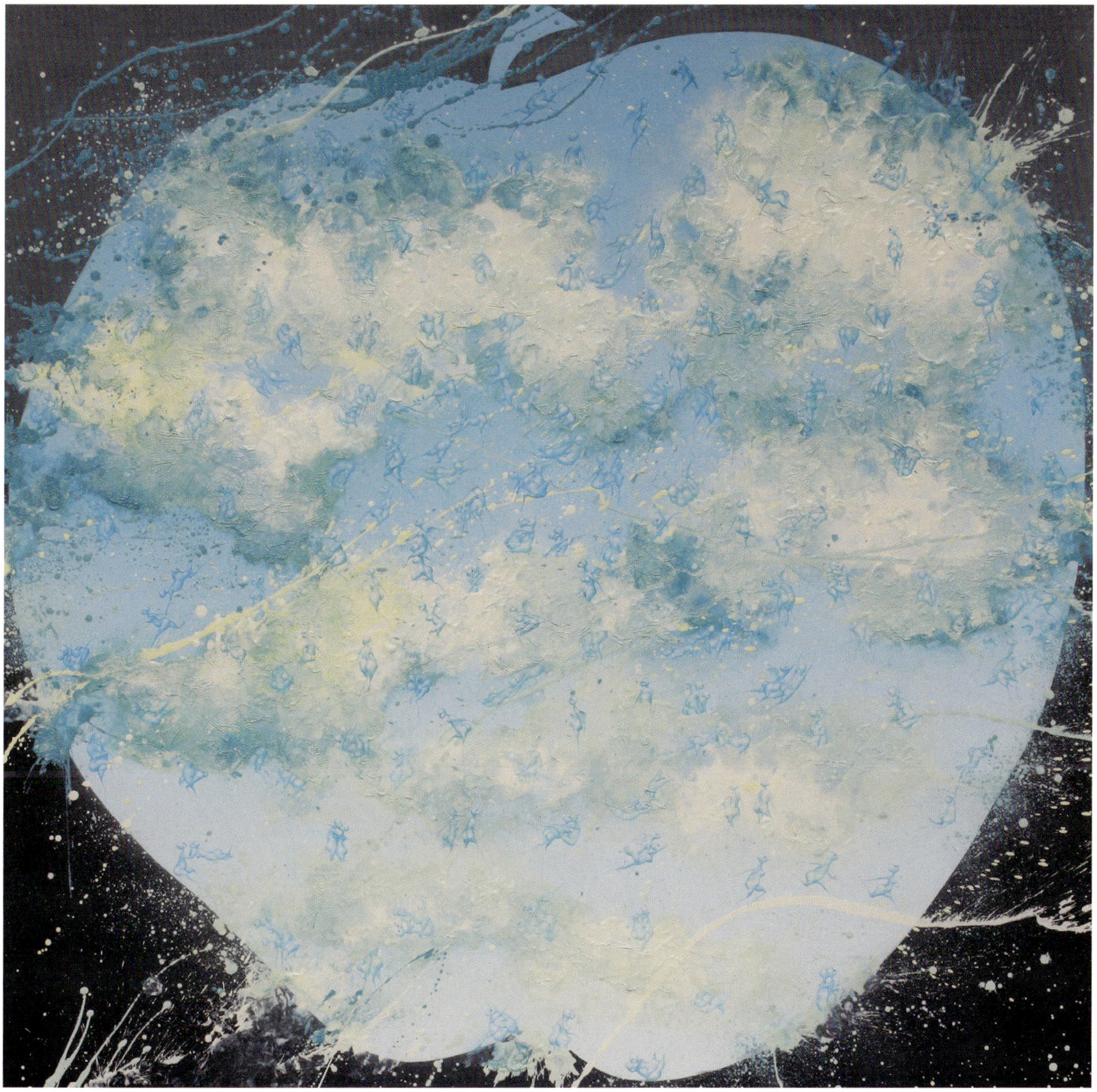

Apple d'Hesperides · 130 x 130 · Oil on canvas

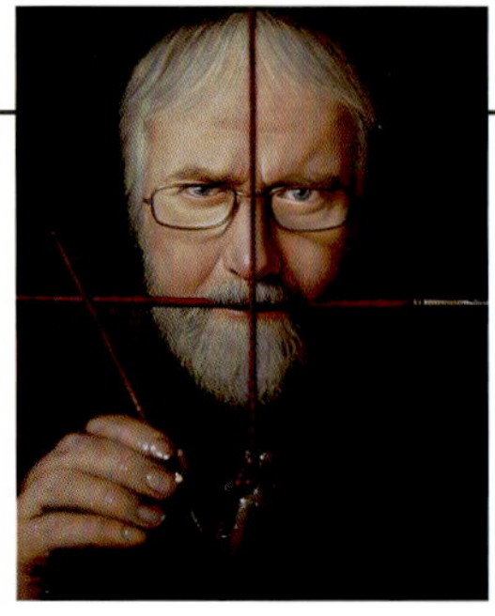

SIEGFRIED ZADEMACK

1952 Germany

www.zademack.com

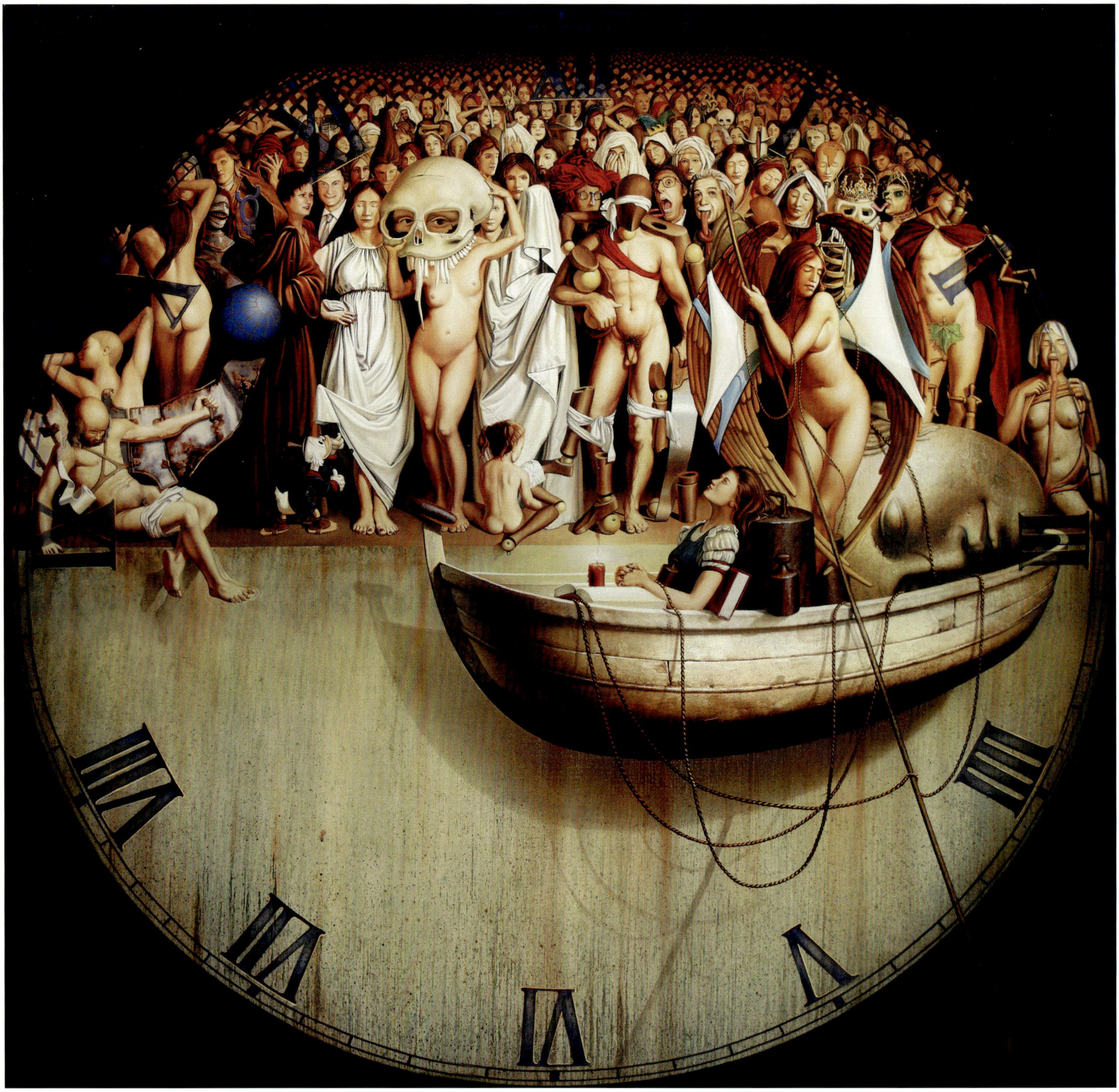

Disembarkation · 120 x 120 cm H · Oil on canvas

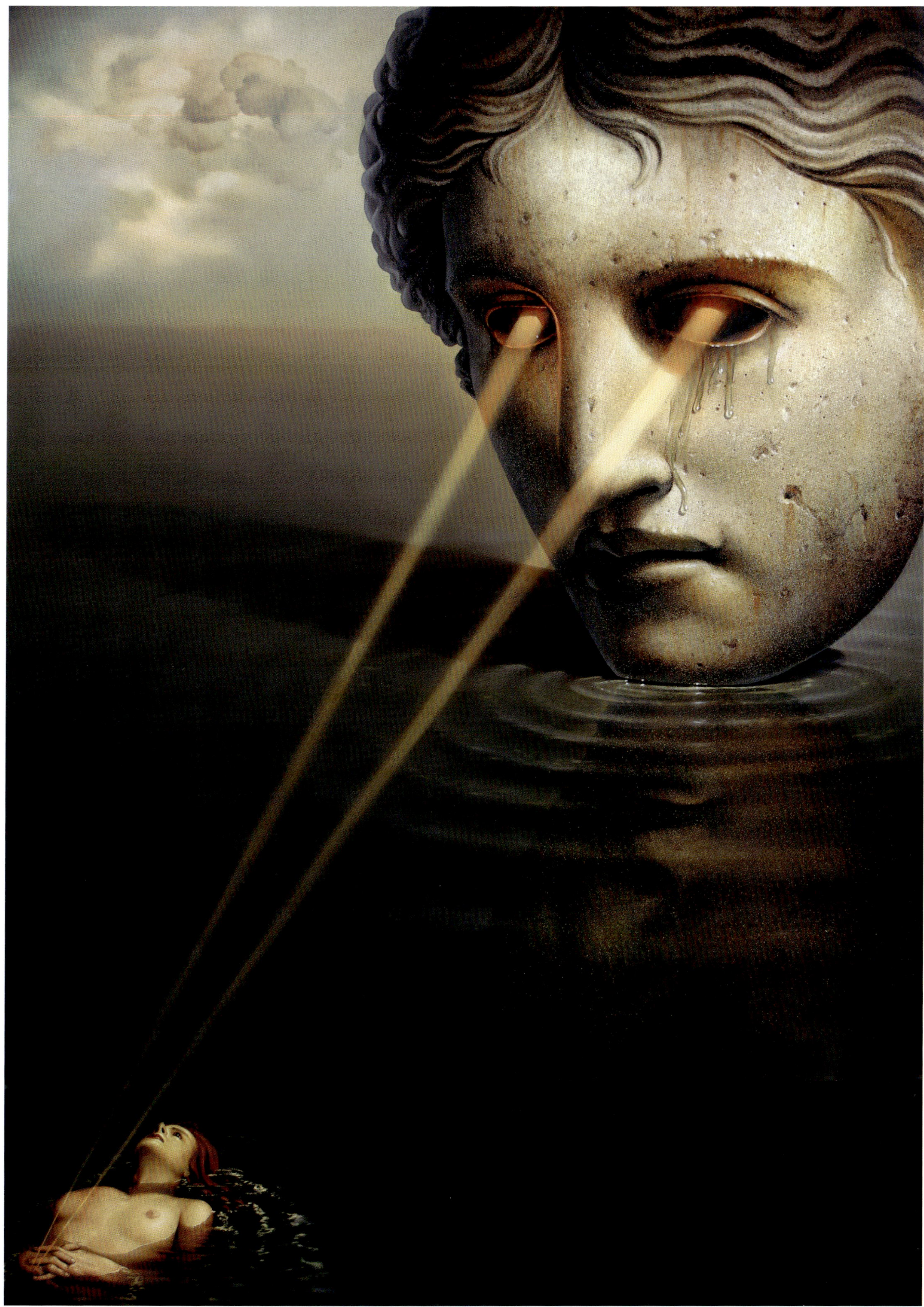

Prayer · 100 x 70 cm H · Oil on canvas

INDEX

Page 5
INTRODUCTION

Page 8
LIBELLULE

Page 12
WOLFGANG HARMS

Page 26
ANJA ALTENBURG

Page 30
BILLIE BAILEY

Page 32
KAROL BĄK

Page 36
JEF BERTELS

Page 38
ROBERT BISSELL

Page 42
DAVID M. BOWERS

Page 46
CLAUS BRUSEN

Page 48
GIL BRUVEL

Page 50
PATRIZIA COMAND

Page 54
KINUKO Y. CRAFT

Page 56
HELLE RASK CRAWFORD

Page 58
PATRICK VAN DER LINDE

Page 60
ZELJKO DJUROVIĆ

Page 62
VAL DYSHLOV

Page 68
COCO ELECTRA

Page 72
MAGDA FRANCOT

Page 74
ANDREAS N. FRANZ

Page 76
GABRIELA GARZA-PADILLA

Page 80
IGOR GRECHANYK

Page 86
LINDA GROEN

Page 88
N. G. HAMMER

Page 90
STEPHANIE HENDERSON

Page 92
MICHAEL HIEP

Page 94
KRZYSZTOF IZDEBSKI-CRUZ

Page 96
LUKÁŠ KÁNDL

Page 100
STEVEN KENNY

Page 102
MARTIN KOLPANOWICZ

Page 106
JACK LIPOWCZAN

Page 110
MICHA LOBI

Page 112
LUDMILA

Page 114
NANNY LUIJSTERBURG

Page 116
BRIGID MARLIN

Page 118
CHIRSTINE MORREN

Page 120
AUTUMN SKYE MORRISON

Page 124
PETER VAN OOSTZANEN

Page 126
JOSÉ PARRA

Page 132
ISABELLE PLANTÉ

Page 134
T.B. RATHBUN

Page 136
JOLANDA RICHTER

Page 138
TIM ROOSEN

Page 140
ISKREN SEMKOV

Page 142
YU SUGAWARA

Page 144
JEAN THOMASSEN

Page 150
TOMMAS

Page 152
CAS WATERMAN

Page 154
RODNEY WOOD

Page 158
OXANA YAMBYKH

Page 162
SIEGFRIED ZADEMACK

IMAGINAIRE IV

Contemporary Magic Realism

First published in Denmark 2011

First edition

IMAGINAIRE IV.
2011, with reg.
ISBN: 978-87-993936-1-9
EAN: 9788799393619
ISSN: 1903-7708

Introduction by Claus Brusen

Special thanks to Libelulle by Françoise and Lukàš Kándl

Set in Garamond Premier Pro
Design and Layout by Tegner Bruno, Aalborg, Denmark
Prepress and Printing by Scanprint, Denmark

Cover: Wolfgang Harms, Rothe Mondvogel. Acrylic and oil on panel
Inside cover "Causa" by Karol Bąk
Backside: A mix of whats inside

Distributed in Europe by Gazelle Book Service, UK

Distributed in North America by Independent Publisher Group

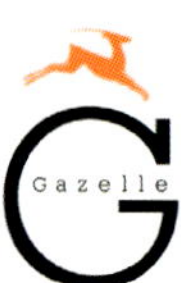

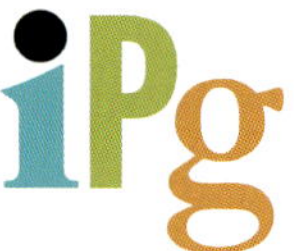

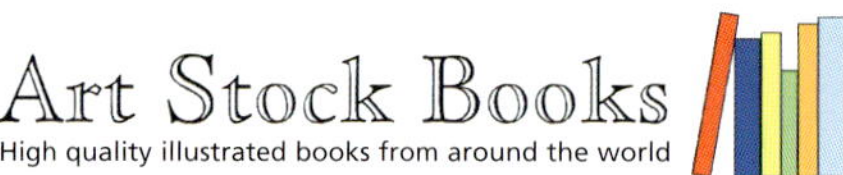

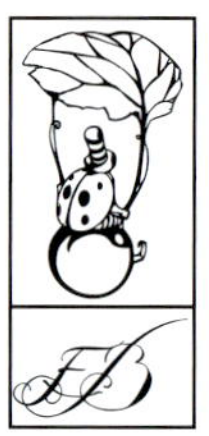

www.fantasmus-art.com

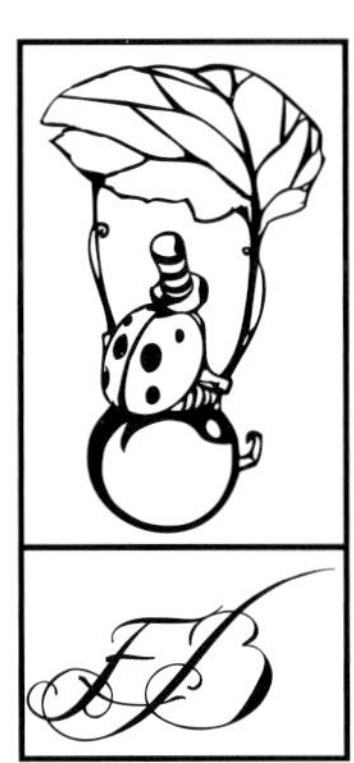

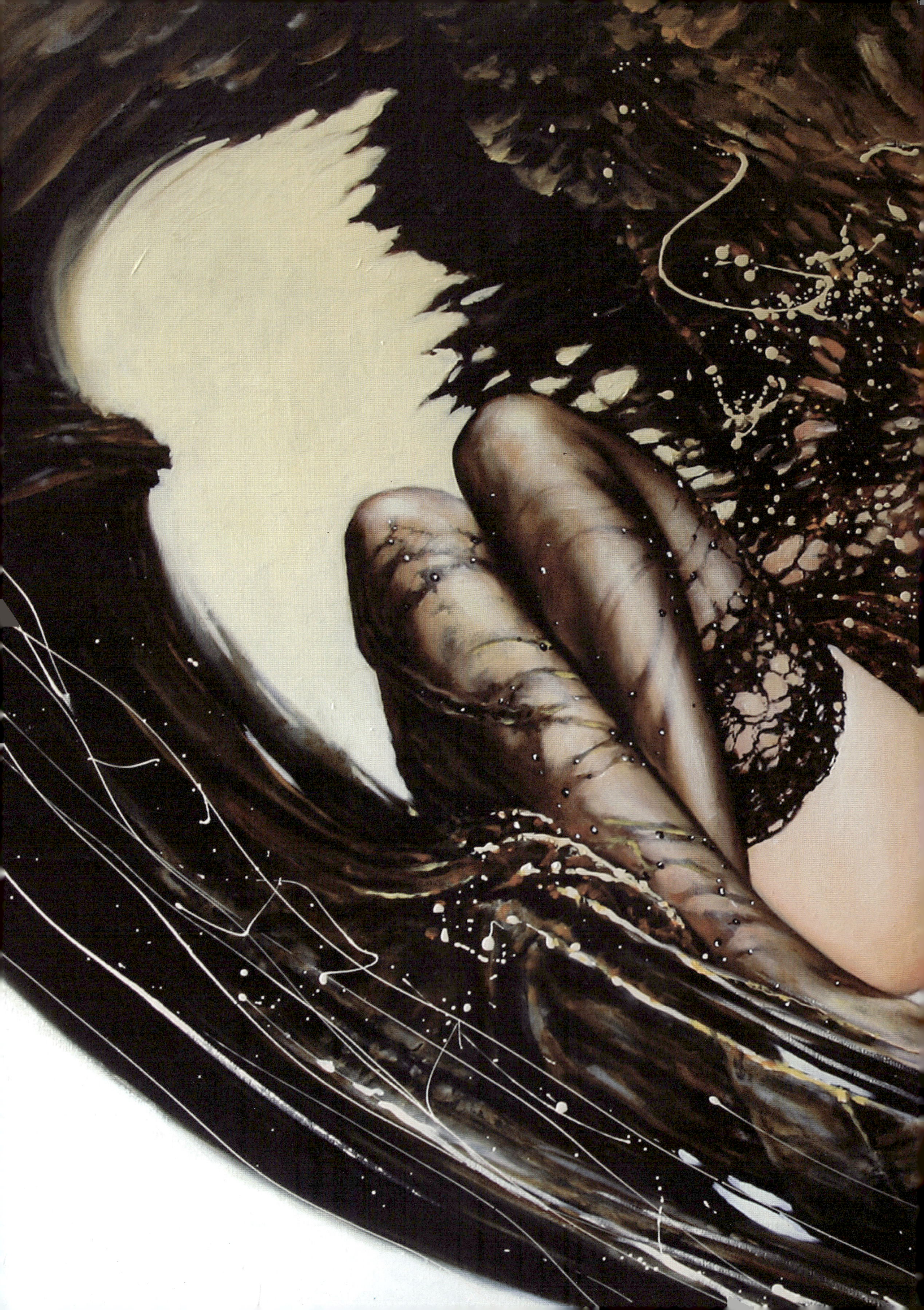